WITH THE STROKE OF A PEN

WITH THE STROKE OF A PEN

EXECUTIVE ORDERS AND
PRESIDENTIAL POWER

Kenneth R. Mayer

PRINCETON UNIVERSITY PRESS   PRINCETON AND OXFORD

Library of Congress Cataloging-in-Publication Data

Mayer, Kenneth R.
With the stroke of a pen : executive orders and
presidential power / Kenneth R. Mayer.
p. cm.
Includes bibliographical references and index.
ISBN 0-691-01204-0 (CL : alk. paper)
1. Executive orders—United States. 2. Presidents—United States.
I. Title.
KF5053 .M39 2001
342.73′062—dc21   00-064264

This book has been composed in Janson

The paper used in this publication meets the minimum
requirements of ANSI/NISO Z39.48-1992 (R1997)
(*Permanence of Paper*)

www.pup.princeton.edu

Printed in the United States of America

10 9 8 7 6 5 4 3 2 1

To Susan

Contents

List of Figures and Tables

Acknowledgments

IN THE COURSE of writing this book I have incurred so many debts that I hardly know how to begin to acknowledge them. I will exhaust the adjectives that I must use to describe this help—crucial, lucid, helpful, critical, generous, professional, invaluable—long before I can properly express my enduring gratitude. The best place to start is to acknowledge the generous financial support I received from the Graduate School Research Committee at the University of Wisconsin, the National Science Foundation (SBR-9511444), the Harry S Truman Library Foundation, the Gerald R. Ford Library Foundation, and the Eisenhower World Affairs Institute. Just as important are the lucid and helpful comments many colleagues and friends have provided. Larry Berman, David Canon, Steven DiTullio, Charles Franklin, Chuck Jones, John Kessel, Martha Joynt Kumar, Ken Meier, Richard Neustadt, Lyn Ragsdale, Bert Rockman, Robert Shapiro, Mary Stuckey, Stephen Wayne, Graham Wilson, and Tom Weko all gave generously of their time and knowledge, as did my fellow participants in the Presidency in the 21st Century Conference (held at Columbia University in 1996 to honor Neustadt's contribution to presidential studies). The archivists and staff at the presidential libraries were a treasure, and endlessly patient with me. A number of current and former government officials graciously consented to detailed interviews; most requested anonymity, but some (particularly former White House counsel Lloyd Cuter) agreed to go on the record. Patrick Murphy, Lisa Nelson, Kevin Price, and Matt Beck provided invaluable research assistance. Malcolm Litchfield at Princeton University Press signed on to this project early, taking a significant risk in the process, and his successor, Chuck Myers, guided the manuscript to completion with a steady and enthusiastic hand. Elizabeth Gilbert was an extraordinary copyeditor, gently correcting my bad writing habits as she went over the manuscript with great care. Louis Fisher and David Gray Adler read the entire manuscript, and provided crucial advice and support; I owe a special intellectual debt to Fisher, whose work spurred my original interest in the legal basis of presidential power.

I reserve the last—and most significant—acknowledgment for my wife, Susan, who has provided an immeasurable amount of support and encouragement, both over the five years I have spent on this project and over the twelve years we have been married. I simply could not have come close to finishing without her, and there is no way I can adequately express how grateful I am (though I know at some point, rubies will help). Asking her to marry me is the smartest thing I have ever done; that she said yes is the luckiest thing that has ever happened to me; and dedicating this book to her is the easiest decision I have ever had to make.

WITH THE STROKE OF A PEN

One

Why Are Executive Orders Important?

He'll sit here, and he'll say "Do this! Do that!"
And nothing will happen. Poor Ike—it won't be a
bit like the Army. He'll find it very frustrating.
　(Harry Truman on Eisenhower, cited in Richard
　Neustadt, *Presidential Power*)

IN JANUARY 1995 President Bill Clinton, House Speaker Newt Gingrich
(R-Ga.), and Senate Majority Leader Bob Dole (R-Kan.) met to discuss
how the United States should respond to a rapidly deepening economic
crisis in Mexico. Faced with the prospect of a complete meltdown of the
Mexican economy, Clinton secured the support of Dole and Gingrich for
legislation to fund $40 billion in loan guarantees for the Mexican govern-
ment.[1] Despite the support of congressional leaders, former presidents
George Bush and Gerald Ford, and Federal Reserve Board chairman Alan
Greenspan, rank-and-file legislators objected to the loan guarantees as a
Wall Street bailout. Prospects for approval evaporated when a group of
prolabor Democrats, still smarting from the 1993 ratification of the
North American Free Trade Agreement, formed an unlikely alliance with
conservative isolationist Republicans to oppose the plan. By January 20
the GOP leadership declared the legislation dead.[2]

In response Clinton unilaterally authorized $20 billion in loan guaran-
tees on his own authority, relying on a little-noticed program called the
Exchange Stabilization Fund, or ESF. Many members of Congress were
outraged, arguing that the ESF, created in 1934 to allow the U.S. government to protect the dollar in international currency markets, was never
intended for such a use.[3] Yet Congress could not stop the president.[4]
Clinton, though humiliated by the Republican sweep in the 1994 elections and weakened by mass defections within his own party, was still
able to commit to a multibillion dollar program without any meaningful
interference.

On August 17, 1998, Clinton testified before a grand jury, empaneled
by Independent Counsel Kenneth Starr, about his relationship with White
House intern Monica Lewinsky and the question of whether he had lied
under oath in the civil lawsuit against him filed by Paula Jones. Although
Clinton had for months denied any sexual relationship with Lewinsky,

he was forced to admit that he had, in fact, engaged in what he called "inappropriate, intimate conduct" with her. The admission (which Clinton repeated in a nationally broadcast television speech that night), ignited a firestorm. His opponents called for his resignation and impeachment, and many of his supporters were furious that he had misled them for months. Clinton's presidency appeared to be teetering on the brink of an abyss.

Three days later, on Thursday, August 20, the U.S. Navy fired dozens of cruise missiles at a terrorist training camp in Afghanistan and a chemical facility in the Sudan suspected of manufacturing nerve gas. Although some congressional Republicans gently raised questions about the *Wag the Dog*–like timing of the strikes (referring to the popular 1997 movie in which a president stages a fake war against Albania in order to divert attention from his sexual affair with a teenager), few offered anything more than tepid criticism. At a time when conventional wisdom believed that Clinton was certain to resign or be impeached, American military forces launched attacks on his word. Clinton also issued an executive order that froze any U.S. assets belonging to Osama bin Laden, whom the United States charged was behind the embassy bombings.[5]

Executive Orders and Executive Initiative

These chronicles of presidential decisiveness and unilateral action are at odds with the prevailing scholarly view of presidential power. Among political scientists the conventional wisdom is that the president is weak, hobbled by the separation of powers and the short reach of his formal legal authority. Presidential power, far from being a matter of prerogative or legal rule, "is the power to persuade," wrote Richard Neustadt in the single most influential statement about the office in the past fifty years.[6] Yet throughout U.S. history presidents have relied on their executive authority to make unilateral policy without interference from either Congress or the courts. In this book, I investigate how presidents have used a tool of executive power—the executive order—to wield their inherent legal authority. Executive orders are, loosely speaking, presidential directives that require or authorize some action within the executive branch (though they often extend far beyond the government). They are presidential edicts, legal instruments that create or modify laws, procedures, and policy by fiat.

Working from their position as chief executive and commander in chief, presidents have used executive orders to make momentous policy choices, creating and abolishing executive branch agencies, reorganizing administrative and regulatory processes, determining how legislation is implemented, and taking whatever action is permitted within the boundaries of their constitutional or statutory authority. Even within the confines of their executive powers, presidents have been able to "legislate" in the sense of making policy that goes well beyond simple administrative activity. Yale Law School professor E. Donald Elliot has argued that many of the thousands of executive orders "plainly 'make law' in every sense,"[7] and Louis Fisher finds that despite the fact that the Constitution unambiguously vests the legislative function in Congress, "the President's lawmaking role is substantial, persistent, and in many cases disturbing."[8]

A short review confirms that executive orders can have profound consequences. In 1939 President Franklin Roosevelt used an executive order to establish the Executive Office of the President (EOP), the touchstone of modern presidential leadership;[9] Clinton Rossiter concludes that this step may have "saved the Presidency from paralysis and the Constitution from radical amendment."[10] Other Roosevelt executive orders were clearly inimical to civil liberties and democratic values, most notably his February 1942 order that authorized the internment of thousands of Japanese Americans during World War II.[11]

Presidents have resorted to executive orders to implement many of the nation's most dramatic civil rights policies. These include Harry S Truman's integration of the armed forces[12] and Dwight D. Eisenhower's calling the Arkansas National Guard into active military service in Little Rock, Arkansas, in order to enforce a court order to integrate Central High School.[13] The American Council on Race Relations reported in 1948 that Truman's military desegregation orders "demonstrate that in government the area of administration and executive authority is equal in importance to legislation and judicial decision" in fostering equal opportunity and civil rights.[14]

Within the civil rights community the executive order became a powerful symbol of presidential commitment to racial equality. Shortly after John F. Kennedy's inauguration, Martin Luther King, Jr., urged the new president to use his executive authority to combat racial discrimination, citing the historical practice of presidents' issuing civil rights executive orders "of extraordinary range and significance."[15] It was through an executive order that "affirmative action" became part of the national consciousness, after President Kennedy used the term in an executive order establishing a Presidential Committee on Equal Employment Opportunity, and thereafter President Lyndon Baines Johnson referred to it in a follow-on order that made eligibility for government contracts conditional upon the implementation of adequate affirmative action programs.[16]

Through executive orders, presidents have almost single-handedly cre-ated the federal government's classification system for national security information, as well as the personnel clearance process that determines whether individuals will have access to that information. Though purely administrative in nature, these rules and procedures have produced dra-matic violations of individual rights and civil liberties, and they have given the president decisive advantages in disputes with Congress over the course of American foreign policy. University of Wisconsin historian Stan-ley Kutler, in his 1997 book on President Richard M. Nixon's White House tapes, traced the origins of Watergate to Nixon's obsession with the leak of the Pentagon Papers, the infamous top-secret study of Ameri-ca's involvement in Vietnam.[17] The extent of presidential control over information has, according to political scientist Robert Spitzer, served as a "key source of presidential ascendancy" in the post–World War II politi-cal environment.[18]

President Truman seized the nation's steel mills in 1952 with Executive Order 10340,[19] a consequential step in itself that became more important when it resulted in the twentieth century's most important judicial state-ment on the limits of presidential power, in *Youngstown Sheet and Tube Co. v. Sawyer*, 343 U.S. 579 (1952).[20] With the order the government took possession of eighty-six of the country's steel mills, representing well over 80 percent of the industry's capacity.

With Executive Order 12291,[21] President Ronald Reagan tried to wrest control over federal regulatory activity from executive branch agencies. The order gave the Office of Management and Budget (OMB) the right to review proposed regulations to ensure that they were justified by cost-benefit analysis and in line with the president's broader agenda. This order, which extended earlier and less successful efforts by presidents Nixon, Ford, and Carter to contain regulatory expansion, "brought agen-cies under presidential control as never before,"[22] and in doing so spurred a "minor revolution" in constitutional theories of presidential authority over administration.[23] George Bush's White House counsel, C. Boyden Gray, noted that Executive Order 12291 was "considered revolutionary at the time . . . and has earned the reputation as one of the most far-reaching government changes made by the Reagan Administration."[24]

A president can declare a national emergency by executive order, a step that authorizes an immense range of unilateral warrants, including—theo-retically—the power to restrict travel, impose martial law, and seize prop-erty, transportation networks, and communications facilities.[25] And even orders that lack such sweeping effect can still be extraordinarily im-portant to particular interest groups or constituencies, who seek substan-tive or symbolic redress for their concerns. Congress, in an attempt to protect its own prerogatives, regularly probes the appropriate limits of the executive's independent power through investigations of particular executive orders.[26]

Technically, although the term was not in use at the time, the Louisiana Purchase was carried out by an executive order.[27]

Presidents and their staffs consider executive orders an indispensable policy and political tool. In the wake of the 1994 congressional elections that gave the Republicans control of both chambers for the first time in four decades, Clinton White House officials predicted a renewed emphasis on "regulations, executive orders, and other presidential tools to work around Capitol Hill, much as Ronald Reagan and George Bush did when the House and the Senate were in Democratic hands."[28] In 1998, as Clinton headed for impeachment, his advisors noted that he would resort to executive orders and other unilateral actions to show that he remained capable of governing. In a statement that both summarized the White House position and served to provoke congressional Republicans, advisor Paul Begala outlined the strategy to *New York Times* reporter James Bennett: "Stroke of the Pen . . . Law of the Land. Kind of cool."[29]

Executive orders often become part of public discourse as both a symbol of energy in the executive and a sign that government is running amok. Contenders for the 1996 Republican presidential nomination promised to issue executive orders as their first presidential acts: Phil Gramm to end the policy of affirmative action in government contracting, Pat Buchanan to reinstate previous bans on fetal tissue research and abortions at overseas medical facilities.[30] In the early phase of the 2000 Democratic presidential primary, former senator Bill Bradley (D-N.J.) and Vice President Al Gore sparred over whether the Clinton White House had been sufficiently aggressive in using executive power to end racial profiling. In a February 2000 debate, Bradley promised to issue an executive order barring racial profiling by the federal government. When Gore promised that he, too, would use the president's power to end profiling, Bradley countered in what would become one of the campaign's testier—and more memorable—exchanges of the primary season:

> MR. BRADLEY: Last month, at the debate in Iowa, when Al said the same thing, that he would issue an executive order, I said, why doesn't he walk down the hall now and have President Clinton issue the executive order? Now, Al, Al said that I shouldn't give President Clinton lectures. I am not giving President Clinton lectures. I am questioning why you haven't done that or why you haven't made this happen in the last seven and a half years.
>
> MR. GORE: First of all, President Clinton has issued a presidential directive under which the information is now being gathered that is necessary for an executive order. Look, we have taken action. But, you know, racial profiling practically began in New Jersey, Senator Bradley. Now, the mayor, the mayor,

the African-American mayor of the largest city in New Jersey said that he came
with a group of African-American elected officials or contacted you to see if
you would help on this, and that you did not. Did you ever call or write or visit
with respect to racial profiling when they brought it to your attention?[31]

The phrase "stroke of a pen" is now virtually synonymous with executive
prerogative, and it is often used specifically to refer to the president's
ability to make policy via executive order. *Safire's Political Dictionary*
defines the phrase as "by executive order; action that can be taken by a
Chief Executive without legislative action." Safire traces the political
origins of the phrase to a nineteenth-century poem by Edmund Clarence
Stedman, but it was in use long before this, at least as a literary metaphor signifying discretionary power or fiat. The phrase became most
widely known during the 1960 presidential election campaign, when
Democrats made an issue of Eisenhower's refusal to issue an executive
order banning discrimination in housing and federal employment. Kennedy promised to do so, committing himself to ending discrimination by
executive order. During the second Kennedy-Nixon debate on October 7,
1960, Kennedy continued his criticism. "What will be the leadership of
the President in these areas," he asked, "to provide equality of opportunity for employment? Equality of opportunity in the field of housing,
which could be done in all federal-supported housing by a stroke of the
President's pen." After several delays Kennedy issued the fair housing
order in November 1962. I discuss this and other civil rights orders in
more detail in chapter six.[32]

Martin Luther King, Jr.'s postelection exhortation to the new president
to use his executive power to combat discrimination, went further. "It is
no exaggeration," King wrote, "that the President could give segregation
its death blow through a stroke of the pen. The power inherent in Executive orders has never been exploited; its use in recent years has been micro-
scopic in scope and timid in conception."[33] The clarity of Kennedy's
pledge and his use of the pen metaphor would eventually prove embarrassing. When Kennedy repeatedly delayed issuing the antidiscrimination
executive order he had promised, civil rights groups reminded him of his
words by mailing him pens by the thousands.

Executive discretion cuts both ways, of course, and opponents of a
particular case of presidential initiative will view these pen strokes quite
differently. After President Clinton issued an executive order that barred
government contractors from hiring permanent replacement workers,[34]
congressional Republicans were in no mood to congratulate him on either
his energy or his dispatch. On the House floor the next day, Representative Bill Barrett (R-Neb.) condemned the president for overturning fifty
years of labor law "with the stroke of a pen."[35]

Observers who are even less sympathetic cast executive orders in an altogether sinister light, seeing in them evidence of a broad conspiracy to create a presidential dictatorship. The common theme of these complaints is that the executive order is an example of unaccountable power and a way of evading both public opinion and constitutional constraints. In the more extreme manifestations, executive orders are portrayed as an instrument of secret government and totalitarianism. The president says "Do this! Do that!" and not only is it done, but the government, the economy, and individual freedom are crushed under the yoke of executive decree.

Truman is said to have issued a top-secret executive order in 1947 to create a special government commission to investigate the alleged flying saucer crash in Roswell, New Mexico (the air force says no such order exists, but not surprisingly the proponents of the UFO-order theory don't believe it).[36] When John F. Kennedy issued a series of executive orders authorizing federal agencies to prepare studies of how they would respond to national emergencies, some saw this as evidence that the government was getting ready to take over the economy and establish a totalitarian regime.[37] The Justice Department in 1963 complained of an "organized campaign to mislead the public" about these orders. The department had presumably grown tired of responding to members of Congress, who referred letters from constituents expressing outrage and alarm over the dictatorship that was right around the corner.[38]

Although the rate at which Clinton issued executive orders dropped after the Republicans won congressional majorities in 1994, critics still accused him of using the prerogative power to turn the presidency into a dictatorship. One review of Clinton's use of executive orders concluded that the president had relied on his decree authority to "act dictatorially without benefit of constitutional color."[39] In his 1997 State of the Union Address Clinton announced his "American Heritage Rivers" initiative, in which federal agency officials would help communities find and apply for environmental grants (the program's details were fleshed out in a series of proposed rules, culminating in Executive Order 13061, issued in September 1997).[40] The program did not commit any funds, create new environmental regulations, change any laws, or impose any requirements at all on local governments or the private sector.[41] Still, conservative property-rights groups claimed it was "a massive conspiracy to extend federal, and perhaps foreign, control over the nation's 3.5 million miles of rivers and streams, over watersheds, even over private riverfront property."[42] Representative Helen Chenoweth (R-Idaho) denounced the initiative as a "flight from democracy," and attempted (unsuccessfully, so far) to stop the program both legislatively and through the courts.[43] During 1995 Senate hearings held in the aftermath of the Oklahoma City bombing, John

Trochman, head of the Militia of Montana, complained that "the high office of the Presidency has been turned into a position of dictatorial oppression through the abusive use of Executive orders and directives, thus leaving Congress stripped of its authority. When the President overrules Congress by Executive order, representative democracy fails."[44]

Despite the apparent importance of executive orders, the political science literature has paid scant attention to them. This position is especially clear within the subfield of presidency studies, which has been dominated by a research paradigm that emphasizes the president's leadership skills and strategic acumen, not the legal basis of presidential power, as the keys to political success. With few exceptions,[45] existing research on executive orders either has been descriptive or has addressed the consequences of particularly important orders.[46] Similarly, the public administration literature "virtually ignores executive orders and proclamations."[47]

More to the point, most of the studies that do exist have minimized the significance of executive orders, viewing them as useful only for routine administrative tasks. The executive order is "limited in its scope and possibilities";[48] "not customarily viewed as a viable tool for major policy initiatives";[49] and "a very limited and temporary alternative for policy initiatives."[50] Mark Peterson argues that although presidents can often use their statutory authority to get at least part of what they want when Congress is uncooperative, "the potential for unilateral action of this kind is limited."[51]

The examples offered here of significant executive orders suggest that this is too limited a view of executive power. My argument is, put simply, that the formal basis of executive power matters to presidents. Both the Constitution and statute endow the president with important and practical legal powers, and the institutional setting of the presidency amplifies these powers by enabling presidents to make the first move in most policy matters, if they choose to do so. By themselves and as a broader indicator of executive authority, executive orders constitute a potent source of presidential power. To cite only one of a number of connections between the two, some of the most important institutions of the president's increasing administrative capacity—including the Bureau of the Budget and its successor, the Office of Management and Budget; the Central Intelligence Agency; the President's Committee on Equal Employment Opportunity; and the Executive Office of the President—have origins traceable to, or have had their powers significantly expanded by, specific executive orders. It is no accident that the first president to make extensive use of executive orders, Theodore Roosevelt, was also responsible for elucidating the modern "stewardship" notion of presidential power; nor that Franklin Roosevelt, whose administration marked the development of the modern institutional presidency, issued far more orders than any other president.

In making this argument about the importance of executive power, I recognize that our "separated system" puts both formal and informal limits on what presidents can do.[52] Presidents come to office in widely varying electoral and political contexts that shape their ability to transform their formal powers into action. Checks and balances were built into institutional structures of the federal government from the beginning, and presidents reeling from a prolonged recession, facing united majority party opposition in Congress, or mired in an unpopular war will find little solace in the powers specified or implied in Article II of the Constitution.

Nevertheless, in most circumstances presidents retain a broad capacity to take significant action on their own, action that is meaningful both in substantive policy terms and in the sense of protecting and furthering the president's political and strategic interests. Some of this authority, particularly in regulatory affairs, has been delegated to the president by Congress,[53] but presidents have also simply assumed many policy-making powers, especially in national security and foreign policy matters.[54] Although the courts do step in to block presidential action on constitutional grounds (with *Youngstown* the most notable case), the general pattern has been more one of judicial deference to executive action than of assertiveness.[55]

My argument about the importance of executive orders builds upon the notion, elaborated by Richard Pious, that "the key to an understanding of presidential power is to concentrate on the constitutional authority that the president asserts unilaterally through various rules of constitutional construction and interpretation."[56] The case I build for refocusing on the president's formal powers makes use of emerging threads within presidency scholarship that place renewed emphasis on the constitutional and statutory bases of presidential power. In addition, presidency scholars are now debating whether the office is best approached through a study of the *presidency* as an institution, with formal rules and structures, or by looking at the characteristics of individual *presidents*. A study of executive orders can make a contribution to this debate.

Executive Orders and the Evolution of the Presidency Literature

If executive orders are such an important element of presidential power, why have political scientists paid so little attention to them? The answer to this question reveals a great deal not only about how political scientists view the presidency but also about the relationship between the legal and political sources of presidential power.

Political scientists have for three decades held that the most interesting aspects of the presidency involve questions of political leadership and strategy, not the constitutional origins of presidential legal authority. The key to understanding the presidency is, in this view, the informal powers of the office: the president's ability to lead public opinion, strike deals with congressional leaders, manage press relations, mobilize constituencies, and conserve political capital. In large part, students of the presidency have tacitly declared the study of law to be nonpolitical, and hence less interesting than the "real" stuff of presidential activity. Institutions, formal powers, and questions of constitutional or statutory interpretation, even when considered important, have been "regarded as the framework within which presidential action [has taken] place—the backdrop to a far more exciting political drama." [57]

In the presidency literature, the distinction between the legal and the political was magnified by the influence of Richard Neustadt's landmark 1960 book *Presidential Power*.[58] Neustadt argued that presidential power lies not in the office's legal authority, but rather in the personal and strategic skill of individual presidents. In a system of "separate institutions sharing power," presidents get what they want not through command or legal authority, but through the ability to persuade others that what the president wants is what is in their own interest.

The "Neustadtian" perspective in *Presidential Power*—what I will refer to as the behavioral paradigm—came to dominate presidency studies as few books have dominated any field of scholarship. It transformed presidential studies, and became all the more influential because of two broader forces that shaped public and academic receptivity to the argument. First, Neustadt's views found support in normative prescriptions of how the president *should* behave. The "power to persuade" model of an activist presidency fit with the notion of the president as a *leader*, at the center of the give and take of political bargaining. FDR and Truman were examples of how to do the job right, Eisenhower an example of how not to behave. This activist approach was well suited to the dynamism and energy of John F. Kennedy, who as president displayed a visible interest in Neustadt's book. The argument also meshed with the notion that the public would be best served via active presidential leadership. The president, as the only elected official with a national constituency and as the embodiment of the national will, was the proper locus for the influence (as distinct from power) to carry out that will.

Second, *Presidential Power* served to demarcate a shift away from traditional avenues of presidential scholarship. Prior to *Presidential Power*, the literature on the presidency focused on the theory and practice of the president's formal legal powers. This body of work reached its pinnacle in Edward Corwin's *The President: Office and Powers*, which was first published in 1940 and appeared in updated editions until 1957.[59] Corwin sought to understand presidential power as conceived by the Framers, explicated in the Constitution, and interpreted through case law. The ambiguities in the original constitutional vestments made the boundaries of presidential power fluid and raised the possibility that the presidency was a "potential matrix of dictatorship,"[60] but throughout Corwin was concerned with the relationship between presidential power and the legal grants of authority. As Corwin himself introduced the book, it is "primarily a study in American public law."[61]

Neustadt changed this emphasis. The first edition of *Presidential Power* appeared at the same time that political science was in the midst of the "behavioral revolution" movement, which emphasized explanation over description in the study of political phenomena. The new approaches placed more emphasis on predicting and explaining actual behavior than on static analysis of institutional or procedural context, and fundamentally changed the way that political scientists looked at the world. Within this shift, *Presidential Power* marked a key transition in presidency studies and became the model of how to analyze the office, institution, and person of the presidency. As Joseph Bessette and Jeffrey Tulis describe it:

> Around the time that the last edition of *The President: Office and Powers* was published (1957), Corwin's work was both substantively and methodologically at odds with far-reaching developments in scholarship on American politics. One of these was the increasing extent to which political scientists were turning their attention away from formal rules and procedures to focus instead on actual political behavior, which, it was argued, was little influenced by laws and constitutions. In the field of presidential studies this new orientation was given its most articulate and influential expression in Richard Neustadt's *Presidential Power: The Politics of Leadership*. . . . The whole thrust of [Neustadt's] analysis was to move us away from formal authority in explaining actual presidential power, for distinctions of the sort employed in constitutional analysis seemed to him to have no effect on presidents.[62]

After Neustadt, scholars turned away from the study of the president's legal powers as the behavioral model deposed the legal model as the dominant paradigm of presidency studies.[63] Political scientists looked not to the Constitution or statutes to understand presidential behavior, but to the foundation of informal presidential power: public prestige and attempts to lead public opinion, professional reputation and style, congressional relations and legislative strategies, decision-making styles, temperament, bargaining skill. *Presidential Power* served as a springboard for decades of research that viewed the presidency in personal rather than legal terms, with a concentration "on questions about the personalities, power, and leadership of specific presidents."[64]

Among political scientists, the power of the argument that legal and constitutional powers were central to the presidency waned as the behavioral model took hold. There were some departures from this trend—Richard Pious did argue, in the late 1970s, "the fundamental and irreducible core of presidential power rests not on influence, persuasion, public opinion, elections, or party, but rather on the successful assertion of constitutional authority,"[65] and Louis Fisher continued to emphasize a public law approach to understanding presidential action—but they were clearly the exception. As recently as 1993 legal scholar Henry Paul Monaghan identified Pious's argument as "a rare dissent among political scientists as to the importance of constitutional law."[66] Political scientist Robert Spitzer argues that political science has, "to a great extent . . . yielded the field of constitutional law to lawyers."[67]

Although Vietnam and Watergate prompted a new wave of interest in the president's formal powers, with renewed concern about the normative question of how far the executive power should reach, most of these analyses were written by law professors.[68] Historians, too, began to look critically at what they saw as the expansion of presidential power, with some faulting Neustadt for conceptualizing presidential power as something distinct from its constitutional roots, and others criticizing the tendency to study presidential power apart from normative ideas about the purposes of that power.[69] The most widely known work in this tradition was Arthur Schlesinger's *Imperial Presidency*, which argued that the presidency had become too powerful, with presidents able to commit to disastrous policies under cover of secrecy and insulation.

Neustadt has been subjected to some criticism, although none has undercut the long-running appeal of his argument. A few scholars have pointed out that Neustadt's analytical framework is static, in that in his model presidents find themselves in a particular set of conditions that they have little say in constructing. In part this was because Neustadt was chiefly concerned with how presidents can be tactically effective given prior constraints. Such a perspective constrained the exercise of leadership by limiting presidents to a short-term view: "Neustadt's presidents do not change the political system in any significant way. The political and institutional parameters of this system appear impervious to the exercise of presidential power; they are transformed by great external forces like economic depression or world war. . . . The assumption that a system is given and that presidents make it work more or less effectively is bound to render the requisites of success elusive, for in their most precise signification, presidents disrupt systems, reshape political landscapes, and pass to successors leadership challenges that are different from the ones just faced."[70]

The enduring influence of Neustadt's argument has meant that questions about the legal basis of presidential power generally and about executive orders in particular have proved far more interesting to legal scholars than to political scientists. The legal literature on executive orders is both deep and broad.[71] Peter Shane and Harold Bruff argue in their casebook on the presidency that "Presidents use executive orders to implement many of their most important policy initiatives, basing them on any combination of constitutional and statutory power that is thought to be available. These orders thus often dwell in Justice Jackson's zone of twilight, where authority is neither clearly present nor absent. Although interstitial, the programs involved may prove surprisingly durable."[72] A 1997 administrative law casebook cautioned that executive orders, even when they lack the force and effect of law, "are compelling documents that agencies ignore at their peril."[73]

Despite the extent of the legal literature, however, there are limits to what these investigations can tell us about broader patterns of presidential decision making. Most legal studies analyze the constitutional issues that executive orders often raise, and typically address the narrow questions of whether the president had the requisite authority to issue a particular order. This literature generally does not tie executive orders to the theoretical issues that advance our substantive knowledge of the presidency (although there are important exceptions). Spitzer attributes the limits of the legal literature to differences in training and outlook among political scientists and lawyers: "The two disciplines [law and social science] involve different emphases in training, intellectual style, and objectives. Lawyers are trained to be advocates; social science training, despite its limitations and flaws, emphasizes exploration."[74] As a result, he concludes, much legal theorizing takes place in a rarified atmosphere divorced from political and historical context.

In any case, the perception remains strong that the legal model is not the best way to answer the most interesting questions about presidents. A leading textbook on the presidency puts it this way: "The legal perspective, although it requires rigorous analysis, does not lend itself to explanation . . . . although studies that adopt the legal perspective make important contributions to our understanding of the American politics, they do not answer most of the questions that entice researchers to study the presidency."[75]

Political science and legal scholarship on the presidency have thus gone in different directions, with the former concerned with the political and personal elements of presidential leadership, and the latter with the formal basis of presidential power. To Bessette and Tulis, "contemporary presidential scholarship is ill-served by this divergence between the legal and political approaches."[76] Constitutional scholar Louis Fisher, one of a handful of scholars whose work has bridged the gap between the legal and political approaches, laments that "too often, law and politics are viewed as isolated sectors of public policy . . . mere mention of a 'legal' dimension seems to stifle further discussion."[77]

As characterized by adherents of the political paradigm, the legal approach to presidential power failed because it held to the notion that the law is a set of objective, external, and autonomous principles that provides definitive answers to questions of presidential power. Moreover, in the political behavior paradigm, the president either has the authority to act unilaterally or he does not, and most of the time he does not, so there is more to gain from studying the informal basis of presidential action—leadership, persuasion, agenda setting, congressional relations, public opinion, and so on—than there is in studying the legal sources of presidential power. Once the relationship between legal authority and presidential power is constructed this way, it is easy to conclude that legal questions are of little relevance to presidents as they pursue their strategic political interests.

The relationship between law and presidential power need not be tied down to either artificially anchored end of the law–politics spectrum. The reality is much more reciprocal: the law both constrains presidential actions and is shaped by them. The president has become, many have argued, far more powerful than the Framers could have envisioned, even though the constitutional provisions regarding the office "have not changed at all since they were ratified in 1787."[78] This is not, however, because presidents have become better at finding ways around constitutional constraints. Instead, it reflects a more complicated dynamic between presidents and the law. The scope of the executive legal power is not fixed, but changes over time in response to evolving doctrines of constitutional interpretation, new institutional arrangements within the executive branch, congressional delegations of statutory authority to the president, history, and precedents established by individual chief executives. Given that the distribution of authority under separation of powers depends on legal interpretations with many characteristics of "common law constitutionalism,"[79] practice matters.

Unilateral Executive Authority

Presidential Power stressed the weakness of the president's legal authority, emphasizing the difficulties of acting unilaterally in a system of separated powers, institutional decentralization, and competition with other actors with their own independent sources of power.[80] This weakness is aggravated by the gulf between what the public expects of the presidency and what occupants can deliver, and the collapse of traditional political structures—especially political parties—that once gave stability and efficacy to presidential leadership. The perceived disintegration of one presidency after another—Johnson (Vietnam), Nixon (Watergate), Ford (Nixon's pardon, recession), Carter (just about everything), Reagan (Iran-Contra), Bush (recession), and Clinton (impeachment)—has led to the conclusion that "the American political system now produces failed presidencies as the norm rather than the exception."[81] The changes wrought by television and the proliferation of interest groups, the decline in U.S. international hegemony after the cold war, the confrontational style of media coverage of the presidency, congressional assertiveness, divided government, a bloated bureaucracy, and persistent budget deficits combine to place the presidency "under siege," incapable of governing except under the most extraordinary circumstances.[82]

In stressing the formal weakness of the president, Neustadt argued that presidential orders, by themselves, lack the necessary practical authority to alter the behavior of others in government. Presidents cannot succeed by issuing commands; they succeed or (more commonly) fail because they are competent political brokers, not because of their formal powers. In fact, Neustadt argued that when a president gets his way by force, it is normally a "painful last resort, a forced response to the exhaustion of other remedies, suggestive less of mastery than of failure—the failure of attempts to gain an end by softer means."[83] An executive order or other legal device, as an instrument of formal authority, does not by itself cause action.

Is this a realistic view? This observation says less about the limits of formal powers than it may seem. In fact, we could make the same argument about legislation, that by itself as an instrument of formal authority it does not automatically cause action. The conclusion, however—that legislation is as a consequence neither material nor interesting—would be rejected immediately. Statutes by themselves do not alter individual behavior; behavioral change is a complex process of implementation by executive branch agencies, interpretation by the courts, enforcement by legal authorities, and acceptance by the public.

Presidents may try to exercise unilateral authority by appealing to "duty, pride, role-conception, conscience, interpersonal identification," or to internalized values or even to loyalty.[84] In the 1990 edition of *Presidential Power*, Neustadt writes that "perceptions of legitimacy and sentiments of loyalty" played a more important role in shaping presidential power than he had earlier believed.[85] Although Neustadt is concerned with the impact these forces have on presidential power stakes—and he considers loyalty, in particular, to be an especially dangerous source of power because of the potential for a Watergate-like catastrophe—these forces play key roles in the president's ability to obtain control via noninstrumental persuasion. In arguing that commands are the only way that presidents can get results without bargaining, the behavioral model of the presidency minimizes the degree to which "many presidential requests are acted upon without bargaining and without commanding," based on "routine compliance."[86]

Ironically, Neustadt cites the steel mill seizure as one of his three cases of presidential command, or instances where a presidential order produced a direct result. In his view, presidential commands, which he considered as evidence more of failure than of success, require among other things that those who receive an order from the president have "control of everything they need to carry it out [and] no apparent doubt of his authority to issue it to them."[87] Actually, as the Supreme Court declared in *Youngstown*, the president did not have the authority to seize the steel mills. In this case, then, a secretary of labor—illegally, as it turned out—seized billions of dollars of private property, and the steel mill owners and workers both acquiesced to that seizure (initially, at least), on the basis of the president's word. Is this evidence of presidential strength or weakness? Although Neustadt recognizes that what counts in these cases is whether the targets of an order believe it to be legal, he also suggests that formal powers may matter as well: "Perhaps legitimacy exerts a stronger influence the more distinct is its relationship to some specific grant of constitutional authority."[88]

Making the argument that the law "matters" to the presidency is not, therefore, the same as arguing that presidential actions are completely determined and controlled by the plain language of the Constitution and statutes. We need not reject the notion that presidents attempt to persuade and bargain in order to argue that those attempts are structured and constrained by the law, or that the president's ultimate authority is vested in the office's legal and constitutional powers.

Evidence exists that presidents often think in constitutional terms, although presidents vary in their attention to legal precedent. Jimmy Carter was particularly concerned about the legal aspects of presidential power, often placing more importance on legal issues than on strategic ones. He "made it known, very clearly, that if there was a legal question in a policy paper, he wanted to know whether the options were lawful or not lawful. . . . He knew that lawyers could 'advocate' any position, but he wanted his Attorney General to tell him what the correct legal answer was, and he was prepared to live by it."[89] The head of the Office of Legal Counsel under Lyndon Johnson connected OLC's review of executive orders to broader questions of the president's legal authority: "The authority of the President to 'make law' by executive order does not exist in mid-air. It must find its taproot in Article II of the Constitution or in statutes enacted by the Congress. In some instances . . . a proposed executive order has been blocked on the ground that it exceeded the legal authority of the

President."[90] The Office of Legal Counsel, according to Douglas Kmiec, who served in the OLC under Ronald Reagan, operates with an institutionalized conservatism when addressing questions of presidential authority, in the form of a "reluctance to sanction practices other than those that are so thoroughly established as to be beyond all legal question."[91] In contrast, Oscar Cox, assistant solicitor general under Franklin Roosevelt, advocated a more aggressive approach to legal interpretation. In a speech in 1942 before the Society for the Advancement of Management in Washington, D.C., Cox argued that during emergencies there is a need for clever lawyers who can come up with flexible interpretations of the law that allow the government to do what it needs to do. Even within the constraints of "our law, our democratic processes, and the social and human values we are fighting to preserve," according to Cox, "the fact remains that our legal framework allows far more latitude for administrative action than is popularly supposed."[92]

When faced with opposition to their policies, particularly in cases where the authority to make the decision is in doubt, presidents will often fall back on constitutional arguments, tying their decision to a specific grant of power in an effort to establish the legitimacy of what they have done. While such appeals are often, no doubt, purely instrumental to the goal of obtaining public support, the fact that presidents make them signifies at a minimum the symbolic importance of the law. Although Truman's 1952 executive order seizing the steel mills cited the president's authority under "the Constitution and laws of the United States, and as President of the United States and Commander in Chief of the armed forces," Truman was less guarded in his initial public statements. In an April 17, 1952, press conference, Truman claimed a virtually unlimited prerogative authority, arguing that he had acted under an open-ended presidential authority to do "whatever was in the best interest of the country." After realizing that this assertion seemed to leave open the possibility of limitless presidential power, even to take over the press if the president thought it necessary, Truman quickly backed away from his statement.[93] To combat the furor raised by the president's initial claim, a few days later the White House released a letter Truman had written to a private citizen, in which he took the position that "the powers of the president are derived from the Constitution, and they are limited, of course, by the provisions of the Constitution, particularly those that protect the rights of individuals."[94]

Such public justifications, as Bessette and Tulis point out, "are often dismissed by scholars as mere rhetoric, attempts to give a cover of legitimacy to actions which have their source in political calculations rather than constitutional analysis."[95] Nevertheless, the perceived need to find some constitutional legitimacy may well condition the choices that presidents make. "It follows," they conclude, "that the written document may mold political behavior by forcing presidents . . . to give serious thought to the constitutional propriety of anticipated actions, even if they have no personal constitutional scruples per se."[96]

Ultimately, the behavioral paradigm of presidential power goes too far in promoting the notion that constitutional and statutory provisions make little practical difference to presidents as they pursue their strategic interests. The emphasis in the legal literature on narrow questions of the constitutionality of particular presidential actions is one reason that political scientists have found legal arguments inapplicable to broader issues of presidential action. It may well be true that "most of what the president do cannot be explained through legal analysis" and that most examples of presidential activity "can only be understood in terms of informal or extraconstitutional powers."[97] A few critical reviews of the behavioral model have pointed out, however, that even the president's informal powers find their ultimate origins within some constitutional provision or grant of power. Neustadt's model found its broadest application in studies of presidential-legislative relations, as scholars sought to identify the sources of presidential influence in Congress. Some aspects of this relationship are modern developments (particularly the expectation that presidents would prepare a comprehensive legislative agenda, which became common only in the twentieth century), but others can be traced back to specific constitutional provisions and are therefore grounded firmly in law (especially the veto, but also provisions that guaranteed presidential independence from the legislature):

> As the specific language of the document written in 1787 has given rise to conflict between the political branches, so has it influenced its nature and scope. The Constitution's qualified veto, for example, ensures that with rare exceptions Congress must make some accommodation to strongly held policy views of the president. Conversely, other constitutional provisions determine that presidents must generally give serious consideration to senatorial views of treaties and appointments. Although the Constitution does not lack ambiguity, it is clear enough on many specific points to define the area and fashion the weapons of congressional-presidential conflict . . . much of the "political" conflict between president and Congress occurs within a horizon of law.[98]

The importance of legal constraints on the presidency has been raised by those who have criticized Congress for relying on an overly legalistic approach to constrain presidential activism. Many conservative legal scholars charged in the 1980s that Congress responded to every instance of presidential activism with legislation that specified in increasingly exhaustive detail all that presidents could not do in foreign affairs, intelligence, or military procurement. The argument was that Congress was engaging in legislative imperialism, encroaching upon the president's legitimate perogatives for partisan purposes. The fact that this debate took place at all is instructive, because it implies the potential efficacy of legal constraints on the presidency. If presidential adherence to the law is merely an afterthought, or if the constraints Congress has tried to impose on the presidency are meaningless, there is no need for concern. Additionally, not everyone agrees that the president will usually win the institutional confrontations with Congress. Michael Horowitz, who served as counsel to the director and chief legal officer in the Office of Management and Budget under Ronald Reagan, concluded that his experience taught him that "Congress is a very potent institution and can do in the presidency. . . . Presidents often have to accommodate Congress because congressional power is real, and it shoots real bullets.⁹⁹ Even so, even those who identify excessive legalism as a problem see a solution in politics, not law: L. Gordon Crovitz and Jeremy Rabkin argue that to many, "the best solution [to excessive legal constraints] is to build up the political strength of the presidency, not to litigate the constitutional rights of the office."¹⁰⁰

Just as the presidency literature divides legal issues from political questions, it also implicitly draws distinctions between politics (where the interesting questions lie) and administration (which is seen as a function of management and implementation, not substantive policy). Much of the literature holds fast to the notion that since executive orders are primarily an administrative tool, they do not have significant political or policy consequences. The implicit argument is that administration has less impact on external interests and encompasses questions separate from, and less important than, broader policy. Without question, though, even purely administrative decisions can have dramatic effects on the public, and students of public administration no longer accept the politics–administration dichotomy. The process by which the executive branch controls what information reaches the public or Congress—on its face largely a question of administrative practice, and one controlled almost exclusively through executive orders rather than through statutes—reaches far beyond agency boundaries. The classification and security clearance systems, and presidential claims of executive privilege, raise critical questions of democratic accountability, the separation of powers, and private rights and civil liberties.

Similarly, presidential efforts to implement affirmative action and labor policy through executive orders have typically involved stipulations barring firms who refuse to abide by the government's policy from bidding for government contracts (see chapter two). In rejecting a Clinton administration effort to bar government contractors from hiring permanent replacement workers, a policy enacted through executive order, the Court of Appeals for the District of Columbia concluded that the order was "quite far reaching," and that it would discourage even nongovernment contractors from hiring replacement workers.[101]

The neglect of executive orders has led to a one-dimensional view of their use. Typically executive orders are viewed as a way for presidents to accomplish on their own what Congress refuses to give them. In fidelity to the Neustadtian argument that command is a sign of failure, Joel Fleishman and Arthur Aufses argue that "in some cases executive orders are as much a reflection of presidential weakness, as of presidential strength. In other words, Presidents may decide to legislate by executive order when they have failed to move desired bills through Congress."[102] But even here there is no consensus. Other political scientists have argued that presidents will rely more heavily on executive orders when they succeed in Congress.[103]

Yet like executive power itself, executive orders do not lend themselves to simple classifications, either as to content or as to motive. At times, presidents have resorted to an executive order strategy because they had no alternative; at others, because it was the most effective way to get what they wanted. Presidents sometimes have issued orders as a way of getting around a Congress that would have surely refused to give them what they wanted. At other times, presidents have relied on executive orders to prevent congressional action, using their powers to preempt legislation and fill power vacuums. Sometimes presidents have issued orders to make a positive statement about policy; at other times they have issued orders under duress as a way to satisfy the immediate demands of important constituencies. How presidents choose to use them depends on context, the policy area, and prior expectations of executive responsibility.

Putting the Pieces Back Together: New Institutionalism and the Presidency

Research on the presidency, I have argued in the preceding section, has mistakenly concluded that executive power generally and executive orders in particular are not important to presidents. The problem is largely attributable to the influence of the behavioral paradigm in presidency research, which has focused more on the personal elements of presidential leadership than on the legal basis of power.

But that is not the only problem. Presidency research has also been criticized for being less theoretical than other subdisciplines within political science, especially in comparison with the literatures on Congress or the bureaucracy. In a pointed 1993 review, Gary King called presidency studies "one of the last bastions of historical, non-quantitative research in American politics," and argued that "although probably more has been written about the presidency than all other areas of American politics combined," a lack of theoretical development has interfered with the formulation and testing of systematic theories.[104] King, along with others, has also called for more basic descriptive work, observing that much of the effort expended by presidential scholars involves looking at "the interesting questions . . . [without taking] sufficient time to verify the prior empirical claims on which those questions stand."[105] The conclusion that executive orders are not important to presidents is precisely this sort of speculation, one that has been widely held but is, I argue, empirically wrong.

One solution to the theoretical problems faced by presidential scholars is to rely on applications of what has become known as the "new institutional economics" as a way of organizing and explaining presidential behavior. The central questions of concern within the NIE literature are why economic institutions emerge and why they take the hierarchical form that they do. As applied to political relationships, NIE considers the interests of the parties involved in any economic or political transaction: the principal, who wishes to achieve a certain outcome, and the agent, the party with whom the principal contracts to produce the desired outcome. The key problem is how the principal can create an incentive structure so that the agent sees it as in his or her interest to act as the principal wishes.[106]

As applied to public (that is, government) organizations, the question is: how are they structured to produce the benefits desired by those who establish them? Political actors establish institutions for a reason—to provide benefits to important constituencies, to carry out imperative administrative and policy functions, to regulate—and politicians are attentive to the central problem of who has the right to define the mission and goals of an institution, and who shall control it. The theme of control permeates considerations of institutional structure: how politicians control bureaucrats, how bureaucrats control their subordinates, how citizens control politicians.

In this respect presidents are no different from any other political principal. What presidents need and work for, argues Terry Moe, is control over governing processes and policies, something they must have given the unique institutional and political situation they find themselves in. In an often-cited passage, he writes that "certain basic factors have structured the incentives of all modern presidents along the same basic lines. The president has increasingly held responsible for designing, proposing, legislating, administering, and modifying public policy. . . . Whatever his particular policy objectives, whatever his personality and style, the modern president is driven by these formidable expectations to seek control over the structures and processes of the government."[107]

The NIE theory of the presidency—or what Thomas Weko calls "rational choice institutionalism"[108]—begins with the assumption that presidents seek control over policy and process, just as rational choice theories of Congress typically assume that legislators seek reelection. Given the importance of institutions and administrative processes to policy outcomes, the epicenter of presidential-legislative struggles is over institutional structure rather than the day-to-day bargaining over particular policy issues. Issues of organization, institutional maintenance, implementation, and processes take precedence.[109] The politics of the presidency is about getting control of the institutions that create and implement policy. Rational choice institutionalism permits a framework that more closely tethers presidential behavior to statutory and constitutional origins, at the same time that it introduces a dynamic element into the evolution of presidential power.

In the struggle for institutional control the president has two main advantages, both of which stem from the president's unique legal powers. The first of these presidential advantages is the formal vestment of executive authority in the office, something far more important than most studies of the presidency have allowed. "The simple fact that presidents are the nation's chief executives endowed by the Constitution and stature with certain formal powers, is of great consequence. For those powers enable them to make lots of important structural choices *on their own* without going through the legislative process. . . . They can organize and direct the presidency as they see fit, create public agencies, reorganize them, move them around, coordinate them, impose rules on their behavior, put their own people in top positions, and otherwise place their structural stamp on the executive branch."[110]

The importance of executive power is enhanced by its inherent ambiguity, and by an increasing level of congressional delegation to the executive branch. Together, these give the president the ability to interpret his responsibilities flexibly and also to shape how statutes are implemented and enforced. In this way executive power is akin to what economists call residual decision rights, which in the private sector "are rights an actor may possess under a contract or governing arrangement that allow him to take unilateral action at his own discretion when the formal agreement is ambiguous or silent about precisely what behaviors are required.[111] Since statutes inevitably leave discretion to the executive, often by design, the president has many opportunities to exercise this residual authority.

Moreover, efforts to check presidential power through legislative restrictions often have had the counterproductive effect of legitimizing the very powers that Congress has tried to limit. I treat this problem in more detail in chapter two, but two examples highlight the problem that Congress faces. When Congress tried to limit the president's ability to carry out covert intelligence operations by imposing reporting requirements in the Hughes-Ryan amendments to the Foreign Assistance Act and the Intelligence Oversight Act in 1980, it inadvertently provided legislative recognition of the president's covert operations authority. The mere fact that Congress required the president to report on such activities was read by the courts as a congressional recognition of the president's right to conduct them. "So once again," concludes Gordon Silverstein, "Congress' attempt to control the executive's actions in foreign policy only provided fresh and unprecedented explicit authorization for executive prerogative."[112]

A similar dynamic occurred in 1977 when Congress tried to limit the way in which presidents exercised emergency economic powers. Since 1917, when Congress passed the Trading with the Enemy Act (TWEA), the president has had the legal authority to regulate aspects of foreign trade in emergency or wartime circumstances. Over the years, presidents had relied on the act to give them an ever-expanding range of authority to exercise control over more and more; Congress played a part in the president's expanding authority by modifying the law to, for example, extend the president's authority to certain domestic situations as well (which it did in March 1933). Between 1933 and 1968, a congressional investigation found, presidents had issued dozens of executive orders and proclamations under the act, with some far removed from what was originally intended: examples included FDR's proclamations closing the nation's banks and prohibiting the removal of gold from the country, FDR's executive orders freezing the assets of enemy nationals, Johnson's executive order restricting capital transfers abroad, and a Nixon executive order continuing certain export restrictions.[113]

As part of a broader congressional effort in the mid-1970s to scale back the scope of the president's emergency powers, Congress enacted the International Economic Emergency Powers Act specifically to reduce the range of the Trading with the Enemy Act.[114] The IEEPA, among other things, required the president to consult with Congress, provided for congressional review, and set procedures for congressional termination of presidential emergency authorities. The most important change was in the president's ability to rely on emergency powers. While the Trading with the Enemy Act authorized the use of the specified powers during wartime or national emergencies (leaving it up to the president to define what, exactly, a "national emergency" was),[115] the IEEPA attempted to restrict the president's use of the act during peacetime. Under IEEPA, the president could only declare a national emergency when the nation faced an "unusual or extraordinary threat . . . to the national security, foreign policy, or economy of the United States."

In a series of executive orders issued on his last day in office, Carter implemented an agreement with Iran to release assets frozen in the United States, as well as to suspend any private claims and terminate any legal proceedings against the Iranian government, in return for the release of American hostages held since November 1979. Despite Congress's clear intent in the IEEPA to limit presidential authority, the Supreme Court held in 1981 that the act authorized the resolution of the Iranian hostage settlement via executive order (in *Dames & Moore v. Regan*, 453 U.S. 654). Chief Justice William Rehnquist interpreted IEEPA not as a restrictive statute, but rather as a sign of "congressional acceptance of broad scope for executive action" in economic emergencies.[116] Harold Koh concludes, "in only one decade, the executive branch had succeeded in extracting from IEEPA the same sweeping delegation of emergency powers that Congress had expressly sought to remove from it after Vietnam."[117]

The second presidential advantage in the institutional setting is the ability to act first, leaving it up to other institutions to reverse what presidents have done. Whether presidents have effective plenary executive authority or not (an open question), there is no doubt that they can take action faster and more efficiently than either Congress or the courts. Congress as a collective organization takes definitive action through the legislative process, which is cumbersome, difficult to navigate, and characterized by multiple veto points. Even when Congress can create and sustain majorities at the subcommittee, committee, floor, and conference stages, the president can use the veto power to raise the bar from a simple majority to a two-thirds majority necessary to enact legislation over the president's objection. The president, at the same time, "has a trump card of great consequence in his struggle against Congress for control of government. He can act unilaterally in many matters of structure."[118] The president, in effect, can often make the first move in these disputes, forcing Congress to take positive action to undo what the president has created. Similarly, the judiciary can overturn executive actions (as it did in rejecting Clinton's 1995 replacement worker executive order), but must wait for controversies to come to it, and definitive resolution can take years. Moreover, even after the judicial decision, enforcement is a matter for the president.

The president's ability to win by default is, like his residual authority, reinforced by judicial doctrines that make it more difficult to challenge presidential action. The so-called *Chevron* rule determines how judges referee presidential-legislative disputes over statutory interpretation, and the rule provides clear advantages to the president. In *Chevron U.S.A v. National Resources Defense Council*, 467 U.S. 837 (1984), the Supreme Court ruled that an agency interpretation of a statute is "controlling unless Congress has spoken to the 'precise question at issue.' "[119] Once the president, through the executive branch, has interpreted a statute, Congress can only override that determination through narrow, explicit legislation on the exact point in question. This requirement places a heavy burden on Congress in confronting unilateral presidential action, given that body's collective nature and inherent bias toward not changing the status quo.

There will of course be exceptions to this rule, cases in which Congress can effectively respond to and circumscribe presidential administrative discretion. Jessica Korn, in her study of the legislative veto, argues that political scientists, legal scholars, and journalists have made far too much of the *Chadha* decision (the 1983 Supreme Court decision that ruled one-house legislative vetoes unconstitutional, with the Court declaring that congressional reversals of executive branch decisions had to go through the normal legislative process) and have neglected the existence of perfectly adequate alternatives to the legislative veto for controlling agency activity.[120] She cites the experience of Reagan's secretary of education William Bennett, who was repeatedly "legislated over" when his administrative decisions ran afoul of the Democratic congressional majority.[121] The 1995 federal court decisions striking down Clinton's replacement worker order and the Supreme Court's 1983 rejection of the line-item veto show that there are limits to even congressional delegation and court deference to the President. And, as Steven Calabresi sees it, it is possible to push this argument too far; he is critical of those who see the combination of judicial deference, congressional delegation, and checks on congressional controls such as the legislative veto as justification for the claim that "newly created doctrines of deference, coupled with much more aggressive use of executive orders and signing statements, [have] led to a situation where the President is able to subvert our whole system of checks and balances by making laws which the Congress must reverse over the President's veto."[122]

Congress's success, though, is conditioned by its collective institutional structure. How then can we predict in which areas the president will be able to operate effectively, and in which he will either lose in direct confrontations or avoid clashes altogether? Silverstein's analysis of separation offers some help: in his view, legislators will more likely organize effectively when they are dealing with issues directly affecting their constituents. Congress, in other words, is most effective when it is acting as a representative institution, because it is more likely to respond to sustained electoral pressure than to vague concerns that the president is encroaching on its administrative or procedural prerogatives. On issues of institutional structure, in particular, and foreign policy, it will be far less able to check presidential authority.

The history of congressional efforts to overturn specific executive orders bears out this observation. Only twice since 1970—in 1972, when

Congress successfully blocked Nixon's effort to resuscitate the moribund Subversive Activities Control Board (by enacting an appropriations rider that prohibited the expenditure of funds to implement Executive Order 11605), and in 1998, when Congress prohibited Clinton from spending any funds to carry out an executive order on federalism—has Congress explicitly invalidated an executive order of any substance. Terry Moe and William Howell identified thirty-six congressional attempts to legislatively countermand executive orders between 1973 and 1997—during a period when presidents issued over 1,400 executive orders—and only one attempt was successful: in 1973, Congress changed the effective date of a Nixon order (E. O. 11777) that provided a pay raise for federal employees.[123] In 1981 John Noyes found only a handful of instances where Congress had explicitly overturned an executive order, with successes limited to presidential action on administration of the Panama Canal Zone, veterans' pensions, and government salaries.[124]

In 1998 Congress suspended one provision of Executive Order 12958, which had automatically declassified all documents more than twenty-five years old.[125] But the provision did not overturn any part of the order, and instead simply required the secretary of energy and the director of the National Archives to devise a plan that would minimize the chance that any "restricted data" would be inadvertently released. And the final version of the law was significantly weaker than the original legislation, proposed by Senator John Kyl (R-Ariz.) and passed by the Senate, which would have required a visual inspection of every page of every document prior to declassification. Archivist John Carlin argued that the Kyl provision would "completely nullify E.O. 12958."[126] In the end Congress opted for a much weaker law that temporarily set back the declassification process by a few months: Clinton submitted the required plan in January 1999, at which point the declassification effort continued.

There are cases in which presidents have backed down in the face of strong congressional resistance—as Clinton did in 1993 when he retreated from his campaign promise to end the ban on gay and lesbian military personnel by executive order[127]—but the general pattern is quite the opposite.

This theoretical perspective offered by the new institutional economics literature provides a way of making sense of the wide range of executive orders issued over the years, and is the centerpiece of my approach. The common theme I find in significant executive orders is control: executive orders are an instrument of executive power that presidents have used to control policy, establish and maintain institutions, shape agendas, manage constituent relationships, and keep control of their political fate generally.[128] Within the boundaries set by statute or the Constitution, presidents have consistently used their executive power—often manifested in executive orders—to shape the institutional and political context in which they sit. There are, to be sure, limits on what presidents can do relying solely on executive orders and executive power, and presidents who push too far will find that Congress and the courts will push back. Yet the president retains significant legal, institutional, and political advantages that make executive authority a more powerful tool than scholars have thus far recognized.

This emphasis on control allows for a longer-term view than that generally taken by informal approaches to presidential leadership. I conclude that presidents have used executive orders to alter the institutional and political contexts in which they operate. The effects of any one effort in this regard may not be immediately apparent, and in many cases presidents succeed only after following up on what their predecessors have done. In this respect I view presidential leadership as both strategic and dynamic, a perspective that brings into sharper relief the utility of executive power to the presidency. I also differ with Neustadt on this score, as he looks at how presidents can be tactically effective within a particular structure context over which they have no control.

For analytic purposes, I divide the uses of executive orders into three levels. At the first level, presidents, relying on their formal and recognized legal powers, simply issue orders that they expect others to obey. Examples of these are the three cases of command Neustadt discusses: Truman's firing of MacArthur; Truman's seizure of the steel mills; and Eisenhower's use of the National Guard and U.S. Army to enforce the Supreme Court's school desegregation decision in Little Rock, Arkansas. In each of these cases, Neustadt argues, "the President's own order brought results as though his words were tantamount to action. He said, 'Do this, do that,' and it was done."[129] This is the sort of command authority that presidents can rarely wield, according to Neustadt. Clearly, though, there are many other examples, a large portion of which have taken the form of executive orders.

The NIE framework, though, posits that presidents can achieve substantive results not simply by giving commands, but by creating and altering institutional structures and processes. At this second level, presidents use their executive authority to shape and alter the institutional landscape in which they reside. Many elements of the institutional arrangements of government, of course, are fixed by constitutional and statutory mandates, and the president cannot as a rule do much about them in the short term (although the history of the shift in the war powers from Congress to the president in the twentieth century is a sign that even constitutional grants of power are not static). Yet residual decision rights still give presidents some flexibility.

Orders in this second category are not "self-executing," inasmuch as the order itself does not lead directly to an immediate action translating presidential words into the desired outcome. Instead, the president creates new processes that alter the organizational position, powers, and incentives of other actors, or that create new institutional structures with new actors; in effect, the president's order channels behavior in order to ultimately produce results.

Put simply, presidents use their authority to reorganize the executive branch and revise administrative processes. In doing so they by design make some policy and procedural outcomes more likely than others. Here is where the presidential advantage over Congress is at its greatest, as presidents have often made unilateral decisions of major import. Examples include Roosevelt's establishment of the Executive Office of the President in 1939, the establishment of wartime agencies during World War II, the various orders that organize government intelligence agencies, and Reagan's 1981 executive order requiring cost-benefit analysis and OMB review of major regulations. These orders fall squarely within the structure of rational choice institutionalism, as they involve cases where presidents have dedicated their efforts and expended scarce political capital to revise processes and institutions, something which if done wisely will spare them and future presidents the need to fight case-by-case political battles in the same areas. By altering institutional arrangements and the incentives that govern individuals, presidents can create structures that favor some outcomes over others.

Presidents will usually have to fight Congress for the right to exert this kind of control, and will sometimes lose, but most of the time they win because of the twin advantages that lie in their being able to move first and in Congress's need to take collective action to counter what the president has done. The dynamic, which has repeated throughout the past hundred years, is as follows: exogenous economic, political, and social pressures serve as the impetus for new government capabilities. The impetus can emerge through the obvious failure of the government to respond to what the electorate sees as pressing needs, the rise of new economic or social institutions that pose challenges to the government's existing administrative ability, through political entrepreneurs who propose new structures, or some combination. Past examples of this process include the initial development of federal government regulatory institutions and civil service organizations in the late nineteenth century and the institutions of the New Deal.

Once the institutions emerge, there is usually a struggle for control between the presidency and Congress over the new capabilities. Congress has at times asserted its control, as it has with the establishment of independent regulatory institutions (whose heads are removable by the president only for cause). Over time, though, successive presidents will often try new strategies to gain control over—or least limit the independence of—these new organizations and capabilities. Traditionally this competi-

tion has taken the form of an iterative game of presidential initiative (usually, though not always, in the form of executive orders) and congressional legislative response.

At the third level, presidents use their unilateral authority as a bargaining tool in an effort to shape the strategic context in which they operate. By taking symbolic stands, placing issues and policies on the public
agenda, and providing political benefits to important constituencies, presidents can dramatically alter the strategic environment in which bargaining takes place. This type of authority comes closest to Neustadt's
"persuasion" model of presidential power. Two recent examples are Clinton's 1995 order that barred government contractors from hiring replacement workers and a 1997 order prohibiting smoking in government
buildings. In the first case Clinton was trying to mend the breach with
organized labor that arose over his support of the North American Free
Trade Agreement (which unions strongly opposed). Even though the president ultimately lost in the courts, he still gained considerable leverage by
making the attempt. In the second case, the president's action was largely
symbolic, and part of an effort to gain public credit by getting on the
"right side" of an important public heath issue.

My focus is on the second and third categories of presidential action.
Although presidents face limits on their ability to mandate direct
change—indeed, in a separated system the lack of such limits would be,
as Montesquieu put it, the very definition of tyranny—the focus in the
presidency literature on the limits of command has obscured the president's ability to use executive authority to gain control of institutions,
processes, and agendas. Even within this more narrow area presidents are
not free to do whatever they want, and in any case Congress or the courts
may step in to reverse what the president has done. I argue, though, that
the president will win more of these battles than he loses, as Congress
fails to overcome the collective dilemma and institutional inertia that
make quick and decisive action difficult. Before I turn to the task of analyzing how presidents have used this power in particular policy areas,
though, it is necessary first to define with more precision what the law
says about executive orders, and provide an accurate and systematic account of the patterns of overall use.

Plan of the Book

In making the case that executive orders have played a critical role in the
development and exercise of presidential power, I proceed as follows. In
chapters one, two, and three, I explore the theoretical and descriptive
aspects of executive orders. This chapter has analyzed what the political

science literature has had to say about the president's formal powers in general and executive orders in particular. As a discipline, political science has moved away from legal analysis as a way of attacking interesting questions about the presidency; our focus has been on the characteristics of individual presidents and their leadership and strategic skills. The lack of attention to executive orders is a consequence of this shift away from looking at the law as an important source of presidential power. I have also offered an application of recent theoretical developments in what has been called the "new institutional economics" into presidency studies. The NIE literature provides a framework that allows a fuller understanding of how presidents have used executive orders to enhance and expand their ability to control both policy and processes. Chapters two and three address the major theoretical and descriptive aspects of executive order use. In chapter two, I investigate the legal theory behind executive orders and other unilateral executive actions and place special emphasis on how courts have interpreted order usage. The thrust of my argument here is that since it has proved impossible to precisely define the scope of presidential power, the details of presidential exercise of that power is of great consequence. Thus a study of executive orders, as a symbol and instrument of executive power, can aid in understanding the reach of the president's practical authority. This chapter also addresses the evolution of how the federal government has disseminated and recorded executive orders and how presidents and their staffs have viewed them.

Chapter three concentrates on systematic description, with a statistical analysis of executive order issuance since the 1930s. My intent here is to identify some of the factors that motivate presidents to use executive orders, and thus gain some insight into the practical utility of orders as a policy and strategic tool. In this chapter I draw on the universe of all orders issued since 1935, as well as a more detailed analysis of a sample of 1,028 orders. Most of the analysis here should be accessible to readers familiar with basic quantitative techniques.

In chapters four, five, and six, I shift to detailed historical analysis of broad categories of orders, based on subject matter and presidential goals. In these chapters I make extensive use of primary documents from presidential libraries and the National Archives. Chapter four, focusing on the establishment and expansion of presidential controls over budget and regulatory policy in the twentieth century, addresses the use of executive orders as a tool of institutional construction. The history of the establishment and development of the Bureau of the Budget beginning in 1921 shows marked parallels with presidential attempts in the 1970s and 1980s to gain control of a rapidly developing federal regulatory power. Even though these two episodes are separated by five decades and took place in dramatically different presidential eras, the similarities suggest a common impetus for presidential assertion of executive authority. Presidents from Taft through Reagan have used executive orders in their efforts to exercise control over budget and regulatory institutions.

Chapter five examines executive orders as a way of protecting presidents' prerogatives in foreign policy. In this policy area more than any other, presidents have used executive orders to preempt and undercut congressional involvement in what has become a field of presidential dominance. The organization of the intelligence community and the procedures for protecting classified information have been almost exclusively a function of executive orders rather than legislation, and presidents have relied on executive order strategies to block congressional action. Most studies of the president's authority in foreign affairs have focused on war powers (or the ability to control the disposition and use of the military in foreign conflicts, whether or not Congress has formally declared war). Presidents have also gained considerable control over the organizational and procedural facets of this power.

In chapter six, I explore the potential for executive orders as a way of circumventing Congress and obtaining results through executive action when legislative action is unlikely. Here the classic examples are the civil rights executive orders, a practice that Roosevelt started with his Fair Employment Practices Commission, which extends through implementation of preference programs in federal contracting, and which places the president directly within contemporary controversies over affirmative action. In this chapter I also consider the question of whether Congress has succeeded in efforts to invalidate executive order strategies through legislation designed to overturn specific orders.

Finally, in chapter seven, I return to the question of what legal and constitutional powers mean to the president. Here I argue that the divergence of behavioral and legal approaches to the presidency constrains our understanding of the office, and that the divergence itself is artificial. It is not necessary to place all of our eggs in one theoretical basket, and there is no reason why the presidency literature cannot integrate different approaches into a meaningful theoretical synthesis. Although no one will ever derive a "unified field theory" of presidential behavior, or a framework that can answer every question we may ask about presidents or the presidency, a renewed focus on the fundamental principles of presidential power—as derived from the Constitution and statutes that grant that formal power—can tell us things about the office and the individual in it that we will otherwise miss.

Two

Executive Orders and the Law

WHAT, PRECISELY, is an executive order? In the most formal sense, an executive order is a directive issued by the president, "directing the executive branch in the fulfillment of a particular program,"[1] targeted at executive branch personnel and intended to alter their behavior in some way, and published in the *Federal Register*. Executive orders are instruments by which the president carries out the functions of the office, and every president has issued them (although there was no system for tracking them until the twentieth century). A 1974 Senate study of executive orders noted that "from the time of the birth of the Nation, the day-to-day conduct of Government business has, of necessity, required the issuance of Presidential orders and policy decisions to carry out the provisions of the Constitution that specify that the President 'shall take care that the laws be faithfully executed.' "[2] The lack of any agreed-upon definition means that, in essence, an executive order is whatever the president chooses to call by that name.[3]

Several authors have offered their own definitions and categories, but they tend to be contradictory. Robert Cash describes executive orders as presidential directives and orders "which are directed to, and govern actions of, governmental officials and agencies."[4] William Neighbors notes that even though the terms "executive order" and "proclamation" are frequently interchanged, executive orders are "used primarily in the executive department, [issued] by the president directing federal government officials or agencies to take some action on specified matters";[5] in contrast, proclamations are "used primarily in the field of foreign affairs, for ceremonial purposes, and when required . . . by statute." Corwin described proclamations as "the social acts of the highest official of government, the best known example being the Thanksgiving Proclamation," which was first issued by Washington but which has been issued every year since 1863.[6]

These distinctions, while accurate on average, are wrong enough of the time to make them less useful for a comprehensive classification. The argument that executive orders are targeted at the behavior of executive branch officials and not the public at large reflects a limited and formalistic perspective of public administration. One could hardly classify in this way Reagan's Executive Order 12291, which fundamentally reshaped the regulatory process, or the series of civil rights orders which directed executive branch officials to use their power and resources to effect substantial and dramatic social change. Presidents have used executive orders to significantly alter baseline "private rights," or the rights of individuals that are commonly understood to be part of an established landscape of private property and personal freedoms. Through executive orders, presidents have shaped the employment practices of government contractors, the travel rights of American citizens, foreign economic policy, private claims against foreign governments, and claims on natural resources on government-owned lands.[7] Terry Eastland, a Justice Department official in the Reagan administration, has noted the blurred line between purely governmental and private effects: "In theory executive orders are directed to those who enforce the laws but often they have at least as much impact on the governed as the governors."[8]

Nevertheless, it is possible to differentiate among the different executive instruments and identify some distinctive characteristics of executive orders. The major classes of presidential policy instruments are executive orders, proclamations, memoranda, administrative directives, findings and determinations, and regulations. Of these, executive orders combine the highest levels of substance, discretion, and direct presidential involvement.[9] Compared with proclamations, which are usually, but not always, ceremonial,[10] executive orders are a "more far reaching instrument for administrative legislation" and have more substantive effects.[11] Presidential memoranda and directives more often address issues that are temporary or are used to instruct agency officials to take specified action in accordance with established regulatory or departmental processes.[12] Determinations and findings refer to particular decisions the president must issue on the record in order to carry out specific authority that has been delegated by Congress to the executive branch. Although these boundaries are fluid, there is little doubt that presidents and their staffs consider executive orders to be the most important statements of executive policy.

It is more useful to think of executive orders as a form of "presidential legislation"[13] or "executive lawmaking,"[14] in the sense that they provide the president with the ability to make general policy with broad applicability akin to public law.[15] For over a century the Supreme Court has held that executive orders, when based upon legitimate constitutional or statutory grants of power to the president, are equivalent to laws.[16] In *Youngstown*, the Court concluded with some force that executive orders lacking a constitutional or statutory foundation are not valid, and longstanding judicial doctrine holds that when an executive order conflicts with a statute enacted pursuant to Congress's constitutional authority, the statute takes precedence.[17]

Since executive orders are a tool of the president's executive power, their reach extends as far as executive power itself. The question of when a president can legally rely on an executive order, therefore, is the same as the question of when the president can bring into effect the executive power generally. It is not a coincidence that many of the most important Supreme Court rulings on presidential power have involved executive orders, including *Youngstown*, *Korematsu v. United States*, *Schechter Corp. v. United States*, *Cole v. Young*, and *Ex Parte Merryman*.

An understanding of executive orders thus requires an investigation into the nature of the president's executive power. My intent is not to derive a comprehensive legal theory of the presidency. Such an effort is not only beyond the scope of what I wish to do, it is also pointless, since decades of scholarship and judicial doctrine have failed to come to definitive conclusions on the subject; it may well be that the constitutional language is indeterminate. My aim is more modest—to identify the main trends in the development of presidential power and connect them to the use of executive orders as an instrument of that power.

Executive Orders and Debates over the Executive Power

The president's authority to issue executive orders comes from three sources: grants of constitutional power, congressional delegations of its legislative authority through statutes, and the possibility that there exist inherent prerogative powers within the office. Within the first two classes of authority, there are powers that are enumerated and others that are implied by the existence of the enumerated powers.

This neat classification, however, obscures important ambiguities. On even such basic questions as whether the opening sentence of Article II ("The executive Power shall be vested in a President of the United States of America") is a description or a grant of power, firm answers remain elusive. Scholars are at odds on a wide range of issues: does the president have any inherent or extraconstitutional powers? Are independent regulatory agencies—whose heads are protected against presidential removal and thus vested with independent executive authority—constitutional? Is the presidency unitary, possessing plenary power over administration?[18] As Monaghan puts it, "very considerable disagreement exists concerning many legal aspects of the presidency."[19]

The classic statement of presidential power is Justice Robert Jackson's analysis in his concurring opinion in *Youngstown*, in which he identified three categories of presidential power:

Presidential powers are not fixed but fluctuate, depending upon their disjunction or conjunction with those of Congress . . .

1. When the President acts pursuant to an express or implied authorization of Congress, his authority is at its maximum, for it includes all that he possesses in his own right plus all that Congress can delegate. . . . If his act is held unconstitutional under these circumstances, it usually means that the Federal Government as an undivided whole lacks power. . . .

2. When the President acts in absence of either a congressional grant or denial of authority, he can only rely upon his independent powers, but there is a zone of twilight in which he and Congress may have concurrent authority, or in which its distribution is uncertain. Therefore, congressional inertia, indifference, or quiescence may sometimes, at least as a practical matter, enable, if not invite, measures on independent presidential responsibility. In this area, any actual test of power is likely to depend on the imperatives of events and contemporary imponderables rather than on abstract theories of law.

3. When the President takes measures incompatible with the expressed or implied will of Congress, his power is at his lowest ebb, for then he can rely only upon his constitutional powers minus any constitutional powers of Congress over the matter. Courts can sustain exclusive presidential control in such a case only by disabling the Congress from acting upon the subject. Presidential claims to a power at once so conclusive and preclusive must be scrutinized with caution, for what is at stake is the equilibrium established by our constitutional system.[20]

The extent of the president's power thus depends on a reading of the president's constitutional powers in relation to any concurrent powers Congress may have, whether Congress has delegated power to the president via statute or whether Congress has acted (either expressly or implicitly) in a manner that contravenes the president's act. This categorization leads to several additional layers of analysis and ambiguity. If the president's powers exist in relation to Congress's powers, we must be able to identify the scope of both in order to understand the extent of either. If the degree of concurrent power depends on the level of congressional "inertia, indifference, or quiescence," we must then be able to define those terms. Finally, Jackson leaves open the possibility that on some questions of presidential power—in the "zone of twilight"—it may well be impossible to identify general principles, as opposed to ad hoc measures that depend entirely on the case-by-case circumstances. This sets the stage for fluid boundaries and also gives the president wide latitude, since Congress will typically be less able to undertake collective action (Moe's argument) either in favor or in opposition to the president.

An example demonstrates the imprecision of presidential power both in theory and in practice. Consider the narrow and relatively straightforward question of whether presidents have the authority to fire executive officers whom they appoint. The president's right to control subordinates stems from the vesting and take care clauses in Article I. The removal power is central to the president's ability to control executive functions, since the president can fire those officials who interfere with administration, and the threat of removal should induce compliance.

The question, while technical, is hardly academic. Congress struggled with this issue from the earliest days of the Republic, debating at length in 1789 whether the president required the Senate's approval to fire officials who were appointed with the advice and consent of the Senate (after a lengthy debate, and a tie vote in the Senate, broken by Vice President John Adams, the Congress acceded to presidential discretion on the matter). Andrew Johnson's refusal to abide by the Tenure in Office Act was the titular reason for his impeachment (although his opponents were looking only for an excuse to move against him).

So-called Unitarians[21] view these vestments as providing for complete control over the executive branch and its activities. To proponents of this view, the executive power necessarily confers upon the president the ability to "control subordinate executive officers through the mechanism of removal, nullification, and executive of the discretion 'assigned' to them himself."[22] Unitarians question in particular the constitutionality of any executive branch office that is not subject to presidential dismissal. The list of suspect offices includes independent regulatory agencies, whose officers are independent of the president, and independent counsels.

Yet for every authoritative law review article that supports the Unitarian thesis, another takes the opposite position. Lawerence Lessig and Cass Sunstein characterize as "just plain myth" the notion that the Framers intended to create a unitary executive with plenary administrative control.[23] Instead, they argue, the Constitution created overlapping executive and legislative powers, with the president clearly in charge of most executive functions but with Congress able to stipulate administrative details of others.

Is it possible to resolve this difference of opinion on the narrow question of the removal power? Probably not. Article II lacks the detail necessary to untangle these questions, and the courts have failed to provide a coherent framework for setting the boundaries of the removal power.[24] In *Myers v. the United States*, 272 U.S. 52 (1926), Chief Justice William Howard Taft ruled that the president had unlimited constitutional authority to remove those executive officers whom he had appointed, a right that Congress could not interfere with. In making this argument, he backed away from a constrained view of presidential power he had articulated ten years earlier.[25]

Holding that the grant of executive power gives the president the power to "secure that unitary and uniform execution of the laws which Article II of the constitution evidently contemplated,"[26] Taft found that the removal power is critical to the president's ability to control the behavior of subordinates. Ten years after *Myers*, in *Humphrey's Executor v. United States*, the Court backed away from the earlier ruling, holding that Congress could limit the president's removal power in certain kinds of offices—those that carry out "quasi-legislative" or "quasi-judicial" functions, as opposed to offices with purely administrative duties.[27] An immediate problem is that the Court never clearly defined what it meant by quasi-judicial or quasi-legislative, and sixty years later an analysis noted these are terms "whose meanings are at best quasi-clear."[28]

Most recently, the Court addressed the removal power in *Bowsher v. Synar*, a case that originated out a provision of the Gramm-Rudman-Hollings deficit reduction law. GRH authorized the comptroller general to impose automatic spending cuts (or sequestrations) when the budget deficit exceeded statutory targets. In this case, the Court ruled that since the comptroller general was an agent of Congress and removable only by congressional action, "Congress in effect has retained control over the executive of the Act and has intruded into the executive function."[29] As such, Congress had improperly exercised executive power and the Court overturned the law. Congress subsequently revised the law, placing the sequestration authority within the Office of Management and Budget.

Critics of these and other rulings on the appointment power argue that the Court shifts between different conceptions of presidential authority without any coherent framework.[30] *Myers* takes a flatly formalist perspective: the Constitution assigns powers exclusively to each branch, and the others may not encroach upon that power. *Humphrey's Executor* adopts a more functionalist view, which considers how a particular distribution of powers furthers the general purpose of general legislative or executive functions.

These questions are not merely hypothetical: Lessig and Sunstein argue that "they assumed special importance in connection with efforts by President Bush to assert close control over government regulation; they have new urgency as a result of likely new efforts by President Clinton to claim authority over a government staffed largely by Republican Presidents. Heated struggles arose between President Bush and Congress over a range of unresolved issues. Similar issues are likely to rematerialize during the Clinton administration, and these debates will undoubtedly raise new issues about exactly how unitary the executive branch can claim to be."[31]

Ultimately there is no conclusive answer to the question of how far the executive power reaches. Even after two hundred years of precedent and judicial opinion, the nature and scope of presidential power remain astonishingly ambiguous. Supreme Court justice Robert Jackson concluded in 1952 in his *Youngstown* concurrence that "a judge, like an executive advisor, may be surprised at the poverty of really useful and unambiguous authority applicable to concrete problems of executive power as they actually present themselves . . . a century and a half of partisan debate and scholarly speculation yields no net result but only supplies more or less apt quotations from respected sources on each side of any question."[32] Among the respected sources on each side of such questions, Jackson went on, "a Hamilton may be matched against a Madison. . . . Professor Taft is counterbalanced by Theodore Roosevelt . . . it even seems that President Taft cancels out Professor Taft."[33] In the end, we are left with competing theories of presidential power and constitutional interpretation rather than a definitive framework.[34]

Constitutional Vestments

Constitutionally, Article II vests "the executive Power" in the president of the United States (although disputes remain over whether this is an affirmative grant of power or merely a description of the language that follows), designates the president as the commander in chief, and gives him the power to negotiate treaties, and to appoint judges, ambassadors, and executive branch officers with the advice and consent of the Senate. The president has the power to grant pardons, and to require executive branch officials to provide written opinions "upon any subject relating to the duties of their respective offices." Article II also authorizes presidents to recommend measures to Congress as they deem "necessary and expedient," and requires them to give information on the state of the Union "from time to time." The broadest grant of authority is contained in the charge that the president "shall take care that the laws be faithfully executed," which contains both limits on presidential behavior (requiring presidents to faithfully carry out the will of Congress as expressed in statutes) and an implied affirmative grant, permitting some discretion in the performance of executive and implementation duties.

Legal scholars have long commented on the imprecision and brevity of Article II's language, especially in comparison with the more explicit and detailed wording of Article I (which defines Congress's power). J. G. Randall, in his comprehensive history of Lincoln's use of the executive power during the Civil War, wrote in 1926 that "there is a certain looseness in the constitutional grant of executive power which is in explicit contrast to the specification of the powers of Congress. It is the 'legislative powers *herein granted*' that are bestowed upon Congress, but it is simply the 'executive power' that is vested in the President. In consequence of the meager enumeration of presidential powers in the Constitution, this branch of our law has undergone a process of development by practice and by judicial decision."[35] The comparative vagueness of the vesting clause, according to Steven Calabresi and Kevin Rhodes, "suggests that the President is to have *all* of the executive power,"[36] a conclusion with implications for defining the scope of implied presidential power.

A second major difference between Articles I and II—the explicit grant of "necessary and proper" powers to Congress, with no analogous grant to the president—has been interpreted as either a recognition that the existence of implied executive power was so plain that it needed no such elasticity to effectuate it, or as evidence that "the domain of implied executive power is Congress', *not* the President's."[37]

Consider the meaning of the vesting clause itself. If the clause is a description, then presidential powers are simply limited to those that are enumerated in the remainder of Article II. If the clause is a more general grant of power, then the president can draw upon a broader range of implied "executive" powers beyond those mentioned in the text. Calabresi and Saikrishna Prakesh analyze the clause in great detail, and find significance in the differences and similarities between the Article II clause and analogous vesting language in Articles I and III. Article I provides that "all legislative powers *herein granted* shall be vested in a Congress of the United States" (§1, emphasis added); Article III that "the judicial power of the United States shall be vested in one supreme Court, and in other inferior courts as the Congress may from time to time ordain and establish" (§1). They conclude that the specificity and conditions in Articles I and III, combined with the relative simplicity of Article II's vesting language, support the contention that "the Vesting Clause of Article II must be read as conferring a general grant of the 'executive power' " to the president.[38] Monaghan, in contrast, finds that "the 'legislative history' of the difference in language between the legislative powers 'herein granted' and 'The Executive power' provides no basis for ascribing any importance to this difference."[39] He attributes the differences to minor changes in drafting rather than any substantive statements about the scope of the executive versus legislative powers.

These disputes are part of a debate that dates from the beginning of the Republic and continues today. Only a few years after collaborating on the *Federalist Papers*, Alexander Hamilton and James Madison became embroiled in a contentious dispute over the president's implied powers. In 1793, shortly after war broke out between France and Great Britain, President George Washington issued his famous Neutrality Proclamation. In the proclamation Washington, who "was convinced that the nation must remain neutral at all costs,"[40] announced that American citizens were not to become involved in the hostilities (by, for example, participating in the seizure of French or British ships), and that the U.S. government would not protect them in the event that they did. Congress was not in session when the issue arose and the cabinet advised against calling a special session, so Washington issued the proclamation solely on his own authority.[41] Even though the constitutional issues were considered in the context of a highly charged political atmosphere, because of strong domestic pro-French sentiment left over from the Revolutionary War, the debate highlighted the ambiguities of the president's legal powers and the clear gaps in constitutional language that made the disputes over presidential power so difficult to resolve. The question raised by the proclamation can be clearly stated: does the president have the authority to declare the *absence* of a state of war, given the clear congressional power to *declare* war?

Hamilton thought so. Following up on his *Federalist* writings which argued for an energetic executive,[42] he identified the president as the locus of foreign policy power, including the power to interpret treaties. In a public debate with Madison, Hamilton argued that the Neutrality Proclamation did nothing but inform citizens of the current state of relations between the United States, France, and Britain. He maintained that the president had only affirmed the existing state of affairs until Congress could make its own determination as to the existence of war or peace.[43] As such, the president had done nothing to encroach upon the congressional war power. Madison disagreed, strongly so, and he attacked Hamilton's theory of presidential power as nothing more than a justification for the president to employ the royal prerogatives of the British monarch. In making this argument, Madison was responding more to the general model of executive power that Hamilton had originally set out than to Hamilton's specific defense of the Neutrality Proclamation (which Madison evidently thought might be justifiable under a limited interpretation of presidential power).[44]

The key constitutional question, which remained unresolved until the end of the nineteenth century, was the extent of the president's *implied* powers, since the Constitution neither affirmed nor denied explicitly that the president could issue such a proclamation.[45] The split between Hamilton and Madison over the president's power, which was taking place in a broader context of which the Neutrality Proclamation was only one part, played a key role in the deepening of ideological splits among governing elites. That schism, according to historian James Rogers Sharp, in turn led to the development of "proto-parties" and to the "broadening of the base of national politics" as Hamilton, Madison, Jefferson, and others tried to solicit popular support for their versions of government.[46]

Since first recognizing the legitimacy of implied presidential powers in 1890, the Supreme Court has expanded the scope of what is implied by the enumerated powers. In the case of *In re Neagle*, 135 U.S. 1 (1890), the Court validated the president's authority to take independent action in executing the law, even when that action has not been expressly authorized by statute. Any "obligation that is fairly and properly inferable" from the Constitution, the Court ruled, has the same status in law as powers specifically mentioned.[47] Peter Shane and Harold Bruff note that *Neagle*, and a similar case arising out of railroad strikes in 1895, *In re Debs*, 158 U.S. 564 (1895), "stated broad support for presidential action taken without statutory authorization."[48]

Two cases of implied powers are especially relevant for a study of executive orders: presidential control over classified information, and presidential assertions of broad authority in intelligence collection. Although I treat these subjects in detail in chapter five, a brief summary of presidential control over executive branch information shows the degree to which presidents have successfully expanded the scope of their implied power.

The Constitution is completely silent on the issue of whether the president has the authority to keep information from the public (and, in the related doctrine of executive privilege, from the other two branches of government). Again there are clear differences in the explicit constitutional vestments in Articles I and II. Article I explicitly grants Congress the right to keep its proceedings closed to the public, requiring that each chamber publish a record of its proceedings, "excepting such parts as may in their judgment require secrecy." There is no analogous language granting the president similar powers. Mark Rozell argues that the lack of specific language in Article II reflects the Framers' opinion that secrecy was such an obvious executive power that they saw no need to mention it.[49] The courts have consistently agreed, holding that the president as a matter of course has access to reports that "are not and ought not to be published to the world,"[50] and that "in the area of basic national defense, the frequent need for absolute secrecy is, of course, self evident."[51]

The doctrine of executive privilege is based on the theory that in order to carry out the executive function, presidents must have the ability to obtain the confidential advice of their advisors. Beginning with Washington's refusal to provide Congress with information pertaining to a failed military mission in 1792, presidents have asserted the right to keep certain information from Congress and the courts. There is no explicit constitutional authorization for such a practice; the Supreme Court has justified its existence as deriving "from the supremacy of each branch within its own assigned area of constitutional duties. Certain powers and privileges flow from the nature of enumerated powers; the protection of the confidentiality of presidential communications has similar constitutional underpinnings."[52] Executive privilege is not absolute, and the courts have stepped in to require disclosure of information related to criminal proceedings or investigations.[53] In 1998 President Clinton asserted executive privilege to bar questioning of two aides, Bruce Lindsey and Sidney Blumenthal, as part of an independent counsel investigation into Clinton's involvement in Whitewater and related matters. In a sealed order issued in early May 1998, a federal judge denied the executive privilege claim and ordered the two to submit to questioning before a grand jury.

In practice, presidents have asserted almost total control over the definition and disposition of classified information, by setting out standards for classification and security clearances in a series of executive orders. Numerous congressional efforts to impose some kind of legislative framework to guide government information policy have had little impact on defense and national security information, which remain the exclusive domain of the executive branch.

Delegated Powers

Congressionally delegated powers make up the second major class of presidential power. Even though Congress may not, at least in theory, transfer its lawmaking power to another branch, it has routinely delegated "substantial discretionary authority to the executive branch" to flesh out the details of policy and implementation.[54] Examples of this delegation have included the power to set tariffs and impose trade restrictions, regulate industries, set agricultural marketing and production quotas, issue environmental protection rules, and specify aggravating factors for punishment under the Uniform Code of Military Justice.

The idea behind delegation is that Congress makes broad policy decisions, and then grants agency officials the discretion needed to effectively define and carry out those policies.[55] Congress's motivations for delegating can range from a recognition that complex regulations require more technical expertise than legislators can realistically provide, to a desire to insulate administration from the parochialism and logrolling inherent in the legislative process, to a desire to transfer blame for a potentially unpopular policy to a bureaucracy.[56]

Judicial doctrine holds that delegation is constitutionally permissible as long as Congress sets out an "intelligible principle" to which the executive branch must adhere in carrying out the delegated powers.[57] Subsequent rulings rendered this standard imprecise, upholding delegations under broad and ambiguous principles. "[The Court has] allowed railroad regulation under 'just and reasonable rates,' broadcast licensing in the 'public interest, convenience, or necessity,' and trade regulation of 'unfair methods of competition.' "[58] The Supreme Court has rejected a legislative delegation of power only twice, both times in 1935. In the second of the two cases,[59] *A.L.A. Schechter Poultry Corp. v. United States*,[60] the Court overturned the 1933 National Industrial Recovery Act, which granted to the president the authority to define "codes of fair competition" that governed wages, working conditions, and trade practices in different industries. The codes themselves were promulgated in a series of 398 executive orders issued between July 1933 and May 1935.[61] The Court ruled that NIRA gave the president too much authority to "[enact] laws for the government of trade and industry throughout the country" without meaningful statutory restrictions.[62] Nevertheless, since then no other Court has enforced this so-called *Schechter* rule, and "attempts to resurrect the nondelegation doctrine have been consistently unsuccessful."[63] That may change, however. In May 1999 the D.C. Circuit Court of Appeals overturned regulations issued by the Environmental Protection Agency pursuant to the Clean Air Act, holding that the agency had failed to articulate an intelligible principle to justify the rules. As such, the pollution regulations "[effected] an unconstitutional delegation of legislative power."[64] Although it was not completely clear from the decision whether the Clean Air Act itself violated the nondelegation doctrine, the case appeared to signify a step back from the long-standing deference the courts had previously shown. In May 2000 the Supreme Court accepted the case for its 2000–2001 term, raising the prospect of a fundamental reevaluation of decades of jurisprudence.

Congressionally delegated powers give the president wide latitude in carrying out statutory provisions, often in ways that Congress did not anticipate. Congress typically places some conditions upon the exercise of delegated power in addition to the general principles required to pass judicial scrutiny. The Administrative Procedures Act of 1946 imposed procedural requirements on executive branch rulemaking and regulatory functions, and Congress often requires detailed reporting and oversight. Even so, these restrictions still leave presidents with substantial maneuvering room and can even backfire, as the courts have often interpreted legislative restrictions on delegated power as explicit authorization of implied presidential authority.

The range of discretion available to presidents through delegated powers, as well as the relationship between executive orders and policy outcomes, is clearly illustrated by government contracting regulations. Presidents have used their implied and delegated powers in this area to make sweeping policies, including affirmative action requirements for government contractors.

Congress, through its power of the purse, establishes and funds programs to purchase goods and services from the private sector. Although legislation stipulates many of the goals and processes of these programs, the actual process of awarding and administering contracts is a classic executive function.[65] Congress has long recognized as much, and even though there is a complex statutory framework that governs procurement broadly, "the development of detailed procurement policies and procedures has generally been left to the procurement agencies" and, by extension, to the president.[66] Within the boundaries and requirements established by law, the president retains the authority to set the conditions under which procurement will take place.

In addition to the constitutional authority as chief executive to administer contract policy within the boundaries set by law, Congress has expanded the scope of this power by explicitly delegating to the president the authority to promulgate contract rules and regulations. In 1949, in response to recommendations that the government centralize and streamline its administrative processes for procurement and management, Congress enacted the Federal Property and Administrative Services Act, or FPASA (40 U.S.C. 471 et seq.). FPASA gives the president the authority to "prescribe such policies and directives" respecting government administration and the management and disposal of government property. Elsewhere in the act, Congress specified its intent "to provide for the Government an economical and efficient system" for procurement and property management.

With this law, Congress gave the president the power to set and administer procurement policy within the boundaries set by statute, and presidents have used it to set many of the conditions under which private companies will receive government contracts. Federal courts have consistently ruled that under the act presidents can make decisions about how the government will carry out its contracting function, as long as the policies are related to the goals of economy and efficiency. Over time presidents have expanded the permissible interpretations of what this means to include policies with broad social and political consequences.

In a 1961 opinion on the president's authority to impose conditions on government contractors, the attorney general concluded that "except to the extent that Congress has either required or prohibited certain types of government contracts or certain provisions to be included in such contracts, the Executive Branch of the Government has discretion to contract in such manner and on such terms as it considers appropriate to the discharge of its constitutional and statutory responsibilities."[67] The government's authority to do this is clear: "No one has a right to a Government contract. . . . Those wishing to do business with the Government must meet the Government's terms; others need not."[68]

Presidents have carried out this power by specifing that in order to be eligible to bid on and receive government contracts, contractors must adhere to particular requirements and conditions. In making these rules presidents have, at various times, required favorable treatment for contractors in labor surplus areas, imposed wage and working-hour requirements, and barred the use of state prisoners as laborers on federal contracts. During the early years of the New Deal, the Roosevelt administration issued an executive order requiring government contractors to comply with codes of fair competition promulgated under the National Industrial Recovery Act.[69] Although this and other NIRA orders became moot when the Supreme Court struck the law down in 1935, it had an enduring legacy, as it served as a blueprint for the Walsh-Healy Act.[70]

Given the scope of government procurement activity and the number of companies involved, such "administrative" rules can have a sweeping effect. The most controversial of these provisions have been those which prohibited contractors from discriminating on the basis of race and which created a variety of oversight mechanisms to enforce the policy (with varying degrees of success). FDR, Truman, and Eisenhower all issued executive orders requiring government contractors to abide by nondiscrimination policies, with authority stemming from "various War Powers Acts and Defense Production Acts passed between 1941 and 1950."[71]

More recently, presidents have asserted their authority through the delegated powers in FPASA to broaden the scope of their contracting power to include general social policy. In 1978 President Carter issued Executive Order 12092, which required government contractors to adhere to wage and price guidelines issued by the Council on Wage and Price Stability.[72] It was the first executive order that explicitly cited FPASA as the authority to "achieve broad national goals through the federal procurement system."[73] The order, and its subsequent implementing regulations, required all contractors receiving more than $5 million to certify their compliance with the wage and price guidelines. Those who refused would be subject to termination on existing contracts and would be ineligible to receive future contracts.

A federal appeals court upheld the president's authority to issue this order in a split decision, ruling that the FPASA grants the president statutory authority over procurement, and that the president's action was not barred by the statute creating the Council on Wage and Price Stability (*AFL-CIO v. Kahn*, 618 F. 2d 784, D.C. Cir.). Of particular relevance was the court's finding that presidents may, under the act, promulgate procurement regulations in order to advance broad social policy, as long as there is a "close nexus" between those policies and the FPASA's stated goals of economy and efficiency. In reaching this conclusion, the court again referred to the acquiescence doctrine. Citing the various nondiscrimination orders issued by presidents since the 1940s, the opinion found it "useful to consider how the procurement power has been exercised under the Act," and took the history of the practice and the absence of congressional resistance as an indication that a broad interpretation of the law was warranted. "Of course, the President's view of his own authority under a statute is not controlling," the appeals court wrote, "but when that view has been acted upon over a substantial period of time without eliciting congressional reversal, it is entitled to great respect."[74]

Executive Order 12092, then, was a valid exercise of presidential power that affected—through a purely administrative rule—billions in procurement dollars and the interests of thousands of current and potential government contractors. Even more, Carter administration officials admitted that the order, though targeted specifically at government contractors, was likely to have economywide effects, because other companies would be forced to lower their own costs in order to compete with federal contractors on private contracts.[75]

Clinton, to his dismay, discovered that this power does not extend indefinitely. In March 1995 he issued Executive Order 12954, which barred federal contractors from hiring permanent replacements for striking employees.[76] Clinton cited the FPASA in the order, claiming that the practice of hiring permanent replacements hurt labor relations and, by inference, contractor productivity. "By permanently replacing its workers," the order stated in a lengthy preamble designed to establish the necessary nexus between replacement workers and economy and efficiency, "an employer loses the accumulated knowledge, experience, skill, and expertise of its incumbent employees. These circumstances then adversely affect the businesses and entities, such as the Federal Government, which rely on that employer to provide high quality and reliable goods or services." No contract over $100,000 would be awarded to a firm if the secretary of labor had certified that any organizational unit within the company had hired permanent replacements.

A coalition of business groups led by the U.S. Chamber of Commerce sued in federal court, challenging the legality of the order on the grounds that Congress had specifically authorized the hiring of permanent replacements in the National Labor Relations Act (NLRA), and that the statute thus preempted the executive order.[77] The appellants challenged the order on two other grounds, that the president had failed to make a finding that permanent replacements in fact had an adverse effect on "economy and efficiency" as required by FPASA, and that the lack of findings constituted an unconstitutional delegation of legislative authority to the president. I focus on the conflict between the NLRA and the executive order because the court considered it "appellants' most powerful argument on the merits" and because it most directly confronts the issue of the reach of executive orders generally.[78]

The court, agreeing with the challenge, overturned two district court decisions that argued that the executive order "was entitled to *Chevron*-like deference and was reasonable because it furthered the statutory values of 'economy' and 'efficiency.' "[79] To the appeals court, the central issue was the conflict between the NLRA and the executive order, as Clinton's order posed issues not raised by other procurement-related orders (such as Johnson's 11246 or Carter's 12092) which did not conflict directly with any statute. Ultimately, the court concluded that Clinton's order was regulatory in nature and that it impermissibly encroached upon labor relations in contravention to the NLRA.

Although Clinton lost in his bid to unilaterally alter labor policy, the judicial rebuff did not constitute a significant departure from the judiciary's typical deference. The court found that an explicit statutory provision (the right under the NLRA to hire replacement workers) trumps a broad but general delegation of authority (the president's power to regulate procurement through the FPASA). Despite the decision's notice of failed legislative efforts to enact a replacement worker policy similar to what was in the executive order, little weight was given to interpreting this congressional "silence." It was not necessary to, and the court did not, retreat from the existing doctrine of acquiescence or deference that might have validated the president if the legislation in question had been less specific.

At the end of the decision the appeals court took issue with the government's claim that the order was narrow in its effect, implicitly undercutting the politics–administration dichotomy: "It does not seem possible to deny that the President's Executive Order seeks to set a broad policy governing the behavior of thousands of American companies and affecting millions of workers . . . the impact of the Executive Order is quite far reaching. It applies to *all* contracts over $100,000, and federal government purchases totaled $437 billion in 1994, constituting approximately 6.5% of the gross domestic product. . . . Federal contractors and subcontractors employ 26 million workers, 22% of the labor force."[80]

Both the IEEPA and the FPASA delegations show the broad range of "residual decision rights" that presidents may exercise, through executive orders, under statutorily defined powers. Although the replacement workers issue shows that the courts will step in to invalidate specific decisions taken under delegated powers, there is less willingness to invalidate the underlying delegations themselves as unconstitutional.

Legislative delegation has become more common since the advent of the modern regulatory state. Critics claim that expansive delegation replaces legislative deliberation with unaccountable bureaucracies, and some legal theorists argue that independent regulatory agencies are unconstitutional. The courts, though, recognized the legitimacy of independent regulatory agencies in *Humphrey's Executor*, and it is difficult to imagine a circumstance in which the judiciary would reconsider its ruling in that case and thereby undercut such a broad scope of government activity.

Inherent Presidential Powers— Executive Prerogative

The third source of presidential power—inherent executive powers—is by far the most controversial, and its existence is disputed. Many legal scholars argue against the notion of inherent powers, concluding that it "is incompatible with the very purpose of a limited, written Constitution."[81] Presidents have nevertheless asserted, particularly during national emergencies, that they possess powers beyond those mentioned in the Constitution. In its strongest form, this argument presupposes the existence of a prerogative power, or the authority "to act on behalf of the United States in the absence of law, or in defiance of it."[82]

Presidents, not surprisingly, tend to view broad executive power more sympathetically once they are in office. Many times, proponents of limited presidential authority adopt a decidedly different stance while in office (as Professor Taft did once he became President Taft). Thomas Jefferson took a very constrained view of the office while serving as Washington's secretary of state, splitting with Hamilton over the Neutrality Proclamation and other issues of executive power. As president, however, he carried out the Louisiana Purchase, expending funds and acquiring territory without any congressional mandate. Taft was involved in several confrontations with Congress over separation of powers issues, at one point even directing his cabinet secretaries to disregard a statute that prohibited them from participating in a centralized budget planning exercise (see chapter four). Another example from the twentieth century is Robert Jackson, who as attorney general argued in favor of the same inherent presidential powers that he would later emphatically reject as a Supreme Court justice. In 1940 Attorney General Jackson argued that the president had the authority to transfer U.S. warships to Great Britain, via executive agreement rather than a treaty, in return for access to British military bases (the so-called destroyers-for-bases deal), even though only two months before Congress had enacted a statute that seemed to prohibit such an exchange. In his legal opinion to the president, Jackson relied heavily on the Supreme Court's 1936 *United States v. Curtiss-Wright Export Corporation* decision (299 U.S. 304), in which Chief Justice Sutherland set out a sweeping theory of inherent presidential prerogative in foreign affairs. *Curtiss-Wright*, said Jackson, "explicitly and authoritatively defined" the president's power in foreign affairs, and permitted Roosevelt to deal with Britain however he saw fit.[83]

Whether or not presidents in theory possess a valid prerogative power, they have repeatedly acted as though they do. Theodore Roosevelt was the first president to suggest that presidents had a limited prerogative power, which he advanced in his notion of the "stewardship" presidency. Roosevelt argued that it was not only the president's right but "his duty to do anything that the needs of the nation demanded unless such action was forbidden by the Constitution or by its laws,"[84] a position that leaves open the possibility that the president can act beyond the law, though not in contravention to it. William Howard Taft was a vigorous critic of this view, deeming it an "unsafe doctrine" because it could be used to justify an unlimited and arbitrary exercise of presidential power.[85] Instead, in his more limited theory of presidential authority, Taft held that "the President can exercise no power which cannot be fairly and reasonably traced to some specific grant of power or justly implied and included within such express grant of power as proper and necessary to its exercise."[86] Some commentators have read Roosevelt to mean that the president has merely implied powers, not prerogative powers. In fact, his view is much stronger, for two reasons. First, Roosevelt explicitly argued that the president could act unless the Constitution or law expressly forbade it. The president could, as a result, not only read the existence of implied powers stemming from enumerated powers, but act in those cases when the Constitution or laws were completely silent. Second, Taft offered his argument in direct opposition to Roosevelt, and Taft clearly recognized the legitimacy of "justly implied" powers.

To historian Forrest MacDonald, the primacy of the stewardship role and its reliance on implied powers was a major impetus to the rise of presidential lawmaking through executive orders and proclamations—"decrees that had the force of law"—as a tool of presidential power.[87] It is no accident that Theodore Roosevelt was the first president to make extensive use of executive orders.[88] Nor is it coincidental that executive orders became more common in the late nineteenth century, precisely at the time when enduring government institutions began to form along with an expansion of state administrative capacity.

Most executive orders in the eighteenth and nineteenth centuries in fact involved routine administrative procedures; the first order, it is generally agreed, consisted of Washington's June 1789 instruction to executive branch heads to submit a "clear account" of their departmental affairs.[89] The bulk of executive orders issued between 1880 and 1900 addressed civil service matters and the disposition of publicly owned land (see chapter three). Theodore Roosevelt issued 1,091 orders during his two terms, nearly as many as had been issued by all previous presidents over the prior 111 years (1,259).

The most powerful historical examples of executive prerogative remain Lincoln's actions in 1861, taken after the outbreak of the Civil War but before Congress convened in July. Acting on his own, Lincoln ordered a blockade of Southern ports, suspended habeas corpus, increased the size of the army and navy, expended government funds in the absence of any congressional appropriation, censored the mail, and imposed restrictions on foreign travel, though "he had no authority to do these things."[90] Lincoln defended his actions by claiming, first, that they were in fact legal and, second, that they were required by the extraordinary danger the Union faced, though the view has long been that these acts were "unconstitutional and extralegal."[91] With respect to his suspension of habeas corpus, Lincoln asked his famous rhetorical question in the context of a broader argument about presidential prerogative: "The whole of the laws which were required to be faithfully executed were being resisted and failing of execution in nearly one-third of the States. Must they be allowed to finally fail of execution, even had it been perfectly clear that by the use of the means necessary to their execution some single law . . . should to a very limited extent be violated? To state the question more directly, Are all the laws but one to go unexecuted, and the Government itself go to pieces lest that one be violated?"[92] Congress ultimately granted retroactive legislative authorization for most of these acts, but taken as a whole, Lincoln's exercise of presidential authority asserted "for the first time in our history, an initiative of indefinite scope and legislative in effect in meeting the domestic aspects of a war emergency."[93]

Franklin Roosevelt made a similar claim of executive prerogative during World War II. In February 1942 Congress passed the Emergency Price Control Act, which gave the president the authority to regulate prices in order to check inflation. The administration felt that provisions governing agricultural rendered the act "unfair and unworkable," because the law restricted the president's ability to impose ceilings on farm products.[94] Over the summer, Assistant Attorney General Oscar Cox proposed that the president's commander-in-chief powers could justify working around the restrictive provisions, much as Roosevelt had done in seizing the manufacturing facilities of North American Aviation in the absence of specific authorization.[95] Cox concluded that "an amendment to the Price Control Act is probably desirable in this connection," and FDR requested the revisions in September 1942.

The way in which FDR asked for changes generated considerable controversy. In an often-cited message to Congress, Roosevelt declared:

I ask that Congress take this action by the first of October. Inaction on your part by that date will leave me with the inescapable responsibility to the people of this country to see to it that the war effort is no longer imperiled by the threat of economic chaos.

In the event that Congress should fail to act, and act adequately, I shall accept the responsibility, and I will act . . .

The President has the power, under the Constitution and under Congressional acts, to take measures necessary to avert a disaster which would interfere with the winning of the war.[96]

Roosevelt was undoubtedly aware of the connections between his assertion of unilateral power and what previous presidents had done during wartime emergencies: Oscar Cox's files on the Price Control Act contain an August 25, 1942, memorandum detailing the use of emergency powers by Lincoln and Woodrow Wilson in the absence of legislation. The memo considered some of Wilson's executive orders "drastic," particularly his order of January 17, 1918, in which "he suspended the operation of practically all industries east of the Mississippi River for a period of five days beginning January 18. . . . This order was promulgated in spite of protests from every part of the country, opinions that the order exceeded the authority of the Executive, and an official resolution of the Senate asking for delay and explanation."[97]

Corwin found FDR's words nothing short of astonishing, interpreting them as a message to Congress that " 'Unless you repeal a certain statutory provision forthwith, I shall nevertheless treat it as repealed' . . . [this message] can only be interpreted as a claim of power on the part of the President to suspend the Constitution in a situation deemed by him to make such a step necessary."[98]

Although Congress did what the president asked, albeit a day late, not everyone accepted FDR's sweeping assertion of power. Senator Robert Taft (R-Ohio), objected in strong terms: "If the President can change the price law by Executive order, he can draft men in violation of the Selective Service Act by Executive order . . . if this doctrine is sustained in wartime it can easily be stretched to cover the post-war period and a whole series of possible later emergencies until we have a complete one-man dictatorship. Then government by the people will have vanished from America."[99] Similarly, Senator Robert LaFollette, Jr. (Prog.-Wisc.) complained that FDR had "placed a pistol at the head of Congress."[100]

Corwin attributes Roosevelt's success in assuming powers far beyond what was constitutionally authorized to the unique emergency that World War II posed, and the fact that the public simply accepted what FDR did. Roosevelt was clearly aware of the importance of having the public believe in the legitimacy of what he was doing. In February 1943 Oscar Cox wrote Harry Hopkins about a recent poll in which 78 percent of the public said it was acceptable for the president, as commander in chief, "to make important decisions before consulting Congress." Cox suggested a public relations effort "to get across to the public some of the historical and other reasons why the Chief Executive, in time of war, has to have a good deal of scope in decisions in the same way that a commanding general in the field does."[101]

Truman, as I noted in chapter one, initially based his steel seizure decision on assertions that the president had virtually unlimited authority to act in emergencies. The solicitor general had claimed that the president had authority to seize the steel mills based "upon nebulous, inherent powers never expressly granted but said to have accrued to the office from the customs and claims of preceding administrations. The plea is for a resulting power to deal with a crisis or an emergency according to the necessities of the case."[102] The majority in *Youngstown* had no difficulty dismissing that argument, holding that no interpretation of either the commander-in-chief power or the take care clause could justify Truman's act of presidential lawmaking. Jackson's concurring opinion specifically rejected the emergency inherent-powers argument.

The Significance of Precedent and Presidential Practice

The ambiguities of executive power provide the president with substantial room—residual decision rights, to use Moe's term—in which to maneuver. The limits on executive orders—that they must be tied to a grant of executive authority, and that they may not contradict a statute—are more flexible than they appear, in large part because the demarcation between executive and legislative powers is not always clear. Legal scholar E. Donald Elliot has criticized the Supreme Court's rulings on separation of powers questions as "abysmal," arguing that Justices have focused far too much attention to questions of whether a particular power is legislative or executive in nature (a task he considers futile and which has not, in his view, provided any definitional clarity), and too little on "abstracting and elaborating theories of what goals separation of powers should serve, and then asking whether a particular function should be deemed to be executive in light of these goals."[103] The lack of any cohesive theory of executive power (or even a precise definition of what, exactly, executive power is) leaves as the only option the practice of defining those powers "implicitly, through a series of ad hoc decisions about specific practices."[104]

Because the specific boundaries between the branches are amorphous, presidents have an incentive to poke at the limits to see how Congress, in particular, will respond. At times presidents can appear to step close to the limits, or even over them, without sanction. No power is more central to the legislative function, for example, than the authority to spend money (the "power of the purse").[105] The president may not spend public money in the absence of a congressional appropriation, nor is it permissible for the President to refuse to spend money that Congress has appropriated. There are times when this restriction does not apply, as when Congress fails to enact either an appropriations bill or a continuing resolution authorizing expenditures; this occurred in 1995, when Congress refused to provide funds for the executive branch during a confrontation with the president over the budget. In these cases, according to a 1981 Opinion of the Attorney General, the president has the authority under the Anti-Deficiency Act to "fulfill certain legal obligations connected with the orderly shutdown of agency operations," and there may be cases where the president may expend funds to carry out the constitutional responsibilities of the office.[106]

As the Exchange Stabilization Fund episode described in chapter one demonstrates, though, presidents can interpret congressional intentions flexibly, using appropriated funds in a manner that Congress clearly did not anticipate. President John Kennedy went even further, establishing the Peace Corps in 1961 by executive order and funding it without any appropriations.[107] To operate the new agency, Kennedy relied on contingency funds provided by the Mutual Security Act until Congress provided a specific authorization seven months later.[108]

The Supreme Court has, in addition, found ways around the apparently unambiguous declaration that statutes take priority over executive orders when the two conflict. In *U.S. v. Midwest Oil Co.*, 236 U.S. 459 (1915), the Court upheld the president's authority, under certain conditions, to issue executive orders or proclamations that have the effect of invalidating a law. At issue in *Midwest* was whether the president could prohibit private entities from purchasing the mineral rights for or title to public lands, when Congress had by law allowed the purchase of such rights. In 1897 Congress had declared that all public lands with petroleum deposits were to be "free and open to occupation, exploration, and purchase by citizens of the United States."[109] In 1909, in response to the rapid depletion of oil reserves on California and Wyoming public lands, President Taft issued a proclamation temporarily withdrawing 3 million acres from any mineral or oil exploitation. Midwest Oil, which had purchased oil rights to some of the land in question, argued that the order unconstitutionally withdrew land that Congress had specified should be open to exploration.

The Supreme Court upheld the president, largely on the grounds that Congress had implicitly accepted the president's authority to make such withdrawals, despite the fact that Taft's order appeared to violate explicit statutory language. Noting that Congress had not challenged 252 presidential withdrawal orders before 1910, the Court reasoned that "the long-continued practice, known to and acquiesced in by Congress, [had] raised a presumption that the withdrawals had been made in pursuance of its consent or of a recognized administrative power of the Executive in the management of the public lands."[110]

The relative institutional capabilities of the presidency and Congress to adapt and respond have also played a role, as have long-standing judicial doctrines that give the president important advantages. In the past few decades the judiciary has through various decisions created a presumption that favors presidential initiative. Unless a presidential act contravenes a clear and explicit statutory or constitutional prohibition that directly addresses the action, the courts are likely to side with the president. In a series of decisions in the 1980s that expanded the scope of executive power, the Supreme Court indicated a willingness to validate executive action in the absence of an explicit congressional prohibition (which must take legislative form), to find implicit congressional consent in legislation that provides authority to the president in tangential policy areas, and to uphold executive interpretations of ambiguous statutes unless Congress has spoken precisely to the issue in point. These patterns hold true in domestic as well as in foreign policy, but take on additional weight in foreign affairs when combined with the traditional deference to presidential action in that arena.

Much of the time, analyses of the president's constitutional power rely on historical evidence of how individual presidents viewed that power and how they put it into practice. Practice matters because of the importance of precedent to the expansion of presidential power, because the parameters of presidential authority have often been shaped by case-by-case judicial review, and because presidents have used their authority (often through executive orders) in order to shape institutional patterns and processes that in turn enhance their ability to exercise administrative control. Each time a president relies on executive prerogative to take some type of action, it makes it easier for a future president to take the same (or similar) action. "The boundaries between the three branches of government are . . . strongly affected by the role of custom or acquiescence. When one branch engages in a certain practice and the other branches acquiesce, the practice gains legitimacy and can fix the meaning of the Constitution."[111]

The difficulty in pinpointing the "correct" distribution of powers contributes to the importance of precedent. This much the judiciary recognizes, as it has long held that custom or long-standing presidential practice can legitimate the exercise of a specific power. The acquiescence doctrine, for example, originated in *Midwest Oil*, in which the Court concluded that President Taft's withdrawal of public lands was authorized by Congress's traditional deference to presidential control in this domain. Although presidents cannot create powers they otherwise do not have through this practice, and the Court has rejected some long-standing practices as unconstitutional (the legislative veto, for example), the doctrine continues to work its way into presidential-legislative relations.[112] Fisher cites congressional acquiescence as a factor in the shift of the war power from Congress to the president, but he sees no practical alternative to relying on custom. A prohibition on the use of custom would require "several hundred amendments to the Constitution and a willingness to keep it in a perpetual state of agitation and flux."[113]

In a concurring opinion in *Youngstown*, Justice Felix Frankfurter offered more details about the acquiescence doctrine, and set out some of the limits as well. "In short, a systematic, unbroken, executive practice," he wrote, "long pursued to the knowledge of Congress but never before questioned, engaged in by Presidents who have also sworn to uphold the Constitution, making as it were such exercise of power part of the structure of our government, may be treated as a gloss on 'executive power' vested in the President by §1 of Art. II."[114] The steel seizure did not constitute such a "systematic, unbroken executive practice," since Congress had spoken clearly on the seizure question over the years, and presidents had only rarely resorted to such action without clear statutory authority.

After analyzing the history of congressional authorization of industrial seizures (which were enacted in sixteen separate laws between 1916 and 1952), Frankfurter concluded that Congress had carefully circumscribed all such grants.[115] There were, moreover, only a few examples of presidential seizures apart from either statutory authorization or extraordinary circumstances. Presidents Franklin Roosevelt and Woodrow Wilson had seized transportation, communication, and industrial facilities, but Frankfurter found that all but three of these seizures (a) took place pursuant to existing law or under a claim that the president was acting pursuant to law or (b) occurred after Congress had declared war.

It is ironic, though, that the majority opinion in the steel seizure case and several of the concurring opinions gave great weight to Congress's refusal to grant Truman the explicit statutory authority to seize the mills. To Lawrence Tribe, "a decisive majority of five Justices treated Congress' silence as speech—its *nonenactment of authorizing legislation* as a legally binding expression of *intent to forbid* the seizure at issue."[116] This potentially significant limit on presidential power, however, was vitiated in *Dames & Moore v. Regan*, the hostage agreement case in which the Court found broad authorization of Carter's use of executive orders to nullify attachments on Iranian-held assets in the United States. As with Truman's steel seizure, the hostage agreements were not explicitly authorized by any statute. However, the Court found implicit authorization in "three not-quite-applicable pieces of legislation."[117] Even though Chief Justice William Rehnquist, in the majority opinion, held that neither the International Economic Emergency Powers Act nor the Hostage Act of 1868 specifically authorized the suspension of private claims against Iran, he did find "both statutes highly relevant in the looser sense of indicated congressional acceptance of a broad scope for executive action in circumstances such as this case."[118] The Court also noted the "history of legislative acquiescence" in upholding Executive orders, despite the fact that the Senate, in particular, had objected to other executive claim settlements, in some cases forcing a renegotiation of terms.[119]

Critics of the acquiescence doctrine note the potential for "bootstrapping" of presidential power, whereby presidents can, over time, accrue power that they should not have simply because they have exercised it enough times. Since the Court has ruled that Congress may only express its disapproval of executive branch action through legislation and not through more informal mechanisms such as the legislative veto,[120] Koh has argued that the rulings, when taken together, "create a one-way 'ratchet effect' that effectively redraws the categories described in Justice Jackson's *Youngstown* concurrence."[121]

The Executive Power and Executive Orders

How do executive orders fit into this framework of presidential power? The legal connection is clear, since federal courts have long considered executive orders to be the equivalent of statutes when they are issued pursuant to the president's legitimate constitutional or congressionally delegated powers.[122] Their validity stems from their status as an instrument through which the president exercises his legal authority; in effect, the president may use an executive order to do anything permitted within the bounds of this authority. Most often, executive orders consist of presidential instructions to officers of agencies and departments, directing them to take specified action. This description is less technical than it may seem, since even administrative rulings can have consequences that reach far beyond executive branch boundaries. Most of the time presidents are free to choose the instrument they wish to use to carry out their executive function (proclamations, administrative directives, findings, executive orders, and so on), although Congress can stipulate that the president use one or another of these instruments for a particular purpose. The federal courts do not distinguish between executive orders and proclamations and hold that the two formats are equivalent for the purposes of carrying out the president's legal authority.[123]

Judicial review of executive orders extends back to *Little v. Barreme*, 2 Cranch 170 (1804). That case originated in a U.S. Navy captain's seizure of a Danish vessel sailing from a French port, based on standing orders from President John Adams. Acting in his capacity as commander in chief, Adams had ordered the navy to seize all vessels traveling to or from France. Adams's order, in turn, was issued pursuant to a statute that authorized the seizure of vessels sailing to French ports. Chief Justice John Marshall found that the capture was not authorized by statute, and ordered the captain to pay damages. The decision established the clear principle that "congressional policy announced in a statute necessarily prevails over inconsistent presidential orders and military actions. Presidential orders, even those issued as Commander in Chief, are subject to restrictions imposed by Congress."[124]

Executive orders have a substantive impact on policy and power, because implementation and administration have substantive impact, and because of the significance of precedent to the exercise of presidential legal authority. The "politics–administration" dichotomy paradigm that once dominated the public administration literature—and, as I note below, found its way into major Supreme Court rulings on the extent of presidential power—has been supplanted by the more persuasive notion that administration inevitably involves politics, insofar as the processes by which agencies implement statutes and programs affect public rights and policy outcomes.

One question that executive orders raise is enforcement, and the ability of private citizens to pursue claims through the courts. Claimants can, of course, challenge the validity of executive orders on the grounds that they exceeded the president's constitutional or statutory authority.[125] Additionally, as a general rule the courts have jurisdiction in disputes arising over executive orders issued pursuant to delegated statutory authority, or those directed at nongovernmental parties. In practice, however, it is almost impossible for private claimants to allege violations of an executive order itself or seek damages as a remedy for violations against another private party.[126] Recent court rulings are consistent on this point, holding that executive orders do not generally permit citizens to insist on judicial enforcement of the orders' requirements.[127] More commonly, aggrieved parties must rely exclusively on administrative remedies to resolve disputes that may arise.[128] An executive order issued as part of a statutory delegation of power, or as part of the process of carrying out a statute, may create enforceable private rights, but only if the statute or the order clearly intended to create such a right.[129] Presidents routinely seek to preempt litigation over their orders, most commonly by inserting within each order a section that denies any intention to create or alter private rights. And if a statute commits a question or determination solely to presidential discretion, the president's actions are not themselves reviewable.[130]

Litigation over whether government agencies have complied with an executive order raises a different set of issues, but here too the courts have been reluctant to step in. As a rule, federal courts have consistently ruled that matters relating to internal management procedures and practices in the executive branch are not subject to judicial review.[131] Even if there are questions about the legality of an executive order, the courts will in most cases refuse to intervene on questions of whether agencies have in fact complied with it.[132] There have been a few cases at the district or appellate level in which the courts ruled that private parties *could* seek judicial remedy in response to agency failure to comply with an executive order, but most of these addressed instances in which the order did not explicitly deny that it created private rights of action.[133]

Executive Order 12291, which required agencies to submit proposed regulations to the Office of Management and Budget and justify them with a cost-benefit analysis, triggered a spurt of federal litigation as private groups alleged that the order illegally interfered with established statutory processes. In most cases courts rejected challenges to regulatory action (or inaction) based on purported violations of 12291 on the grounds that the order created no judicially enforceable private rights.[134] In others, the courts evaded the issue of the legality of the order, upholding or rejecting agency action on other grounds.[135] Noyes argues that the Court's unwillingness to infer the existence of private rights in executive orders places limits on presidential power (since the power to create private rights has typically been lodged in the legislature).[136]

The formal process for issuing executive orders is itself outlined in two executive orders. Order 11030 and 11354 specify the format of orders and proclamations, and require that orders be reviewed by the Office of Management and Budget.[137] If the director of the OMB approves the order (part of OMB's central clearance function that it first assumed in the 1930s), he or she transmits the order to the Department of Justice for legal review (a task performed by the Office of Legal Counsel). After presidential signature, orders are sent to the Office of the Federal Register, and once published have the force and effect of law.

There is no penalty for avoiding this process: presidents and their staffs are free to skip one or more steps, and orders 11030 and 11354 prescribe no sanction for violating their terms. As a result, when the White House is under time pressure it routinely bypasses the formal routine. The most commonly skipped step is formal clearance by the Justice Department, with the OMB staff typically relying on informal legal guidance as a substitute. Examples of important orders issued without complete formal review include Reagan's Executive Order 12291 (cost-benefit analysis requirement for federal regulations in February 1981)[138], and Eisenhower's Executive Order 10730 (placing the Arkansas National Guard in the active military in September 1957).[139] The most common reason for rushing through the process is the desire to issue orders quickly either at the end of the president's term or at the start of an administration.

In contemporary practice, executive orders typically either originate from the advisory structures within the Executive Office of the President or percolate up from executive agencies desirous of presidential action. For particularly complex or far-reaching orders, the White House will solicit comment and suggestions from affected agencies on wording and substantive content. Simple executive orders navigate this process in a few weeks; complex orders can take years, and can even be derailed over an inability to obtain the necessary consensus or clearances.

The history of one particularly controversial and complex executive order highlights the process. In January 1979 President Carter signed an executive order that required government agencies to contemplate the environmental impact of their actions on foreign soil.[140] The order arose out of a protracted wrangle between the foreign affairs/defense and environmental agencies about the foreign application of the National Environmental Policy Act (NEPA). The dispute involved months of negotiations in the midst of litigation and the threat of legislation. Throughout the process, the themes of maintaining presidential control over a rapidly developing process, and interagency coordination, are apparent.

Congress enacted the National Environmental Policy Act in 1969 as part of a broad effort at environmental protection. Its most notable feature was a requirement that federal agencies prepare an environmental impact statement (EIS) for all "major Federal actions significantly affecting the quality of the human environment."[141] From the outset questions arose over whether this provision applied to agency actions outside the territorial United States, or just those taking place within the United States. The act itself was ambiguous on this point. Although the statute made no specific mention of foreign applicability, it noted the broad scope of environmental problems in its references to the "human environment," and it required federal agencies to consider "the worldwide and long-range character of environmental problems."[142]

Environmental groups insisted that this language required agencies to prepare an impact statement on foreign activities, and in 1973 a consortium of groups filed a lawsuit to force the Atomic Energy Commission (AEC) and the Export-Import Bank to require an EIS for the nuclear power export program.[143] Court decisions were inconclusive, generally assuming NEPA's applicability to foreign actions although none issued a binding ruling to that effect.[144]

Within the Executive Office of the President, the Council on Environmental Quality, or CEQ—the unit established within the EOP to oversee agency compliance with NEPA—took the position that NEPA in fact applied to the foreign actions of federal agencies.[145] This put the council squarely at odds with those agencies that insisted on a purely domestic application of the environmental impact statement requirement, including the Nuclear Regulatory Commission, the Export-Import Bank, and the departments of Defense and State.[146] Objections, both inside and outside of government, centered on the fear that applying NEPA abroad would undercut foreign policy objectives, intrude upon the sovereignty of foreign countries by administering U.S. law on their territory, and interfere with foreign trade and economic development programs.

Carter himself was reported to favor some sort of requirement that the agencies consider the environmental effects of their foreign actions, but the White House spent much of 1977 and 1978 struggling to find the best way to proceed. Carter had raised the visibility and impact of the dispute in 1977, when he expanded CEQ's authority by issuing an executive order that authorized the council to promulgate binding regulations on NEPA implementation abroad. This was a departure from previous council decisions, which had been issued as less binding departmental guidelines or memoranda.[147] While this change in nomenclature would have no impact on how the courts viewed NEPA itself, it would create "a second and independent obligation" for agencies stemming from the requirements of the executive order.[148]

When CEQ issued draft regulations in January 1978 to implement the order, it "drew instant opposition from the State, Defense, Treasury, and Commerce Departments, as well as the ExImBank, the Nuclear Regulatory Commission, and the Office of Special Representative for Trade Negotiations."[149] Faced with adamant opposition from this powerful set of agencies, Carter quickly backed off from the idea that CEQ would disseminate governmentwide regulations.

Nevertheless the administration had to do something, because two other issues had arisen by the time CEQ had released the draft regulations. First, the Export-Import Bank was facing a new lawsuit challenging a wide range of export loans and licenses on the grounds that the bank had failed to issue an EIS for environmentally sensitive actions.[150] Although previous court decisions had avoided the question of extraterritorial NEPA requirements, the White House feared that the government had only a "minimal chance of winning the suit," and that a ruling against Eximbank would present all government agencies with court-defined guidelines rather than rules set by the administration.[151] To those agencies strongly opposed to CEQ's regulations, the prospect of a judicial mandate was even more distasteful than what the council had proposed. The litigation was all the more threatening since the Justice Department was palpably unenthusiastic about defending ExImbank's position that it was exempt from all NEPA requirements: in a January 1978 memo to White House Counsel Robert Lipshutz, the Office of Legal Counsel had conceded that NEPA probably did, in fact, apply to foreign actions. "Although NEPA does contain references to 'the Nation' and to 'Americans' as noted by ExImbank," wrote Assistant Attorney General John Harmon, "its thrust is, without doubt, toward requiring federal agencies to consider the impact their actions may have upon man's global environment."[152]

Second, Carter wanted to avoid legislation regarding the application of NEPA, and especially to head off Senate legislation that would exempt Eximbank from the environmental impact statement requirement. Although administration officials opposed statutory exemptions, and wanted agencies to think about the foreign environmental consequences of their policies, they also feared that a legislative mandate exempting agencies from NEPA would undercut the Administration's environmental policy. Officials argued before Congress that the executive branch needed flexibility in determining how to consider environmental effects.[153] "The Administration's goal," one account concluded, "is to find a middle ground that will reflect sensitivity to the environmental effects of U.S. actions abroad without hobbling the efforts of American exporters to compete in foreign markets."[154] To do nothing, Lipshutz told the president, would leave the issue to the courts and Congress to decide.[155]

By July 1978 the CEQ and Department of State had spent several months negotiating on the text of a draft executive order, through which the president would set the procedures for considering the environmental effects of agency action. Although they agreed on the outline and intent of the order, they could not resolve certain major differences. The sharpest disputes arose over the breadth of the order and the degree to which it would be subject to judicial review. CEQ pushed for a broad order with few exceptions, while State and other agencies involved in foreign policy wanted blanket exemptions for certain types of exports, including nuclear fuel and hazardous products that were tightly regulated in the United States. Although all agencies opposed opening the order to judicial enforcement, State was particularly adamant, refusing to support the draft order unless it had written assurance that the Justice Department would take the position that the order was unreviewable by the courts.[156]

Carter himself resolved the outstanding issues when they were presented to him on August 18, more or less splitting the difference between the agencies: he exempted nuclear programs from the order (State's preferred position), but broadened the application to other toxic products and tightened the language that permitted agencies to bypass the order (CEQ's position).[157] CEQ chairman Charles Warren, in a case of bureaucratic bean-counting, pointed out to Vice President Walter Mondale that Carter "went with CEQ 3 times, State 2 times, and [middle-ground language] 2 times." Warren was especially concerned about rumors that Carter was reconsidering two of his pro-CEQ decisions, and he cautioned that if Carter backtracked, the order would "[reflect] the environmentally sensitive option in only 1 out of 7 cases," something that "would be poor public policy and have serious political consequences."[158]

The most significant decision Carter made about the draft order was to remove all references to NEPA in the citation of authority, and base the order on the president's constitutional power. Carter did this in order to reduce the likelihood that the order would become entangled in the legal fights over NEPA and its implementing regulations, and to restrict the order's scope.[159] The text makes this clear, stating that "while based on independent authority, this Order furthers the purpose" of NEPA and other environmental laws, and exempting seven major categories of agency activity.[160] At the same time, the order did not require agencies to adhere to NEPA when considering extraterritorial action with significant environmental consequences. Instead it called for a more concise level of documentation and analysis, the most comprehensive of which had little in common with the environmental impact statements required for major domestic actions.[161]

Given the controversy over 12114's drafting it is hardly surprising that the order, once it was finally issued in January 1979, failed to settle the question of how agencies were to review the environmental consequences of their foreign actions. Implementation has been uneven, with some agencies adopting a loose interpretation that conflicts with the intent of both NEPA and the order, allowing them to circumvent the need to conduct environmental analyses.[162]

In practice, the federal courts have been reluctant to rule one way or the other on whether the order is the final word on government actions abroad. In some cases, courts have rejected claims that agencies had failed to adequately consider the environmental consequences of their foreign actions, but these findings were generally reached on procedural grounds, not on a broader reading of 12114's reach.[163] In 1993, however, a federal court ruled that the National Science Foundation was required to prepare an EIS on its plan to incinerate waste at an Antarctica research station, Executive Order 12114 notwithstanding. But even in this case the court based its decision not on the coverage or exclusivity of order 12114, but on the narrower question of whether the presumption against extraterritorial application of U.S. laws applied to actions in Antarctica, a sovereign region.[164]

Executive Order 12114 has not resolved the fundamental issue of how far NEPA extends beyond U.S. borders, nor have judicial interpretations of either NEPA or 12114.[165] The order has, however, protected agencies against at least some legal challenges, both by explicitly denying that it creates private rights of action and by creating procedural protections. In *Greenpeace U.S.A. v. Stone*,[166] Greenpeace sued the U.S. Army, claiming that the army had not prepared an adequate EIS covering a proposed shipment of chemical weapons from Germany to the Johnson Atoll in the Pacific Ocean for disposal. The court ruled that the army's adherence to the procedural requirements of Executive Order 12114 was a factor in its decision to reject the claim: "The court is persuaded under the *specific facts* of this case that the Army's compliance with Executive Order 12114 is to be given weight" in evaluating the merits of the lawsuit.[167]

E.O. 12114 did succeed in one respect, in a manner entirely consistent with the new institutional economics theoretical framework: it altered the legal landscape, and thus forced Congress to enact an explicit modification to NEPA if it were to resolve the underlying ambiguities in the statute that gave rise to Executive Order 12114 in the first place. In accordance with judicial doctrine, this required that Congress specify that NEPA does apply to extraterritorial actions by U.S. government agencies, something legislators have repeatedly tried and failed to do. Whatever the shortcomings of 12114, it has repeatedly trumped congressional efforts to overturn it, or to allow legal challenges to presidential action taken on its authority.[168]

The story of Executive Order 12114 is hardly exceptional, and the extent of presidential involvement reveals the importance that the White House places on orders as a significant policy-making tool.

Executive orders are a potent instrument of presidential authority. Their importance stems from the ambiguities of the president's constitutional powers, the deference to the president shown by the judiciary, and both legal doctrines and political realities that give the president a significant edge in disputes with Congress. No one is quite sure how far the executive power reaches; although the broad boundaries are clear enough, it has proved impossible to construct precise guideposts along those boundaries that allow us to predict with any certainty whether a president is about to step over the line. But what we do know—or should recognize—is that executive orders provide a window into the exercise of presidential power. Presidents think about them; staffers wrangle over them; executive branch officials worry about them. It makes sense, then, to survey the landscape in more detail to analyze how presidents have used them.

Three

Patterns of Use

ANY COMPREHENSIVE understanding of executive orders as a class of presidential decision requires some basic descriptive work: How many orders have presidents issued? Are there any consistent patterns with respect to the subject matter of orders? Does the frequency of orders vary with a president's political situation? To understand how presidents have used executive orders as an instrument of executive power, it is necessary to place orders into categories and analyze the external forces that spur their issuance. This chapter attempts to discern patterns in how presidents have used executive orders over time.

Tracking Executive Orders

The complexity of the process surrounding Executive Order 12114, described in chapter two, belies the notion that executive orders typically involve routine administrative matters with few substantive consequences. But the complex administrative procedures that govern the drafting and clearance of modern executive orders stand in sharp contrast to the informal methods that were used to keep track of them before 1935. Until the format and publication of executive orders were standardized in the 1920s and 1930s (in a series of presidential instructions that themselves took the form of executive orders), it was often unclear which presidential actions, exactly, constituted an executive order. Presidents have issued executive directives and commands from the earliest days of the Republic, but there has never been a uniform style. As a result, executive orders were issued and recorded in a haphazard manner:

> Often a President would write "Approved," "Let it be done," or "I approve the accompanying recommendation and order that it be effected," or similar words at the end of a recommendation drawn up by a Cabinet member. Sometimes an Executive order was signed by a secretary at the order of the President. . . . Other orders were signed by the Secretary of State in the absence of both the President and the Vice President. . . . Others were orders signed by department heads, and they purported to have the same effect as if they had been signed by the President. . . . Executive Order 396 [of 1906] is not even

dated. It is simply an endorsement on a letter written by Senator Knute Nelson, of Minnesota, making a certain woman eligible as a classified laborer in the Department of Agriculture.[1]

Initially there was not even a systematic process for collecting and recording executive orders.[2] Through the eighteenth and nineteenth centuries, each department kept its own files of orders, and presidential documents have found their way to a variety of places, including the Library of Congress, the National Archives, and individual collections of presidential papers. The federal government began printing executive orders in "slip" form in 1895, meaning that the orders were issued as loose-leaf pages that could be included in legal document collections; the series was, however, far from comprehensive.[3]

In 1905 the State Department created a repository for executive orders and asked executive branch agencies to submit their individual collections. In 1907 State organized this collection chronologically, and assigned numbers to each order beginning with the earliest order in its files (issued by Lincoln in October 1862, establishing military courts in Louisiana[4]) and ordering each successive order sequentially. Orders issued since then were assigned new numbers in this series, which is now known as the "numbered series." To this day, executive orders are numbered according to their placement in this sequence. The numbering system was confusing as well, since officials often discovered old order series well after they had been issued. In these cases the practice was to assign fractional numbers or letters to orders that could not otherwise be squeezed into the series in the proper sequence.

Yet even this record is far from complete, because many orders were issued but not transmitted to State.[5] The original compilation of unnumbered orders contained only 1,500 out of an estimated total of between 15,000 and 50,000, and all sources agree that there are no differences at all in substance, coverage, or significance between the numbered and the unnumbered series; the sole distinction is that orders that were transmitted to the State Department by 1907 received a number, and those that agencies failed to send over were not. As of December 1999 the numbered series stood at 13144. There are as many as 40,000 executive orders and proclamations that are excluded from this count.[6]

As the size of the federal government and scope of regulatory authority grew, the inadequacy of the State Department record-keeping system became increasingly clear. In 1929 Hoover issued an executive order (E.O. 5220) that required all orders to be transmitted to the State Department, but compliance was a problem, and the process did not provide anything approaching universal access.[7] As the number of orders exploded during the first two years of Franklin Roosevelt's administration, the system collapsed. The problem, according to an American Bar Association report, was that

> the practice of filing executive orders with the Department of State is not uniformly or regularly followed. . . . Some orders are retained or buried in the files of the government departments, some are confidential and are not published, and the practice as to printing and publication of orders is not uniform. Some orders are made known and available rather promptly after their approval; the publication of others may be delayed a month or more, with consequent confusion in numbering. The comparatively large number of recent orders which incorporate provisions purporting to impose criminal penalties by way of fine and imprisonment for violation is without numerical precedent in the history of the government.[8]

Erwin Griswold counted nearly 3,000 NRA administrative orders promulgated by the National Recovery Administration in its first year, with many found only in the thousands of press releases from the organization that issued a particular order. The Department of Commerce counted 466 executive orders between 1933 and 1936 that dealt exclusively with NRA codes.[9]

Ultimately there were so many poorly catalogued and unpublicized orders that it proved impossible in some cases to know whether a given executive order was in effect or not (a problem for executive branch officials as well as for the public).

In one case that was to serve as a metaphor for the legal chaos that stemmed from the lack of coordination and effective record keeping of administrative actions and executive orders, the government prosecuted an individual for violating a regulation that had actually been rescinded by an executive order, but nobody knew it. The executive order at issue in this case—*United States v. Smith*—resulted from poor draftsmanship and inadequate clearance procedures.

The National Industrial Recovery Act authorized the NRA to promulgate codes of fair competition for private industry, and the NRA issued the codes as executive orders under delegated authority. Unlike executive orders originating in the White House, the NRA orders were neither reviewed by the Department of Justice nor filed with the State Department.[10] The code adopted for the oil industry, issued in August 1933, set production quotas for each state and allowed the states to allocate production rights among in-state oil companies. In a September 1933 executive order, Roosevelt amended the code to prohibit the interstate transfer of oil produced in violation of the state production quotas. In *Smith*, the government charged an individual with producing excess oil in violation of the code. Smith's defense was that the code was an unconstitutional intrusion into intrastate commerce, and a federal district court agreed, dismissing the case in March 1934. The Justice Department appealed directly to the Supreme Court.

During preparation for oral argument on this and related cases involving challenges to the oil code, a government attorney discovered that Roosevelt's September 1933 executive order had inadvertently dropped the enforcement language from the code. As recounted by Supreme Court justice Robert Jackson, "[the] executive order amending a section of the code read: 'Section 4 of Article III is amended to read as follows,' and then followed only the first paragraph of that section in amended form. The second paragraph, containing the criminal provisions, was not set forth. Of course the intention was to retain the second paragraph of the original without amendment, and both the government and industry had been acting on that understanding. But technically, the amendment should have read '*The first paragraph* of Section 4 of Article III is amended to read as follows'. . . someone had been careless in draftsmanship."[11] Although all official copies of the code continued to include the "missing paragraph," the deletion of the enforcement provision meant that the government was prosecuting Smith for violating a law that did not exist. In something of a panic, Harold Ickes, secretary of the interior and administrator for the petroleum industry, wrote FDR in September 1934 that "the presence of the paragraph in the code is essential to its proper enforcement . . . [the Justice Department] feels that it must rely on this Executive Order if it is to save the case."[12] The error was quickly corrected by another executive order, but the government had to drop the Smith prosecution days before oral argument.

This was not the end of it, however. During Supreme Court oral argument in a subsequent case arising from the petroleum code, *Panama Refining Co. v. Ryan* 293 U.S. 388 (1934), the lawyer for Panama Refining (who had also been Smith's attorney), raised the issue of the nonexistent code to protest against the "viciousness of governing folks by executive order."[13] What followed was, in Corwin's words, "an interesting fifteen minutes in Court, albeit a bad quarter of an hour" for Assistant Attorney General Harold Stephens, as the Justices grilled him on the slipshod procedures for recording and promulgating executive orders and regulations.[14]

Soon after the Hot Oil debacle, Harvard Law School professor Erwin Griswold published an influential article calling for the establishment of an "Official Gazette" that would serve as a public record of all executive and administrative orders, rules, and directives.[15] The idea of a gazette had been floating around government agencies for some time, and a March 1934 Department of the Treasury legal counsel memorandum recommended such an official publication, noting that "the actual issuance of executive orders and regulations is accompanied with rather amazing informality," with dissemination of any particular order dependent on whether newspapers chose to publicize it.[16]

The Federal Register Act (now at 44 U.S.C. § 1501 et seq.) solved this problem, requiring publication of all generally applicable executive orders and proclamations. Beginning in March 1936, every executive order has been published, except for those that are either classified or apply to specific individuals. Although the act requires the courts to take notice of the contents of the *Register*, and publication is taken as evidence of required public notice of regulations and executive acts, the *Federal Register* itself has no substantive effect on the law or presidential powers.[17] Orders themselves are collected in an annual annex to the Code of Federal Regulations, but are not codified or cross-referenced in any systematic fashion.

Not everyone agrees that publication in the *Register* is sufficient for the public notice that ought to be reasonably required for complex statutes and regulations. In his dissenting opinion in *Federal Crop Insurance Corporation v. Merril*, 322 U.S. 380 (1947)—in which the majority ruled that publication of a crop insurance regulation in the *Register* was sufficient public notice, even though farmers who were unaware or misinformed about the regulation lost their insurance when they unknowingly violated the rule—Justices Jackson and Douglas thought it an "absurdity to hold that every farmer who insures his crops knows what the Federal Register contains or even knows that there is such a publication. If he were to peruse this voluminous and dull publication as it is issued from time to time in order to make sure whether anything has been promulgated that affects his rights, he would never need crop insurance, for he would never get time to plant any crops."[18] Nevertheless the *Register* serves as the definitive source for presidential executive orders, and the precision and regularity of coverage permits an accurate count of how many orders have been issued and when they have been released.

In figure 3.1, I display a graph of the number of executive orders issued by month since March 1936. Several features of the series stand out: a sharp rise and subsequent drop-off in orders between 1941 and early 1943; a surge from 1945 to 1948 and again from 1951 to 1952. From there the monthly series settles down in a roughly stationary pattern, with periodic spikes indicating high levels of presidential activity in some months, and a slight drop again after 1980.

These patterns themselves are instructive, as they counter the perception that executive orders are routine and nonsubstantive, and refute a standard explanation for why the number of orders dropped permanently during the 1950s. Without question, executive order issuance rises and falls in response to significant events.

The 1941–1942 rise in order issuance is due to the administrative preparations for and conduct of the war effort, combined with the exercise of

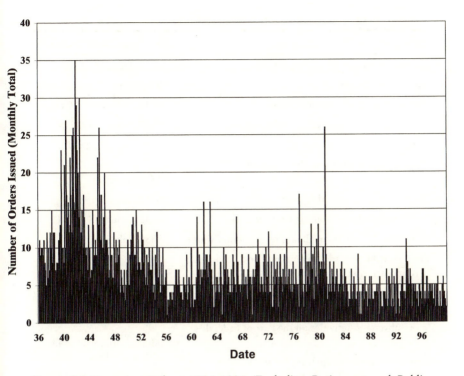

Figure 3.1 Executive Orders, 1936–1995 (Excluding Retirement and Public Lands)

sweeping emergency powers delegated to the President by the First and Second War Powers Acts. In 1942 alone Roosevelt cited these acts in 62 separate executive orders, and the Office of War Information calculated that between July 1939 and June 1942 Roosevelt issued 286 executive orders related to the war.[19] By creating organizations within the Executive Office, and by taking advantage of the temporary emergency powers delegated by Congress, Roosevelt was able to vastly expand the scope of independent presidential authority, and he exercised those powers in large part through executive orders.

Table 3.1 lists the wartime agencies created between 1940 and 1945. Some, like the National War Labor Board, the Office of War Mobilization, and the Office of Price Administration, assumed major roles in the war effort. Corwin concluded that Roosevelt far overstepped the proper limits of legitimate authority in conducting the war effort, going well beyond the authority delegated by the First War Powers Act.[20] Indeed, even within the administration some agreed that they were pushing presidential powers to the limit. The official history of the Office of Price Adminis-

TABLE 3.1
War Agencies Created by Executive Order, 1940–1945

Agency	Order Number and Date
Advisory Board on Just Compensation	9387, October 15, 1943
Alaska War Council	9181, June 11, 1942
Civilian Production Administration	9638, October 4, 1945
Committee for Congested Production Areas	9327, April 7, 1943
Committee on Fair Employment Practice	8802, June 25, 1941
Defense Communications Board/Board of War Communications	8546, September 24, 1940
Division of Defense Aid Reports	8751, May 2, 1941
Division of Defense Housing Coordination	8632, January 11, 1941
Economic Defense Board/Board of Economic Warfare	8839, July 30, 1941
Food Distribution Administration/ Food Production Administration	9280, December 5, 1942
Foreign Economic Administration	9380, September 25, 1943
Interdepartmental Committee to Consider Cases of Subversive Activities on the Part of Federal Employees	9300, February 5, 1943
Interdepartmental Committee for the Voluntary Payroll Savings Plan for the Purchase of War Bonds	9135, April 16, 1942
Interim International Information Service	9608, August 31, 1945
Interim Research and Intelligence Service	9521, September 20, 1945
Management Labor Policy Committee	9279, December 5, 1941
National Defense Mediation Board	8716, March 19, 1941
National Housing Agency	9070, February 24, 1942
National Patent Planning Commission	8977, December 12, 1941
National Railway Labor Panel	9172, May 22, 1942
National Wage Stabilization Board	9672, December 31, 1945
National War Labor Board	9017, January 12, 1942
Office of Alien Property Custodian	9095, March 11, 1942
Office of Censorship/Censorship Policy Board	8985, December 1941
Office of Civilian Defense	8757, May 20, 1941
Office of Community War Services	9338, April 29, 1943
Office of Defense Health and Welfare Service	8890, September 3, 1941

TABLE 3.1 (cont.)
War Agencies Created by Executive Order, 1940–1945

Agency	Order Number and Date
Office of Defense Transportation	8989, December 18, 1941
Office of Economic Stabilization	9250, October 3, 1942
Office of Economic Warfare	9361, July 15, 1943
Office of Facts and Figures	8922, October 24, 1941
Office of Inter-American Affairs	9532, March 23, 1945
Office of Lend-Lease Administration	8926, October 28, 1941
Office of Price Administration	8734, April 11, 1941
Office of Production Management	8629, January 7, 1941
Office of Scientific Research and Development	8807, June 28, 1941
Office of War Information	9182, June 13, 1942
Office of War Mobilization	9387, May 27, 1943
Petroleum Administrator for War	9276, December 2, 1942
President's Committee on Deferment of Federal Employees	9309, March 6, 1943
President's War Relief Control Board	9205, July 25, 1942
Publications Board	9568, June 8, 1945
Retraining and Reemployment Administration	9427, February 24, 1944
Solid Fuels Administrator for War	9332, April 19, 1943
Supply Priorities and Allocations Board	8875, August 28, 1941
Surplus War Property Administration	9425, February 19, 1945
War Food Administration	9334, April 19, 1943
War Production Board	9024, January 16, 1942
War Refugee Board	9417, January 22, 1944
War Relocation Authority	9102, March 18, 1942
War Shipping Administration	9054, February 7, 1942

Source: Bureau of the Budget, *The United States at War: Development and Administration of the War Program of the Federal Government*, War Records Section, Bureau of the Budget, Historical Reports on War Administration, no. 1, 1946, 521–535.

tration, in noting that FDR had imposed price controls by executive order in advance of a legislative authorization, observed that "since it was not subjected to a court test, we shall never be quite sure whether it was a lawful exercise of authority or a usurpation."[21] Of the myriad wartime agencies responsible for economic policy and control, only the Office of Price Administration had explicit congressional authorization. Roosevelt created the rest relying solely on his executive and emergency powers, with Congress going along "in response to manifest public necessity."[22]

Since many of these agencies lacked specific statutory authorization, they posed peculiar problems, especially concerning enforcement of their various directives and orders in the absence of appropriate legislation. One way around this problem was to characterize the agencies as purely informative or advisory, rather than adjudicative or executive. Agencies could issue advisory opinions without relying on a statutory mandate. Technically the objects of those opinions were free to ignore them, although in practice there were consequences for disobedience. Corwin flatly rejected the "advisory" finesse, noting that for the National War Labor Board and the War Production Board, "the advisory character of the agency was for the most part a sham and pretense, its *governing capacity* the substantial reality."[23] In other cases the agencies used indirect sanctions, threatening to withdraw draft exemptions for striking workers or imposing "voluntary" fines and other penalties that companies acquiesced in even though the sanctions lacked any legal authority and were "little short of blackmail."[24]

The number of orders dropped sharply after 1942, a pattern attributable to the elimination of two major classes of executive orders: routine orders covering individual exceptions to civil service rules and orders managing public lands. The decline in public land and civil service orders resulted from changes in the law that allowed the president to either delegate decision authority to subordinates or issue blanket orders that covered a class of decisions. In 1930 Congress had established a mandatory retirement age for federal employees, but authorized the president to exempt individuals from this provision by executive order if they occupied temporary positions. As the number of emergency and temporary employees grew as World War II approached, the administrative costs of granting individual exemptions grew to the point where they made little sense given the gravity of the president's wartime duties: only days after Pearl Harbor, FDR issued four separate orders exempting individuals from the retirement age. To help relieve the burden, Roosevelt granted automatic exemptions to all presidential appointees in January 1942,[25] and the number of orders fell immediately: in the twelve months prior to this order, FDR issued seventy-eight retirement exemption orders; in the twelve months after the order, he issued fourteen. The following May, Roosevelt extended the blanket exemption to broad classes of regular civil service personnel.[26] Truman added more blanket exemptions in 1947 and 1948, but presidents continued to issue occasional individual orders for employees outside the covered classifications (an average of about one every nine months). In December 1978 Carter eliminated the exemption orders altogether by delegating authority to the newly created Office of Personnel Management: the last exemption order was dated August 22, 1978.[27]

Public land orders have a similar history. Throughout the nineteenth century, presidents used executive orders to establish Indian reservations, townships, and lighthouse areas and to reserve land for military use. Many of the withdrawals were made pursuant to explicit congressional delegations, but presidents also issued hundreds of executive orders withdrawing land solely on the basis of their executive authority. In a move designed to curtail Theodore Roosevelt's zeal for reserving public lands for conservation purposes, in 1907 Congress barred the establishment of new national forests in the Northwest, without much success since Roosevelt withdrew 16 million acres just before he signed the legislation.[28]

In 1909 President Taft withdrew 3 million acres in California and Wyoming to preserve what was thought to be a substantial oil reserve. Although he did this without any statutory authority, the Supreme Court upheld the withdrawal in *United States v. Midwest Oil Co.* (236 U.S. 459), establishing the principle that a presidential action, even taken in the absence of explicit statutory authorization (or taken in apparent contravention of the law), can be valid in the face of congressional acquiescence. Since, the Court ruled, presidents had over the years issued hundreds of orders withdrawing land solely on their executive authority and Congress had done nothing, Congress had given implied authorization to the practice. Considered by some to be "Taft's most audacious official act,"[29] the withdrawal played a role in Congress's attempt to roll back the president's power over public lands. The Pickett Act, enacted in 1910, codified the president's withdrawal power while imposing some restrictions on its exercise.[30]

By the 1920s over half of all executive orders dealt with public lands, with presidents issuing an average of more than ten per month between 1925 and 1939. The explicit delegation of powers to the president expanded with the passage of the Taylor Grazing Act, and FDR reserved lands for military use as World War II approached. After Pearl Harbor FDR needed to free himself from the need to issue so many of these often trivial orders, and in April 1943 he delegated his authority to withdraw and manage public lands to the secretary of the interior.[31] From that point, Roosevelt and then Truman issued one public land order every other month. In 1952 Truman made this transfer more permanent, formally delegating authority under the recently passed Presidential Subdelegation Act.[32]

Presidents have issued public land orders since then, but they tend to involve more substantive policy disputes and often take the form of proclamations rather than executive orders. For example, in 1978 President Carter unilaterally withdrew 55 million acres of public land in Alaska, using a series of proclamations to designate the land as a national monument.[33] In the late stages of the 1996 presidential campaign, President Clinton issued a proclamation withdrawing 2 million acres in the Grand Staircase–Escalante National Monument to prevent coal mining on the land.[34]

The number of orders grew again after May 1945, when Truman rescinded many previous orders governing wartime regulations or agencies, lifted wartime controls, and managed the process of demobilization.[35] Orders rose again, although less sharply, during the Korean War as the president once more had to manage the move to a wartime footing. In issuing his wartime orders, Truman relied mainly on the Defense Production Act of 1950, which gave him renewed authority to implement economic controls. The delegation was, however, less sweeping than what Roosevelt had during World War II.

After Eisenhower took office in 1953, the number of orders dropped permanently. Between 1936 and 1952 presidents had issued an average of 186 orders per year, but since 1953 the average has been 60 orders per year. Apart from the elimination of routine civil service and public land orders, legislation enacted in 1950—the Presidential Subdelegation Act— explicitly permitted the president to delegate specific authority to other executive branch officials, in effect allowing these officials to act in the president's name.

Although Glendon Schubert dismissed the Subdelegation Act as "devoid of meaning," since in his view it gave pointless legislative recognition to authority the president already had, Bureau of the Budget officials saw it as a substantive way of streamlining administrative processes.[36] Presidents have relied on the act in issuing dozens of orders delegating routine matters to other officials, revising and transferring those grants of authority and generally freeing themselves from the sort of trivial orders that swamped FDR. Two examples are the establishment and administration of customs ports of entry and the administration of the Coast Guard, two functions delegated to the secretary of the treasury in 1951 and 1955, respectively.[37]

One type of order more common now are those that establish emergency investigative boards to mediate labor disputes in the transportation industry. The Railway Labor Act allows the president to create, via executive order, an emergency board if a railroad or airline labor dispute threatens to "substantially disrupt" commerce. Since the act became law in 1926, there have been more than 225 of these emergency boards, although there were only a handful before 1940 and few were established by executive order before 1946. The act is silent as to which instrument presidents are to use to set up emergency boards, and the practice was to rely on proclamations rather than executive orders in the 1920s and 1930s.[38] During World War II Roosevelt delegated his emergency authority to the National Railway Labor Panel, itself established by Executive Order 9172.[39]

The way in which presidents have used advisory commissions shows the connections between purely administrative tasks, substantive policy, and the importance of symbolism to the presidency. Presidents have long relied on outside boards, commissions, task forces, and councils to provide policy advice, often to take advantage of broad expertise but also as an effort to obtain independent advice from outside existing institutional channels or to create support for presidential policy.[40] Moreover, at times presidents have sought simply to create institutional policy structures via presidential commissions when no suitable home existed in federal agencies or when Congress had refused, or would likely refuse, to appropriate money.

Many of these commissions have had extremely high profiles and were established by executive order: a recent review listed the Commission to Investigate Pearl Harbor (the Roberts Commission), the Commission to Investigate the Assassination of President Kennedy (the Warren Commission), the National Advisory Commission on Civil Disorders (the Kerner Commission), and the Special Review Board on the Role of the National Security Council in the Iran-Contra Affair (the Tower Commission).[41] To this list we can add, at a minimum, the Committee on Administrative Management (the Brownlow Commission) and the President's Commission on Strategic Forces (the Scowcroft Commission). Although presidents can use other administrative mechanisms to create commissions, even simply announcing their formation without any specific legal instrument, "important commissions, those which are widely publicized and which deal with broad and pressing questions of public policy, are more likely to be created by executive order or statute."[42]

Although the use of these commissions would at first appear mostly trivial, not only have they precipitated constitutional confrontations (as the Commission on Economy and Efficiency did in 1912, discussed in chapter four), but Congress has long viewed them as a general threat to its legislative prerogatives and powers of the purse. Congress has moved several times to limit the president's use of independent commissions without statutory authorization, normally by denying the president the ability to spend funds on such efforts and often in response to particular commission activities. In 1842, after President John Tyler appointed a commission of private citizens to investigate corruption in the New York

Customshouse, Congress prohibited the president from paying for commissioners or commission activities unless Congress had appropriated funds. The attorney general ruled that this provision could not prevent the president from appointing commissions, although it could keep him from paying for them.[43] Congress tried the same tactic again in 1909, this time in response to Theodore Roosevelt's establishment of a Council on Fine Arts to devise plans for federal buildings and grounds. With an amendment to an appropriations bill, Congress once more prohibited the use of funds to pay the salaries or expenses of any commission unless Congress had authorized its creation.[44]

In creating the organizations he used to manage the war effort, FDR established many of them as presidential "advisory" bodies to finesse their lack of statutory authorization. In an effort to rein in these committees, particularly the Fair Employment Practices Committee, Congress in 1944 enacted the so-called Russell amendment, which prohibited the president from expending any funds on "any agency or instrumentality, including those established by Executive order" for longer than one year.[45] Despite this legislative restriction, which remains in force, presidents have continued to make extensive use of commissions, and even pay for them out of their discretionary accounts when Congress has refused to provide funding.[46]

Through the 1950s and 1960s Congress tried several more times to restrict the use of presidential advisory committees, but the efforts were largely preempted by presidents establishing their own guidelines using executive orders. In 1950 the Department of Justice issued guidelines for advisory committees, in response to their rapidly increasing number.[47] The guidelines recommended that advisory committees have statutory authorization, have a government-specified agenda, use full-time government employees as chairs, keep full records of all meetings, and serve only in an advisory capacity. A 1962 executive order required all federal advisory committees to adhere to the guidelines, but congressional sentiment that the order was loosely enforced led to renewed pressure to constrain presidential discretion. This time around, though, the concern was less with the constitutional issues raised by advisory committees than with the openness of the advisory process.[48] With restrictive legislation moving rapidly through Congress in 1972, President Nixon again tried to head off congressional action by issuing another executive order on advisory committees that made minor changes to the earlier order.[49] The effort failed to appease Congress, which enacted the Federal Advisory Committee Act (FACA) in late 1972.

Under the FACA, advisory committees must hold open meetings and report on their findings, and the president must submit an annual report detailing the activities of all federal advisory bodies. While the focus on disclosure rather than funding restrictions was viewed at the time as a more effective way of ensuring a degree of congressional oversight, Congress has shown no inclination to press the issue further by, for example, imposing direct restrictions on the president's ability to create and use commissions. "In general," concludes Thomas Wolanin, "Congress has been unwilling or unable to limit the President's authority to create commissions."[50]

Executive Order Subject Matter and Importance

This pattern of order issuance rising and falling in response to external events, changes in administration, and revised administrative procedures points to two conclusions. First, it suggests that there is in fact a substantive component to executive orders, for if they were indeed routine there is no reason to expect that they would reflect anything but administrative "noise" independent of important external variables. Second, contrary to the position in the literature about the unimportance of orders, executive orders have very likely become *more* substantive over time as entire classes of routine orders are no longer issued. Although presidents obviously issue fewer orders now than they did in the 1930s and 1940s, the percentage of those of orders devoted to substantive goals is higher.

In this section I provide support for the argument that executive orders have become more important to presidents over time. As I noted in chapter one, political scientists have traditionally viewed executive orders as merely a routine administrative tool, not as an instrument for making important policy decisions. Lyn Ragsdale and John Thies found that the percentage of policy executive orders applicable to the general public—as opposed to administrative, ceremonial, public land, or civil service orders—has grown over time, from almost 0 percent in the 1920s to 80 percent in the 1980s.[51] They did not attempt to classify orders by significance, however, although they did check a sample of 200 orders to see if presidents made a public statement about the order, finding that presidents mentioned two-thirds of the orders in their sample.

The analysis here relies on a random sample of 1,028 executive orders issued between March 1936 and December 1999, drawn from the entire set of all executive orders issued. This sample, which covers 17.6 percent of the approximately 5,800 orders issued since March 1936, can be used to generate inferences about the total population of orders. Although it is possible to classify the entire set of orders by category (as Ragsdale has done),[52] the sample allows for a more detailed (and tractable) investigation into the question of what fraction of orders can be considered significant.[53]

The first task is to classify the executive orders in the sample based on subject matter. I created the following exhaustive and mutually exclusive categories. When an order addressed multiple issues or crossed policy boundaries, I assigned it to the category that best described the order's primary focus:

Civil service: Orders dealing with civil service appointments, retirement exemptions, administration of federal personnel, salary, holidays, and so on. I also included personnel loyalty orders and any orders dealing specifically with Foreign Service management or personnel.

Public lands: Orders that withdrew land for public use, restored public lands, revoked previous land orders, or that established or altered the boundaries of public lands, migratory waterfowl refuges, or airspace reservations.

War and emergency powers: Orders that created or abolished wartime agencies, addressed the exercise of special wartime administrative functions, took possession or control of private economic entities, or established emergency preparedness procedures for federal agencies.

Foreign affairs: Orders dealing with export controls, foreign economic policy, foreign trade, foreign aid, foreign affairs and diplomatic relations generally, establishment of international or treaty-based organizations, management of territories (Philippines, Puerto Rico, the Canal Zone), and immigration.

Defense and military policy: Orders dealing with military personnel, classified information, organization of the intelligence community, administration and reservation of military lands and reservations, and defense policy generally.

Executive branch administration: Orders creating boards, commissions, or interagency councils; orders that delegated presidential power or transferred powers from one agency to another, established civilian awards, administered tax policy (including inspection of tax returns), affected the organization of the Executive Office of the President, administered customs, law enforcement, and commemorative orders; contracting.

Labor policy: Orders creating emergency boards and boards of inquiry to investigate labor disputes, and orders managing federal government labor policy.

Domestic policy: Orders that dealt with domestic policy generally, including energy, the environment, civil rights, the economy, and education.

Tables 3.2 and 3.3 show the overall distribution of executive orders in the sample by subject area and across time. Overall, from 1936 to 1999, more than 60 percent of the orders dealt with general executive branch administration, the civil service, or public lands. Most of the remaining orders concerned the president's foreign affairs and war powers, with only a small percentage dealing with domestic and labor policy.

These patterns change when orders are broken down by time period. Table 3.3 shows the distribution of orders across categories for each decade, from the 1930s to the 1990s (the 1930s includes four years, from

TABLE 3.2
Executive Order Subject Categories, 1936–1999

Type of Order	Percentage of Orders in Sample
Executive branch administration	25.5
Civil service	19.6
Public lands	15.6
Defense and military policy	11.9
Foreign affairs	11.3
War and emergency powers	7.1
Labor policy	5.4
Domestic policy	3.8

Note: Percentages are drawn from a random sample of 1,028 orders. Margin of error is +/ –2.6.

1936 to 1939). Several patterns are immediately apparent, especially the sharp drop in the percentage of orders devoted to public land and civil service issues. Over three-fourths of orders in the 1930s dealt with these issues, with nearly half devoted to public lands alone.[54] In the 1990s there were no public land orders, and only one order in eight dealt with the civil service. As I noted above, presidents no longer issue these orders, having delegated these responsibilities to subordinates. The number of orders devoted to war and emergency powers has gone down considerably since the 1940s and 1950s, with the higher figures obviously attributable to the extraordinary impact of World War II and the Korean War.

The percentage of executive orders that deal with foreign affairs, executive branch administration, and domestic policy has grown significantly since the 1930s. Part of this is undoubtedly due to the rise of the presidency as an institution, since as presidents have taken on more and more administrative responsibility they have come to rely on the executive order as an instrument of policy making. Within this category of executive branch administration, the three most common orders are those that established presidential boards and commissions, those devoted to mostly routine administrative tasks (transferring functions from one agency to another, creating agency seals, setting travel reimbursement rates, initiating management reforms), and those specifically delegating presidential powers or designating the executive branch officials responsible for carrying out congressionally specified duties.

The second area of relative growth in executive orders is in foreign and military affairs. In these areas the absolute number of orders has remained roughly consistent, but they have become a larger percentage of all orders over time (from 12 percent in the 1940s to nearly 50 percent in the 1990s).

TABLE 3.3
Executive Order Subject Categories by Decade, 1936–1999 (Sample of 1,028 Orders)

	1936–1939	1940s	1950s	1960s	1970s	1980s	1990s
Civil service	30.5%	21.8%	13.8%	11.9%	22.0%	13.1%	12.0%
Public lands	46.1	18.4	10.5	5.0	2.5	1.0	0.0
War and emergency powers	0.0	19.3	3.3	4.0	1.7	1.0	0.0
Foreign affairs	9.6	7.6	9.9	11.9	10.2	20.2	22.7
Defense and military policy	2.4	12.7	27.6	10.9	6.8	6.1	11.9
Executive branch administration	10.8	13.6	28.3	36.6	44.9	41.4	36.6
Labor policy	0.0	4.4	5.9	13.9	3.4	10.1	5.3
Domestic policy	0.6	2.2	0.7	5.9	8.5	7.1	9.3
Number of orders in sample	167	316	152	101	118	99	75
Number of administrations	1	2	2	4	3	3	2
Significant orders	1	50	14	14	26	23	21
Percentage	0.6%	15.8%	9.2%	13.9%	22.0%	23.2%	28.0%

Significant Executive Orders

The second, and more important, task is to determine which orders constituted "significant" policy making by the president. This is, to be sure, an inexact and subjective process, but it is possible to outline some basic criteria that permit distinctions between, for example, an order exempting an individual from mandatory retirement from one that imposed a loyalty program on federal employees. One way to start is to investigate how other researchers have approached this task, most commonly with regard to legislation.

David Mayhew, in his landmark book *Divided We Govern*, constructed an inventory of major legislative enactments from 1946 to 1990. He used a two-stage process, first noting whether contemporary observers considered a law significant (largely on the basis of journalistic accounts). In a second pass, Mayhew looked at retrospective evaluations by policy experts in various fields: Did legislation generate scholarly work? What did those experts think about the legislation? On the basis of these criteria, Mayhew identified 267 acts as particularly important.[55]

Mark Peterson, in his study of presidential-congressional relations, coded presidential policy initiatives as innovative and/or as part of an important overall program. Importance was a function of whether specialized sources (*Congressional Quarterly, CQ Almanac, National Journal*) mentioned the policy, and the level of innovation a function of whether the proposal involved a large departure from existing policy or constituted a new program. In his sample of presidential proposals, Peterson found that over one-fifth dealt with "issues of the greatest consequence."[56]

In considering whether an executive order was significant, I used a somewhat looser version of Mayhew's selection process, and asked the following questions. First, did the order receive attention at the time from the press or from other political actors or institutions? At times the journalistic coverage has focused more on the subject of an order than on the order itself. When Eisenhower placed the Arkansas National Guard under federal control in order to force the integration of Little Rock schools, his action took place within a much broader legal and political process. Press accounts at the time tended to focus not on the fact that Eisenhower had issued an executive order, but rather on the substance of what he did.[57] In looking at press attention, I considered both the national press (the *New York Times, Washington Post*, or *Wall Street Journal*) and more specialized publications covering politics or specific professional fields.

In addition, I considered whether Congress considered an order important enough to hold committee hearings or whether specific legislation to override the order made it to the floor of either chamber. Congressional hearings, in particular, have long been recognized as an important barometer of which issues legislators deem significant.[58] Again, some orders receive more congressional attention than others, and many pass unnoticed, but it is not at all unusual for legislators to become attentive to those orders perceived to threaten congressional authority or prerogative.

Second, have students of law or the presidency referred to the order (or a class of orders) and argued its importance in their writings? This is a way of replicating Mayhew's "second sweep" measurement of expert opinion on an order. As I noted in chapter one, the legal literature is extensive, the social science and history literatures less so. Nevertheless, the extent to which an order receives mention in one or more of these forums is an indicator of importance. For example, I counted all of the emergency seizures of private property—whether during wartime or not—as significant. Although some of these seizures made the news at the time and others did not, Rossiter considered them as a whole a "spectacular display [of] the President's power of martial rule."[59] Similarly, Corwin dealt at length with the wartime property seizures as an example of presidents' intrusion into the clearly legislative territory of industrial policy.[60] In addition, I reviewed the law review literature to determine whether an order received any attention from legal scholars.

Third, did presidents themselves consider the order important, as evidenced by their public statements or emphasis in the public record? Different presidents placed varying emphasis on executive orders. Carter and Reagan tended to publicize most of their orders, placing them in their *Public Papers* publications. Others did not routinely publicize their orders, instead releasing order texts and public statements only for orders that they considered especially noteworthy. I counted as significant those orders about which a president made a nonroutine statement (which did not include routine press releases).

Fourth, did the order trigger federal litigation? A few orders have generated legal challenges of major importance—the steel seizure case, *Korematsu*, *E.P.A. v. Mink*. A lawsuit is an indication that a plaintiff considered the order a sufficiently important infringement on some right or interest to take on the cost and time of seeking judicial remedy. And a Supreme Court or appeals court decision is clear evidence that the judiciary considers the case important and controversial as a matter of law. Executive Order 11246, for example, has been cited in over three hundred federal district court cases since 1965. I counted litigation over an executive order that is catalogued in either the *Nexis* or Westlaw databases.

Finally, does the order create a new institution with substantive policy responsibility, expand or contract significant private rights, or constitute a significant departure from existing government policy? Again I distinguish between orders creating ceremonial or symbolic organizations (such as the American Battle Monuments Commission) and those establishing or reorganizing agencies with substantive duties (such as the Office of War Information or the Office of Strategic Services).

I counted an order as significant if it met at least one of the conditions outlined here: press attention, congressional notice, presidential emphasis, litigation, or creation of institutions with substantive policy responsibility. Most significant orders met more than one criterion. To be sure, this process involved subjective judgments, but I adopted throughout a conservative view of what constituted a significant order. When there was ambiguity about whether an order was significant or not, I considered it insignificant. I considered as insignificant orders that exempted individuals from retirement or other civil service requirements, and all but four public land orders. In making the significance/insignificance designation, I erred on the side of underestimating the number of significant orders.

According to these criteria, 149 of the 1,028 executive orders in my sample—or about one in seven—qualify as significant (table 3.6, at the end of the chapter, contains a list of these orders, giving the number, date, and title of each). Obviously, some types of orders are more likely to be significant than others. Executive orders devoted to war and emergency powers, for instance, are almost by definition more important than those addressing civil service or public lands. The distribution of significant executive orders confirms this: nearly 60 percent of the important orders dealt with national security construed broadly (war and emergency powers, military policy, or foreign affairs). In domestic policy, the most common use of significant orders was to establish presidential boards or advisory commissions (fifteen orders), to administer or make rules for government administration (ethics, for example; ten orders), and to set civil rights and environmental policy (six orders each).

The purposes of significant executive orders become much clearer when the distribution is broken down by decade; these data are shown in figure 3.2. The figure shows the percentage distribution of each type of order, by decade. (I collapsed labor, civil service, and public land orders into the domestic policy category, because there were only a handful of orders in each). In the 1940s, roughly 65 percent of the significant executive orders in my sample addressed war and emergency powers. Most of these orders consisted of government takeovers of businesses during World War II or orders establishing government agencies. As the World War II and Korean emergencies receded, the distribution of significant orders became more even across categories.

The biggest change in the series, from the 1940s and 1950s, is that domestic policy and executive branch management orders have become

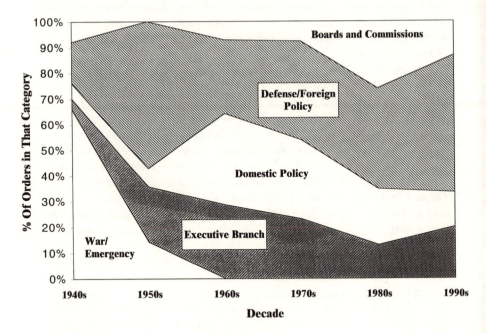

Figure 3.2 Executive Order Subject Area, by Decade

far more important as a significant policy tool. In the 1940s, only 10 percent of significant orders fell into these two categories; in the 1960s, nearly 70 percent did. Currently, roughly one-third of significant orders address domestic or executive branch issues.

In figure 3.3 I show the estimated frequency of significant executive orders that have been issued since the 1940s. In this graph, I estimate the average number of significant executive orders issued in each year, based on the results of the sample analysis. Although my estimates are based on an analysis of the 1,028-order sample, the randomness of the sample allows me to make inferences about the entire universe of orders. Such statements are estimates, and they will be accurate within a statistical margin of error.

Figure 3.3 shows that since the 1970s, presidents have issued, on average, more than one significant order per month (roughly fourteen per year). While the number of important executive orders is half of what it was in the 1940s (with the difference attributable to World War II), it has grown since the 1950s and 1960s. The persistence and uniformity of the pattern is a strong indication that executive orders have become more important over the last few decades, not less.

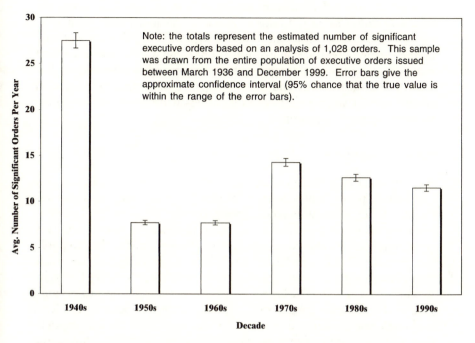

Note: the totals represent the estimated number of significant executive orders based on an analysis of 1,028 orders. This sample was drawn from the entire population of executive orders issued between March 1936 and December 1999. Error bars give the approximate confidence interval (95% chance that the true value is within the range of the error bars).

Figure 3.3 Estimated Number of Significant Orders, Annual Averages

Explaining Why Presidents Use Executive Orders: A Statistical Approach

Another method of analyzing the factors behind executive orders is an event count/time series analysis. This statistical method confirms the substantive importance of executive orders. If, on the one hand, executive orders are an important element of executive authority, then the way presidents use them should vary in predictable and systematic ways as a function of a president's overall political and strategic situation. If, on the other hand, executive orders are not used to make policy, then they should be issued independently of political context. The existing literature on executive orders has come to divergent conclusions about the factors behind their use. For example, while some studies have concluded that presidents will rely more heavily on executive orders when they face opposition in Congress, others have maintained that legislative success prompts presidents to issue more orders.[61] At the same time, there is general agreement that the number of orders is inversely related to presidential partisan strength in Congress.

One way to resolve these uncertainties is to step back and consider executive orders as an indicator of executive flexibility and initiative in policy making. This allows me to derive hypotheses by drawing not only on the existing literature on executive orders but also on the insights of recent work on the presidency which argues that what presidents seek is control over institutions and processes (some of which I addressed in chapter one). I suggest that executive orders will vary according to the following general conditions.

PRESIDENTIAL PARTY

If orders are a useful policy tool, then presidents with a more active view of executive power should be more likely to use them than presidents less inclined to aggressively pursue a policy agenda. While political party is not a perfect proxy for activism, Democratic presidents have historically been more inclined to favor expansive government policies than Republican presidents, and so presumably would be more likely to issue orders for substantive policy purposes. Kennedy established the Peace Corps by executive order, and FDR began the practice of using orders to promulgate civil rights policy emphasized by successive Democratic presidents (although Eisenhower and Nixon did so as well). Even though Republicans took a more sympathetic view of a strong executive during the Reagan and Bush years, this was based more on their belief that Congress had encroached on proper executive branch powers, especially in foreign affairs; it did not reflect anything approaching an activist governing philosophy in the traditional sense.[62] Although Dennis Gleiber and Steven Shull suspected that liberal presidents would issue more orders than conservative presidents, they found only a very weak relationship. They argued that since all presidents need to use executive orders to implement legislation and achieve other necessary goals, their use "may be more uniform across presidents."[63]

The first expectation about the frequency of orders is that Democratic presidents will issue more executive orders than Republican presidents.

BEGINNING- AND END-OF-TERM EFFECTS

Presidents, when they take office, usually try to place their immediate stamp on executive branch processes and policies. Executive orders are an excellent way to do this, since they allow presidents to alter organizational relationships and administrative routines. Although some scholars have found no pattern to order frequency over a president's term,[64] presidents have issued numerous significant orders early in their administrations. Clear examples of this practice are Reagan's Executive Order 12291, which he issued three weeks into his first term, and Clinton's Executive Order 12836, issued in his second week, revoking two Bush-era orders that were unpopular with labor unions.[65] The incentive to make changes will be greater when party control of the White House has changed, as incoming presidents distinguish themselves from their predecessors and "hit the ground running."

If presidents use executive orders at the beginning of their terms, they may well do the same at the end, to put a legacy in place. Outgoing presidents can use executive orders to obligate their successors to various courses of action by making appointments, establishing new departmental rules, and carrying out implementation tasks. The new president can reverse course, but this entails issuing new executive orders that revoke the earlier ones (which is yet another reason to suspect a beginning-of-term effect). Again, this pattern should be especially marked when a president is leaving office to a successor of the opposite party, because it is then that the pressure to complete action is highest.

Even a cursory investigation uncovers a robust pattern of last-minute orders issued in a president's final days in office. During the last few months of the Ford administration, the White House processed executive orders without going through the normal review channels. Normally executive orders must be cleared through both the OMB and the Office of Legal Counsel in the Department of Justice. Yet this process was skipped for a number of orders that administration officials wanted to issue prior to January 20, 1977.[66] Ford, who issued seven orders his last full day in office, reflected a pattern that was far from unique. Carter issued twenty-two orders in his last week, and ten on his last day.

Carter's final orders highlight the unilateral authority they can reflect. All ten of the orders Carter issued on his last full day in office, January 19, 1981, addressed the agreement with Iran to secure the release of the American hostages held there since November 4, 1979. Negotiations had continued throughout the campaign and into the transition period with little support from the incoming administration. On the nineteenth, Carter announced that the Iranian government had agreed to release the hostages in return for the release of Iranian assets frozen in the United States and the establishment of an arbitration process to settle private claims against Iran. Legal scholars speculated that any agreement that had such a sweeping impact on private interests would require legislation to carry out, but Carter implemented the agreement relying wholly on the executive power.[67] Carter's authority to unilaterally make and carry out the executive agreement with Iran and issue the implementing executive orders was upheld by the Supreme Court in *Dames & Moore v. Regan,* 453 U.S. 654.[68]

Carter issued these orders on his final day in office as a lame-duck president who had been humiliated in a landslide defeat. Even so, he was able to write the final chapter of "one of the most dramatic exercises of presidential power in foreign affairs in peacetime in United States history"[69] with no interference from Congress, the courts, or even the new president.

A second set of expectations about executive orders is that presidents will issue orders more frequently at the beginning and end of their terms, especially when party control of the White House has switched or will switch.

CONGRESSIONAL AND PUBLIC SUPPORT

Since executive orders are a unilateral presidential tool, presidents may use them to compensate for congressional opposition.[70] This theme arises from histories of the civil rights orders, which have maintained that Democratic presidents used executive orders because they knew that Congress would refuse to pass legislation.[71] Presidents may also use executive orders to preempt legislation or undercut Congress in other ways. When faced with the certain prospect of legislation imposing sanctions on South Africa in 1985, President Reagan successfully fractured a veto-proof coalition of Democrats and moderate Republicans by imposing weaker sanctions by executive order. In doing so, he "managed to avoid a major legislative defeat and the further embarrassment of an almost inevitable veto override,"[72] although Congress overrode Reagan's veto of sanction legislation the following year. Presidents have restructured the intelligence community through executive orders, in part to undermine congressional efforts to reorganize the community via statute.

For the same reasons, presidents who have low levels of public approval may be more likely to resort to executive orders. Doing so offers a way of getting around other institutional actors who might be emboldened in their opposition to what they perceive as a weak White House, and also provides presidents with a method of position-taking, framing policy questions, or delivering on promises made to key constituencies.

The existing literature provides inconclusive support for these expectations. As noted above, researchers have reached contradictory results on the relationship between congressional support and order frequency. George Krause and David Cohen find no statistically significant relationship between popularity and order frequency, although the regression coefficient has the expected sign.[73] In contrast, Phillip Cooper argues that presidents are likely to use executive orders "as instruments of expediency to circumvent administrative law,"[74] behavior that would be consistent with a tendency to rely on orders to compensate for a lack of public and congressional support.

The third expectation about executive orders is that presidents will tend to issue more of them when (a) they lack strong support in Congress, and (b) they experience low levels of popular support.

CAMPAIGN EFFECTS

If executive orders are suitable for major policy initiatives, it is reasonable to expect incumbent presidents to take full electoral advantage of them. In chapter one I offered examples from the 1996 presidential campaign, in which Republican contenders Gramm and Buchanan promised specific executive orders on their first day, if they were elected. Of more substance were candidate John F. Kennedy's promises during the 1960 campaign to issue various civil rights orders as president (I return to this subject in chapter six).

Presidents are, of course, aware of the advantages that incumbency provides, especially the ability to "look presidential" in contrast to challengers who must overcome the threshold barrier of appearing to be of presidential caliber. By issuing executive orders in the course of a campaign, an incumbent president can focus attention on issues that play to his strengths, provide benefits to key constituencies, and create a public image of action and decisiveness. During the 1980 campaign Carter's staff was well aware of the advantages of well-publicized presidential action, and hoped to time an executive order to secure maximum advantage. Carter was preparing to issue an order establishing a federal council to coordinate environmental policy in the Lake Tahoe region. The order was ready in September 1976, and domestic policy adviser Stu Eizenstat wanted the president to sign the order while on a campaign visit to California. "Your trip to California presents an excellent chance to highlight key environmental issues of your Administration," Eizenstat wrote. "A signing ceremony [for the Lake Tahoe executive order] . . . should get wide coverage, [and] would be well received throughout *many* voting constituencies in California."[75]

In the months before the 1996 election, President Clinton issued executive orders that created an Advisory Commission on Consumer Protection and Quality in the Health Care Industry (E.O. 13017, September 9, 1996); implemented procedures to collect delinquent child support payments (E.O. 13019, October 3, 1996); and provided funding and White House administrative support for Native American Tribal Colleges and Universities (E.O. 13021, October 23, 1996). Although not all of these decisions received national news coverage, they all got some play in the media.[76]

The final expectation about executive orders is that presidents will issue more orders when they are running for reelection than they do at other times in their terms.

Having set out four hypotheses about how executive order frequency should vary, I now turn to the task of defining the statistical model that I will use to test them.

The Data and Model

The data for analysis are monthly totals of executive orders issued from April 1936 to December 1999. Monthly data on the number of executive orders from 1936 to 1987 are from the Congressional Information Service index to executive orders. Data from 1988 to 1994 are from the annual index of the *Federal Register*, and 1995–1999 data are from the on-line database maintained by the National Archives.[77] I omitted orders that exempted individuals from mandatory retirement or orders that addressed a specific tract of public land. Mandatory retirement orders were identified by inspection, and public lands orders from an annual index in the *Register*.

Since the number of executive orders issued in any month can only take non-negative integer values, with an average of six per month between 1937 and 1999, an event-count model is the appropriate method of analyzing the series. I expect the event-count series to be over dispersed, because each event (the occurrence of one executive order) increases the probability of observing another event in any given time period: executive orders are commonly issued in clumps, external events that spur order issuance may well be responsible for multiple orders, and presidents often revise specific orders several times by issuing additional orders. Consequently, I use a negative binomial event-count model.[78]

The negative binomial model used here incorporates the formula in William Greene's *Econometric Analysis*, whose parameterization includes a dispersion parameter α, in addition to the coefficient vector $\exp(x\beta)$ to account for the positive contagion in the order sequence.[79] α is assumed to be > 0. In the Poisson model, which requires independence between the individual events, $\alpha = 0$. Poisson processes are thus a special case of the negative binomial where the dispersion parameter is 0, a result that permits checking the validity of the negative binomial specification using a likelihood ratio test (as a double-check of the estimated values of $\alpha = 0.04$ in the tables).[80] The test statistic is shown in the tables as the "LR

Test against Poisson," and clearly indicates that the negative binomial specification (indicating positive contagion) is correct.

The coefficient vector is

$$\mu_i = \exp(x_i\,\beta),$$

where

$$x_i\,\beta = b_0 + b_1 Orders_{t-1} + b_2 Orders_{t-3} + b_3 Orders_{t-12} + b_4 \overset{\textit{First Year}}{\textit{Party Change}}$$

$$+ b_5 \overset{\textit{First Year}}{\textit{No Party Change}} + b_6 \overset{\textit{Last Month}}{\textit{Party Change}} + b_7 \overset{\textit{Last Month}}{\textit{No Party Change}}$$

$$+ b_8 Campaign + b_9 No\ Campaign + b_{10} \overset{\textit{Truman}}{\textit{Unified Govt.}} + b_{11} \overset{\textit{Truman}}{\textit{Divided Govt.}}$$

$$+ b_{12} \overset{\textit{Eisenhower}}{\textit{Unified Govt.}} + b_{13} \overset{\textit{Eisenhower}}{\textit{Divided Govt.}} + b_{14} \overset{\textit{Clinton}}{\textit{Unified Govt.}} + b_{15} \overset{\textit{Clinton}}{\textit{Divided Govt.}}$$

$$+ b_{16} FDR + b_{17} JFK + b_{18} LBJ + b_{19} Ford + b_{20} Carter + b_{21} Reagan$$

$$+ b_{22} Bush + b_{23} \overset{\textit{Presidential}}{\textit{Popularity}}$$

$$+ \sum_{i=0}^{23} w_i^a X_{t-i}^a + \sum_{i=0}^{23} w_i^b X_{t-i}^b + \sum_{i=0}^{23} w_i^c X_{t-i}^c + \sum_{i=0}^{23} w_i^d X_{t-i}^d$$

where

Orders$_t$	= the number of executive orders issued in month t from April 1936 to December 1999, excluding public land orders and orders exempting individuals from civil service rules
Orders t–1; Orders t–3; Orders t–12	= lagged values of the dependent variable, with lags of 1, 3, and 12 months
First Year, Party Change	= 1 during the first year of a new administration, when party control has changed from previous administration; 0 otherwise
First Year, No Party Change	= 1 during the first year of a new administration when party control has not changed from previous administration; 0 otherwise
Last Month, Party Change	= 1 during last month of outgoing president's term, when incoming president is from the other party; 0 otherwise

Last Month, No Party Change	= 1 during last month of outgoing president's term, when incoming president is from same party; 0 otherwise
Campaign	= 1 in January-October of presidential election year, when incumbent president is running for reelection; 0 otherwise
No Campaign	= 1 in January–October of presidential election year, when incumbent president is not running for reelection; 0 otherwise
FDR, JFK, LBJ, Ford, Carter, Reagan, Bush	= 1 during each president's administration, respectively; 0 otherwise. Nixon is the excluded dummy variable.
Truman Unified, Eisenhower Unified, Clinton Unified	= 1 during periods of each administration when president's party controlled Congress (unified government); 0 otherwise
Truman Divided, Eisenhower Divided, Clinton Divided	= 1 during periods of each administration when opposition party controlled Congress; 0 otherwise
Presidential Popularity	= Six-month moving average of presidential approval rating, as measured by the Gallup Poll, beginning in January 1949. Monthly presidential popularity ratings for 1949–1994 from Ragsdale, using interpolation to calculate missing values when no poll was conducted in a given month, and averages when a month included multiple polls. Ratings for 1995–1999 taken from the Gallup Poll.[81] The six-month moving-average calculation does not carry over from one president to the next; values for the first five months of a new president's administration were calculated using the formula

$$\frac{Popularity}{Moving\ Average_j} = \sum_{i=1}^{j} \frac{Popularity_i}{j}, \qquad j = 1, \dots, 5$$

X^a, X^b, X^c, X^d	= intervention effects (see below)
$w_i^a, w_i^b, w_i^c, w_i^d$	= weights for the lagged values of $X^a, X^b, X^c,$ and X^d, respectively

I used the <nbreg> command in Intercooled STATA 4.0 to derive the coefficient estimates.

Estimating Intervention Effects

The last four terms of μ_i (the terms with the X's and w's), constitute an Almon polynomial distributed lag estimation of the impact of four discrete events that had strong effects on the number of orders issued. These events are (1) the German invasion of Poland in September 1939, which led Roosevelt to declare a limited state of emergency and begin preparations for war; (2) the Japanese attack on Pearl Harbor in December 1941; (3) the German surrender in May 1945, which accelerated the demobilization process; and (4) the start of the Korean War in June 1950. Each of these events had an immediate and large effect on order issuance, with the impact trailing off over approximately the following two years. As I argue above, presidents often react to crises by utilizing delegated emergency powers, consolidating their administrative authority, and implementing extraordinary measures. Executive orders have historically been a key mechanism for this activity, and presidents issued unusually large numbers of orders in the buildup to World War II, postwar demobilization, and in the early stages of the Korean War. Since these events have little to do with "politics," per se, failure to account for them could result in seriously flawed coefficient estimates.

Each intervention effect is coded as one in the month of the shock, with the assumption that the effect of the shock dissipated over a two-year period. In estimating the effect the external shocks had on the number of orders, I assume that presidents reacted swiftly to each by immediately issuing executive orders, and that the effect of the shock wore off slowly over a two-year, or twenty-four-month, period. I estimated the lag weights using an Almon lag, which approximates the true lag structure by fitting a polynomial curve to the data.[82] Choosing a two-year lag structure was arbitrary, but it presents a reasonable fit with the plotted data, and in any case the estimates for the substantive variables were unchanged by using different lag structures. Moreover, the lag structures for the interventions are substantively unimportant on their own; what is important is to control for their effects so that they do not contaminate the other variables in the event-count model.

Because the X variables are modeled as dummy variables that take the value one at a single time only, the weight structure becomes simple; the 96 coefficients in the lagged variables can be expressed with only ten variables as follows:

$$\sum_{i=0}^{23} w_i^a X_{t-i}^a = a_0 + a_1 i + a_2 i^2 \qquad \sum_{i=0}^{23} w_i^b X_{t-i}^b = b_0 + b_1 i + b_2 i^2$$

$$\sum_{i=0}^{23} w_i^c X_{t-i}^c = c_0 + c_1 i \qquad \sum_{i=0}^{23} w_i^d X_i^d = d_0 + d_1 i$$

with the X's and i's $= 0$ for all periods not part of the two-year lag following each intervention. For each set of coefficients, the variable i is the number of lags between the intervention and the current period. I incorporated into the model new variables based on the right-hand side expression.[83]

Results

The results of the estimation procedure for the entire series appear in table 3.4. The negative binomial specification is correct according to a likelihood ratio test of the negative binomial model compared with the alternative and more restrictive Poisson specification.

The coefficients in table 3.4 show unambiguously that the frequency of executive orders varies with the president's political environment. In event-count models the effect of an independent variable with coefficient β is $\beta\theta$, where θ is equal to the expected value (or average) of the dependent variable.[84] Different presidents issued orders at significantly different rates, with Republicans typically less likely to issue orders than Democrats; Nixon is the omitted variable, so the other presidents are placed relative to his administration. The coefficients for the Reagan (-0.269) and Bush (-0.378) are large and in the expected negative direction, and the coefficients for all Democratic presidents except Clinton are positive, although only Kennedy (0.220) shows a significant relationship. Between 1936 and 1995, presidents issued an average of 6.03 executive orders per month; setting θ to this value produces an estimate of $6.03 \times -0.269 = 1.6$ fewer orders per month for Reagan and 2.3 fewer for Bush, or about 19 fewer orders annually for Reagan, 27 fewer for Bush.

Although the start of a new president's term has no demonstrable effect on the number of orders issued (the coefficient does, however, have the expected positive sign), the end-of-term effects are dramatic: outgoing presidents who are leaving the office to successors of the opposition party issue nearly six additional orders ($6.03 \times 0.915 = 5.52$) in the last month of their term, nearly double the average level. This is the largest effect in the model except for the intervention coefficients corresponding to the beginning and end of World War II. There is no corresponding increase in order frequency when presidential turnover does not involve a shift in party control. This is persuasive evidence that executive orders have a strong policy component, as otherwise presidents would have little reason to issue such last-minute orders.

Presidents who are campaigning for reelection issue more orders than they would otherwise; although the coefficient for the campaign effect is insignificant, in election years where the president is not running for reelection the frequency of orders drops. In comparison, then, presidents issue more orders in the last year of their term when they are campaigning than they do when they are not campaigning: approximately 1.4 per month, or 14 over the course of the January-October election year period. This fits well with the notion that executive orders allow presidents to shape the public agenda and maintain ties with important constituencies during campaigns.

Presidential popularity has a large and significant effect on the frequency of orders. As presidents become less popular they tend to issue more orders, a result consistent with the hypothesis that executive orders provide a way for presidents to act on their own without relying on other institutions or actors. Again, using the 6.03 monthly average for the complete series, each 10-point drop in a president's six-month moving average popularity rating results in approximately one additional order every three months, or four per year; a 30-point drop spurs one additional order per month. Monthly popularity ratings, in contrast to the six-month moving average, had no effect on order frequency, indicating that presidents respond more to sustained changes in popularity rather than to short-term variation. Presidents use executive orders as a compensatory strategy to make policy decisions when their public standing declines.

The polynomial and lag specifications proved to be reasonable approximations of the actual series behavior. Using the estimates for the effect of World War II, or the b coefficients, the immediate estimated impact of Pearl Harbor on executive order issuance was $[1.38 - 0.129 + (0.002)^2] \times 6.03 = 7.54$ additional executive orders per month (again, using the formula $\beta\theta$, with θ set to the mean value of orders over the entire series, 6.03; β is the coefficient estimate, 1.25 in this case). However, the number of executive orders issued in the months leading up to December 1941 was decidedly higher than the overall average of 6.03 orders per month: over the two years prior to Pearl Harbor, Roosevelt had issued an average of nearly 15 executive orders per month. Although θ is normally set to the overall average of the dependent variable, it is also appropriate to set it at different levels if we have a prior belief that the expected value will be higher at some times than at others; the same coefficient β will have different effects depending on from where the dependent variable is starting. If I make the reasonable assumption that other things being

TABLE 3.4
Event-Count Results: Dependent Variable Orders, April 1936–December 1999

Independent Variable	Coefficient Estimate	Standard Error	t-statistic
Orders $_{t-1}$	−.0088*	.0048	1.84
Orders $_{t-3}$	.0066	.0045	1.45
Orders $_{t-12}$	.0132***	.0047	2.83
F. Roosevelt	.1044	.1526	0.68
Truman Unified	−.0191	.1165	0.16
Truman Divided	.0435	.1580	0.28
Eisenhower Unified	.2054	.1256	1.64
Eisenhower Divided	−.1688*	.0926	1.82
Kennedy	.2203*	.1170	1.88
Nixon	−.0504	.0939	0.06
Ford	−.0586	.1172	0.50
Carter	.1152	.1029	1.12
Reagan	−.2697***	.0877	3.08
Bush	−.3783***	.1114	3.40
Clinton Unified	−.1488	.1372	1.09
Clinton Divided	−.4223***	.1012	4.18
First Year, Party Change	.0472	.0730	0.65
First Year, No Party Change	−.0591	.1015	0.58
Last Month, Party Change	.9148***	.1470	6.22
Last Month, No Party Change	.2626	.4925	0.49
Campaign	−.0501	.0644	0.78
No Campaign	−.2269**	.1118	2.03
Presidential Popularity	−.0058***	.0022	2.65

equal, the expected number of orders in December 1941 would have been 15, I estimate that Pearl Harbor and the U.S. entry into World War II is then responsible for $15 \times 1.25 = 18.75$ additional orders that month, a figure close to the actual increase from 15 to 35 between November and December 1941.

To ensure that the popularity effects are not an anomaly due to the measurement's beginning in 1949 (since the popularity variable is set to 0 before then), I reestimated the model for the January 1949–December 1999 period. The results, shown in table 3.5, confirm that the relationships are robust: all of the coefficients that had a statistically significant impact over the complete series had a comparable effect in the truncated

TABLE 3.4 (cont.)
Event-Count Results: Dependent Variable Orders, April 1936–December 1999

Independent Variable	Coefficient Estimate	Standard Error	t-statistic
Almon Polynomial Lag Coefficients			
a_0	.5421**	.2285	2.37
a_1	−.0286	.0395	0.73
a_2	.0018	.0015	1.12
b_0	1.3816***	.2225	6.21
b_1	−.1295***	.0405	3.19
b_2	.0029*	.0017	1.75
c_0	1.0288***	.251	4.09
c_1	−.0469***	.0129	3.62
d_0	.6357***	.1871	3.40
d_1	−.0237**	.0120	1.98
Constant	1.9297		
Log Likelihood	−1762.0		
Observations	756.0		
Pseudo-r^2	.130		
Est. α	0.04		
LR Test against Poisson, $\chi^2(1) = 20.87, p < 0.001$			

* $p < 0.1$. ** $p < 0.05$. *** $p < 0.01$.

series; in fact, several became larger. Not only is presidential popularity not an artifact, but the other relationships in the model cannot be attributed to the extraordinary impact of World War II.

Estimating the impact of divided government produces a surprising result. Simply testing for differences between presidents under divided and unified government is no different than testing for differences between Democratic and Republican presidents, because of the consistent Democratic control of Congress: between 1936 and 1999, Democratic presidents enjoyed unified control twenty-nine years out of the thirty-six they served; Republicans, by contrast, faced divided government twenty-five of twenty-seven years.

Instead I look for differences among those presidents who faced both divided and unified government during their terms. For Truman, divided government had no impact on the number of orders he issued; both coefficients are small, the same sign, and indistinguishable from zero. Both Clinton and Eisenhower, however, issued more executive orders when they had majorities in Congress, in contrast to what the conventional

TABLE 3.5
Event-Count Results: Dependent Variable Orders$_t$, January 1949–December 1999

Independent Variable	Coefficient Estimate	Standard Error	t-statistic
Orders $_{t-1}$	−.0077	.0075	1.03
Orders $_{t-3}$	.00004	.0074	0.01
Orders $_{t-12}$	.0120*	.0072	1.66
Truman	−.0256	.1181	0.22
Eisenhower Unified	.2144*	.169	1.69
Eisenhower Divided	−.1570	.0960	1.64
Kennedy	.2333*	.1202	1.94
Nixon	−.0503	.0991	0.51
Ford	−.0816	.1237	0.66
Carter	.1272	.1105	1.15
Reagan	−.2673***	.0906	2.95
Bush	−.3911***	.1165	3.36
Clinton Unified	−.1608	.1436	1.12
Clinton Divided	−.4210***	.1044	4.03
First Year, Party Change	.0286	.0789	0.36
First Year, No Party Change	−.0245	.1106	0.22
Last Month, Party Change	.8798***	.1552	5.67
Last Month, No Party Change	.2087	.4937	0.42
Campaign	−.0757	.0822	0.92
No Campaign	−.1700**	.1336	1.27
Presidential Popularity	−.0062**	.0027	2.27
Almon Polynomial Lag Coefficients			
d $_0$	.6441***	.1920	3.36
d $_1$	−.0206*	.0124	1.66
Constant	2.0258		
Log Likelihood	−1368.4		
Observations	612.0		
Pseudo-r^2	.061		
Est. α	0.04		
LR Test Against Poisson, $\chi^2(1) = 10.18$, p < 0.01			

* $p < 0.1$; ** $p < 0.05$; *** $p < 0.01$.

wisdom predicted. Eisenhower issued over 1.2 more orders per month (6.03 × .205) when the Republicans controlled Congress in 1953 and 1954, compared with the remainder of his term when the Democrats had majorities in both chambers. For Clinton the relationship is even stronger: nearly 2.5 fewer orders per month after the Republican 1994 midterm sweep. These estimates are consistent with the overall frequency of Clinton's orders: from an average of 54 per year in 1993–1994, to an average of 40 per year from 1995 to 1999.

Clinton's drop in orders since 1995 is a particularly intriguing result, since in the wake of the 1994 elections Clinton White House officials predicted a renewed emphasis on "unilateral executive actions that circumvented Congress."[85] Even more curious was Clinton's response to his impeachment and trial: in 1998, he issued fewer executive orders (38) than he had in any previous year of his administration except 1997.

The conflicting effects of popularity and divided government present something of a puzzle. If, as I hypothesize, presidents use executive orders to compensate for political weakness in other areas, why does low popularity stimulate more orders while weakness in Congress does not? One possibility is that the dynamic between the presidency and Congress is too complex to be fully accounted for by a simple relationship between party differences and institutional collisions. Split party control may make bipartisanship more difficult, but it does not make it impossible, as Mayhew noted in his argument that divided government does not hinder significant lawmaking activity.[86] Charles Jones found numerous examples of legislative activity where the president retained the initiative on legislative proposals under divided government, either because the issues in question were deemed too important to be left to partisan wrangling, or because opposition was suppressed by the belief that the president had a mandate. Partisanship obviously plays a role, but Jones concludes that "when it comes to making laws in Washington, it is never done solely in the White House, it is sometimes done largely on Capitol Hill, and it is normally done with a substantial amount of cross-institutional and cross-partisan interaction through elaborate sequences featuring varying degrees of iteration."[87]

Unified government, in any case, does not eliminate the role executive orders play in presidential-congressional disputes (and Jimmy Carter demonstrated that even party majorities on the Hill do not always count for much). Clinton's early experience with his campaign promise to issue an executive order ending the military's ban on gay and lesbian service members is a telling example. There was no question that Clinton had the necessary authority to issue the order ending the ban immediately, because the issue was and remains a matter of internal Department of Defense policy and thus under the president's direct control.[88] Nevertheless Clinton backed down in the face of congressional and military resistance. The White House worried that issuing the order would further undermine Clinton's already tenuous relationship with the military services, and provoke Congress into enshrining the ban in statute.[89] President Kennedy faced the same sorts of questions about his 1960 campaign promise to issue an executive order banning discrimination in federal housing programs. Because of concern that the order would alienate key southern legislators, it was delayed several times, and finally issued quietly in November 1962 (see chapter six).

The analysis confirms some prior expectations about executive orders: Democratic presidents issue more than Republican presidents; presidents issue more at the end of their terms, when they are running for reelection, and when they lag in public opinion polls. Presidents turn to executive orders as a governing and policy tool when they need administrative flexibility and agenda control. Surprisingly, divided government has the opposite of the anticipated effect, as presidents issued more executive orders when they had congressional majorities and fewer when the opposition party was in control.

The frequency of executive orders is thus a function of the president's political environment. A president's popularity, the stage of his term, the election cycle, and whether or not he is leaving the office to the opposition party all affect the number of orders in predictable and consistent ways. In addition, significant executive orders are far more frequent than the conventional wisdom recognizes. Although, to be sure, even significant executive orders will normally be of less consequence than major legislative action, their frequency—about one per month over the last thirty years—belies the notion that executive orders are a minor tool for routine administrative decisions.

TABLE 3.6
Significant Executive Orders from Sample

Order	Date Signed	Title/Description
7856	Mar. 31, 1938	Rules Governing the Granting and Issuing of Passports in the United States
8233	Sept. 5, 1939	Prescribing Regulations Governing the Enforcement of the Neutrality of the United States
8344	Feb. 11, 1940	Withdrawal of Public Land for Classification—Alaska
8629	Jan. 7, 1941	Establishing the Office of Production Management
8683	Feb. 14, 1941	Establishing Naval Defensive Sea Areas around Naval Airspace Reservations
8693	Feb. 25, 1941	Prescribing Regulations Concerning the Exportation of Articles and Materials
8751	May 2, 1941	Establishing the Division of Defense Aid Reports in the Office for Emergency Management of the EOP
8773	June 9, 1941	Government Possession and Control—North American Aviation, Inc.
8785	June 14, 1941	Regulating Transactions in Foreign Exchange and Foreign-Owned Property
8802	June 25, 1941	Equal Employment in Government Contracting, Establishing the Fair Employment Practices Committee
8890	Sept. 3, 1941	Establishing the Office of Defense Health and Welfare
8944	Nov. 19, 1941	Government possession and control, Grand River Dam Authority
9017	Jan. 12, 1942	Establishing the National War Labor Board
9040	Jan. 24, 1942	Adding duties to the War Production Board
9083	Feb. 28, 1942	Transfer of authority for maritime functions
9102	Mar. 18, 1942	Establishing the War Relocation Authority
9253	Oct. 9, 1942	Administration of Contracts of the Immigration and Naturalization Service
9279	Dec. 5, 1942	Mobilization of National Manpower, Administration of Selective Service System
9337	Apr. 4, 1943	Transfer of authority to withdraw public lands to the Secretary of the Interior
9341	May 13, 1943	Government possession and control, American Railroad Co. of Puerto Rico
9351	June 14, 1943	Government possession and control, Howarth Pivoted Bearings Co.
9387	Oct. 15, 1943	Establishing Advisory Board on Just Compensation
9425	Feb. 19, 1944	Establishing Surplus War Property Administration

TABLE 3.6 (cont.)

Order	Date Signed	Title/Description
9427	Feb. 24, 1944	Establishing Retraining and Reemployment Administration
9437	Apr. 18, 1944	Revocation of Executive Order 9165 (Protection of Essential Facilities from Sabotage and Other Destructive Acts)
9459	Aug. 3, 1944	Government possession and control, Philadelphia Transportation Co.
9474	Aug. 31, 1944	Government possession and control, Ford Colleries Co. and Rochester and Pittsburgh Coal Co.
9476	Sept. 3, 1944	Government possession and control, certain coal companies
9484	Sept. 23, 1944	Government possession and control, Farrell Cheek Steel Co.
9505	Dec. 6, 1944	Government possession and control, Cudahy Brothers Co.
9508	Dec. 27, 1944	Government possession and control, Montgomery Ward & Co.
9511	Jan. 12, 1945	Government possession and control, Cleveland Electric Illuminating Co.
9523	Feb. 18, 1945	Government possession and control, American Enka Corp.
9570	June 14, 1945	Government possession and control, Scranton Transit Co.
9593	July 25, 1945	Government possession and control, Springfield Plywood Corp.
9595	July 30, 1945	Government possession and control, United States Rubber Co.
9607	Aug. 30, 1945	Revoking 48-hour minimum workweek
9608	Aug. 31, 1945	Termination of Office of War Information
9621	Sept. 21, 1945	Termination of Office of Strategic Services and transfer of its functions
9622	Sept. 21, 1945	Revocation of Executive Order 9103 (Publication and Use of Federal Statistical Information)
9639	Sept. 29, 1945	Government possession and control, certain petroleum companies
9661	Nov. 29, 1945	Government possession and control, Great Lakes Towing Co.
9672	Dec. 21, 1945	Establishment of National Wage Stabilization Board, Termination of the National War Labor Board
9674	Jan. 4, 1946	Liquidation of War Agencies
9691	Feb. 4, 1946	Resumption of peacetime civil service regulations
9801	Nov. 9, 1946	Removal of wage and price controls
9808	Dec. 5, 1946	Establishment of the President's Committee on Civil Rights
9863	May 31, 1946	Designation of certain international organizations as having diplomatic privileges

TABLE 3.6 (cont.)

Order	Date Signed	Title/Description
9981	July 26, 1946	Establishing the President's Committee on Equality of Treatment and Opportunity in the Armed Services
9989	Aug. 20, 1948	Transferring authority over blocked assets to the attorney general
10028	Dec. 12, 1949	Defining Noncombatant Service and Noncombatant Training
10152	Aug. 17, 1950	Incentive Pay for Hazardous Duty
10161	Sept. 9, 1950	Delegating functions under the Defense Production Act
10173	Oct. 18, 1950	Protection of vessels, harbors, ports, and waterfront facilities of the United States
10193	Dec. 16, 1950	Providing for the conduct of the mobilization effort
10210	Feb. 2, 1951	Authorizing exercise of powers in Title II of First War Powers Act, 1941
10251	June 7, 1951	Suspension of eight-hour law for certain Department of Defense personnel
10277	Aug. 1, 1951	Amending regulations regarding protection of vessels, harbors, ports, and waterfront facilities of the United States
10352	May 19, 1952	Amending regulations regarding protection of vessels, harbors, ports, and waterfront facilities of the United States
10433	Feb. 4, 1953	Further providing for administration of Defense Production Act
10460	June 16, 1953	Telecommunications authority of the director of defense mobilization
10483	Sept. 2, 1953	Establishing the Operations Coordinating Board
10621	July 1, 1955	Delegating functions to the secretary of defense
10816	May 7, 1959	Safeguarding information in the interests of the defense of the United States—amendment of previous executive order
10842	Oct. 6, 1959	Creating board of inquiry on labor disputes in the maritime industry
10903	Jan. 9, 1961	Delegating authority—regulations relating to overseas allowances and benefits to government personnel
10924	Mar. 1, 1961	Establishing the Peace Corps in the Department of State
10938	May 4, 1961	Establishing the President's Foreign Intelligence Advisory Board
10939	May 5, 1961	Ethical standards for government officials
11076	Jan. 15, 1963	Establishing the President's Advisory Commission on Narcotic and Drug Abuse
11098	Feb. 14, 1963	Amending Selective Service regulations

TABLE 3.6 (cont.)

Order	Date Signed	Title/Description
11141	Feb. 12, 1964	Declaring a public policy against discrimination on the basis of age
11296	Aug. 10, 1966	Evaluating flood hazards in federal buildings and properties
11327	Feb. 15, 1967	Authority to order ready reserve to active duty
11375	Oct. 13, 1966	Amending Executive Order 11246, equal employment opportunity
11404	Apr. 7, 1968	Restoration of law and order in the state of Illinois
11435	Nov. 11, 1968	Designating the secretary of interior to administer criminal and civil law in Native American territories
11458	Mar. 3, 1969	National Program for Minority Business Enterprise
11490	Oct. 28, 1969	Assigning emergency preparedness functions
11512	Feb. 27, 1970	Federal space planning, acquisition, and management
11514	Mar. 5, 1970	Protection and enhancement of environmental quality
11527	Apr. 23, 1970	Amending Selective Service regulations
11593	May 13, 1971	Protection and enhancement of the cultural environment
11615	Aug. 15, 1971	Stabilization of prices, rents, wages, and salaries
11636	Dec. 17, 1971	Employee-management relations in the Foreign Service
11697	Dec. 17, 1973	Inspection of income tax returns by the Department of Agriculture
11785	June 4, 1974	Amending Executive Order 10450—security requirements for government employment
11796	July 30, 1974	Regulation of exports
11808	Sept. 30, 1974	Establishing the President's Economic Policy Board
11810	Sept. 30, 1974	Regulation of exports
11832	Jan. 9, 1975	Establishing National Commission on the Observance of International Women's Year, 1975
11888	Nov. 24, 1975	Implementing the Generalized System of Preferences
11911	Apr. 13, 1976	Preservation of endangered species
11958	Jan. 18, 1977	Administration of arms export controls
11992	May 24, 1977	Establishing the Committee on Selection of Federal Judicial Officers
12041	Feb. 25, 1978	Amending the Generalized System of Preferences
12059	May 11, 1978	Establishing the United States Circuit Judge Nominating Commission
12072	Aug. 16, 1978	Federal space management
12088	Oct. 13, 1978	Federal compliance with pollution control standards
12114	Jan. 4, 1979	Environmental effects abroad of major federal actions

TABLE 3.6 (cont.)

Order	Date Signed	Title/Description
12133	May 9, 1979	Drug policy functions
12139	May 23, 1979	Foreign intelligence electronic surveillance
12143	June 22, 1979	Maintaining unofficial relations with the people of Taiwan
12160	Sept. 26, 1979	Enhancement and coordination of federal consumer programs
12183	Dec. 16, 1979	Revoking Rhodesian sanctions
12202	Mar. 18, 1980	Establishing the Nuclear Safety Oversight Committee
12217	June 18, 1980	Federal compliance with fuel use prohibitions
12232	Aug. 8, 1980	Historically black colleges and universities
12250	Nov. 2, 1980	Coordination of nondiscrimination laws
12264	Jan. 15, 1981	Federal policy on export of banned or significantly restricted substances
12279	Jan. 19, 1981	Transfer of Iranian assets held by domestic banks
12288	Jan. 29, 1981	Terminating the Wage and Price Regulatory Program
12296	Mar. 2, 1981	Establishing the President's Economic Policy Advisory Board
12331	Oct. 20, 1981	President's Foreign Intelligence Advisory Board
12340	May 25, 1980	Amendments to the Manual for Courts Martial
12369	June 30,1980	Establishing the President's Private Sector Survey on Cost Control in the Federal Government (Grace Commission)
12400	Dec. 3, 1983	Establishing the President's Commission on Strategic Forces
12434	July 19, 1984	Alaska Railroad rates
12502	Jan. 28, 1985	Establishing the Chemical Warfare Review Commission
12525	July 12, 1985	Emergency authority for export controls
12541	Dec. 20, 1985	Continuation of export control regulations
12544	Jan. 8, 1986	Blocking Libyan government property in the U.S. or held by U.S. persons
12548	Feb. 14, 1986	Grazing fees on federal lands
12615	Nov. 19, 1987	Performance of commercial activities by the federal government
12632	Mar. 23, 1988	Federal labor management relations program
12661	Dec. 27, 1988	Implementing the Omnibus Trade and Competitiveness Act of 1988
12262	Dec. 31, 1988	Implementing the U.S.-Canada Free Trade Act
12675	Apr. 20, 1989	Establishing the National Space Council
12708	Mar. 23, 1990	Amendments to the Manual for Courts Martial

TABLE 3.6 (cont.)

Order	Date Signed	Title/Description
12722	Aug. 2, 1990	Blocking Iraqi government property and prohibiting transactions with Iraq
12724	Aug. 9, 1990	Blocking Iraqi government property and prohibiting transactions with Iraq
12730	Sept. 30, 1990	Continuing export control regulations
12735	Nov. 16, 1990	Chemical and biological weapons proliferation
12740	Nov. 29, 1990	Waiver under the Trade Act of 1974 with respect to the Soviet Union
12806	May 19, 1992	Establishing a fetal tissue bank
12834	Dec. 20, 1993	Ethics commitments by executive branch appointees
12839	Feb. 10, 1993	Reduction of 100,000 federal positions
12853	June 30, 1993	Blocking Haitian government property and transactions with Haiti
12864	Sept. 15, 1993	Establishing United States Advisory Council on the National Information Structure
12874	Oct. 20, 1993	Federal acquisition, recycling, and waste prevention
12897	Feb. 3, 1994	Garnishment of federal employees' pay
12937	Nov. 10, 1994	Declassification of selected records with the National Archives
12958	Apr. 17, 1995	Classified national security information
12961	May 26, 1995	Establishing the President's Advisory Committee on Gulf War Veterans' Illness
13010	July 15, 1996	Establishing the Commission on Critical Infrastructure Protection
13021	Oct. 19, 1996	Tribal colleges and universities
13047	May 20, 1997	Prohibiting new investment in Burma
13080	April 7, 1998	American Heritage Rivers Initiative Advisory Committee
13103	Sept. 30, 1998	Computer software piracy
13112	Feb. 3, 1999	Invasive species
13132	Aug. 4, 1999	Federalism

Four

Executive Orders and the Institutional Presidency

THE PRESIDENCY is more than the person who occupies the office of president; it is also the set of institutions and processes that shape the behavior of the people who work within them. Viewing the office from this perspective helps shift our attention away from the characteristics of individual presidents and toward structures that remain more or less the same from one administration to the next. It also offers a way to link presidential influence to specific legal powers, since a central component of the president's formal authority is the ability to control institutions and processes. Presidents may not be able to say "do this, do that" and then sit back and wait, but they do have the ability to create, adapt, and modify institutions and organizational processes in ways that maximize the chances that policy and political outputs will match their own preferences.

In this chapter I will trace the use of executive orders as an instrument of institution building and control. Presidents, especially in the twentieth century, have used executive orders both to create and to gain control of institutions that are now crucial to presidential leadership. By creating new organizations, expanding the scope and powers of existing institutions, and unilaterally altering crucial administrative procedures, presidents have been remarkably successful in gaining control of the government's institutional apparatus, outmaneuvering Congress, and only rarely being blocked by the courts (as, for example, occurred in the *Myers* decision).

As I noted in chapter one, the president—despite the checks and balances of the separation of powers—retains important advantages in struggles over institutional structure and process. The president can often move first, leaving it up to the other branches to undo what has been done. Presidents, acting in this capacity as unitary decision makers, are more likely to have complete information about what, precisely, they are trying to accomplish, and can more easily conceal their true intentions from other actors. The validity of these statements—which to this point in my argument are more assumptions than anything that has been empirically proved—will become clear in the course of the case studies that follow in this and the next two chapters.

The history of the presidency's institutionalization is replete with stories of legislators or bureaucrats who seriously misjudged the consequences of reform, and of presidents who attempted to conceal the true nature of their motivations. The two most important presidential institutions, the Bureau of the Budget (BoB, which evolved into the Office of Management and Budget in 1971) and the Executive Office of the President, were both established amid poorly understood intentions, unplanned consequences, and even intentional obfuscation. The chief architect of the EOP, Louis Brownlow, admitted that when he wrote the initial drafts of Executive Order 8248 (which established the EOP), he purposefully obscured language that established a unit called the Office of Emergency Management (OEM), which was to serve as the legal foundation for multitudes of presidential wartime agencies.

In its famous 1936 report, the President's Committee on Administrative Management (PCAM) had called for an extensive reorganization of the executive branch and an expansion of the president's administrative powers. In January 1937 FDR submitted legislation incorporating many of the PCAM's recommendations, in a reorganization proposal that would have significantly expanded the president's control over regulatory, fiscal, and personnel policy. It was poorly received in Congress, and opposition continued to build throughout 1937 and 1938, in part because Roosevelt had committed to his ill-fated "court packing" plan in the interim.[1] Critics saw reorganization and court packing through the same lens, viewing both as "evidence of Roosevelt's dictatorial ambitions," and congressional leaders declared the bill dead in May 1938.[2] FDR tried again in 1939, finally succeeding with a reorganization bill that gave the president less sweeping powers—Congress extended reorganization authority for two years, barred the president from reorganizing independent regulatory agencies, and retained the power to reject any reorganization plan with a concurrent resolution.[3] FDR signed the legislation in April 1939 and issued his first reorganization plan with E.O. 8248 five months later.

Because of the fate of the 1937 reorganization bill, Brownlow was especially sensitive to how the press and public might react to the establishment of the Executive Office had they known the full implications of the order's language. He acknowledged later that his plan to establish the OEM within the context of E.O. 8248 would provide the legal authority "for the erection of the major part of the governmental machinery used for defense in war. It was a novel and unprecedented feature in that it permitted the government to act immediately in time of an emergency."[4]

But few people besides Brownlow and FDR knew this at the time. The reorganization effort as a whole, beginning in 1937, was presented "to Congress and the public in a way that sought to camouflage its constitutional implications,"[5] and E.O. 8248 continued in the same vein. OEM was listed as the sixth organizational unit within the Executive Office of the President; it was not identified by name; and the remainder of the order said nothing about its structure or functions (the other five units were all explicitly defined in section II of the order). The language, purposefully vague, stipulated that the president could establish, "in the event of a national emergency or threat of a national emergency, such office for emergency management" as he might determine.[6]

Brownlow likened the OEM provision to a "rabbit stowed in the hat": when the order was issued, "the little rabbit came out . . . but was so disguised in small print, with no capital letters, that it occasioned no remark on the press or in [general discussion]."[7] The *American Political Science Review*, which at the time regularly published short articles describing the changes that were occurring in executive branch organization, noted the order but did not include any reference to the OEM provision.[8]

It was not until May 1940, when Hitler invaded the Low Countries, that Roosevelt activated the OEM, thus "[pulling] the rabbit out of the hat for keeps."[9] In between the expiration of the Reorganization Act of 1939 (in January 1941), and the passage of the First War Powers Act in January 1942, FDR used executive orders in the absence of legislative authority to establish dozens of wartime agencies within the OEM. It was a pattern of presidential bootstrapping; each successive order or action was based on a previous order, with the trail ending at E.O. 8248. Once Congress had delegated critical wartime powers to the executive branch the OEM was no longer needed as a legal anchor, since FDR could then act pursuant to a statute, but even then it served as a key symbol of presidential control and as an "extension of congressional approval" of whatever FDR put within it.[10]

BoB's official history of the war mobilization effort praised "the soundness of the broad administrative strategy of maintaining presidential initiative in matters of emergency government organization. The legal basis for this initiative had been provided with considerable prevision in 1939 in actions laying the basis" for the OEM through presidential action.[11] To others, though, these agencies were a far more sinister embodiment of unlimited presidential power, reminiscent of court packing and the 1937 reorganization bill. Corwin argued that FDR was well aware of the constitutional problems the executive creations raised, and that he tried to evade them by relying on the OEM umbrella to justify presidential action.[12]

But neither Congress nor the courts were willing to step in during a national crisis. When Congress objected to what it perceived as a presidential power-grab, FDR used the immense prestige of a key official to overwhelm legislators:

The Senate sub-committee on Appropriations did not like this method of creating new agencies, and senators, at a hearing in 1941, raised sharp questions as to whether they had been legally authorized. Roosevelt was able to rely on the prestige of the first Director General of the Office of Production Management, William Knudsen, to neutralize opposition. When Knudsen entered the room at a Senate hearing to discuss OPM appropriations, "senators rose to greet him, forgot their inhibitions, and passed the appropriations for the whole array of emergency agencies. . . . If there had been any doubt about the authority for creating these agencies, the act of appropriating funds gave a sanction to their legality and we were in business.[13]

In the one court case to move beyond the district courts, the D.C. Court of Appeals ruled that the agencies created via presidential authority were informatory or advisory, not legislative, and thus were valid exercises of presidential power.[14]

The pattern of misread intentions and poorly understood consequences was true as well for the BoB, which was enthusiastically endorsed in Congress despite expressed fears that it would lead to an excessive growth of executive power. In this case Congress simply misjudged what the institution would mean, even though proponents of the bureau were hardly quiet about its implications for presidential power. According to Moe, "While there were some fears of presidential encroachment on legislative powers, the act was neither intended nor expected to alter the balance between the two branches and was largely viewed by Congress as a means of helping rationalize its own previously chaotic budgetary process. What proved to be a truly important reform in the development of American political institutions was feasible precisely because its far-reaching political consequences were unanticipated."[15]

This era provides a key test of the new institutional economics predictions about the president's ability to trump Congress in this struggle for institutional control. I analyze two distinct episodes that display the same dynamic—the rise of presidential budget power in the early twentieth century, and presidents' efforts after 1970 to put their stamp on regulatory policy. In both cases, although they are separated by decades and occurred in distinctly different periods in presidential power, the pattern was the same. The rise of new economic and political forces spurred new governmental institutions. In the early twentieth century, the issue was how best to craft a government budget. Later, the issue was how to respond to new environmental problems and pressure for more government regulation of business. In both cases, Congress and the president competed for control of the administrative and regulatory machinery that resulted. And in both cases the president's ability to move first, combined with Congress's relative inability to respond effectively, tilted the competition in favor of the executive.

The Presidential Budget Power

The story of the events leading up to the Budget and Accounting Act of 1921—which established the Bureau of the Budget—provides the archetype of the dynamic I seek to illuminate; while there were earlier examples of expanding presidential power, most notably during the Jackson and Lincoln administrations, they were temporary episodes in an otherwise unexceptional story. Most nineteenth-century presidents lacked the inclination to assert their executive power, and they lacked the resources necessary for strong leadership. The federal government was small, and its powers were hemmed in by narrow interpretations of the commerce clause. Government positions were doled out as congressionally controlled patronage. The president's ability to exert leadership was limited, because there were no administrative mechanisms or organizational processes that enabled him to supervise or control the executive branch. "Amid a growing executive branch and a Congress becoming more capable of specialized work through committees," writes Peri Arnold of the late nineteenth century, "the president still limped along with staff support comprising a handful of clerks and a secretary or two."[16] That assessment would change with the adoption of the budget law. "The modern presidency, judged in terms of institutional responsibilities," concludes James Sundquist, "began on June 10, 1921, the day that President Harding signed the Budget and Accounting Act."[17]

The pattern of nearly continuous growth of presidential power in the twentieth century required as a precursor the late nineteenth-century expansion of national government administrative capacity.[18] The needs of a rapidly industrializing society outstripped the abilities of both state and federal governments to deal with them, and out of this grew a new set of regulatory institutions, administrative practices, and patterns of state-society relations.

Inevitably the creation of new institutions and the assumption of new powers led to disputes over who or what would control them. As Skowronek puts it, "after 1900, the doors of power opened to those who saw a national administrative apparatus as the centerpiece of a new governmental order. The central question in institutional development was correspondingly altered. It was no longer a question of whether or not America was going to build a state that could support administrative power but of who was going to control administrative power in the new state that was to be built."[19] In the late nineteenth century presidents had few opportunities to exert their executive authority through any institutional prism; the administrative capacities necessary for that did not exist. Congress was the dominant force, and "administration" took place without much presidential influence. In this decentralized environment, executive branch organizations were more closely tied to their patrons in Congress than they were to the president.[20]

But the growth of a national administrative capacity would provide the presidency with a potential resource for leadership. Political elites who favored a strong set of government institutions "[knew that] the presidency, above all other positions within the old order, stood to gain from a real opportunity to reconstitute institutional power relationships so as to support an expansion of national administrative capacities. The bureaucratic remedy promised the chief executive his own national political constituency, independent institutional resources, and an escape from the limitations" of existing political relationships based on decentralized party power.[21]

A key piece in this institutional structure was the power to oversee and coordinate the federal budget. Since the exercise of virtually every federal government function requires, at some level, spending money, the power to shape the budget implies the power to shape policy. The rise of a national budget and the organization created to administer it were to be centerpieces of presidential power after 1921. Several scholars have noted the impact of the budget act itself on the presidency,[22] but there have been few contemporary investigations of the foundation that was laid over the previous decade and how specific cases of executive initiative broke new ground in the struggle for budgetary control.

The sharp rise in expenditures around the turn of the century demonstrated the flaws in the existing budget process. The trend during this period is well documented; spending more than doubled between 1880 and 1904, an increase attributable to spending on rivers and harbors, pensions, the Spanish American War, and construction of the Panama Canal.[23] At the same time, changes in congressional procedures in 1880 and 1885 decentralized spending authority to numerous committees, stripping the Appropriations Committee (itself established in 1865) of its power to control distributive pressures in the legislature.[24]

Presidential control was lacking as well. Traditionally each executive department developed its own budget, often in close contact with relevant committees in Congress. These budget estimates were then sent to the Treasury Department, which did little more than compile the individual documents into a Book of Estimates and transmit the result to Congress. There was nothing in the way of centralized presidential control, no coordination among agencies, and no attempt to relate expenditures to revenues. Expenditures were not classified in any coherent way, and it was impossible to determine how much the government was spending on any particular function or common program. Under the existing system, as the Commission on Economy and Efficiency described it, executive branch officials were "acting as the ministerial agents of the Congress rather than as representatives of the President."[25]

One consequence of such a loosely constructed process is that the budget estimates were frequently wrong. Agencies would often run out of money halfway through the year and require supplemental appropriations to avoid shortfalls. Congress, unhappy with what it saw as both carelessness and lack of respect for its own powers of the purse, began in the early twentieth century to enact more detailed budget legislation, as well as laws (such as the Anti-Deficiency Act in 1906, which prohibited agencies from spending money that they did not have) designed to limit executive branch leeway.[26]

The consensus was that the budget process was broken and needed reform, but any significant changes confronted the problem that reforms would inescapably alter the distribution of political power between the president and Congress, not only over programs and policy but also in terms of control over administrative activities. The existing system placed Congress at the center and gave executive agencies a high degree of autonomy from the president. Giving the president more control would necessarily reduce the influence of those who benefited from this arrangement. These contrasting forces set the stage for a constitutional confrontation over the president's authority to control the executive branch. To Taft, budgeting was a central executive function, and he argued that a centralized budget would enhance accountability by placing responsibility on the president as head of the executive branch.

Congress not surprisingly took a different view, seeing its spending power as a cornerstone of its constitutional position in government. Congressional concerns were heightened because of earlier disputes with the presidency over control of the executive branch. These conflicts revolved around executive orders issued by Taft and Theodore Roosevelt in an early effort to get control of what would eventually be known as central clearance. Both presidents sought to control the ability of government personnel to communicate directly with Congress. In January 1902 Roosevelt issued an executive order forbidding any executive department employee from lobbying for salary increases or trying "to influence or attempt to influence in their own interest any other legislation whatever either before Congress or its committees," except through their department or agency heads. In 1906 Roosevelt extended this order to include employees of "independent Government establishments."[27]

Taft continued this effort with his own order, extending the prohibition to include every "bureau, office, or division chief," all subordinates, and all military officers stationed in the District of Columbia (Executive Order 1142, November 26, 1909). This order also prohibited officials from responding to congressional requests for information, unless they obtained the approval of the department head. Congressional reaction was swift, and legislators responded by cutting "deeply into [Taft's] budget requests, forcing him to come back later for supplemental appropriations."[28]

But Taft did not give up. As part of his broader effort to gain control over administration, in 1910 he asked Congress for funds to establish a commission to study government administration and recommend improvements. From the outset, however, Taft anticipated that one of the recommendations of the Commission on Economy and Efficiency would be an executive budget.[29]

When Taft attempted to follow through on the commission's recommendation for an executive budget, the result was nothing short of a constitutional confrontation between Congress and the president over who would control the vital budget function. Surprisingly Taft, who later was to take a formalistic view of constitutional powers as chief justice of the Supreme Court (particularly in *Myers v. United States*), in this case argued from a functional perspective that did not rely on explicit constitutional powers. In a letter to the secretary of the treasury, Taft outlined his position. "If the President is to assume . . . any responsibility for either the manner in which business of the Government is transacted," Taft wrote, ". . . it is evident that he cannot be limited by Congress to such information as that branch may think sufficient for his purposes. In my opinion, it is entirely competent for the President to submit a budget, and Congress cannot . . . prevent it. . . . And this power I propose to exercise."[30] Congress, which was already chafing against Taft's efforts to get control of the expanding civil service, was in no mood to cooperate on the budget; to many legislators, presidential control of the budget was meant an abdication of one of Congress's basic constitutional responsibilities as well as an abandonment of its best method of constraining excessively energetic presidents. The prospect of an executive budget posed a direct challenge to congressional authority and autonomy. "Critics of executive budget-making considered it a diminution of legislative power. "Uncle Joe" Cannon, Speaker of the House from 1903 to 1911, warned that an executive budget would signify the surrender of the most important element of representative government. " 'I think we had better stick pretty close to the Constitution with its division of powers well defined and the taxing power close to the people.' Edward Fitzpatrick, author of a budget study in 1918, characterized the executive budget concept as a step toward autocracy and a Prussian style military state."[31]

Taft submitted the report of the Commission on Economy and Efficiency to Congress in June 1912. In an accompanying message, Taft made it clear that in his view the president had the constitutional authority to prepare and submit a coordinated executive budget, the current practices notwithstanding. Even so, Taft recognized the importance of working

with Congress. Preparing such a budget without congressional cooperation would be inefficient (since agencies would still have to prepare their
budgets for the Book of Estimates) but still permissible: "Although the
President has the power to install new and improved systems of accounts
and to require that information be presented to him each year in such
form that he and his Cabinet may intelligently consider proposals or estimates; although the President, under the Constitution, may submit to the
Congress each year a definite well-considered budget, with a message calling attention to subjects of immediate importance, to do this without the
cooperation of the Congress . . . would entail a large expenditure of public money in duplication of work."[32]

When Taft instructed executive branch agency heads to prepare budget
estimates in accordance with the commission's recommendations, Congress retaliated with a law that prohibited executive branch officials from
preparing any budget documents except those that were specifically required by law. Taft responded with an executive order directing agency
heads to submit the draft budget proposals in accordance to his directions
anyway, the law notwithstanding.[33]

Although Congress paid no attention to Taft's executive budget, his
actions had a significant impact on the forces that ultimately resulted in
the establishment of a presidential budget system in 1921. One account
of Taft's influence maintained that although Congress rejected his attempt
to implement the key recommendations of his Commission on Economy
and Efficiency, his efforts still constituted "a great service in raising this
important issue and focusing the attention of the public, as a whole, on
this problem. It also furnished the supporters of the National Budget System the ground-work with which they could carry on the fight."[34] For a
president generally considered to be weak, especially in the shadow of
Theodore Roosevelt, Taft managed to play a key role in laying the foundation for a major expansion of executive power.

The presidents involved in efforts to institute a national budget (Taft,
in particular) recognized from the outset that the new capability would
provide a significant advantage over Congress in controlling executive
branch activity. Both Taft and Wilson saw that significant separation of
powers questions were at stake, and outside pressure for a national budget
was part of a broader effort to replace legislative parochialism and chaos
with the "neutral competence" of "scientific" presidential management.
Although to Congress the act was a way of ordering a haphazard system,
there were clear signs that Congress would be giving up much more than
it believed at the time.[35]

Proponents of the budget system made no secret of their view that it
would enhance presidential power, and some wanted to strip Congress
of the power to amend presidential budget requests altogether. Charles

Wallace Collins, writing in 1916, argued that in an effective executive budget system, "the legislative branch . . . yields to the executive the legislative initiative in matters of finance [and] refrains from adding any amendments by way of increasing any of the items or changing their purpose or adding any new items without the consent of the executive."[36] Further, a central tenet of the executive budget movement was that "the functional demands of modern administration required coherent administrative organization placed in the president," even if Congress had to delegate that authority to do it.[37]

The pressures of World War I made it clear that Congress would one way or another have to provide the president with some sort of budget power. Outlays rose by nearly 2,500 percent between 1916 and 1919, from $713 million to $18.5 billion, and what had been a $48 million surplus in 1916 became a $13.3 billion deficit.[38] In 1919, soon after the war ended, Congress enacted budget legislation which gave the president central budget control. And, in any case, congressional supporters of the executive budget minimized its impact on legislators' prerogatives. The committee report on the first version of the bill argued that "this bill does not in any way abridge the authority of Congress over appropriations. Congress will be at liberty, as now, to revise or increase the budget estimates or add new items to them. What attitude Congress takes on this question is not a matter of legislation but of rule. It is within the sole province of each House of Congress to decide whether it will modify the existing rules and committees established for the consideration of appropriations bills."[39]

The 1919 legislation, though, contained two provisions designed to minimize the degree of congressional abdication. The first provision was the location of the Bureau of the Budget in the Department of the Treasury, the executive department considered most faithful to congressional sentiment. By putting the BoB here, Congress ensured some check on presidential influence. According to Sidney Milkis, "the Budget Act of 1921 did significantly enhance the President's authority to oversee the expenditures of the executive departments and agencies, but the effect of this legislation was blunted by the placement of the newly created Budget Bureau in the Treasury Department rather than directly under the supervision of the president himself. This tended to circumscribe the administrative power of the president and to retain the autonomy of executive departments and agencies from the oversight of the White House."[40] The Treasury Department had a long history in the cross fire of presidential congressional disputes: During Jackson's presidency, he and Congress clashed over who had the authority to direct the secretary of the treasury to handle the nation's finances. "Congress frequently treated the Secretary of the Treasury as *its* agent, delegating to him—rather than the President—the responsibility for placing Government money either in the national bank or in State banks."[41]

Second, the newly established comptroller general, an officer of Congress with the responsibility for auditing executive branch spending, would be immune to presidential removal. Woodrow Wilson vetoed the first budget act in 1919 because of this provision, arguing that it was an unconstitutional usurpation of executive powers by a legislative agent. Two years later, Congress passed a revised act without this provision, which was signed into law by Warren Harding.

Almost immediately the new BoB took on responsibilities going well beyond simple budget preparation, congressional intent notwithstanding. Most of these steps were initiated by executive action alone, through executive orders, administrative directives, and BoB orders issued in the president's name. The first director, Charles M. Dawes, established procedures and departments to coordinate the activities of a number of agencies that were disposing of surplus property from World War I. The assumption of these duties was no accident, since "increased control over administration was the Bureau of the Budget's ambition from its inception. . . . From the beginning Dawes understood the bureau's potential as an executive weapon. Despite the fact that the new law was not to take effect until fiscal year 1923, the Harding administration quickly devised a budget for fiscal year 1922. This was done without formal authority and rested on President Harding's orders, implemented through the new bureau."[42] Dawes's diary of his activities during the first year of the BoB is an account of his ambitious attempts to make full use of the bureau's potential.[43] He cites as one of his accomplishments "the reorganization of the routine business of government through the use by the president of the Budget Bureau as an agency of executive pressure, and the creation by executive orders of coordinating machinery out of the body of the existing business organization."[44] Incremental expansion of executive authority was a key element of the BoB's assumption of these new duties. Dawes's first report to Congress noted that the president was "determined to assume his full responsibility as the head of the governmental business organization, and directed the Director of the Bureau . . . to immediately suggest to him such improvements in existing governmental business methods as could be legally inaugurated by him through Executive orders."[45]

In December 1921 Dawes tried to expand the BoB's reach to include general legislative clearance, directing agencies to submit all legislative proposals with any financial impact to the bureau, which reserved the right to make recommendations to the president (in Budget Cirular no. 49). Here Dawes was asserting authority not found explicitly in the Budget and Accounting act: the act gave the president the authority to review only budget requests and estimates, but Dawes, construing this language broadly, maintained that the BoB should review legislation that could have any effect on government spending, which was to say just about everything. This step, if not specifically required by the law, was "necessary for a full compliance with its spirit."[46]

The bureau's position constituted "a new assertion of presidential control over agencies," and the cabinet secretaries made it clear that they objected.[47] Within a month Dawes had retreated, insisting that the BoB had no interest in policy, but was concerned only with "routine business" and providing a "convenient machinery" for transmitting the president's policies to Congress.[48] Still, the primary force behind BoB's withdrawal was the concern among cabinet secretaries about their autonomy (a dispute that was to emerge anew after 1939, amid fears that the new formal staff structure within the Executive Office of the President would interpose itself between secretaries and the president), rather than any concerns expressed by members of Congress.

But Dawes never formally rescinded Budget Circular no. 49, and in 1924 the BoB under Calvin Coolidge "seized on this empty order [circular no. 49] and within it built a strong and well enforced, if narrowly defined accessory to central budgeting," requiring central clearance on all legislation with clear budgetary implications.[49] FDR repeatedly expanded BoB's clearance authority to include executive orders (1933), all agency legislative proposals (1934),[50] and coordination of agency recommendations on enrolled bills (1939).

In expanding central clearance beyond simply budget preparation, presidents acted solely on the basis of their executive authority. A 1937 internal BoB memorandum made this clear, noting that the statutory charter for the bureau did not provide the necessary authorization: "There is no authority whatever in the Budget and Accounting Act for our procedure with respect to reports on legislation. . . . The authority we have over [these] reports comes from Executive authority and *not* from any Act of Congress."[51] The expansion was driven by the president's desire for more coordination with and control over agency activities, and at least until 1939 involved gradual expansion rather than any dramatic overhaul of administrative procedures. Perhaps because of the incremental and procedural nature of the changes, there is little evidence of strong congressional objections. In any case, Congress had more important battles to wage with Roosevelt over court packing and reorganization.

Despite FDR's repeated delegations to the bureau, it was far from ideal as an instrument of presidential administrative power. It was chronically short of money and understaffed, problems identified by the President's Committee on Administrative Management (the Brownlow Committee) as impediments to the bureau's ability to function as an effective presidential agent.[52] From the outset, the bureau had suffered under the self-imposed spending constraints established by Dawes and retained by his successors. Arguing that the bureau could hardly preach economy to the rest of the government if it did not practice the same itself, Dawes took great pride in putting BoB on a bare-bones budget. But this insistence on frugality "almost destroyed the usefulness of the Bureau," because there was not enough money to employ sufficient staff.[53]

The Brownlow Committee recommended that BoB be reconstituted so that it was larger and more powerful, and made more accountable to the president. In Executive Order 8248, Roosevelt moved BoB into the Executive Office of the President, making it a direct agent of presidential control, solidifying its importance as an agent of central clearance. During World War II, BoB grew dramatically—with its staff increasing from forty to six hundred—and it assumed broader authority granted by both executive orders and legislative delegation.[54] "Between 1940 and 1943," writes Larry Berman, "the Budget Bureau constituted the sole staff support for the President in managing the defense and, later, the war effort."[55] As I noted earlier, FDR's creation of the Office of Emergency Management within the EOP gave him a crucial pillar to which he attached dozens of wartime organizations. By 1945 the bureau had added to its mandate oversight responsibility for federal statistical programs (Federal Reports Act of 1942), coordination of government mapping and chart-making activities (Executive Order 9094, March 10, 1942), review of public works projects (Executive Order 9384, October 4, 1943), and budgetary clearance of government corporations (Government Corporations Control Act of 1945).[56]

In 1954 Richard Neustadt described the expansion of central clearance this way: "For more than thirty years now, central clearance has persisted, its history marked by a long series of 'accidental,' unforeseen accretions. Nothing once absorbed has been wholly displaced; each new element somehow encompasses the old ... overall, here is a record of great growth, successful adaptation—this under six successive Presidents, through every variation in national and governmental circumstance since Harding's term of office."[57] The presidential budget and growth of BoB power illustrates the pattern: societal and political pressures serve as the impetus for a new government capability; Congress and the president compete over the question of control; the president prevails and uses the new capability in unanticipated ways to develop even more power, and Congress can do little to stop him. Over time, the new powers—once so controversial—become institutionalized as a routine and accepted part of the presidency. The pattern has played out in a number of situations, across presidents and eras, and has less to do with specific presidential initiative than the motivations and incentives, relative positions, and inherent institutional qualities of Congress and the presidency.

Regulatory Review

The push for a presidential budget between 1910 and 1921 parallels in rough outline a dispute that was to occur sixty years later over presidential attempts to rein in newly empowered regulatory institutions. Again the pattern was the same: social and political pressures resulted in a new set of institutions and government capability, with a corresponding struggle over who was to control them. In this case the question was control of a rapidly expanding regulatory capacity in the 1960s and early 1970s. Successive presidents, starting with Nixon, began to assert control over the new institutions and processes, issuing a series of executive orders that imposed procedural requirements on agencies when they issued new regulations, with each successive presidential order putting in place more substantive procedural constraints.

The history of presidential efforts to control regulatory agencies actually goes back much further, although the scope of the problem emerged in sharp relief only as the capacity of these agencies expanded rapidly in the 1960s and 1970s. Regulatory agencies have always posed unique problems, because unlike cabinet departments, Congress has purposely insulated them from presidential control; this insulation has typically been achieved by protecting high-level agency officials from removal.[58] The problem of control had emerged by the 1930s, when the Supreme Court ruled (in *Humphrey's Executor*) that Congress could create regulatory agencies that were independent of direct presidential influence. The Brownlow Committee saw these agencies as a "headless fourth branch" of government lacking accountability to the president, and recommended incorporating them into the cabinet departments. An accompanying report gingerly suggested that rulemaking be subject to the same central clearance procedures as executive orders and legislative proposals; that is, that the Bureau of the Budget coordinate and clear regulations.[59]

As part of the second Hoover Commission in the 1950s, Eisenhower requested a memorandum detailing his authority over the operations of regulatory commissions (the report concluded that the president's authority was ambiguous, probably extending to the executive functions of the agencies but not to their quasi-legislative or quasi-judicial functions).[60] The issue arose again in the 1960s, albeit indirectly, when Kennedy issued an executive order prohibiting racial discrimination in federally funded housing. Kennedy, and then Johnson, considered extending the nondiscrimination rule to cover lending activities of federally insured banks and savings and loans. Such a step presumed that the President indeed had the authority as chief executive to superimpose a requirement on the independent agencies that regulated banking (the Federal Deposit Insurance Corporation, the Federal Savings and Loan Insurance Corporation, and the Board of Governors of the Federal Reserve). After being repeatedly advised that the legal prospects were dubious at best, neither president forced the issue.

Presidents had thus long been concerned about their ability to control regulatory activity. But the problem became acute by the early 1970s, after Congress created a raft of new agencies, including the Consumer Product Safety Commission (established in 1972), the National Highway Transportation Safety Administration (1970), the Occupational Safety and Health Agency (1970), and the Environmental Protection Agency (1970). These new agencies had much broader regulatory authority than the organizations created in the first two waves of economic regulation (in the late nineteenth century and the 1930s), because they were responsible for regulating across broad sectors of the economy rather than specific industries.[61] That presidents began to assert control over this new set of institutions was no coincidence, as they "came to realize that their grip on the course of domestic policy hinged to a considerable extent on their ability to influence the thousands of rules that put programs into action."[62]

These attempts to gain control of regulatory agencies were closely related to efforts to reorganize the Bureau of the Budget into a more effective tool of presidential power. By the mid-1960s, various study groups and review committees had concluded that the bureau could no longer keep up with its growing workload.[63] Shortly after taking office, Nixon created an Advisory council on Executive Reorganization, known as the Ash Council after its head, Roy Ash. The council recommended, among other things, that the Bureau of the Budget be reorganized to give the president broader authority over executive branch management. The council also considered the status of the independent regulatory institutions, concluding that they were unaccountable, unable to keep up with rapid technological developments, chronically short of competent staff, and wedded to rarified procedures that failed to account for economic realities.[64] In this respect, the Ash Council reached the same conclusions that the Brownlow Committee had come to four decades earlier.

Despite significant congressional opposition to the notion of expanding BoB, Nixon prevailed, in part because the reorganization process gave him a key advantage. For decades, Congress had repeatedly delegated to the president broad authority to reorganize executive branch activities.[65] Typically Congress would have the final say on reorganization proposals, usually by reserving the right to disapprove reorganization plans before they could take effect. But this required Congress to respond to presidential initiative, rather than take the initiative itself, and therefore put it at a disadvantage. When Nixon implemented the Ash Council recommendations, he relied upon the reorganization authority that Congress had granted him in 1969. After a "massive lobbying effort" by the administration, Congress could not muster majorities to pass a disapproval resolution. In July 1970 Nixon transferred BoB's authority to the newly created Office of Management and Budget (via Executive Order 11541).[66]

Nixon initiated efforts to gain control of these new regulatory institutions by instituting a "quality of life" review program within the newly formed OMB. In a clear parallel with the expansion of the BoB's budget review powers, the regulatory review process began in 1970 when George Shultz, OMB director, simply asserted that the OMB had the authority to "review *and clear*" proposed EPA regulations.[67] This position conflicted with the legal status of regulatory agencies, since Congress had explicitly delegated authority to the heads of the agencies, not to the president. Even in those cases where the agency head served at the pleasure of the president (unlike the heads of independent agencies, such as the Federal Trade Commission or the Securities and Exchange Commission, who could only be dismissed for reasons specified by Congress), it was not clear that the president could intervene in day-to-day activities. In the face of the legal and political problems raised by Shultz's original stance, the quality of life process dropped references to clearance and focused instead on interagency review of proposed regulations.[68]

Under the review program, agencies had to submit major regulations for interagency review thirty days prior to publication of the proposed rules in the *Federal Register*. Although the program ostensibly applied to regulatory activity generally, it was specifically targeted at the Environmental Protection Agency, and no other agency ever had any of its regulations reviewed.[69] The EPA was a particular concern because it had quickly grown into a large, powerful organization with "perhaps the broadest statutory authority of any regulatory agency."[70] But the OMB did little more than "[coordinate] the review process by circulating draft regulations to all interested agencies," and "did not wield any decision making power."[71] Critics claimed, however, that the added layers of bureaucratic review created significant delays, and that some major environmental regulations were stalled for two years. In addition, the interagency discussions were not part of the public record, which raised concerns about openness and accountability.

President Ford expanded the scope of regulatory review, and instituted the first formal procedures. Ford not only continued the quality of life review process, but in Executive Order 11821 he required agencies to prepare an "inflationary impact statement" of major regulations.[72] Both the OMB and the Council on Wage and Price Stability had authority to review the statements, although they could not force agencies to revise regulations.[73] But the existence of a formal process opened the door to litigation by groups who wished to challenge the adequacy of the analyses: in April 1975 a federal district court issued a preliminary injunction blocking a proposed Department of Agriculture regulation on beef grading, ruling that the agency had prepared a deficient impact analysis.[74] On appeal, though, the Eighth Circuit overturned the injunction, holding that Executive Order 11821 "was intended primarily as a managerial tool for implementing the President's personal economic policies and not as a legal framework enforceable by private civil action."[75] Despite this decision, Ford took the precaution of renaming the inflation impact statement the "economic impact analysis," to distinguish it from "environmental impact statements" required—and often litigated—under the National Environmental Protection Act.

The effectiveness of Executive Order 11821 was limited because Ford, choosing not to force the issue of presidential control, opted for a voluntary program in which agencies were encouraged to prepare regulatory analyses but faced no sanctions for refusing or failing to do so.[76] Still, the order represented an improvement in extending review to more agencies and by improving the "experience and professionalism of executive branch regulatory reviewers."[77]

Carter continued to expand the scope of presidential review, and tried to balance the need for economic analysis with a desire to minimize delays. In part his regulatory reform efforts were also motivated by a desire to fend off legislation pending in Congress that would have subjected all regulations to cost-benefit requirements. The White House feared that the proposed bills were designed to undercut the rulemaking process altogether (all of the major bills tracked by the administration were sponsored by Republicans who were considered opponents of strong government regulations). In August 1977 OMB director Bert Lance cautioned Carter that "without a strong Administration program, we will be pre-empted by Congress, where several initiatives—some of them quite pernicious— are gathering momentum."[78] A February 1977 Council of Economic Advisers memorandum warned that a legislated requirement "would create serious problems associated with analysis of nearly all regulations, rather than just 'major' regulations, and could swamp agencies with paperwork. Furthermore, it opens every regulation to judicial review, with its attendant litigation costs and delays."[79]

Over the next thirteen months, the Carter White House drafted a new executive order on regulatory reform, issuing Executive Order 12044 in March 1978.[80] Similar to the Ford and Nixon processes in its broad outlines of coordinating regulations via presidential instruments, the Carter program included two innovations. First, it specifically required agencies to prepare a cost-benefit analysis for major regulations, thereby shifting the terms of the debate from a rule's inflationary impact (under Ford) to whether a regulation was worth the cost. Second, Carter established two organizations within the White House specifically to monitor compliance and direct the regulatory review efforts (the Regulatory Analysis Review Group, or RARG, and the Regulatory Council).

Like FDR and Eisenhower before him, Carter puzzled over whether regulatory review should extend to the independent regulatory agencies, and in November 1977 he asked specifically for public comment on that issue. It did not take long for him to get an answer. Within a month, the Chairmen and ranking minority members of six key Senate committees wrote the president that "it is our unqualified view that . . . the Executive Order cannot lawfully be applied to the independent regulatory commissions. To do so would violate the intent of Congress that the Executive Branch not control the rules these agencies issue."[81] All of the independent commissions except the Nuclear Regulatory Commission objected to the idea that the order could apply to them. Despite a Justice Department opinion that the president could impose *procedural* requirements on the independent agencies, the OMB advised Carter to back down, arguing that "a confrontation with Congress over this Order is not worth the political costs" and suggesting that the president instead work with Congress to resolve the constitutional questions.[82]

Despite Carter's extension of regulatory review, by the end of the 1970s, critics were pointedly noting that none of the executive orders on regulation included any sanctions. The quality of life reviews, inflation impact analyses, and Carter's program to improve government regulation were toothless, either essentially "hortatory interagency advisory and review systems lacking centralized control and enforcement authority, or ad hoc intercessions into particular rulemakings by the President or White House staff at his behest."[83] The new procedures were designed to encourage agencies to think about economic consequences and cost-benefit considerations in the early stages of the rulemaking process. But the result, more often than not, was that agencies went their own way, with especially controversial rules triggering interagency disputes that had to be resolved in the White House.

President Reagan dramatically altered the political landscape with his regulatory order, issued in February 1981.[84] Executive Order 12291 required executive branch agencies to justify proposed rules and regulations using cost-benefit analysis, and prohibited regulatory action unless "the potential benefits to society for the regulation outweigh the potential costs" (E.O. 12291, § 2 (b)). Agencies had to prepare a regulatory impact analysis and submit it for review to the Office of Management and Budget, which had the authority to "recommend the withdrawal of regulations which cannot be reformulated to meet its objections."[85] The review authority was placed in the Office of Information and Regulatory Affairs

(OIRA), a unit within the OMB created by the Paperwork Reduction Act of 1979 to coordinate agency efforts to collect data from business.

Reagan's order gave new power to the OMB, and it "went way beyond the Nixon, Ford, and Carter administrations in applying cost-benefit analyses . . . to stymie agency rule making."[86] In practice, regulatory review served to shield the rulemaking practice from public view, as initially OMB officials did not keep written records regarding their contacts with either agencies or other interested parties regarding the new central clearance function. The review process, argue Joseph Cooper and William West, "operated largely through informal, off the record contacts. Indeed, [OMB] not only has kept much of its written comments confidential, but it has usually preferred oral communications over the phone or through small staff conferences to written correspondence."[87] This further centralized presidential control, because it limited the possibilities of judicial review.

Executive Order 12291 had elements of the "unintended consequences" that derive from presidential interpretations of statutes. Congress created OIRA to limit the amount of data that the government could force business to provide. James Miller, Reagan's first OIRA director, noted his intent to use the Paperwork Reduction Act provisions to limit the regulatory power of independent agencies (to which the order did not apply): "Nearly every substantial regulation involves, as part of its enforcement mechanism, a requirement for filling out forms or maintaining specific records. And under the new paperwork act, all agencies, including the independents, must clear all the forms they wish to use through OMB—specifically, by delegation, with the administrator of the Office of Information and Regulatory Affairs, which means me . . . the act does give OMB considerable authority."[88] Thus, if the unfettered constitutional authority was lacking to give the president the ability to force agencies to reach particular rulemaking outcomes, there was statutory authority—unwittingly delegated by Congress—for the president to accomplish the same goals indirectly, by denying agencies the ability to collect the necessary information.

The order also demonstrates the impact of presidential initiative, as it altered the existing institutional arrangements unilaterally and forced Congress to take active measures to try and recapture the ground it had lost to the president. One reason Reagan took the executive order route is that Congress would have refused to voluntarily grant such a measure of control, and attempts to seek legislative reform of regulatory institutions failed throughout the Reagan presidency.[89] The chronology of 12291 suggests that a legislative alternative was never considered. The order was issued on February 17, 1981, less than one month after Reagan was inaugurated; the Office of Legal Counsel in the Justice Department issued its opinion on the proposed order on February 13. Administration officials had been planning the order from the earliest days of the transition, and it could not have been thought of as a contingency plan pending failure to get legislation through Congress. It was a preemptive move, motivated by the assumption that legislation would have failed. Once the tenor of the administration's regulatory approach became clear, the White House could not expect any support from a Democratic Congress that had been responsible for the regulatory structure that the order attempted to rein in.

The legal analysis of Executive Order 12291 highlights the ambiguities of the president's executive power, and although the order did not explicitly apply to the independent agencies, it once again raised the difficult constitutional question of whether or not the executive branch is unitary. Since the order itself cites no specific statutory or constitutional provision as the basis for the president's authority to issue it (the preamble begins, "By the authority vested in me as President by the Constitution and laws of the United States of America"), it relies on a unitary picture of presidential authority—the idea that the president, as chief executive, has the authority to manage and control the activities of all executive branch officials and agencies (at least insofar as permitted by statute). The Office of Legal Counsel argued that there was both legal and political justification for this position. "Because the President is the only elected official who has a national constituency," concluded OLC, "he is uniquely situated to design and execute a uniform method for undertaking regulatory initiatives that responds to the will of the public as a whole."[90] Further, the OLC argued that the president had the constitutional authority to "supervise and guide" executive branch officials in the conduct of their duties, and to "require them to report on the costs and benefits of proposed action" as part of the Constitution's Article II, section 2, language that allows the president to "require the opinion, in writing, of the principal officer in each of the executive departments, upon any subject relating to the duties of their respective offices."[91] This language is remarkably similar to the reasoning used in 1921 as justification for legislative clearance in the Bureau of the Budget—that the president had constitutional authority to direct executive officers, a power base from which the clearance function could be inferred.[92]

Executive Order 12291 produced unusually sharp disagreement on basic theoretical questions (the practical disputes over the order were even more pointed), and is perhaps the most controversial executive order of the past three decades. Some legal scholars considered the order unconstitutional on its face as an impermissible "act of Executive legislation in violation of the separation of powers principle."[93] The main constitutional objection was that the underlying assumption of E.O. 12291—the unitary executive and presidential control of all executive branch functions—was flawed. Critics of 12291 argued that the Constitution allowed Congress to create agencies that exercised their authority independently of the president. Once this axiom is accepted, then presidential attempts to control these activities are an invalid exercise of the president's executive power. A secondary objection was that the order violated the provisions of the Administrative Procedures Act (APA), the statute that establishes the legal framework for rulemaking processes. Under the APA, agencies must comply with a variety of procedures designed to make the regulatory process fair, responsive, and public.[94] E.O. 12291 allowed the OMB to influence the rulemaking process without public notice of its activities, and in several high-profile cases the office was accused of allowing industry groups, trade associations, and other outside interests to influence its assessment of proposed rules. In 1984, after OMB rejected an EPA analysis of a proposed rule for asbestos exposure, a subsequent congressional investigation discovered that OMB staffers had talked secretly with industry representatives (who were, not surprisingly, opposed to strict regulations) and with EPA officials. There was no public record of these contacts.[95]

Others, however, were equally emphatic that the actions in 12291 "fall squarely within the president's constitutional authority."[96] Two earlier OIRA directors maintained in 1986 that "the strictly legal questions raised by the review program are not very difficult, and none of the legal attacks has been or is likely to be successful."[97] Cass Sunstein notes that a key provision of the order—a qualification in section 2 that the requirements of the order are applicable "to the extent permitted by law— renders it difficult, if not impossible, to make a plausible argument that the order is unlawful on its face."[98] It also had the effect of almost automatically preempting legal challenges, since by definition the order could not be used to justify any attempt to circumvent a statute.[99] Although the courts held that the OMB could not delay indefinitely regulations that were otherwise required by statute, in no case did any court rule that the principle of presidential review violated any law or constitutional provision.[100]

In 1985 Reagan issued a second regulatory review order, 12498, which required regulatory agencies under the jurisdiction of 12291 to publish an annual index of "anticipated regulatory actions."[101] The OMB was given the authority to review this list to ensure that agency actions were consistent with administration policy and to sort out problems of duplicative or conflicting rules. A key advantage in requiring such a compilation is that the OMB was thus given advance warning of the rules that would eventually come before it for formal review, and therefore could prepare for any disputes that might be expected. One critical analysis concluded that the order "grants OMB virtually unbridled power to supervise or veto almost any agency's activity without public scrutiny."[102]

Executive Orders 12291 and 12498, then, are classic examples of the ways in which the ambiguities of executive power lead to disputes when presidents assert authority in new forms, and of Justice Jackson's argument that disputes over executive power traffic mainly in "more or less apt quotations from respected sources on each side of any question."[103] Despite the controversy, though, Reagan was able to change the debate from whether the president had the authority to conduct regulatory review to what to do about it once the president acted as if he did. And the forces behind Reagan's regulatory review program understood that E.O. 12291's importance extended beyond a strictly legal interpretation:

> Although agencies retain legal authority to issue regulations over the objections of OMB or even the president under E.O. 12291, the architects of the Reagan order believed that review would carry substantial force. To begin with, they felt that agency heads, who were chosen by the president on the basis of loyalty to his program, would be disposed to accept direction by his agents. Moreover, they were confident that in cases of conflict agencies would be hesitant to insist on their formal prerogatives due to OMB's substantial powers over their operations with respect to budgeting, personnel ceilings, information gathering, and clearance for congressional contacts and requests. As former OIRA administrator James Miller stated, "If you're the toughest kid on the block, most kids won't pick a fight with you."[104]

By taking action unilaterally, Reagan put Congress in a defensive position in which it had to respond to executive initiative in order to undo what the president had done. To Moe, Executive Order 12291 is a textbook case of Congress's inability to countermand unilateral executive action. Despite intense Democratic opposition, Congress was unable to alleviate the order's impact or undercut OIRA's authority, through either the legislative or the appropriations processes. The only concessions Congress won were an agreement in 1986 to require Senate confirmation of OIRA's head and increased public disclosure of OIRA activities. These concessions, argues Moe, "were not serious ones considering that, if legislative opponents had really been able to exercise power, they could have put OIRA out of business."[105] Moreover, the reforms left undisturbed "manifold opportunities for informal communication and influence."[106] Even after legislative authorization for OIRA lapsed in 1989, both Bush and Clinton were able to get funding for it annually and Congress reauthorized the office in 1995.

President Bush left in place the basic structure of the Reagan order, but created yet another organization to enhance presidential control and further insulate the centralization efforts from congressional interference.

Under the authority of Executive Orders 12291 and 12498, Bush transferred OIRA's regulatory review power to a Council on Competitiveness, located in the White House and chaired by the vice president. Although the council's main function was to resolve disagreements between OIRA and agencies, it quickly became mired in disputes over its role in the broader regulatory review process. Because the council was a creature of executive authority only, and existed as an interagency task force within the White House Office, it repeatedly claimed an executive privilege when asked about internal procedures or contact with agencies or nongovernment groups. Once again critics charged that the regulatory review process "undermine[d] the most basic precepts of democratic government" by operating in relative secrecy and providing opportunities for *ex parte* contacts outside the normal channels of the regulatory process.[107] Even so, Congress could not muster majorities to restrict the council's activities.[108]

Still, in a few cases Bush administration officials overreached, and had to backpedal in the face of congressional and public objection to particular stances. In one notorious 1992 incident, OIRA administrator James MacRae advanced the theory that the cost of regulations alone might contribute to additional deaths in the general population, a position that could undermine the basic notions of regulatory policy. According to this reasoning, businesses that must absorb the costs of regulation either pass those costs on to their customers (lowering income among consumers) or cut wages (lowering income among their workers). In addition, if a particular job becomes less risky as the result of government regulation, then the "risk premium" that employers must pay for that work will drop.[109] Reduced income, in turn, had been tentatively linked in some controversial studies to reduced life expectancy.

Relying on OIRA's central clearance authority under 12291, and citing the research that found a relationship between income levels and life expectancy, MacRae asked the Occupational Safety and Health Administration (OSHA) to reestimate the costs and benefits of a proposed regulation on exposure limits for various industrial chemicals.[110] OSHA estimated that its proposed rule would cost $163 million annually and save between eight and thirteen lives each year. MacRae, using an estimate that each $7.5 million in regulatory costs could result in one additional death as a result of lowered income levels, countered that the rule could cause twenty-two additional deaths through reduced income, resulting in an overall net increase of eight to fourteen deaths per year.[111]

It was a novel interpretation of regulatory costs, and the assistant secretary of labor for policy—a Bush appointee—could scarcely conceal her astonishment at what she termed an "unprecedented" request for a reevaluation of the proposed rule using OIRA's methodology. The department refused to back down, citing its obligations under OSHA's statutory mandates.[112] Other Labor Department officials were blunt in their criticism, calling OIRA's position "bizarre" and "ridiculous" (the director for health and safety at the AFL-CIO considered the request "really loony").[113] MacRae was quickly summoned before the Senate Committee on Governmental Affairs, where his reception was no friendlier. Senator Herb Kohl (D-Wisc.) likened MacRae's position to that of "a villain twirling his mustache and laughing as he forecloses on a widow's mortgage on Christmas Eve."[114] The General Accounting Office concluded that MacRae had overstated the degree to which the "risk-risk" model of regulation was accepted as valid, misinterpreted the economics behind the mortality estimates of regulatory costs, and misread the law.[115]

Despite the intense controversy of the Reagan and Bush regulatory review efforts—one account of the ongoing struggle concluded that "no feature of modern U.S. government has been more controversial over the last decade than review of agency rules" by OMB[116]—White House influence in agency activities is now an accepted part of the regulatory process. Although Clinton abolished the Council on Competitiveness upon taking office, he "most assuredly did not get rid of regulatory review. Indeed, he saw [it] as essential to presidential leadership."[117] During his first year in office Clinton issued his own executive order on regulatory review (E.O. 12866, September 30, 1993), which made some procedural changes to OMB review but "maintain[ed] much of the substantive focus of the Reagan orders, including the emphasis on cost-benefit analysis as the basic foundation of decision."[118] Clinton's order restricted OMB review to "major rules" (defined as those likely to impose more than $100 million in costs), and imposed a ninety-day time limit for OMB to complete its assessment of the regulatory impact analysis. OIRA personnel maintain that the Clinton order corrected some problems with 12291, particularly in its record-keeping requirements and strict time limit for OMB review. The focus on major rules allows OIRA to focus its limited resources on fewer reviews, with the number of rules reviewed dropping by almost 75 percent from the 1980s.[119] At the same time, the percentage of proposed rules that undergo some sort of change during the review process has gone up, from about 14 percent of all reviewed rules under Reagan to 38 percent in Clinton's first term.[120] Clinton has issued follow-on executive orders detailing additional factors that agencies must consider when drafting regulations, such as the impact rulemaking activities have on poor and minority populations, children, and tribal governments.[121]

In this way regulatory review moved along the same path as the budget power after 1921, with once-controversial activities becoming routine. Even opponents of regulatory review concede as much: in 1994 the litigation director of Public Citizen, a nonprofit group generally supportive of federal regulation, testified before Congress that "I, for one, am no fan of centralized regulatory review. In the past, regulatory review has often been a means by which an Executive Branch hostile to the mission that Congress has assigned to agencies can thwart that mission and subvert through unrecorded, back-room deal-making what the Administrative Procedure Act establishes as an open regulatory process. . . . Having said that, it is clear that centralized regulatory review is now a fixture."[122]

And as in the budget process, the congressional response was slow in coming and not very effective. After the 1994 midterm election rout of the Democrats, the new GOP congressional leadership moved quickly to recapture some of the ground lost to the president over the previous fifteen years. At stake were not only key institutional prerogatives in domestic policy but also the position that regulatory review under Clinton had been less effective than it had been under Reagan and Bush. In 1996 Congress established a review process in which agencies are required to transmit major regulations to the General Accounting Office, which in turn reports to Congress on whether the proposed rule has conformed to all applicable executive orders and statutes.[123] Congress then has an opportunity to disapprove of the proposed regulation by enacting a Joint Resolution of Disapproval (replacing the one-house legislative veto, which the Supreme Court invalidated in *I.N.S. v. Chadha*). In theory, then, Congress has created its own review mechanism, designed to ensure agency accountability to Congress.

But almost everyone agrees that the congressional review procedure has had virtually no effect. Congress lacks the expertise and staff to do anything with the reports that the GAO provides;[124] only a handful of disapproval resolutions have been introduced in the three years since the process was established, and none has come close to passing even one chamber.[125] Only a year after the Congressional Review Act (CRA) became law, legislators followed up with two more proposals designed to bolster congressional control over the regulatory process. The first would establish a regulatory equivalent of the Congressional Budget Office, called the Congressional Office of Regulatory Analysis, which would provide independent assessment of proposed regulations (H.R. 1704, introduced May 22, 1997). The second would subject *all* regulations to a congressional vote, with implementation barred unless the proposal received majority approval from both the House and the Senate (H.R. 1306, introduced March 12, 1997). Representative Sue Kelly (R-N.Y.), sponsor of H.R. 1704, argued that her bill was necessary because of flaws in the CRA process. In addition to staff problems, she noted that the executive branch enjoys important informational advantages over Congress that hinder effective legislative oversight. "Nearly all of Congress' information about the impact of new regulations [reported under CRA] comes from the agencies who are developing them. This information is often unreliable because agencies have a vested interest in downplaying the negative aspects of the regulations they have proposed. As a result, Congress is at a disadvantage when trying to determine just how a particular regulation will impact the economy, making it that much more difficult to effectively implement the CRA."[126] In a reprise of arguments used in many other contexts, opponents of a stronger congressional role claim that the executive orders on regulatory review obviate the need for a legislative response.[127]

The ongoing dispute between the executive branch and Congress over which is better suited to oversee regulatory agencies obscures the more basic question of whether centralized regulatory review gives the president effective control over agency decision making. Have Executive Orders 12291, 12498, and 12866 really made a difference? Not surprisingly, OIRA is quick to point out the advantages of presidential oversight, claiming that OMB's involvement is aboveboard rather than secret, consultative rather than confrontational, and that it serves as a true oversight mechanism as opposed to simply an additional veto point. Under 12866, argued OIRA head Sally Katzen in 1996, regulations are "better supported by relevant data and analysis, more carefully reasoned, more cost effective, and more reflective of a fair balancing of the competing concerns involved."[128]

Katzen's assessment, though, is hard to verify. In an audit of regulatory review, the General Accounting Office found that it was often impossible to determine whether changes to draft regulations were made in response to suggestions by the OMB. Agencies often failed to keep complete records about what occurred during the review process, even though E.O. 12866 requires that they compile, for public release, a comprehensive index to all substantive changes that occur (agencies are also supposed to document whether any given change was the result of an OMB suggestion).[129]

Conclusion

The parallels between regulatory review and the national budget are clear enough. In both cases, the creation of a new capability or the need for new administrative structures produced a struggle between the president and Congress over control. George Eads, who chaired Carter's RARG, indeed saw both in "budgetary" terms: "In a real sense, [Executive Order 12291] marks the final emergence of regulation as a governmental function deserving the same level of attention as the raising and spending of money. We do not yet have a formal regulatory budget, but enough basic budget-like controls are now in place, at least on paper, to permit the president to shape regulatory programs singly and overall." In both cases, presidents asserted that the Constitution gave them the authority to exercise control over agency activities. And in both cases the congressional response was muted, delayed by decades, and mostly ineffective.

The expansion of the central clearance functions over budget and regulatory matters are hardly the only instances in which political pressure has spurred growth in the institutional presidency; since its establishment, the Executive Office of the President has become larger, more specialized and internally complex, and more autonomous.[130] What began as an advisory structure to serve as the president's "eyes and ears" has become an institution—a bureaucracy—in its own right. While a larger EOP provides the president, in theory at least, with a more effective tool for supervising the executive branch as a whole, that capability comes at a price. As the EOP becomes larger, it becomes more difficult for the president to control. More formal internal structures impose constraints on presidents, who will find it harder to mold the institution in accordance with their personal decision-making styles and temperament. In principal-agent terms, the Executive Office was created to help the president—as principal—to oversee and manage executive branch agencies—the agent. But where the EOP was initially considered as an extension of the president's will, it has more and more assumed the character of an institution that the president has trouble controlling.[131] Complicated organizational arrangements, multiple layers, and unwieldy procedures can serve mainly to insulate the president from the information and people needed to make good decisions. A large staff imposes new burdens while not necessarily relieving presidents of old ones. Many presidential scholars, starting with George Reedy, have argued that the growth of the presidential institution has been bad for the office.[132]

More recently Matthew Dickinson has lamented that contemporary presidents have been unwilling to adopt FDR's informal, freewheeling, competitive advisory structures. Ultimately, in this line of reasoning, a large presidential organization actually decreases presidential control "by diffusing bargaining resources and increasing management costs," thereby reducing the president's ability to influence outcomes.[133] As evidence, he argues that since the 1960s presidents have been increasingly likely to make "poor bargaining choices, based in part on the advice of their White House staff–dominated advisory organizations."[134]

This conclusion is at odds with the argument I make in this chapter that presidents have enhanced their control over government activities by expanding the boundaries of White House and Executive Office institutions. The historical evidence simply does not support the position that the presidency has been weakened by the institutionalization of the office.

An enlarged Executive Office creates some problems, to be sure, as presidents must spend time and effort controlling it, but that hardly means that the president would be better off with a less formal or smaller administrative support structure. In the two cases identified here—budget and regulatory review—centralization was driven by successive presidents' desire for control over rapidly expanding administrative processes.

Failures and success occur independently of staff structures, in any case. Roosevelt's staffing arrangements did not prevent him from making some poor decisions—the ill-advised court-packing proposal, the 1937 reorganization plan, the internment of Japanese Americans, his threat to act unilaterally if Congress failed to revise the Economic Stabilization Act—that undercut his own bargaining authority or ran against the grain of civil liberties and constitutional structure. Clinton promised to reduce the White House staff by 25 percent, although the initial cuts failed to meet that goal and did not appear to improve the president's bargaining position much.[135] Indeed, the impeachment debacle showed that presidents are capable of making horrendous choices, even when the White House staff recognizes the danger and does its best to protect presidents from their own worst tendencies. In 1996 several White House staffers and Secret Service agents had protested that Monica Lewinsky's frequent presence around the Oval Office was inappropriate. Because of these concerns, Deputy White House Chief of Staff for Operations Evelyn Lieberman decided to move Lewinsky out of the White House (although she cleared the action with Chief of Staff Leon Panetta). In April Lewinsky was transferred to a job in the office of the assistant secretary of defense for public affairs.[136]

In January 1997 Clinton resumed the relationship with the help of his personal secretary, Betty Currie, who went to great lengths to conceal Lewinsky's presence from White House staff.[137] Both Clinton and Curry thus purposefully evaded a staff that had sensed, correctly, that something was amiss. Although this episode does not necessarily provide much guidance about how to structure presidential advisory networks or staff relations, it does suggest that not all presidential missteps can be traced to shoddy staff work.

From a theoretical perspective, institutionalization is beneficial as well. If presidents must expend effort to control subordinates—an unexceptional conclusion—then they benefit from arrangements that lower the cost of control. Formal organizational arrangements, specialization, hierarchy—in short, institutions—are mechanisms for lowering these costs; indeed, the "theory of the firm" is built around the notion that institutions are often more efficient than specific contractual relationships in solving the problem of monitoring subordinates.[138] The expansion of budget and regulatory clearance fits within this framework. By insisting on some degree of White House clearance of budget and regulatory matters, and establishing institutional processes that have carried out these functions, presidents have lowered the cost of monitoring and controlling the behavior of executive branch agencies. The path toward greater control has been evolutionary, with successive presidents adapting and extending what their predecessors have done. There have been failures, particularly when a president has reached too far, too fast (as Taft did with his insistence on an executive budget before Congress was ready, or as Harding found out when the Bureau of the Budget pushed for central legislative clearance before the agencies were ready), but the pattern has been consistently one of gradual accretion of control within the presidency. Even if the institutional arrangements are not ideal—presidents still lack effective control over independent regulatory agencies, and departments can still circumvent the White House on budget matters by mobilizing congressional and interest-group supporters—there is no doubt that presidents prefer the newer arrangements to the old. In this regard, more control, even imperfect control, is better than less.

Five

Executive Orders and Foreign Affairs

IF THE PRESIDENT's domestic policy power has grown steadily but incrementally since the 1930s, in foreign affairs it has grown explosively. Indeed, few dispute the pattern of increased presidential power in foreign affairs over the past fifty years. Although congressional-presidential disputes over the war powers have had the highest profile in this area, executive orders have played a role in the day-to-day expansion of presidents' institutional capacity as well. In this chapter I analyze two cases that reveal the same patterns of gradual evolution, exploitation of residual decision rights, and the importance of moving first that I covered in the previous chapter on the budget and regulatory institutions. In much the same way, presidents have asserted almost complete control over the organization of the national intelligence community and the classification process protecting government information from public disclosure. Throughout the twentieth century, presidents have succeeded in expanding their power, particularly with respect to Congress, with little interference. The pattern identified at the beginning of this book—presidential initiative continually outflanking congressional efforts to impose a statutory regime—is readily apparent.

The issues of information secrecy and intelligence organization involve fundamental questions about representative government and the separation of powers. An absolute government prerogative to keep information from Congress and the public undercuts both congressional oversight and public accountability. Critics are quick to charge that the ability to classify information is a crucial element of presidential power and that it almost inevitably leads to abuses. In *The Imperial Presidency*, Arthur Schlesinger argued that by the end of the 1960s "the religion of secrecy had become an all-purpose means by which the American Presidency sought to dissemble its purposes, bury its mistakes, manipulate its citizens and maximize its power."[1] More recently, the 1995 Commission on Protecting and Reducing Government Secrecy concluded that "secrecy can [have] significant consequences for the functioning of government itself. Information is power, and it is no mystery to government officials that power can be increased through controls on the flow of information."[2]

The availability of information, then, and the procedures for restricting the distribution of that information are central issues of government power, national security, and political legitimacy. Unfettered presidential control of information creates an imbalance between the executive and Congress, especially in foreign affairs, when Congress is denied access to information necessary for constitutionally permitted oversight activities.[3] Information controls have been a "key source of presidential ascendancy."[4] Presidents also benefit from their use of executive privilege, in which the executive denies information not only to the public but to Congress as well. Such actions raise "major concerns [about] the rights of citizens and government accountability."[5]

The structure and function of the nation's intelligence organization raise the same sort of issues, not only because of the secrecy inherent in these activities, but also because of the close nexus between intelligence and law enforcement and the tension between presidential control of critical foreign activities versus public and congressional accountability. In addition, both intelligence organization and information classification get to the core of presidential power, since they lean heavily on the president's inherent executive authority.

Congress "Wins" One: The Subversive Activities Control Board

Ironically, an example of the president's strength at the intelligence/secrecy nexus is actually a case of unsuccessful presidential action—Nixon's attempt to revive the moribund Subversive Activities Control Board (SACB) via an executive order. It is one of the few executive orders of any substance to be explicitly repudiated in Congress since 1970. Congress forced the president to back down by enacting an appropriations restriction that prohibited the executive branch from spending any funds enforcing the order. Still, the degree of effort required to overturn the order is indicative of the hurdles that Congress must overcome to prevail over the president in a head-to-head confrontation.

Congress created the Subversive Activities Control Board via the Internal Security Act of 1950, charging it with investigating communist organizations and empowering it to designate groups as communist, communist-front, or communist-infiltrated. A designation triggered a number of restrictions on the organization and its members, including a requirement that the group register with the attorney general and disclose its membership and finances, and a stipulation that no one belonging to a "subversive" group could hold a government job.[6] In 1953 the board designated the Communist Party as such a group, prompting the party to argue that the act was unconstitutional. After protracted litigation, including multiple board rehearings and lower court evaluations, the Supreme Court upheld the statute as constitutional, although it left open the possibility that the registration requirements might violate the Fifth Amendment right against self-incrimination; in 1965 the Supreme Court rejected the registration requirements on this basis.[7] In practice, the inability to mandate registration of members left the board with "virtually nothing it could constitutionally do."[8]

In 1968 Congress attempted to resuscitate the board by repealing the mandatory registration requirement, instead allowing the board simply to declare that certain organizations were communist or that certain individuals were affiliated with communist organizations (Public Law 90–237). In *Boorda v. Subversive Activities Control Board* (421 F.2d 1142 D.C. Cir. 1969), the District of Columbia Court of Appeals issued an emphatic ruling that such schemes were impermissible; when the Supreme Court refused to hear the government's appeal, the board was once again left with nothing to do.[9]

The White House, however, began preparations to revitalize the emasculated SACB which, they feared, would be eliminated by Congress unless it had a meaningful workload.[10] By early 1970 Nixon aides were trying to link the board to the president's power over the requirements for government personnel security clearances; the idea was that the SACB would henceforth be empowered to identify organizations to which federal employees, or prospective employees, could not belong (or, more precisely, designate organizations in which membership would be one of the factors that could be taken into account when deciding whether an individual was suitable for a government job). If the board could not publicly identify certain groups as communist, it could still accomplish much the same goal by declaring that members of those groups could not obtain government jobs or security clearances. Under the then-current executive order governing security clearances (E.O. 10450, April 1953), the attorney general was authorized to identify such groups anyway, so all that was required was a transfer of this power from the attorney general to the SACB. This strategy evaded the constitutional problems that had enfeebled the SACB, and would revive the attorney general's list, which had not been updated since 1955. As described by the head of the Internal Security Division of the Department of Justice:

> Under [the proposed] procedure, the resulting designation of organizations would be done in connection with the Federal Employee Security Program. Knowledgeable and active membership in a designated organization would be one of many factors for the head of a federal agency to consider in determining whether the employment of a particular individual is consistent with the interests of national security. This will remove many of the constitutional difficulties that are created by listing such organizations solely for the purpose of informing

the public, as the courts will probably allow the Government more latitude to list certain organizations when it is done to strengthen employment security programs and to further the Government's interest in insuring the loyalty of its own employees.[11]

William Rehnquist, who was then assistant attorney general in the Office of Legal Counsel, described the order as "essentially an exercise of the President's power to prescribe regulations for the employment of individuals as will best promote the efficiency of the Civil Service."[12]

It was a titanic finesse. With the existing path blocked by the courts, Nixon simply repackaged the same policy in a form more closely tied to executive prerogative, putting the revised system in place on July 8, 1971, with Executive Order 11605.[13]

The congressional reaction was swift, and in one of the only instances in which legislators have expressly overturned an executive order, Congress was able to shut down the SACB by cutting off appropriations. Within days of the executive order, Senator Sam Ervin (D-N.C.) introduced both legislation prohibiting the SACB from spending any money executing the powers granted to it by E.O. 11605 and a "Sense of the Senate" resolution stipulating that the president had "usurped the legislative powers conferred on Congress by the Constitution" and infringed upon Americans' First Amendment rights.[14] In 1972 Congress included Ervin's legislation as an appropriations rider to the State, Commerce, Justice et al. appropriations bill. The Nixon administration finally gave up in 1973, conceding the issue by not requesting any funds for the board.[15]

What accounts for Congress's success in eliminating the SACB, and what distinguishes this from the far more common outcome in which the president wins? Part of the explanation is that the board lacked any concrete constituency, which meant that supporters had no political base to mobilize. This, in turn, was due to the board's failure to do much of anything in its twenty-two years of existence (the only organization that it found to be communist was the Communist Party itself, and the board was unable to require it to register). Its annual budget was minuscule ($350,000 to $450,000 at the end), and Ervin argued that the board members did little "except draw their breath and their salaries."[16] Apart from staunch anticommunists and die-hard conservatives, no one supported the SACB. Stymied time and again by successful court challenges, the board limped along, and even within the Nixon White House there was opposition to the effort to resurrect it. Others in the administration felt that the board was mostly symbolic and probably doomed anyway, order or no order.[17]

In this context the successful legislative effort to countermand Executive Order 11605 was exceptional, and it ironically demonstrates the presidency's strength more than its weakness. Here was a case of clear presidential overreaching, of using presidential fiat to blatantly evade congressional and judicial limits and revive an unpopular and anachronistic relic of the McCarthy era. Legislative opposition to the order arose in the context of other disputes with Nixon over impoundment, assertions of executive privilege, prosecution of the Vietnam War, and wiretaps.[18] The controversy over the SACB took its place at the beginning of the legislative procession that would culminate in congressional repudiation of Nixon via the War Powers Resolution, the Budget and Impoundment Control Act of 1974, and the impeachment inquiry. Even so, it took Congress a year to succeed at a time when Nixon was weakened by the rapidly growing Watergate scandal, and the president ceded the issue by not asking for further appropriations instead of provoking an institutional confrontation. There have been only a handful of comparable congressional successes since.

Classified Information and Personnel Security

What is especially striking about debates over classification and secrecy is that presidents have asserted almost complete command over the institutions and processes that both produce and protect secret information.[19] For six decades presidents have determined what information can be classified, specified the levels at which information can be classified, set the standards for classifying and declassifying information, designated who is authorized to classify information, and determined how classified information will be protected. In doing this they have relied on their inherent constitutional authority as commander in chief and chief executive, and have seen little interference from either Congress or the courts. Although Congress has made a few attempts to impose statutory limits on the president's classification authority (most notably the 1966 Freedom of Information Act and, more recently, the President John F. Kennedy Assassination Records Collection Act of 1992), the efforts have been piecemeal. In practice, classification remains an outpost of almost absolute executive prerogative.

Advocates of this presidency-centered process argue that unambiguous constitutional vestments—the vesting clause and the take care clause, in particular—give presidents exclusive control over all executive branch information and preclude any congressional interference. Supporters of presidential control point also to numerous statutory provisions that explicitly delegate to the president the power to keep some information secret. The first such statutes were enacted in the early twentieth century,[20] but the largest delegations occurred during the cold war. Those who favor broader congressional participation counter that Congress's authority to "raise and support armies," "provide and maintain a navy," and "make rules for the government and regulation of the land and naval forces" gives legislators an important role. Moreover, the congressional oversight responsibility requires that Congress have access to information necessary to evaluate executive branch activities.[21]

The legal and constitutional arguments concerning the balance of congressional-executive authority over classification suggest strongly that the pure presidency-centered view is overdrawn. Even so, the constitutional language is far from conclusive on the question, which means that it is up to Congress and the president to fight for control.[22]

The degree of presidential control over classification is more the result of an institutional competition between the president and Congress than any coherent legal or administrative theory that locates this power exclusively within the executive branch. Since World War II, presidents have expanded the scope of their authority over classification policy because they have proved more adept than Congress in gaining control of a rapidly developing policy area. Although Congress has a legitimate constitutional role to play, it has been unable to assert its prerogatives. That failure has more to do with its institutional characteristics than any definitive constitutional interpretation. Presidents, put simply, have been able to outmaneuver the legislature, seizing effective control over information by repeatedly moving first and interpreting statutory guidelines to their own advantage. Congress, as a collective decision-making institution, has a much harder time taking action, and legislation on the subject often must overcome a presidential veto. When Congress has acted, moreover, it more often than not has augmented presidential authority, usually by creating new categories of classified information or specifying the penalties for revealing secrets.[23]

The history of congressional-executive interaction on this point is clear: when Congress authorizes the president to classify information, these delegations have been exploited to expand the reach of executive power far beyond what Congress intended. When Congress is silent, presidents move to take control on their own initiative. And when Congress enacts laws designed to restrict the executive branch's authority to keep information private, presidents have been able to maneuver within the statutory guidelines to maintain their authority.

A short history of the classified information system will show how the secrecy regime came to reside almost exclusively in the executive branch. In the eighteenth and nineteenth centuries, government information controls were fragmentary and ineffective. Some military documents from the War of 1812 and the Civil War were marked "secret" or "confidential," but there was no officially recognized classification system.[24] Military security during the Civil War was so notoriously inept that Confederate commanders came to rely on Northern newspapers for information about Union army tactics and troop movements.[25]

The War Department established the first agencywide classification system in 1917, creating a three-tiered formula ("secret," "confidential," and "restricted" classifications) patterned after the systems then used by the French and British military.[26] To further control the wartime distribution of information, President Wilson created by executive order (E.O. 2954, April 13, 1917) a censorship panel called the Committee on Public Information (called the Creel Committee, after Chairman George Creel), and gave it the power to control publicity surrounding military activity.[27]

The trend toward presidential hegemony accelerated sharply in 1940, when Franklin Roosevelt issued the first of what would become a series of executive orders that firmly established presidential dominance of the classification process. Executive Order 8381 (March 22, 1940) gave civilians in the defense agencies the authority to classify many different categories of defense information.[28] In issuing this order, Roosevelt relied on a statute that authorized the classification of information relating to military installations and equipment (to prevent, for example, unauthorized photography), but the president went well beyond the intent of the authorizing statute by extending its coverage to a complete array of military information, including "books, pamphlets, documents, reports, maps, charts, plans, designs, models, drawings, photographs, contracts, or specifications . . . and all such articles or equipment which may hereafter be so marked with the approval of or at the direction of the President." The legislative history of the authorizing statute, argue Richard Ehlke and Harold Relyea, "provided no indication that Congress anticipated or expected that such a security classification arrangement would be created."[29]

During the war Roosevelt continued to use executive orders to gain fuller control over information, although most national security information remained under the direct control of the military services.[30] FDR established the Office of Censorship in 1941 (Executive Order 8985, December 18, 1941), giving it the authority to control communications originating within the United States to foreign countries.[31] The office issued a Code of Wartime Practices, in which it identified information that should not be published without consultation with the government. In June 1942 Roosevelt brought all government information functions under one organization, the Office of War Information, which he also created through an executive order (E.O. 9182, June 13, 1942).[32]

After 1945 wartime security concerns were supplanted by cold war fears of espionage and subversion, and Truman was quick to centralize control within the White House. The National Security Council recommended a governmentwide program for protecting classified information in 1948 as part of an overall internal security program.[33] On the basis of these recommendations, Truman subsequently issued two orders that solidified presidential control over the classification process. The first, Executive Order 10104 (February 1, 1950), added the "top secret" category to the existing three-part system, established standards for each level of classification, and authorized military agencies to classify information.[34] The second, Executive Order 10290 (September 24, 1951), allowed civilian agencies to classify information and extended protection to information related to "national security" instead of the narrower "national defense" criteria used previously; in doing so Truman "completely overhauled the security classification program,"[35] replacing an ad hoc system of "widely varying sets of regulations" in departments with a centralized system ultimately controlled from the White House.[36]

Truman's classification orders were widely criticized at the time as overly broad. Under them, agencies having little to do with national security—such as the Smithsonian Institution, the Railroad Retirement Board, and the Migratory Bird Conservation Commission—could classify information. The sharpest criticism arose over the ability to classify information on the basis of the need to protect "national security," and the authorization of the designation "restricted" to apply to a broad range of information that "required protection against unauthorized use or disclosure."[37] In practice this category permitted the classification of information that had little connection to national security, and produced some undeniably preposterous cases of overclassification. For example, in the 1950s the Army War College prepared an annual guide to the U.S. government consisting of basic information on the separation of powers, the Constitution, and the organization of the executive branch. It quoted extensively from the Constitution. In July 1953 the college asked the White House to check the accuracy of revisions to a new edition of the book, the pages of which were classified "restricted."[38] Evidently the army considered the Constitution and the U.S. *Government Manual* military secrets.

In response to the criticisms of E.O. 10290, shortly after taking office Eisenhower asked Attorney General Herbert Brownell to recommend revisions.[39] Brownell concluded that 10290 was "so broadly drawn and loosely administered as to make it possible for government officials to cover up their own mistakes and even their wrongdoing under the guise of protecting national security."[40] In November 1953 Eisenhower scaled back the Truman program with his own executive order. Executive Order 10501 restored the narrower "national defense" criterion for classification, eliminated the "restricted" classification level, reduced the number of agencies that could classify information, and instituted a procedure for declassifying documents that no longer warranted protection.[41]

The more restrictive Eisenhower order did little, however, to reduce secrecy levels. A series of congressional hearings in the late 1950s highlighted some persistent absurdities:

1. The army had classified some 1940s research into the bow and arrow, calling it a "silent flashless weapon." A report on the research was classified "confidential" in 1944, and was not declassified until 1958 after the House Committee on Government Operations asked for a review.

2. The navy had classified a study of shark attacks, including a 1916 Brooklyn Museum report on sharks in the waters around New York City.

3. The Department of Labor had classified statistics on the amount of peanut butter purchased by the military, on the grounds that the information would allow an enemy to estimate the number of service personnel. At the time, however, the Department of Defense was issuing monthly reports detailing military personnel strength.[42]

These were not the only examples to emerge during the 1950s of excessive secrecy applied to demonstrably mundane information. When the movie *On the Beach* was released in 1959, the Eisenhower administration became concerned that the film's depiction of nuclear war could create pressure for radical disarmament measures (the film was about an American submarine that surfaced after World War III had destroyed much of the earth). A cabinet paper outlined a public relations strategy to counter the film's impact.[43] It was classified "confidential."

The framework established by 10501 lasted with minor changes until 1972, when Nixon replaced it with an order of his own (E.O. 11652, March 10, 1972).[44] Although in rough outline the two orders were similar, the Nixon order represented, at least superficially, an attempt both to reduce the level of classification and to tighten enforcement. Executive Order 11652 reduced the number of agencies and personnel with the authority to classify documents at the top secret level and required faster declassification of most documents. At the same time, though, it broadened the definition of what could be classified from the "national defense" justification in 10501 to a "national defense or foreign relations" criterion. Arthur Schlesinger warned that this was a "far more spacious standard," and additionally expressed concern that 11652 "pretended to supply a basis for criminal prosecution in cases of unauthorized disclosure," something that an executive order by itself could not do.[45] Although the Nixon administration portrayed the order as a significant step toward increased openness, there is no doubt that the original order was motivated by the desire to control leaks (especially to Congress), restrict access to classified information, and bring diplomatic and foreign affairs information under the umbrella of the classification system.[46]

Immediately after taking office, President Carter began considering proposals to increase openness in government.[47] In July 1978 he issued a new classification executive order (E.O. 12065, July 3, 1978) that placed much more emphasis on reducing secrecy than previous orders.[48] The order stipulated that information could be classified only when its unauthorized release would cause "identifiable damage" to national security, and imposed for the first time a balancing test in declassification review, requiring agency officials to weigh the public's interest in knowing information against the potential damage from release. The order also required a presumption against classification when there was "reasonable doubt" about the need to maintain secrecy. Procedurally, the Carter administration broke with precedent by circulating the draft order to congressional committees asking for public comment.

The Carter order also established a new interagency organization to coordinate and implement secrecy policy, the Information Security Oversight Office (ISOO). Prior to the establishment of ISOO, the oversight of classification policy was the responsibility of an Interagency Classification Review Committee located in the General Services Administration. Carter's National Security Council found the committee "weak" and "moribund," and recommended that it be replaced by a more powerful organization located within the Executive Office.[49] Although ISOO remained within the General Services Administration, primarily because officials within the Office of Management and Budget argued that OMB lacked the necessary expertise to run the office, it came under close supervision by the National Security Council.[50]

Reagan too sought to place his stamp on executive branch classification policy, but reversed the trend toward increased openness. His classification order (E.O. 12356, April 6, 1982) repudiated Carter's policy by eliminating the balancing test and requiring presumptive classification when there was any doubt about the need for secrecy.[51] Reagan also eliminated the mandatory declassification procedures in previous orders, allowed agencies to reclassify previously available information, and imposed some secrecy requirements on government grantees in the private sector.[52] Reagan administration officials argued that the revisions were needed to provide more protection for defense information and to correct deficiencies in the Carter order that made it harder for the government to prevail in legal challenges to government refusals to release files.[53] Critics of the Reagan order charged that it reversed thirty years of precedent by "expanding the conditions for classification, requiring the application of official secrecy whenever possible, and maintaining records under security protection in perpetuity."[54]

Clinton in turn replaced E.O. 12356 with his own classification order, which put renewed emphasis on declassification and imposed more stringent limits on what may be classified.[55] Unlike previous orders, 12958 required original classifiers to identify themselves and explain on a "why line" the justification for classifying a document; it also made management of classified information a factor in personnel evaluations. In the most significant declassification step ever taken, the order automatically declassified all documents of "permanent historical value" over twenty-five years old, whether or not they had been reviewed. Departments may appeal automatic declassification decisions to an Interagency Security Classification Appeals Panel, comprising senior executive branch staff, but in order to prevail appeals must meet one of nine narrow exemptions.

The number of pages declassified annually between 1981 and 1998 makes clear the impact that executive orders have on declassification activity. By 1983, the year after Reagan issued his executive order, the number of pages declassified dropped by almost three-fourths from 1981 levels (from 28.7 million to 8 million pages), and the rate of declassification remained relatively stable throughout the 1980s. The Clinton order changed this pattern, dramatically increasing the number of documents declassified (from 11.5 million pages in 1994 to 193 million in 1998).[56]

The reliance on executive orders to control the classification regime has produced policy that has shifted quickly and significantly from one order to the next, with three major changes in twenty years. Such rapid change has interfered with sustained progress in declassifying documents, and there is nothing to prevent a new president from suspending the current declassification program by issuing a new executive order rescinding 12958.

The 1995 Commission on Protecting and Reducing Government Secrecy concluded that the transience of orders encourages agency officials to resist implementation, in the hope that an order they oppose will be replaced by one more favorable toward classification. Compliance with the presidential regulations, moreover, has been a persistent problem, especially when presidents have insisted on more openness rather than less. In 1956, three years after Executive Order 10501 established a strict three-category classification system (top secret, secret, confidential), government agencies were still using at least thirty-six separate designations to identify information not classified but withheld from the public.[57]

Security Clearances and Loyalty

The president's authority to define classified information leads directly to the authority to determine who may have access to that information. As a result presidents can set the standards for personnel security clearances, something they have done (in parallel to the series of orders on classification) with executive orders. In the 1940s and 1950s, Truman and Eisenhower extended this authority, notoriously, to apply a broader "loyalty" standard to all federal government employees as a way of fighting subversive infiltration of the executive branch.

The president's ability to create a loyalty program stems from the general executive power, which includes the power to hire and fire employees at will, subject to limitations that Congress has imposed through, for example, the Civil Service Act and nondiscrimination laws, and constitutional protections against arbitrary and capricious government actions.[58]

In 1947 Truman established, via Executive order 9835, a comprehensive loyalty standard for federal employees (the order was based in large part on the work of the Temporary Commission on Employee Loyalty, which Truman had established via executive order in November 1946).[59] The order required a loyalty investigation of every federal employee, not just those who occupied sensitive positions or who had access to classified information, and stipulated that people could be fired if "on all the evidence, reasonable grounds exist for the belief that the person involved is disloyal to the Government of the United States."[60] The order set out different categories of activity that could lead to a finding of disloyalty: sabotage or espionage, treason, advocating violent revolution, unauthorized disclosure of classified information, acting to promote a foreign government over the interests of the United States, and, most chillingly, "membership in, affiliation with, or sympathetic association with" any group designated as subversive by the attorney general.[61] Each agency established a Loyalty Board, which reviewed cases referred to it by the FBI. In cases involving evidence of suspected disloyalty, employees could ask for a hearing before their agency's board.

Shortly after taking office, Eisenhower followed up with a loyalty-security program of his own, which he set out in Executive Order 10450 on April 27, 1953.[62] To distinguish his program from Truman's, Eisenhower merged loyalty considerations with the screening of employees as security risks. Working from a key grant of congressional authority created in 1950 (in which the heads of agencies involved in national security affairs could summarily dismiss employees for security reasons), Eisenhower extended summary dismissal rights to all federal agencies. The order also revised the standard for determining who was eligible for government employment, requiring agency heads to ensure that employment of any given civilian was "clearly consistent with the interests of national security." E.O. 10450 required agency heads to classify jobs as either sensitive or nonsensitive, and required a more intensive investigation of people filling sensitive positions.

E.O. 10450 established a more enduring and robust security program, not only by falling back on explicit congressional authority but also by tying the loyalty issue more closely with the president's authority in national security affairs and by shifting the emphasis from loyalty to security risks (administration officials felt they were on especially firm footing in relying heavily on a congressional grant).[63] Many of its provisions remain in force, despite several amendments by subsequent executive orders.

Court decisions, though, have created procedural protections that, for all practical purposes, eliminated "loyalty" as a condition for employment. Critics charge that these rulings have "thoroughly undermined" the legal doctrine that government employment is a privilege, not a right.[64] The Supreme Court took an initial step in 1952, declaring that mere affiliation or membership in a subversive organization was not grounds for dismissal; the government had to show that an individual *knew* about the organization's activities and purpose.[65]

In the 1956 landmark *Cole v. Young* opinion, the Supreme Court rebuffed Eisenhower's effort to extend summary dismissal authority to all federal agencies, holding that Congress had authorized such actions only for positions related to national security.[66] Without such plenary authority, the president had to rely on the normal civil service process to dismiss employees from nonsensitive positions, under which civil servants had important procedural protections (such as the right to an appeal and, for veterans, the right to a hearing).[67] *Cole* had the effect of limiting summary dismissals on loyalty grounds only to those positions that were involved in national security (in practice, notes Lewy, loyalty actions all but ended, with only sixteen cases pursued since 1956).[68]

Three years later, in 1959, the Supreme Court ruled in *Greene v. Elroy* that in the absence of an explicit presidential or congressional delegation, the Department of Defense could not deny security clearances to employees of federal contractors without due process protections, including the right to confront and cross-examine witnesses against them.[69] The *Greene* decision, given its immediate effect on the security clearance process for private contractors, put the Eisenhower administration in a difficult position. The White House, it was clear, had to respond, and Eisenhower's advisors debated whether they should seek legislation or fall back on an executive order to redefine the industrial security program. Legislation would provide a firmer legal basis, but Assistant Special Counsel Phillip Areeda argued that the mere fact of the president's request for legislation might imply an absence of presidential power. This implication would tend to preclude independent Executive action if Congress failed to act during the current session. . . . The appearance of executive impotence would also tend to limit future Presidential discretion in this area and related security programs."[70] In February 1960, eight months after the *Greene* ruling, Eisenhower issued Executive Order 10865, establishing a defense industrial security clearance program that provided the procedural protections the Court found lacking.[71] The order remained in effect forty years later.

By the end of the 1950s the loyalty program, insofar as it applied to all government employees, had run its course, eroding as a result of Joseph McCarthy's ignominious end, documented abuses of civil liberties, judicial constraints, and mounting criticism from the public (and from the legal, scientific, and academic communities). Nixon's failed try at reviving the SACB, privacy laws passed in the early 1970s, and continued court challenges settled the issue. What remains is a program that requires a suitability evaluation before an individual is granted a security clearance (pursuant to Executive Order 10450). Still, the process is controlled—to the extent permitted by the constitutional protections that the courts have insisted upon—by the president, through executive orders and departmental regulations. Clinton continued the practice of earlier presidents by issuing Executive Order 12968 on August 7, 1995.[72] In it, Clinton updated some of the standards in 10450, including explicit nondiscrimination language, and a stipulation that sexual orientation, by itself, cannot be considered in clearance determinations. The order also established a common set of standards for all federal agencies, but "it does not supersede Executive order 10450 . . . in effect, it simply adds another regulatory layer to the personnel security system."[73]

There can be no doubt whatever that the loyalty-security orders of the 1940s and 1950s had a dramatic and harmful effect on civil liberties and individual rights. The records of various loyalty board hearings display government power at its most brutally intrusive and, oddly, most absurd. Despite assurances that the loyalty investigations would not turn into a "witch hunt," the practical difficulties in screening over 2 million employees, along with the ambiguities in the order, produced the very hysteria that Truman was hoping to fend off. The abuses and criticisms of the program are now well known: employees suspended in advance of any disloyalty findings, the use of uncorroborated secret evidence, Justice Department prosecutions that appeared motivated by a desire to serve up enough heads to sate congressional appetites, loyalty board members reaching disloyalty findings because they feared for their own jobs "if they acted according to their own best judgment and cleared some of the employees."[74] The boards were composed of poorly trained people who were trying to carry out vague and inconsistent policy, and the large number of boards (over 150) led to huge variations in what were considered appropriate avenues of inquiry. A 1955 compilation of illustrative loyalty hearings shows federal employees questioned about, among other things, their political beliefs, reading habits, favorite newspaper columnists, reli gion, relatives' political leanings, opinions about the Korean War, knowledge of Yiddish, attitudes toward the poor, and views concerning racial equality in a way that obliterated any semblance of due process or limited government.[75]

It is not surprising that these ham-fisted investigations failed to significantly improve internal security. This is so despite evidence from the recently declassified "Venona" files proving that the Soviet Union was, in fact, engaged in a systematic espionage campaign against the U.S. government, and that bona fide security concerns played a larger role behind Executive Order 9835 than originally recognized.[76] The Defense Department's own evaluations—as recently as the early 1990s—concluded that most spies turn to espionage for economic, not ideological, reasons, and generally only after long careers in the defense community (this was clearly true of John Walker and Aldrich Ames, the two most damaging espionage cases of the past several decades).[77] Trying to ensure loyalty or suitability at the initial clearance stage does nothing to prevent this type of threat, and diverts attention from those individuals more likely to commit espionage.

The Congressional Response

At various times during this history of presidential control over information and personnel clearances, many members of Congress have repeatedly expressed dissatisfaction with the government's classification policy. Congressional objections typically focused on overclassification, use of classification policy to hide mistakes, and executive branch refusals to provide information to Congress. Yet attempts to create a statutory framework and give Congress a more prominent role in the classification process have, with only a few exceptions, failed, and when they have not failed have still left the president enough maneuvering room to minimize the impact of statutory controls. In 1956 legal scholar Harold Cross, an ardent proponent of government openess, held that in matters of secrecy and classification, "the dearth of congressional enactments has left the field wide open for executive occupation,"[78] and little has changed since then. Congressional oversight of the implementation of the classification orders has been "virtually nonexistent."[79]

Although there is little question that Congress has at least some authority to regulate classified information, legislative remedies have been frustrated by a dynamic of presidential initiative seen in the other areas of competition between the institutions. The president, by taking advantage of his ability to move first and of Congress's relative inability to take collective action, has been able to use his discretionary authority to fend off legislative encroachment. Congress has repeatedly failed to muster majorities to overturn or revise any of the relevant executive orders or enact an overall statutory classification system, despite numerous attempts.

One reason Congress has had such difficulty acting is that presidents have been able to preempt legislation via strategically timed executive orders. In 1972, when Congress reviewed the classification process in the wake of the Pentagon Papers and broader concern about executive branch secrecy, Nixon stopped the legislation by issuing Executive Order 11652. At the time of Nixon's order, two congressional committees were considering a statutory classification system, but neither managed to send legislation to the floor of the House. Critics charged that Nixon intentionally undercut the legislation by issuing the order.[80] More recently, the Senate Select Committee on Intelligence abandoned plans to report a statutory classification bill in 1995 because the Clinton administration had announced that it was working on a replacement for Executive Order 12356.[81]

The same dynamic operated with security clearances as well as with the loyalty program imposed by Truman and Roosevelt. Here, too, policy was affected by the congressional-presidential competition for influence. The antecedents of "loyalty" policy extend at least to World War I, when President Wilson issued a confidential order to department heads permitting them to fire employees if their continued presence "could be inimical to the public welfare by reason of . . . conduct, sympathies, or utterances, or because of other reasons growing out of the war."[82]

Legislation defined the process in the interwar years, with Congress anxious to reassert its authority after the wartime emergency passed.[83] In 1939 Congress passed the Hatch Act, which, among other things, prohibited federal employees from belonging to any group that advocated the overthrow of the U.S. constitutional form of government. Congress followed up with legislation granting summary dismissal power to the Navy and War departments, and laws that barred payment of federal funds to people belonging to subversive organizations.[84]

There is little doubt that Truman's loyalty order was prompted by a desire to head off further congressional action; he established the Temporary Commission on Employee Loyalty in the context of Republican charges that his administration was soft on communism, and he explicitly intended for the commission to "take the ball away" from the House Committee on Un-American Activities, which was conducting its own loyalty investigations.[85] And once he had established the commission, "he was in effect committed to a new loyalty program. The Commission's concerns were sure to have become known; and if Truman had rejected them, Congress probably could not have been restrained from acting on its own."[86] Harold Hyman, who wrote the definitive work on loyalty tests throughout American history, argued that the order "struck a new note in the expanded concept of executive powers. In all previous peacetime loyalty-testing experience, Congress rather than the president had taken the lead."[87]

In this Truman probably did forestall more draconian legislation. "Politically, the effect of Executive Order No. 9835 was indeed pronounced," writes Truman biographer David McCullough, "as *Time's* Capitol Hill Correspondent, Frank McNaughton, described in a confidential report to his editors: 'The Republicans are now taking Truman seriously . . . [his] order to root out subversives from government employment hit a solid note in Congress, and further pulled the rug out from under his political detractors.' "[88] In July 1947 the House of Representatives debated legislation that would have in effect established a statutory loyalty program, making the loyalty program in 9835 a law, but opponents of the bill claimed that it was motivated only by Republican desire to recapture the loyalty issue, which Truman had defused by issuing 9835. "The President's Executive Order stole the Republican thunder," argued Representative Adolph Sabath (D-Ill.). "This bill is merely a belated effort of the Republicans to get back in the groove of their Red-baiting campaign."[89]

Still, Truman remained enormously sensitive to congressional (and Republican) pressure to beef up the loyalty program beyond what was in Executive Order 9835, although he insisted that Republican charges of disloyalty within the government were a "red herring" designed to deflect criticism of Congress's lackluster legislative record. Nevertheless, in response to charges that the existing loyalty program was ineffective (and after the chair of the Civil Service Commission expressed frustration that ambiguous loyalty cases were being resolved in favor of the employee[90]), Truman reversed the evidentiary presumption with Executive Order 10241, issued in April 1951.[91] The new order revised the standard for dismissal to permit action when, "on all evidence, there is reasonable doubt as to the loyalty of the person involved." This language shifted the burden in these ambiguous cases onto employees: under 9835, the government had to show that an employee was disloyal. Under 10241, the employee would have to show that she was loyal. Writing in the *Harvard Law Review*, John Lord O'Brien called this shift "a final abandonment . . . of the protection traditionally accorded the individual,"[92] and former attorney general Francis Biddle wrote Truman that the new order "will be treated in many agencies as an open invitation to start the very 'witch hunt' the President has been so anxious to avoid"[93]

Similarly, Eisenhower's revision of the Truman loyalty program was spurred, in part, by a desire to maintain executive control over the policy and, in particular, to ward off congressional efforts to investigate alleged loyalty problems in the executive branch.[94] Political scientist Robert N. Johnson, writing in 1956, noted that "the gradual subsidence of spectacular Congressional investigations in the loyalty-security field is due mainly to the fact that, since Eisenhower's inauguration, the executive branch has taken precisely the position on these questions that the extremists in Congress had previously advocated, thus stealing their thunder."[95]

In defining classified information, presidents have also taken advantage of their flexibility to interpret statutes to their advantage and control information through unilateral action, a pattern that was clear from the beginning of the Republic but accelerated sharply after World War II. From 1789 to 1949, agency control of records and information originated in a so-called housekeeping statute, actually a variety of acts passed between 1789 and 1872, that provided the authority to maintain and control the disposition of records. When codified in 1875 into a single law, the statute gave agency heads the authority to issue regulations regarding "the custody, use, and preservation of the records, papers, and property appertaining" to department operations. Although this statute "was never intended to give Federal officials the authority to keep their records hidden from public view," it was often used to do just that.[96] As I noted above, Roosevelt based his classification order on a 1938 statute that prohibited the photographing or drawing of military or naval installations and equipment, even though Congress clearly did not anticipate such a broad interpretation.

Congressional concerns about the government's rapidly expanding administrative capacity led to the passage of the Administrative Procedures Act in 1946 (5 U.S.C. §§ #551–559). The act, which mandated public comment and record keeping for many types of departmental actions, was also intended to counteract what Congress saw as excessive secrecy in the executive branch within the civilian agencies. Nevertheless it allowed agencies to refuse public release of information if "secrecy is required in the public interest" and required individuals requesting information to show that they had a legitimate need for it. These catch-all exceptions allowed agencies to withhold information virtually at will, and Congress did not revise the law for nearly twenty years, succeeding finally with the 1966 Freedom of Information Act.

The Freedom of Information Act (or FO1A, 5 U.S.C. § #552) remains the broadest congressional effort to impose statutory information controls on the executive branch. It eliminates the public interest justification for keeping information secret, and requires agencies to release all information except when it falls into one of nine exempt categories. Of most relevance here is the exemption that allows agencies to maintain secrecy when information is "specifically required by executive Order to be kept secret in the interest of the national defense or foreign policy." This language was designed to be more restrictive than the "public interest" exemption in the APA, which it replaced, but it in practice has served to legitimate presidential control over national security information. By expressly recognizing the president's authority to control information policy via executive order, the legislation actually enhanced executive branch discretion:

> By empowering the executive branch to define the types of information which may be protected under the FOIA's national security exemption and to amend the criteria at will, Congress has eliminated a possible check against the executive's power to withhold information. In the FOIA's eight other exemptions, Congress establishes the criteria for exemption and thus defines the scope of the executive's power to protect information. In the national security exemption, however, Congress vests total control in the executive to define the scope of its power to protect information. The allocation of control over national security matters to the executive conforms to the separation of powers doctrine. Nevertheless, the elimination of this check creates the potential for abuse by the executive. For example, the President could establish criteria for exemption from the FOIA which are so broad as to permit agencies to withhold any information they want, regardless of the public interest in the disclosure of that information.[97]

The original FOIA statute did not allow any review of decisions to classify information. Classified information, as defined by presidential executive order, was explicitly and automatically exempted from release. In *EPA v. Mink*[98] the Supreme Court held that the executive order exemption was controlling, and that the law made no provision for judicial review of the original classification decision.

In response to the *Mink* decision, Congress revised the FOIA in 1974 to tighten the national security exemption. The revised language, enacted over President Ford's veto, permitted *in camera* judicial review of classification decisions, henceforth exempting from release material required by executive order to be kept secret and which "is in fact properly classified pursuant to such executive order."

The more restrictive language has not, however, led to enhanced judicial scrutiny of classification decisions.[99] One reason is that Congress made it clear that the courts were expected to defer to the executive on classification decisions.[100] Subsequent federal court decisions adhered to this legislative intent and established the principle that the courts will accord "utmost deference" to agency determinations.[101] Only once has a federal court ordered the disclosure of classified information in an FOIA lawsuit, and no court has ever mandated the release of classified military or diplomatic documents where the government adhered to the procedural requirements of the applicable executive order.[102] A 1996 guidebook for FOIA litigants identified the difficulties in challenging classification decisions: "As social policy, deferral to the classification decisions of government can be debated, as it has been under the Watergate and Iran-Contra controversies, but as a purely legal matter, the deck is stacked heavily against disclosure and deference to the classification decision strengthens the agency's hand."[103]

And even with the more restrictive language in FOIA designed to make it easier to force the executive branch to release information, strange cases remain. In 1977, after reading in a story in the *Washington Post* that the president's tennis scores were treated as "top secret" information, the mayor of New Carrolton, Maryland, made a Freedom of Information Act request for "the tennis scores of the President and his doubles partner, Mr. Lance, in a match with Hamilton Jordan and Tim Smith on Sunday, August 14, 1977." The White House replied using its standard language in FOIA requests: "Whereas the President is, as you know, committed to the principle of open government, Congress in initially enacting in 1966, and then amending the Freedom of Information Act in 1974, made it clear for several valid reasons that the President, the White House Office, and the President's principal advisers were not intended to be covered by the Act. Accordingly, the information you requested is not available."[104] It appears that the White House wasn't kidding.

Congress retains the ultimate authority to force the president's hand through its power of the purse, but this power is a blunt instrument, has rarely been brought into use, and even then has been only partly successful. Members of Congress objected strenuously to a Reagan administration effort to expand the nondisclosure agreements that cleared employees had to sign as a condition for receiving their security clearances. At issue was a change in the wording of the document, in which individuals agreed not to divulge not only classified information but "classifiable" information as well.[105] Critics charged that this could be used to discipline those who released unclassified information that was later deemed to be secret, thus opening the door to post hoc sanctions, and the congressional reaction was swift: in an appropriations rider to an Omnibus Continuing Resolution for fiscal year 1988, Congress barred the executive branch from spending money to "implement or enforce" the secrecy agreements if they contained the disputed language. Congress approved the same language again the following year.[106] The administration backed down in early 1988, issuing revised regulations that dropped the "classifiable information" provision.

Although Congress ultimately forced the wording change in the secrecy agreements, it had no success on the related question of whether the nondisclosure agreements could impede congressional access to executive branch information. The question is whether employees of the executive branch can reveal classified information to Congress without the authorization of their superiors. The executive branch has consistently maintained that Congress has no such right to classified information. This question presents a set of issues different from those related to secrecy from the public, since in this case members of Congress are presumptively cleared to see classified data, and existing procedures govern the transmission of highly classified intelligence information to congressional oversight committees.

The recent case of State Department official Richard Nuccio shows that the executive branch retains decisive control on this point.[107] During 1994 congressional hearings into U.S. policy toward Central America, Nuccio, a member of the State Department's Bureau of Inter-American Affairs, testified that the United States knew nothing about alleged illegal activities by the Guatemalan military. At issue was a charge by Jennifer Harbury, a U.S. citizen, that in 1992 the military had tortured and murdered her husband, a guerrilla leader named Efraim Bamaca Velasquez. After reviewing classified cables from various agencies, however, Nuccio found evidence that a CIA-paid informant and the Guatemalan military may have been involved both in the death of Velasquez and in the murder of Michael Devine, a U.S. citizen. In March 1995, after learning the identity of the informant, Nuccio informed Representative Robert Torricelli (D-N.J.) about what he knew, including the informant's name. Torricelli then released this information to the *New York Times*.[108] Not surprisingly, the story provoked a firestorm of criticism embarrassing to the CIA, but it also raised questions about the propriety of Torricelli's releasing classified information to the press as well as his public identification of an intelligence asset.[109]

Nuccio, though, became the target of disciplinary action. The State Department reprimanded him for revealing the information, and placed his security clearance on probationary status. A federal prosecutor began investigating whether Nuccio violated the Intelligence Identities Protection Act of 1982 (now Title VI of the National Security Act), which prohibits cleared individuals from revealing the identity of any "covert agent."[110] Although Nuccio was cleared of any criminal violation, the CIA found the State Department's sanction of Nuccio insufficient and revoked Nuccio's clearance altogether, thus barring him from seeing any intelligence-related information. It did this even though CIA director John Deutsch admitted that the agency was remiss in not informing Congress of the alleged human rights abuses (he also fired two top officials and disciplined several others for their part in the scandal, after an investigation by the CIA inspector general).[111] This move effectively ended Nuccio's career, since without access to classified information he was unable to do his job.

To Nuccio's supporters, his was a brave act of uncovering official corruption and cover-up: they noted that it was Torricelli who ultimately revealed the information, and that Torricelli himself was cleared to receive the information Nuccio provided. Torricelli had his own difficulties stemming from the episode, facing an ethics charge alleging that he violated House rules by releasing the information to the *Times* (the Ethics Committee took no action, holding that the relevant rule was ambiguous on key points).[112] Others pointed out the risks of individuals' determining on their own whether to divulge classified information, whatever their motivation. The Office of Legal Counsel took an absolute position, arguing that the president must have "ultimate and unimpeded authority over the collection, retention, and dissemination of intelligence and other national security information in the Executive Branch. There is no exception to this principle for those disseminations that would be made to Congress or its Members."[113]

In response to the affair, the Senate moved to protect future whistleblowers who release classified information to Congress. Its version of the fiscal year 1998 Intelligence Authorization Act included provisions designed to protect individuals who disclose information—no matter what the level of classification, and no matter from which agency—to legislators on the relevant congressional oversight committees, or to an employee's own congressional representative. The Senate Select Intelligence Committee Report on the bill claimed that duly elected members of Congress were automatically cleared to receive any classified information covered under Executive Order 12356.[114] The act passed the Senate on a 98–1 vote, but the Clinton administration announced that it would veto any bill with such a provision as a violation of the president's constitutional authority, and the disclosure language was dropped in conference committee with the House.[115] The official administration position was that any bill that permits executive personnel to provide Congress with information without going through proper channels is "an unconstitutional infringement on the President's authority as Commander in Chief and Chief Executive."[116]

The Senate tried twice more in 1998 to enact similar legislation. A slightly more restrictive provision was incorporated into the Senate version of the fiscal year 1999 Intelligence Authorization Act, and passed by a similarly lopsided vote (93–1), but once again the House balked. Senator Richard Shelby (R-Ala.) also introduced a bill that would have provided broad protections to members of the intelligence community who disclose classified information to Congress, but the Senate took no action.

In the end, Congress did enact a law that gave some protection to whistleblowers in the Nuccio mold, although the provisions were far weaker than what the Senate had originally passed in 1997. The final version of the fiscal year 1999 Intelligence Authorization Act included language that protected Central Intelligence Agency personnel who report to the congressional intelligence committees regarding issues of "urgent concern." But potential whistleblowers must first notify the director of the CIA that they intend to make such a report, and receive direction "on how to contact the intelligence committees in accordance with appropriate security practice."[117] But the law creates an additional channel through which information can flow from the agency to Congress: employees are permitted to register their concerns with the inspector general, who then has the authority to investigate and report to the CIA director. The director, in turn, must forward the inspector general's report to Congress. The language was a compromise reflecting the tension between Congress's desire for the information it needs to carry out its oversight function and worries over a presidential veto (a certainty if the disclosure language was too strong), along with a desire to prevent damaging leaks. But it is telling that Congress chose to integrate the whistleblower protection law into the inspector general process rather than provoke a constitutional confrontation with the president over the issue.

In the 1990s Congress enacted laws and introduced legislation that facilitated the release of information, but these bills ultimately allowed the executive branch to keep documents secret or edit disclosed documents in the interest of national security. The best-known recent case is the President John F. Kennedy Assassination Records Act of 1992, in which Congress stipulated that all agencies send assassination records to the National Archives for preservation and review. All records were to be made public, except those that the president certified required continued classification. Later examples from the 105th Congress include H.R. 2635, the Human Rights Information Act, which seeks the release of information on human rights abuses in Central America; S. 1379, the Nazi War Crimes Disclosure Act, which seeks the disclosure of information in government files on war crimes; and S. 1232, which seeks the release of physicist Glenn Seaborg's journal while head of the Atomic Energy Commission. (Seaborg's journal was originally declassified by the AEC but was then reclassified when the AEC became part of the Department of Energy).

Despite what may appear to be a trend toward increased openness, Congress has shown no inclination to fundamentally revise the classification system. Senator Daniel Moynihan (D-N.Y.) offered comprehensive reform legislation in 1997 that would have put the entire classification system under a statutory footing (S. 712, the Government Secrecy Act), but his bill attracted only a handful of sponsors and died quietly in 1999.[118] I noted in chapter one Congress's effort to stall the declassification provisions in Clinton's E.O. 12958, by tightening the standards for reviewing documents set for release. Even this legislative push, though, was temporary and did little but ask the president to report on what the executive branch was doing. On the whole, classification policy remains, and will almost certainly continue to be, an area of clear presidential dominance and control.

Control over Intelligence Organization

Control of the intelligence community has always been an executive function. From the earliest days of the Republic, presidents have had a free hand in structuring the intelligence community as they saw fit, establishing intelligence priorities, granting authority to units within the community, and creating new organizations on their own. Much of the time, this authority has been implemented through executive orders. Even when Congress has tried to impose statutory limits and requirements, presidents have maneuvered within these constraints to maintain executive control. Presidents have used their executive authority to reorganize the intelligence community, establish entirely new organizations and oversight mechanisms, and prescribe standards for intelligence activities. When challenged, presidents have issued executive orders to stall or preempt pending congressional action.

Intelligence organizations created without any congressional involvement include the National Security Agency (established in October 1952 in a classified presidential memorandum); the National Reconnaissance Office (established in August 1960); the Defense Intelligence Agency (established by Defense Department directive in August 1961); and the Defense Mapping Agency (created in a 1971 intelligence community reorganization). In addition, presidents have created a variety of oversight boards and commissions relying entirely on their own authority. These units include the President's Board of Consultants on Foreign Intelligence Activities (Executive Order 10656, February 8, 1956) and the President's Foreign Intelligence Advisory Board (Executive Order 10938, May 6, 1961).[119] Much of the intelligence community lacks any specific statutory charter outlining its functions; that has been left for individual presidents to determine. With few exceptions, there are no statutory restrictions on how the intelligence agencies may conduct their activities. Some of the most important intelligence functions are shrouded in legal ambiguities, with imprecise boundaries between what is permitted and what is not. Virtually every postwar president—Truman, Eisenhower, Kennedy, Nixon, Ford, Carter, Reagan, and Clinton—has used executive orders to reorganize the intelligence agencies, to define the scope of allowable activities, and to put his own stamp on intelligence policy.

Presidential control over intelligence functions and classified information are closely related, because of the importance of maintaining secrecy (both from the public and from Congress). Because intelligence, virtually by definition, requires secrecy, presidential control is closely tied to the president's authority over information and classification, a power explicitly recognized by the courts. In *Chicago and Southern Airlines v. Waterman Steamship Corp.*, the Supreme Court not only supported the executive nature of intelligence but also justified the judiciary's reluctance to become involved in congressional-legislative disputes on the issue:

> The President, both as Commander-in-Chief and as the nation's organ for foreign affairs has available intelligence services whose reports are not and ought not to be published to the world. It would be intolerable that courts, without the relevant information, should review and perhaps nullify actions of the executive taken on information properly held secret . . . even if courts could require full disclosure, the very nature of executive decisions as to foreign policy is political, not judicial. Such decisions are wholly confided by our Constitution to the political departments of the government, executive and legislative. . . . They are decisions of a kind for which the judiciary has neither aptitude, facilities nor responsibility and which has long been held to belong in the domain of political power not subject to judicial intrusion or inquiry."[120]

Origins of the Intelligence Function and the Emergence of Presidential Control

The "intelligence community" is defined as the agencies that collect, analyze, and disseminate intelligence information. Numerous organizations play roles, and the boundaries and respective jurisdictions are imprecise: the military services have their own intelligence units, as do the Treasury, Energy, and State departments. Alongside are the National Security Agency (responsible for communications security and electronic eavesdropping), the National Reconnaissance Office (satellite surveillance and imaging), the FBI, the Defense Intelligence Agency, the Drug Enforcement Administration, and the CIA. With such a large and diverse set of units, coordination—among the different agencies, between the organizations that collect and analyze intelligence information and the organizations that use it—is an ongoing problem.

The constitutional origin of the president's control over intelligence is ambiguous, determined more by tradition, executive initiative, and congressional acquiescence than by any explicit grounding in the law. Proponents of executive authority argue, as the Supreme Court did in *Waterman*, that the president has an inherent constitutional authority to conduct foreign policy, that information collection and clandestine activities are natural and wholly appropriate extensions of that power, and that Congress may not intrude into the president's domain. Congress, conversely, has repeatedly asserted a more restrictive interpretation of presidential authority (though without much success). The Church Committee, organized in the mid-1970s to investigate intelligence activities, argued that intelligence should be governed by both Congress and the president with the same system of checks and balances that applied to any other policy area. The Senate Select Committee on Intelligence took the same position in 1980, noting that "there is no mention in the Constitution of intelligence activities. Whatever constitutional authorities may exist must follow from other constitutionally conferred duties, such as the power of the President to act as commander-in-chief, and to make treaties with the advice and consent of the Senate,"[121] with the president's power balanced against the broader congressional legislative powers.

In practice, however, the constitutional elements of the debate have been displaced by a consistent pattern of congressional acquiescence and presidential preemption. Congress has typically ceded the ground to the president by enacting broad statutory delegations of power and by an inability to take the initiative on intelligence matters. In a pattern at the core of executive institutional power, presidents have moved to fill in the gaps in authorizing legislation with their own interpretations, outflank congressional efforts to impose more substantive restrictions, and maintain the initiative in important policy areas. This pattern has existed since the origins of a standing intelligence function within the military in the nineteenth century, but became much more marked with the union between the intelligence function, presidential control of information, and the national security apparatus erected with World War II.

Executive orders proved useful as the primary means of controlling intelligence, for two reasons. The first was the close proximity of intelligence to core executive powers. The second was that most presidential decisions about the way the intelligence community should operate involved the coordination of intelligence functions across departments. As such, executive orders, a recognized tool of administrative organization and procedural change, were a natural source of authority. The intelligence function already existed within various agencies, and because of the wartime environment in which it initially expanded, Congress was in no position to object. Postwar presidents used executive orders to move the authority from one organization to another. After 1945, the World War II emergency that had played such an important role in congressional deference on security issues was replaced by the cold war, which rendered Congress similarly unwilling to challenge presidential ascendancy. Here, too, presidential authority was less open to question, and once the precedent of executive control was firmly established it was that much harder for Congress to assert its own powers to control the organizations that emerged. Finally, the secrecy of the organizations and powers subverted congressional control. Since Congress cannot oversee activities about which it knows nothing, presidents have successfully used their ability to control information dissemination to avoid before-the-fact congressional participation in sensitive intelligence operations. Intelligence coordination thus stood at the intersection of individual presidential powers, with the combination proving a potent instrument of executive autonomy.

The organizations that handled intelligence in the nineteenth century were almost exclusively established by administrative action by executive branch officials, without legislative recognition (the Secret Service, created by statute in 1863 to investigate "frauds upon the revenue," was an exception). At the outbreak of the Civil War, the government "lacked any centralized intelligence organization, and, in desperation, scrambled to establish a piecemeal makeshift secret service."[122] With the creation of the U.S. Army Signal Corps (by statute, 12 Stat. 64 at 66), the army moved into cryptography and, by extension, the collection of intelligence information.[123] Yet the intelligence structure was "totally dismantled" at the end of the war.[124] From this point until the creation of the Office of Naval Intelligence in 1882 (again, by administrative order, issued by the secretary of the navy), intelligence collection was ad hoc.[125] Three years later, in 1885, the secretary of war established a tiny unit to collect military intelligence on foreign powers, one office and one clerk, which would become the Military Information Division within the army's Adjutant General's Office.[126] However small these offices were, they marked the beginning of a standing intelligence function within the military. When Congress did become involved by legislating on intelligence and related matters in the nineteenth century, the "statutes were so vaguely written that they left much latitude to executive implementers."[127] The FBI got its start in 1908 when the attorney general reacted to statutory restrictions on the use of Secret Service agents for criminal investigations, by creating a Bureau of Investigation; Congress appropriated funds a few years later.[128]

Few statutes governed anything related to intelligence before 1947, and the president had virtually complete control. Foreign and domestic intelligence activities were linked via Hoover's Federal Bureau of Investigation (itself more an executive than a statutory creation), which focused on domestic subversion. In July 1941 Roosevelt appointed William Donovan as Coordinator of Information (COI), responsible for collecting and analyzing "all information and data which may bear upon the national security." The establishment, by presidential directive, of this position "was a landmark in American government. It was the first peacetime, civilian, centralized intelligence agency."[129] Roosevelt's directive was "purposely vague"about the COI's responsibilities, and Donovan spent considerable time over the next few years battling with other agencies in government in jurisdictional disputes.[130] Congress, however, was conspicuously absent from these organizational issues, as it had begun to defer completely to FDR as World War II approached. The intelligence community thus developed well beyond congressional control.

In June 1942 Roosevelt issued Executive Order 9182, reconstituting the COI as the Office of Strategic Services (OSS), which assumed clandestine operational duties in addition to information collection and analysis functions.[131] The OSS, which was under the direct control of the Joint Chiefs of Staff (JCS), was intimately connected to the broader military function and thereby closely aligned with the president's war powers. Although the military was originally opposed to the creation of the COI, by the end of 1941 Donovan's OSS was sufficiently robust that the services had begun to recognize its value, and the Joint Chiefs wanted to preserve military influence over its intelligence operations.[132] Donovan, in turn, saw a partnership with the Joint Chiefs as a way of avoiding subordination of OSS functions to the military services. Roosevelt's order specified that OSS would "collect and analyze such strategic information as may be required by the United States Joint Chiefs of Staff" and "plan and operate such special services as may be directed" by the JCS.[133] This latter grant was a clear authorization (veiled as it was) for OSS to engage in clandestine operations: within a week of OSS's creation, the JCS specified that one function of the OSS was "to prepare plans for and to execute subversive activities" under the direction of the Joint Chiefs.[134]

As the government began planning for postwar organization, controversy erupted over the fate of the OSS and the intelligence services: the military services wanted to maintain control over the intelligence organization, while Donovan was pushing for an independent intelligence structure not under the control of any agency or military department, and with a direct line of communication to the Executive Office of the President.[135] In Donovan's view, the postwar intelligence organization would be permanent, would be a "central, independent intelligence service headed by an appointee of the President . . . responsible to the President," and would be responsible for intelligence production and coordination as well as control of secret operations.[136] In November 1944 Donovan sent Roosevelt a memorandum with a draft executive order establishing a central intelligence service within the Executive Office of the President. In language that would work its way into later orders as well as into the National Security Act of 1947, this early draft specified that the new service, among its other duties, would perform "such other functions and duties relating to intelligence as the President may from time to time direct," and stipulated that the organization would have "no policy or law-enforcement functions, either at home or abroad." The draft also charged the new intelligence service with conducting "subversive operations abroad."[137] The disposition of the postwar intelligence organization was left unresolved when FDR died in April 1945.

Truman abolished the OSS in September 1945 by executive order (E.O. 9621) and divided its organizational assets between the State and War departments; in accordance with the preferences of the Bureau of the Budget, Truman asked the State Department to take the lead in planning for postwar intelligence organization.[138] Others in the administration, particularly Admiral Sidney W. Souers and the Joint Chiefs, opposed the establishment of central intelligence within the State Department, arguing instead that the new intelligence organization should be directly under the president, rather than within an agency, in order to ensure that the president would receive unbiased advice not tailored to the interests of any one agency or policy. In December 1945, Admiral Souers wrote Truman aide Clark Clifford that under the JCS plan, the intelligence authority "would be set up under the President, and therefore on a higher level than that of any single department. As a result, no one department could influence unduly the type of intelligence produced. Furthermore, more balanced control could be expected, as no single department would be dominant."[139] This is indeed very close to the pattern of emerging presidential control over executive branch activities predicted by the new institutional economics literature, although in this case the impetus was a concern by the military departments that they not lose control of the intelligence function to the State Department.

In a January 1946 presidential directive Truman established the Central Intelligence Group (CIG), composed of representatives of the War, State, and Navy departments and headed by a director of central intelligence appointed by the president. The name of the unit was carefully chosen to get around legislative restrictions on funding independent executive branch agencies in the absence of legislative authorization (from the Independent Offices Appropriation Act of 1945): "It is generally held that the change of name for the new central intelligence organization from agency to group was made because the word 'Group' would have to suffice pending an Act of Congress to place the new organization on a statutory basis. There were legal connotations to the word 'Agency' which, according to the Bureau of the Budget, made its use impossible until such legislation had been obtained."[140] The directive continued the emphasis on reorganization within the executive branch, establishing "not an agency with a head and a body . . . but something closer to an executive secretariat."[141]

The CIG was designed to function as a coordinator and unbiased evaluator of intelligence information produced by the departments (indeed, the very reason for a centralized organization was the tendency of the agency-centered intelligence units to produce information heavily slanted toward the particular policy biases of their parent agencies). From the beginning, though, it took on a distinctive presidential character, and allowed the president and his staff to work around, when necessary, the existing intelligence offices. CIG succeeded in warding off State Department efforts to prevent it from delivering its own intelligence summaries to the president, and by spring 1946 the National Intelligence Authority (NIA, a board consisting of the secretary of state as chair and the secretaries of war and navy) began asking the CIG to perform its own independent research analysis and authorized the conduct of covert activities. CIG was thus transformed into an "intelligence producer," allowing it to "compete with the Departments [for intelligence] without the problem of departmental obstruction."[142]

Even so, Admiral Souers, the first director of central intelligence (DCI), noted the difficulties in running an intelligence organization in the absence of enabling legislation, which among other shortcomings prevented the CIG from entering into contracts for necessary services and operations. Souers was well aware of the problems of stepping into such an organizational muddle relying solely on a presidential order as his grant of authority.[143] Through the spring of 1946, officials in the BoB and Justice Department expressed concern that the directive establishing the CIG lacked sufficient legal basis, and a draft executive order was prepared to allay these concerns. But the order was never issued, as "all parties appear to have been satisfied that the President's Directive had legal standing without an executive order."[144]

Souers recommended that "the National Intelligence Authority and the Central Intelligence Group should obtain enabling legislation as soon as possible, either as part of a new national defense organization or as a separate agency, in order that (1) urgently needed central intelligence operations may be effectively and efficiently conducted by the Central Intelligence Group, and (2) the National Intelligence Authority and the Central Intelligence Group will have the necessary authority and standing to develop, support, coordinate, and direct an adequate Federal intelligence program for the national security."[145] The second DCI, air force general Hoyt Vandenberg, continued to press for legislation to ease the CIG's administrative problems; he was also motivated by a desire to transform the CIG from an interdepartmental group to "a large, vigorous, independent central intelligence agency. For this he needed legislation."[146] By July 1946 Vandenberg's staff had drafted and sent to Clark Clifford legislation to establish an independent CIA.

Intelligence officials clearly considered legislative action to serve as a way to legitimize their activities; it in no sense reflected attitudes that Congress had a legitimate role to play in the intelligence process. Congress's job was to provide a legal imprimatur, and then get out of the way.

The portion of the National Security Act of 1947 that established the CIA was taken almost verbatim from Truman's 1946 directive establishing the Central Intelligence Group; at one point, an early version of the bill incorporated the order by reference, although "there was objection to that as bad legislative practice."[147] The act which established the Central Intelligence Agency almost as an afterthought, authorized the new organization to advise on, coordinate, and analyze intelligence policy and information; one reason for the lack of specificity was fear that excessive detail would generate opposition to the agency and thereby jeopardize the entire unification bill. The final statutory authorization also charged the CIA "to perform such other functions and duties related to intelligence affecting the national security as the National Security Council may from time to time direct." Described by Clark Clifford as a "carefully phrased 'catchall' clause," the language was deliberately ambiguous to avoid advertising intentions, even though it was understood that the "such other functions" would include covert activities.[148]

The legislative history of the National Security Act makes clear the limits of Congress's ability to respond effectively to presidential initiatives. There was, in fact, opposition within Congress—especially in the House—to the broad and ambiguous grants of authority in the intelligence sections of the legislation; several members argued that the CIA's responsibilities and power should be explicitly and carefully defined. Members complained that incorporating the president's order by reference would allow succeeding presidents to modify the CIA's authority at will, and Representative Mitchell Jenkins (R-Pa.) objected specifically to allowing the president to use executive orders to delineate the CIA's powers.[149]

The House Committee on Military Affairs revised the legislation submitted by the president, but "really only rewrote and shifted paragraphs around, added one new function, and ascribed all the functions not to the DCI but to the CIA."[150] The House also inserted a clause requiring that the director of the CIA be a civilian, but the Senate refused to accept that provision, and the conference bill restored the original language that the director be appointed from "among the commissioned officers of the armed services or from among individuals in civilian life." The substance of the legislation, however, was not much different from the original administration submission: "Congress certainly thought in 1947 that it had contributed significantly to the soundness of the act when it insisted upon spelling out both the functions of the restrictions on the agency. In both cases, however, it had done nothing more than what CIG was most anxious to do and everybody else quite prepared to do."[151]

Since the statutory establishment of the CIA in 1947, Congress has struggled with—and presidents have exploited—ambiguities in the enabling legislation. The implicit authorization of covert activities is but one example. The act was also silent on the relationship of the various components of the intelligence organization to one another. To the Church Committee, Congress in the 1947 act was seeking to put intelligence on a statutory footing, in order to "reduce the reliance on 'comprehensive and undefined' Presidential power that had previously been the source of authority" for conducting foreign intelligence operations; further, the committee maintained that the act did not intend to authorize, explicitly or otherwise, covert activities.[152]

The history of executive-legislative relations on intelligence is one of the president filling the gaps in the authorization and imposing his own interpretation of ambiguous statutory language. Much of the controversy surrounds the authority of the CIA to conduct covert activities, which go far beyond intelligence collection and include foreign operations—the CIA defines them as "any clandestine operation or activity designed to influence foreign governments, organizations, persons or events in support of United States foreign policy"[153]—and the authority of the CIA to conduct investigations of domestic individuals or groups that may be operating as foreign agents. The early legislation establishing the CIA is silent on these issues, neither unambiguously permitting nor prohibiting such activity, and both the CIA and the NSC have exploited the interstices. Time after time, the Congress has been unable to clarify its intent or place explicit limits on intelligence activities; despite several efforts to pass charter legislation that would clarify the responsibilities and organizational structure of the intelligence community, the president retains a substantial degree of "residual decision rights" to structure the community as he likes.

The record is clear that from the CIA's earliest days presidents were attentive to the issues raised by congressional attempts to oversee intelligence activities. Soon after the CIA's establishment, some legislators were calling for more congressional involvement. In April 1948 Congressman Edward Devitt (R-Minn.) introduced legislation that would have created a Joint Committee on Intelligence and made a lengthy speech on the House floor introducing his bill. In his remarks, he claimed that Rear Admiral Roscoe H. Hillenkoetter, director of the CIA, supported the idea of the committee. The White House took note of Devitt's remarks, with presidential advisor John R. Steelman suggesting to Truman that "perhaps someone should have a talk with Admiral Hillenkoetter about this matter."[154]

Presidential Control of the Intelligence Community by Executive Order

Presidents have consistently opposed congressional restrictions on their ability to conduct intelligence functions, an opposition based more on broad separation of powers issues and a desire to maintain control rather than on the substance of any proposed legislation. Presidents have repeatedly and successfully preempted congressional efforts to impose a formal statutory framework on the intelligence agencies, and most of the legislation ultimately enacted has represented, at best, marginal reforms. Even when Congress has passed legislation, presidents have responded by using their organizational flexibility to outmaneuver congressional attempts to control—or even look into—intelligence activities.

For example, the second Hoover Commission—established by Eisenhower to review the organization of the executive branch and propose reforms—recommended that Congress look into legislative oversight of the intelligence agencies. The Hoover Commission criticized what it saw as an excessive reliance within the intelligence agencies on covert operations, and urged more vigilant congressional oversight. The report of the intelligence task force expressed concern "over the absence of a satisfactory machinery for surveillance of the stewardship of the CIA" and proposed a centralized congressional oversight committee as a way of "reestablishing the relationship between the CIA and the Congress so essential to and characteristic of our democratic form of governance, but which was abrogated by the enactment of Public Law 110 [the National Security Act of 1947] and other statutes relating to the agency."[155]

Working with this recommendation, Senator Mike Mansfield (D-Mont.) introduced legislation in 1955 that would have established a Joint Oversight Committee. The bill encountered strong opposition from senior senators, especially those with existing jurisdiction over the intelligence agencies. Allen Dulles, CIA director, laid out his objections to the legislation in a lengthy classified memorandum to the National Security Council. He contended, not surprisingly, that existing mechanisms within the executive branch provided adequate oversight, and he cautioned that a separate congressional oversight committee could actually lead to congressional oversight:

> A basic fact which must be borne in mind in analyzing this problem is that the establishment of a separate Congressional Committee whose only functions related to the conduct of foreign intelligence activities would inevitably mean a closer scrutiny by a much broader membership of Congress of the activities of the United States Government in this field. . . . If the membership, and particularly the staff, of a new Congressional Committee has no other functions other

than those relating to foreign intelligence, it is inevitable that the demands on the executive branch for information, operational and otherwise, will be considerably greater than under present arrangements. The actual needs of the CIA for substantive legislation are neither frequent nor extensive enough to occupy a major amount of time of a congressional committee or staff. . . . To do its job the staff would undoubtedly attempt a thorough and continuous review of all agency activities and thus become involved in the most sensitive of clandestine activities.[156]

The legislation failed, although the Senate Appropriations Committee did establish a separate subcommittee on the CIA in 1957.

President Eisenhower, moreover, by establishing the President's Board of Consultants on Foreign Intelligence Activities, or PBCFIA, by executive order,[157] was able to deflect calls for congressional action. Although the Hoover Commission had recommended that such a board, consisting of private citizens, be set up to advise the president on intelligence matters, the board was also designed to stop Mansfield's oversight legislation.[158] A Senate report criticized the board as inadequate, noting that it would report only to the president and would ultimately strengthen "the already tight control of the Executive over the CIA."[159] The passivity of the board was noted in its first briefing to the president, in which James Killian, PBCFIA chairman, began by explaining that "the Board members were only part-time advisors and did not claim any superior judgment over the responsible officials," and that the board's goal was to "strengthen the hands of [intelligence] officials."[160]

Successive presidents modified the PBCFIA via executive orders, since the board was an advisory unit attached solely to the Executive Office of the President. Members of the board resigned after Kennedy's election in 1960, and Kennedy did not reconstitute the board until after the Bay of Pigs debacle, renaming it the President's Foreign Intelligence Advisory Board.[161] Nixon revised the board's charter in 1969, renaming it (yet again) the President's Intelligence Advisory Board.[162] Carter abolished the board altogether in assigning its functions to the Intelligence Oversight Board (IOB), which Ford had created in *his* intelligence order.[163]

The specifics notwithstanding, the intelligence executive orders themselves were part of a concerted effort to preempt legislation that would have established tighter congressional control and more specific restrictions on the conduct of intelligence agencies. The connection was explicit for Ford's executive order on intelligence organization (E.O. 11905, February 19, 1976), which was issued in the aftermath of high-profile investigations of intelligence abuses including, among other things, surveillance and infiltration of domestic groups, interception of mail, assassination attempts, and destabilizing foreign democratic governments. The Senate convened a committee to investigate the allegations (the Church Committee), and pressure was again building for some sort of comprehensive legislative overhaul and more extensive congressional control over intelligence operations. As Eisenhower did in the 1950s, though, Ford was able to deflect the move toward a legislative charter by establishing his own investigating body (the Rockefeller Commission) and issuing his intelligence executive order, which reorganized the top levels of the community and instituted some prohibitions on intelligence operations. "The entire exercise," writes Frank Smist, "was an attempt by the administration to prevent legislative action that would permanently inscribe congressional oversight into law."[164]

Carter continued this pattern of presidential preemption. Although Carter publicly supported the idea of charter legislation, which was under congressional consideration during much of his term, he and his senior advisors supported "broad and clear statutory authority for the intelligence agencies but not a level of legislative detail that would infringe on [the president's] authority or hamper the agencies' effectiveness and flexibility."[165] Both Vice President Mondale and CIA director Stansfield Turner advised Carter that acceding to a legislative charter posed significant risks, which the president could deflect by continuing the executive order strategy: "The danger with endorsing charters is that the legislative drafting could get out of control in the Congress and result in excessive legislative detail that would limit flexibility in the use of intelligence agencies and hamper their effectiveness. However, the Congress is moving ahead. . . . Our judgment is that you should take the initiative on the principle of endorsing charters and legislation."[166] The Senate Select Committee on Intelligence was already drafting charter legislation, but agreed to delay the process while the administration conducted its own study of intelligence organization. In August 1977 Carter announced that although he still supported the idea of charter legislation, he would proceed with his own reorganization through executive order.[167]

The distinctive feature of Carter's intelligence executive order (E.O. 12036), which he issued in January 1978, was a lengthy list of prohibitions on intelligence activities.[168] It significantly extended the restrictions that Ford had included in Executive Order 11905, and remedied what Carter's advisors felt were loopholes in 11905's prohibitions. The Ford order, for example, prohibited foreign intelligence agents from "infiltration or undisclosed participation within the United States in any organization for the purpose of reporting on or influencing its activities or members" except for some situations involving law enforcement investigations.[169] Carter attorney general Griffin B. Bell considered this language wholly inadequate. "While appearing to narrowly restrict infiltration," he wrote the president, "it actually allowed unrestricted infiltration for unspecified purposes."[170] One example: Ford's order explicitly excluded the FBI from the provision. To remedy this flaw, Carter's order included a much broader and more detailed ban, extending it to all government employees, and requiring approval by the attorney general of all such operations.[171] In addition, Carter's order prohibited the intelligence community from engaging in medical experimentation, participating indirectly in banned activities, and conducting or assisting in law enforcement investigations within the United States (except in certain situations involving foreign intelligence agencies, terrorists, or international drug traffic). The order "was primarily concerned with restrictions and oversight."[172]

Within one year of taking office, Reagan replaced Carter's intelligence order with his own, Executive Order 12333 (December 8, 1981).[173] In it, Reagan shifted the emphasis from placing restrictions on intelligence operations to providing positive grants of authority. Bretton Sciaroni, who served as counsel to the president's Intelligence Oversight Board, described the contrasts between the two orders:

> President Carter's Executive Order on intelligence, the successor to President Ford's Order, was cast largely in negative terms, emphasizing what the intelligence community *could not* do in its operations, rather than what it *could do*. . . . President Reagan's Orders eased some of President Carter's restrictions, and set forth what *could* be done by the intelligence community. When he issued the new Orders, President Reagan stated that they were 'designed to provide America's intelligence community with clearer, more positive guidance and to remove the aura of suspicion and mistrust that can hobble our intelligence efforts.' "[174]

One major difference between the orders, which would assume additional significance in the Iran-Contra affair, is that the Carter order limited "special operations"—meaning covert operations—to agencies within the intelligence community, and further stipulated that only the CIA could conduct such activities unless the president determined "that another agency is more likely to achieve a particular objective" (E.O. 12036, § 2–306). The order also prohibited intelligence agencies from soliciting third-party individuals, organizations, or government agencies to "undertake activities forbidden by this order or by applicable law" (E.O. 12036, § 2–307). Had this restriction been in place, the Reagan administration would not have been able to claim, as it did in a memorandum written by IOB counsel Sciaroni, that the Boland amendment (about which more below) did not apply to the NSC because the NSC "was not a member of the intelligence community and that the legislation to which the Boland Amendment was attached did not affect the NSC."[175] Reagan's order dropped the language limiting special operations to intelligence community agencies, although it replicated the language limiting such activities to the CIA unless the president determined that another agency—this time not just those in the intelligence community—was more likely to achieve an objective (E.O. 12333, § I.8(e)).

This pattern of presidential initiative and flexibility stands in sharp contrast to Congress's largely ineffective attempts to enact meaningful restrictions and oversight. Even the intelligence reforms of the 1970s—without a doubt the most important in congressional history—proved clumsy and unproductive. In response to the same events that triggered Ford's intelligence order, Congress tried to rein in what it saw as an out-of-control intelligence community. In 1974 Congress amended the Foreign Assistance Act of 1961 to require written presidential authorization and reporting of intelligence operations (distinguished from the act of collecting intelligence information).[176] Section 662, known as the Hughes-Ryan amendment, stipulated that no funds be spent on operational activities "unless and until the President finds that each such operation is important to the national security of the United States and reports, in a timely fashion, a description and scope of such operation to the appropriate committees of the Congress." In enacting these "finding" and "reporting" requirements, Congress followed what would become a standard legislative refrain: if Congress could not control or prevent covert operations, it could at least insist on some accountability by making the president certify that they were necessary and report them.

But presidents found the provision easy to outmaneuver, as the limits of this language make clear: it does not require advance notification and places no restrictions on the scope of permissible operational activities. More important, presidents discovered that in enacting Hughes-Ryan, Congress had inadvertently given formal legal notice that covert activities did, in fact, exist and that the president was implicitly authorized to conduct them. Presidents could henceforth point to statutory language permitting "operations in foreign countries, other than activities intended solely for obtaining necessary intelligence" as conceding the legitimacy of the very type of activity that Congress was trying to control.

The same thing occurred six years later, when Congress tried again to enact specific charter legislation for the intelligence community. By the time Congress was finished with proposed charter legislation in 1980, "a comprehensive 263 page charter . . . [was] trimmed down into the two-page Intelligence Oversight Act of 1980 . . . which did little more than codify the executive practice followed by the Carter Administration over the previous four years."[177] In the 1980 act, Congress reduced the number of committees to which the president had to report, required the president to keep these intelligence committees "fully and currently informed" of all existing and anticipated intelligence activities, and required reporting of intelligence operations (meaning covert activity) in a "timely fashion."

In any case, the notification and finding provisions failed to prevent the abuses that emerged from the Iran-Contra scandal. Although it is not my intent to offer a comprehensive analysis of the events of 1984–1987, the history shows how easy it was for the president and those acting on his behalf to maneuver within the congressionally imposed boundaries on the conduct of covert intelligence operations (as well as to ignore those restrictions that proved burdensome).[178]

At the heart of Iran-Contra was the question of whether units within the executive branch had broken the law in providing assistance to the Nicaraguan Contras, a group fighting against the existing regime there. In October 1984 Congress enacted (with the president's signature) a provision intended to stop U.S. support for the Contras. The Boland amendment specified that no money available to "the Central Intelligence Agency, the Department of Defense, or any other agency or entity involved in intelligence activities" could be used to support the Contras. In place, then, were three explicit provisions designed to restrain intelligence activities: the need for the president to issue a finding for covert operations, the need to report those operations to Congress, and Congress's use of its power of the purse to prohibit a specified activity.

However one views the ensuing events—as either a constitutional crisis or a policy dispute—there is no question that the legislative restrictions were ineffective in preventing the White House from doing what it wanted to do. The contours of the events are clear enough: after the Boland amendment, the National Security Council took over the covert operations. Money for Contra aid came initially from wealthy individuals and foreign countries. Eventually Col. Oliver North hit on the idea of selling U.S. weapons to the Iranian government at marked-up prices, and funneling the profits to the Contras. This would have the additional benefit of, North hoped, securing the release of American hostages being held in the Middle East.

What is clear is that the executive branch had no trouble circumventing the legislative proscriptions. With the CIA barred from providing support, the operational center moved to the National Security Council (which, the administration would later argue, was not an intelligence agency and thus not covered by the Boland amendment). With expenditures barred, NSC personnel raised money from wealthy individuals, from foreign countries, and finally from the sale of weapons to the Iranian government. The need for the president to issue a finding led to retroactive actions, in which the president signed findings that justified covert operations well after those operations were under way. In other cases, operations went forward with no finding at all. The requirement that covert operations be reported to Congress was interpreted broadly and sometimes ignored.

The Minority contribution to the *Report of the Congressional Committees Investigating the Iran-Contra Affair* is instructive, since it shows how elusive effective congressional oversight can be. In defending the president, congressional Republicans argued that (1) the Boland amendment did not apply to the National Security Council, since that body was not part of the "intelligence community" as defined in other statutes and executive orders;[179] (2) the Hughes-Ryan findings need not be in writing;[180] and (3) presidents can delay congressional notification for as long as they deem necessary.[181]

Indeed, the Office of Legal Counsel wrote in 1986 that Congress had little power in the intelligence field. In an analysis of whether Reagan had complied with the law when he failed to notify Congress of the Iran-Contra initiatives, OLC argued that the president had "presumptively exclusive authority in foreign affairs," and that the "timely notification" provisions should "be read to leave the President with virtually unfettered discretion to choose the right moment for making the required notification" to Congress.[182] That is to say, presidents would be well within the law to interpret "timely" as never.

In the aftermath of Iran-Contra, Congress attempted once again to reassert its oversight authority. In 1989 it established the position of inspector general within the CIA, and required the IG to report biannually on problems found within the intelligence community.[183] In 1991 Congress replaced the reporting requirements of Hughes-Ryan with more specific provisions enacted after the Iran-Contra failure. The new language requires the president to immediately report to Congress any illegal intelligence activities, including covert action, and specifies new requirements for presidential determinations regarding covert activities. Unlike Hughes-Ryan, which was unclear on whether findings had to be oral or written, and on when the findings had to be issued, the new language is far more precise. The 1991 revision required determinations to be in writing, prohibited retroactive findings that justify an activity that has already taken place, requires specific mention of the government organization authorized to engage in the activity, and prohibits any activities that violate the Constitution or statutes.

The struggle between Congress and the executive branch over the structure and organization of the intelligence community continues, as has the pattern of presidential dominance. Although Congress plays a more central role in intelligence policy than it did before the Church Committee, and has relied on the Permanent Select Committees on Intelligence to "bring about an equal partnership between the legislative and executive branches,"[184] it has had only minor successes in direct confrontations with the president. Support for executive primacy remains strong.

Congress tried several more times in the 1990s to impose organizational reforms, and even to create a statutory charter, but legislators had no more success than they did in the 1980s (or 1970s, or 1950s). Once more presidents relied on their executive authority to fend off congressional action. In late 1991, in response to congressional efforts to again take up the issue of intelligence reorganization and charter legislation, President Bush issued National Security Review Directive 29, which called for a comprehensive assessment of intelligence organization. Based on the results of this review, Bush initiated several administrative reforms but also used the opportunity to deflect calls for congressional action. In testimony on two proposed bills under consideration in the Senate, CIA director Robert Gates argued for executive action over legislation: "We have responded substantially in nearly all of the areas identified in the proposed legislation as in need of change, and yet we have done so in a way so that if in a year or two we are determined that further adjustment is needed in these structures, we can do so quickly and efficiently, without the need to seek new statutory authority."[185] In 1992 Gates created several internal CIA task forces, which recommended some minor reforms, but the main function was to once again deflect congressional reform (in 1992 both House and Senate intelligence committee chairs introduced legislation that would have created a unified intelligence structure under a director of national intelligence, an effort that was opposed by both the CIA and the defense agencies because it would have reduced their control over intelligence assets).[186]

But concern over the details of administrative structure were supplanted—spectacularly so—by the Aldrich Ames espionage fiasco, which became public in 1994. Over a decade of spying, Ames, a high-level employee in the CIA's Directorate of Operations, had revealed to Soviet intelligence key details about U.S. operations, including the names of top-level spies in the Soviet Union. When an investigation uncovered tepid CIA responses to warning signs that something was amiss—Ames's payment of hundreds of thousands of dollars in cash for a house, for example, or spending $30,000 per month on credit card bills—the agency had to defend itself against charges that it had "consistently provided the government with faulty assessments and tolerated inexcusable security breaches in its ranks," and was redundant in a post–cold war world.[187]

One congressional response was the establishment of the Commission on the Roles and Capabilities of the United States Intelligence Community authorized as part of the fiscal 1995 Intelligence Authorization Act. The commission was charged with a broad review of the intelligence function (the authorizing legislation stipulated nineteen separate questions covering virtually every aspect of intelligence roles, missions, organization, and resources).

The commission, in its final report, came out decisively in favor of continued executive dominance. It recommended a wide range of new or revised executive orders that would, among other things, expand the jurisdiction of intelligence agencies to include global criminal activity and proliferation, and clarify the use of intelligence assets in international law enforcement investigations. More important, it called on the president to implement the commission's overall recommendations via a new executive order on intelligence, to replace Reagan's Executive Order 12333.[188] On congressional oversight, the commission took a careful stance, recognizing the importance of "rigorous and intensive" review of the intelligence community.[189] Nevertheless the report also catalogued the negative aspects of oversight, citing the "informed witnesses" who argued that "oversight by the Congress has become so burdensome and intrusive that it is having a negative effect on intelligence operations."[190] Although the report did not say as much explicitly, it discouraged Congress from tinkering with the statutory authority of intelligence agencies and argued repeatedly that the best route to reform was reorganization within the boundaries of the existing laws. The one change suggested in congressional oversight was to eliminate limits on how many years members of the House and Senate select intelligence committees could serve.[191]

In 1995 and 1996, the staff of the House Permanent Select Committee on Intelligence conducted its own review of intelligence organization. Their report, released in 1996, advocated more centralization of authority within the DCIA, although not to the point of consolidating all intelligence functions into a single organization. Even though the report's focus was specifically on "issues which might require legislative remedies," it did not make any major recommendations on, for example, charter legislation, congressional notification on covert activities, or congressional restrictions on the conduct of intelligence activities.[192]

Congress did make some minor organizational changes in 1996, as part of the fiscal year 1997 Intelligence Authorization Act. But the final legislation was "drastically scale[d] back" from the initial versions, which had significantly enhanced the DCIA's power over budgets and appointments.[193] The Senate had originally included a provision that would have required disclosure of the overall intelligence budget, which was removed in conference; the House version contained language that barred the CIA from using journalists as spies, but the conference bill added a provision that allowed the DCIA to waive the restriction.[194]

Since the 1970s Congress has played a larger role in overseeing the conduct of intelligence activities. Nevertheless legislators have shown great reluctance to impose a legislative framework on what has been, for five decades, a predominantly executive area. For all of the attention Congress has devoted to intelligence oversight, it still has not imposed clear statutory guidelines that define impermissible intelligence agency activity, created a statutory charter for the CIA or other intelligence community agencies, or defined the organizational relationships and authorities of the various agencies.

Congress Rethinks the Executive Order Ban on Assassinations

A final example shows that Congress remains unwilling—or unable—to significantly alter the pattern of executive control over intelligence. A key part of Ford's intelligence reorganization executive order was the provision barring intelligence agencies from "engag[ing] in, or conspir[ing] to engage in, political assassination."[195] With the stroke of his pen, Ford instituted a prohibition that every succeeding president has acceded to. It represented a significant reform, and the first presidential effort to impose a public, external restraint on the intelligence community. As for the authority to issue such an order in the absence of any explicit legislative grant, presidents have cited their constitutional powers as commander in chief and chief executive, as well as the 1947 National Security Act's broad and ambiguous charge that the CIA may carry out "such other functions" as the National Security Council "may from time to time direct."

Ford's ban on assassination had some patent shortcomings as did the executive orders that followed. They failed to define "political assassination," did not specify the penalties for violating the provision, and can be circumvented under a variety of conditions. One author has argued that the provisions would be nullified in the event of a declaration of war, action taken in self-defense under Article 51 of the United Nations Charter, or an assassination ordered directly by the president.[196] The Army's judge advocate general concluded that although assassination is barred by executive order, "its intent was not to limit lawful self defense options against legitimate threats to the national security of the United States or individual U.S. citizens. Acting consistent with the Charter of the United Nations, a decision by the President to employ clandestine, low visibility or overt force would not constitute assassination if U.S. military forces were employed against the combatant forces of another nation, or a terrorist or other organization whose actions pose a threat to the security of the United States."[197]

Despite the evident ambiguities, the ban immediately became an important symbol of U.S. high-mindedness. As an executive order, however, it has always been and remains vulnerable to a future president's decision to rescind it, and questions persist about its applicability in specific cases of U.S. military action. Some scholars have argued that the order is the worst possible mechanism for implementing such a policy, because its ambiguities create uncertainties that can hamper legitimate operations: "Possibly the worst state of affairs surrounds the domestic executive order outlawing assassination. Setting forth a prohibition without clearly delineating what it means is arguably more damaging than having no order at all. Not only does the absence of definitional guidelines render the order subject to abuse through exceedingly narrow interpretations . . . it has the potential to inhibit valid operations out of fear that the ban might be violated. The failure of the executive order to outline exactly what it prohibits has set planners and operators adrift."[198]

In 1986, for example, Reagan ordered a military strike against Libya in retaliation for that country's support for specific terrorist activities. U.S. aircraft attacked, among other targets, Libyan leader Muammar Qadhafi's headquarters and home. The administration denied that it was trying to kill Qadhafi, although it did point to Article 51 of the UN Charter as authorizing the operation.[199] Later on, however, officials argued that Qadhafi *was* a legitimate target when he was present at a military installation.[200] The debate centered on some semantic distinctions: would his death have been assassination if he had died as the result of an attack not specifically designed to kill him? Michael Schmitt, for one, argues that this interpretation is "inconsistent with the Church Report, the proposed [congressional] legislation, and analysis under international law."[201]

The Persian Gulf War raised a similar set of issues. When the air force chief of staff publicly identified Iraqi president Saddam Hussein as a legitimate military target, Secretary of Defense Richard Cheney fired him; even so, State Department counsel Abraham Sofaer declared that Hussein's death would not be illegal if it occurred during a military operation.[202]

The same issue arose once again in 1993, when President Clinton ordered a cruise-missile strike against the Iraqi intelligence headquarters. Clinton defended the strike as justified under UN Article 51, based on evidence that the Iraqi government had plotted to assassinate former president George Bush.[203]

As I noted above, there is no question that Ford's intelligence order was motivated by his desire to preclude Congress from enacting more stringent legislation concerning the intelligence community. Nevertheless, Congress has on many occasions tried to push through a statutory prohibition on assassinations, with legislative provisions much harsher than those in the executive orders. Senator Frank Church introduced S. 2825 in 1975, which would have made it illegal to assassinate a foreign official outside the United States. In 1976 a House bill set a prison term of one year for any intelligence operative who kills someone. S. 2525, the Intelligence Reorganization Act of 1978, went much further, prohibiting the killing of "any foreign official because of such official's office or position or because of such official's political views, actions, or statements" during peacetime, and making violation punishable by life imprisonment. In 1980 both chambers considered legislation that would have given statutory affirmation to Carter's executive order on intelligence.[204] None of these efforts succeeded.

To add to the confusion, at other times legislators have tried to rescind the executive order prohibition, arguing that the ban undercuts U.S. security interests by unnecessarily hampering military and intelligence activities. In 1991 Representative Bob McEwen (R-Ohio) introduced a resolution indicating congressional support for revoking the assassinations ban in Executive Order 12333 until Saddam Hussein complied with all applicable UN Security Council resolutions.[205] More recently, a public debate about the wisdom of the assassinations ban followed renewed concern about Hussein's capability to develop nuclear, biological, or chemical weapons, and the U.S. attacks against Osama bin Laden. The argument was that the ban required U.S. officials to initiate large-scale military attacks when their real goal was to kill a particular person. A bipartisan coalition of legislators—including Senators Dianne Feinstein (D-Calif.) and Orrin Hatch (R-Utah) and Representatives Lee Hamilton (D-Ind.) and Bob Barr (R-Ga.)—began questioning the ban,[206] and Barr introduced legislation (H.R. 4681) that would nullify all executive order proscriptions on assassination.

In the end, Congress has failed to either restrict or expand the president's authority to order assassinations. The ban, like most intelligence policy as a whole, remains a matter of executive prerogative, subject to evasion, rescission, or modification as the commander in chief sees fit.

The executive-legislative struggle over the control of government secrecy and the conduct of intelligence operations repeats the pattern observed in budget policy and regulatory reform: the development of new state capabilities, an ongoing struggle for control over this new power, and a clear trend toward presidential ascendance. Unlike budget or regulatory policy—whose antecedents are clearly legislative in character—intelligence and classification powers emanate largely from implicit presidential vestments, something that makes effective legislative control even more difficult. Despite numerous attempts at establishing some sort of statutory framework, Congress has only minimal success in constraining executive activism. The executive order has been the president's tool of choice both for exercising control over these vital government functions and for deflecting congressional interventions.

Six

Executive Orders and Civil Rights

IN PREVIOUS CHAPTERS I have documented the ways in which presidents have used executive orders to create or alter institutions and processes that have grown central to executive leadership; to carve out new policy responsibilities in the face of congressional acquiescence and to protect those responsibilities from congressional encroachment; and to solidify their control over executive branch administration. All of these patterns are consistent with what the new institutional economics framework predicts. In each case presidents, by relying on their inherent or delegated legal authority and in some cases by exceeding it, have managed to outmaneuver Congress and take advantage of the discretion that inevitably accompanies broad and general grants of constitutional and statutory authority. In the competition for control over institutions, presidents have significant advantages stemming from their relative unity contrasted with Congress's collective processes, and from judicial readings that usually favor executive authority even when Congress tries to contain it.

But the ability to create and alter is a two-edged sword, since organizations, once they are established, may be able to deflect presidential pressure by creating their own constituencies and mobilizing political supporters. In other words, presidents might establish a new institution or process only to find that it resists their (and future presidents') efforts to direct it. This is the classic principal-agent problem at the core of economic institutionalism: how can a principal (a president, in this case) be sure that an agent (a policy or advisory organization) will faithfully implement his policy wishes? Or how can a president control structures and institutions left over from a previous administration? The existing theory of executive orders and presidential prerogative offers the stock answer that what was enacted by executive order can be undone by simply issuing another order. As the history of presidential involvement in civil rights shows, the process is not so simple. Over several decades, presidents expanded the scope of federal civil rights protections, using their constitutional and statutory powers to institute new policies by executive order. Not all of these policies were effective. Many, though, had a substantive impact on racial equality, and most helped shape the public debate on civil rights.

In making the case that the president played a key role in using executive orders to promote a civil rights agenda in the three decades before the Civil Rights Act of 1964, I do not wish to fall into the trap of historical determinism—of oversimplifying the convoluted and complex chain of events, issues, and personalities that shaped civil rights policy into a rigid cause-and-effect argument about presidential power. When explaining historical events political scientists, according to Russell Riley, are especially prone to attribute too much importance to individual initiative by presidents, and his work challenges the thesis that presidents were especially active in civil rights, in any case.[1] "Presidential contributions toward the processes of black equality," he concludes, "have tended to be overstated, [while] presidential contributions to the process of suppressing movements for racial equality have tended to be understated."[2] More specifically, Riley objects to the notion that presidents elevated civil rights out of a concern for justice and equality; rather, he argues, presidents were responding to shifts in political pressure that *forced* them to take seriously the demands of groups pushing for racial equality.

The progression of civil rights executive orders between 1941 and the 1970s also indicates that presidents may indeed have trouble controlling the institutions that they create by executive orders. The succession of civil rights orders tended to commit future presidents to the path that had already been established, and it is now impossible for a president to undo even the most controversial policies that have arisen through executive action. Affirmative action, or the taking of race into consideration in contracting, employment, and college admissions, emerged most sharply out of a 1965 executive order and the implementing regulations that followed over the next five years. In the 1980s, despite concerted opposition from the Justice Department under Ronald Reagan, affirmative action survived repeated attempts to scale it back. In the 1990s, as state-level action and federal court decisions narrowed the scope of permissible affirmative action (or eliminated it altogether), Clinton struggled to keep control of what had become an explosive political issue.

In other areas of presidential policy making, what was once controversial eventually became accepted as normal operating procedure. With affirmative action the pattern was reversed, as what was initially relatively noncontroversial has become the rallying point for opponents and a litmus test for supporters. Yet the programs and institutions endure, an object lesson in the structural politics of institutional control.

Each successive presidential step—in contracting, in housing, in employment, in the military—set a precedent establishing the government's authority to counter long-standing discrimination. In each of these areas, congressional action followed presidential action—often by several decades, but it did follow, in every case. From the perspective of present-day politics, it can be difficult to appreciate how difficult executive action—in some areas that we now consider to be not even remotely controversial, in others that remain contentions—was at the time.

The early efforts to proceed via executive order, notes historian Hugh Davis Graham, "were halting and largely ineffectual" until Kennedy's decision to establish the President's Committee on Equal Employment Opportunity in 1961. "But all of these efforts contained within them the seeds of successful future attempts, eventually on a massive scale."[3] Executive orders ultimately cleared the path toward the statutory accomplishments of the 1960s.

In the last thirty years, executive orders have become less important because of the scope of legislative activity. The watershed moment for civil rights in the United States was undoubtedly 1964–1965, when Congress passed two of the most important laws ever enacted. The Civil Rights Act of 1964 and the Voting Rights Act of 1965 constituted the most significant progress on civil rights since Reconstruction. The 1964 act, writes Graham, "was by any comparative measure a spectacular accomplishment,"[4] and Lyndon Johnson considered the Voting Rights Act as his "greatest accomplishment."[5] The Fair Housing Act of 1968 went far beyond the provisions of Kennedy's housing order in barring discrimination by organizations and individuals involved either directly or indirectly in federally assisted housing.

Yet alongside this record of legislative achievement, the presidency played a key role in using executive power to advance civil rights. Indeed, there are few areas in which executive orders have played a more significant role in effecting dramatic and widespread policies. Prior to the legislative juggernaut of 1964 and 1965, civil rights had been almost an exclusively executive domain, with each president since Franklin Roosevelt putting the weight of presidential authority behind administrative attempts to end racial discrimination (though not all of the efforts were successful). And although most of the fundamental questions of the civil rights era are settled, those that remain—particularly with respect to the divisive question of affirmative action—ultimately revolve around the appropriate exercise of executive branch, and therefore presidential, authority to pursue social goals.

Reliance on Executive Power

The presidency was the first of the three federal institutions to enter the civil rights field after Reconstruction, with the courts following (with the Supreme Court's *Brown* decision in 1954) and Congress having the final say, first with the Civil Rights Act of 1957 and ultimately with the 1964 Civil Rights Act and the 1965 Voting Rights Act. With executive orders and other forms of intervention, presidents forged the path that ultimately produced the 1964–1965 acts. In the remaining areas of unresolved conflict over racial preferences and affirmative action, moreover, presidential initiatives still set the agenda. My thesis is that presidential initiative played a decisive role in broadening the scope of civil rights policies, in a sequence of increasingly effective presidential responses, which ultimately pulled along both the courts and Congress.

After Reconstruction, presidential action was the logical starting point for a renewed assault on racial discrimination, since most other avenues had been closed off by a combination of judicial interpretation and congressional intransigence. In the notorious 1896 *Plessy v. Ferguson* decision, the Supreme Court held that the Fourteenth Amendment of the Constitution did not prohibit discrimination by state governments; that decision, along with a series of cases in which the Court struck down federal civil rights laws as unconstitutional (the *Civil Rights* cases), left Congress unable to enact a statutory end to discrimination by either state governments or private entities, even if it had the inclination.[6] One of the few options left was a "limited fight against segregation" in those areas "within the sphere of federal jurisdiction," including discrimination in federal government activities themselves.[7] This path led directly to the president.

Franklin Roosevelt was the first twentieth-century president to take the civil rights issue seriously, but this was not for any lack of trying on the part of civil rights organizations; the notion that the president could spur progress in civil rights had existed well before the New Deal. These early efforts to prompt presidential action got nowhere, partly because presidents in the early twentieth century were hardly sympathetic to the cause of equal rights, and partly because presidential power itself was commonly viewed as more limited before the New Deal. In any case, no president, Democrat or Republican, could afford to alienate the South by pushing too hard on civil rights, and the chief executive often mirrored the dominant racial attitudes of the time. As a result, "no twentieth-century Republican president had measured up to the Lincoln legacy."[8]

In 1905 Theodore Roosevelt declared his support for segregationist policies in his notorious Lincoln Day speech, and followed up by ordering summary dishonorable discharges for several companies of African-American soldiers after reports that the city of Brownsville, Texas, had been looted.[9] Calvin Coolidge and Herbert Hoover rebuffed efforts to secure federal antilynching legislation, and also refused requests that they create a presidential commission on the economic and social conditions of blacks.[10]

Democratic presidents offered no more hope. Although Woodrow Wilson received an unusually large number of minority votes in 1912, his secretary of the treasury and postmaster general quickly reinstated the pre–Civil War practice of segregation in their respective departments.[11] In 1913 and 1914 William Monroe Trotter, publisher of the African-American newspaper *The Guardian*, tried to persuade Wilson to end these practices by executive order.[12] Not only did this effort fail, but it prompted Wilson to publicly declare his view that segregation was beneficial to both whites and blacks; moreover, Wilson regarded Trotter's attempt to use black support for him in the 1912 election as leverage to obtain the order as "blackmail."[13]

Congress had, in fact, taken a few tentative steps in the early 1930s, enacting language for a variety of New Deal programs that barred discrimination based on race, but the provisions were interpreted loosely and even then hardly enforced.[14] Nondiscrimination language written into the original civil service statute in 1883, and reaffirmed in 1940, went unenforced because there was no entity charged with implementation, and no penalties for violating the law.[15] Indeed, southerners did not object strongly to the legislative proscriptions because they considered the laws irrelevant.[16]

Yet it remains an interesting question why civil rights groups first looked to the presidency as the key authority for making progress in this area. By the 1930s, of course, legislative hostility to significant civil rights legislation was firmly entrenched, largely a function of southern opposition to federal intervention of any kind. One explanation is that civil rights emerged as a permanent fixture on the federal agenda at precisely the same time that presidential power—exemplified by the transformative politics of FDR and the necessities of wartime emergency—grew to unprecedented levels. The dramatic shift of black voters from the Republican to the Democratic Party, black migration to the North, and the realignment of black voters to the Democratic Party by 1936 created an opportunity to demonstrate the importance of minority votes to the party's political fortunes.

Roosevelt's first term, in fact, resulted in the near unanimous view that the New Deal offered blacks very little, and that it often made their situation worse. Roosevelt's support for nondiscrimination was by no means assured, given his concerns about alienating southern Democrats in Congress whom he needed for higher-priority New Deal legislation.[17] In the words of Thomas Corcoran, a close presidential advisor, "when Roosevelt came in 1933, there were many more things to worry about than what happened to civil rights . . . we weren't concerned about civil rights."[18] FDR repeatedly refused to support antilynching legislation, and established the Fair Employment Practices Committee (FEPC) only after proponents threatened a large—and potentially embarrassing—public protest in 1941. Nevertheless, there were glimmers of hope that Roosevelt might be open to using executive power: early on, the administration declared that there would be no discrimination in New Deal programs, although in practice there were "plenty of loopholes for" racial bias.[19] Secretary of the Interior Harold Ickes ended segregation in departmental bathrooms and cafeterias, and he insisted that the Public Works Administration hire blacks for skilled positions.[20] Roosevelt's pathbreaking FEPC order had an antecedent in executive action he took in 1935, when he issued an executive order prohibiting the just-created Works Progress Administration from discriminating "on any grounds whatsoever."[21] But throughout the 1930s the FDR administration "had responded intermittently and usually timidly" to the demands of civil rights groups.[22] In part, argues Alan Brinkley, this was because the dominant conception of New Deal liberalism defined social problems as a function of class rather than of race. Instead of special remedies for discrimination, the "best hope for aiding oppressed minorities was economic reform."[23]

Yet there is no doubt that the 1930s proved to be a crucial decade in the establishment of an executive civil rights strategy. In casting their lot with Roosevelt, African Americans traded in their seventy-year Republican loyalties and became a visible constituency to a party and a president committed to an active federal role in economic and social policy. As the crisis in Europe intensified and the United States began mobilizing for war, civil rights groups turned their attention to black employment in the defense industry, a matter squarely within the domain of executive branch authority. This combination—the need for full mobilization, the application of direct public pressure, and a focus on eliminating discrimination within federal government activities—resulted in the executive order strategy.

The beginnings of a presidency-based civil rights strategy was clearly the establishment—through Executive Order 8802—of the Fair Employment Practices Committee in 1941.[24] Although the committee itself was ineffective in enforcing nondiscrimination, it did, critically, establish civil rights as a central federal policy issue.[25] Writing in 1953, Louis Ruchames called Executive Order 8802, which established the FEPC, "the most important effort in the history of the country to eliminate discrimination in employment by use of government authority."[26] From that point on, civil rights groups *expected* presidential leadership in civil rights policy, at the minimum.

The creation of the FEPC also demonstrates how civil rights groups used the techniques of mass politics to place civil rights on the presidential agenda, ushering in the era of civil rights executive orders. After meetings in 1940 between FDR and officials of the National Urban League and the National Association for the Advancement of Colored People (NAACP) produced no demonstrable change in discriminatory practices within the defense industry, A. Philip Randolph "concluded that he and other black leaders had exhausted the conference method of handling black problems," and that more direct strategies were needed.[27] Randolph began organizing a mass demonstration to be held in the capital city, scheduled for the summer of 1941. The newly organized March on Washington Committee put FDR on notice that it expected a broad assault on discrimination, to be implemented through executive orders. It asked for an executive order barring contract awards to any company or government arsenal that practiced racial discrimination; orders abolishing discrimination in the military and in worker training programs; an order abolishing discrimination in all federal government agencies; and legislation that would prevent unions from barring admission to blacks.[28]

At a time when World War II was in full force and Roosevelt had already declared an unlimited national emergency, the March on Washington Movement (MOWM) changed the political calculus on civil rights questions. The president was forced to recognize that the costs of doing nothing on civil rights had grown large, and he concluded that he could not risk the international embarrassment of such a display "at a time when the semblance of unity was most essential to national prestige."[29] The costs of acting had also diminished, however, because Roosevelt's concern with placating congressional southerners had waned as the war brought into sharper relief the full measure of the president's emergency powers.

Although the MOWM failed to achieve its goals (indeed, Roosevelt failed to issue any of the requested orders), its leaders did accept a compromise whereby FDR created the Fair Employment Practices Committee by executive order in return for cancellation of the march. In Executive Order 8802, Roosevelt affirmed an administration policy of nondiscrimination in vocational training programs, mandated a nondiscrimination clause in all defense contracts, and established the FEPC to receive complaints about discrimination. It was, concludes Gerald Rosenberg, a demonstration "that blacks had the power to exert pressure on government."[30]

Because it was solely an instrument of executive power, however, the FEPC was hamstrung and made no significant progress. It lacked any powers of investigation, and did not have the power to cancel contracts for violating the nondiscrimination provision (this was left to the individual contracting agencies). The FEPC was limited to the tasks of holding hearings (although it could not compel testimony) and publicizing discrimination claims. The committee had no staff to speak of, and it faced great opposition within the executive branch itself, where "federal managers instinctively resented a new watchdog agency whose very inquiries seemed to insult both their competence and their sense of fairness."[31] The newly formed committee held a series of public hearings in late 1941 and early 1942, but quickly faced criticism from all sides. Supporters of a strong FEPC blasted the committee for not taking stronger action against clearly evidenced racism in major defense contractors, while opponents—especially in the South—viewed the FEPC with great suspicion.

In July 1942, without warning, Roosevelt transferred the FEPC from the Office of Production Management to the War Manpower Commission, a move that ended the FEPC's status as an independent presidential agency and left "little doubt . . . that its purpose was to restrict the committee's activities."[32] Despite Roosevelt's assurances that the step was designed to strengthen the committee and give new life to Executive Order 8802, within six months the FEPC disintegrated. After the head of the War Manpower Commission, Paul McNutt, canceled FEPC hearings scheduled for January 1943, a majority of the FEPC members and a number of staff attorneys resigned. Thus did the "the first FEPC essentially [collapse] amid mutual recriminations."[33]

But civil rights groups refused to accept the demise of the FEPC quietly. Public protest against the ineffectiveness of the first FEPC, and of Roosevelt's tepid support, led to Executive Order 9346 in May 1943. The order reestablished the FEPC under the president, expanded its jurisdiction to cover labor unions, provided the committee with a fulltime staff, and granted it additional powers to take action in response to charges of discrimination.[34] The reconstituted FEPC was more active than its predecessor, and disputes over its future moved to Congress. As early as 1942, legislation was introduced to establish a permanent FEPC,[35] and by 1944 opponents of the committee were moving to eviscerate it. In 1944 emboldened congressional conservatives, led by Representative Howard W. Smith (D-Va.), created a Special Committee to Investigate Executive Agencies. Although the ostensible purpose of this committee was to reassert congressional prerogatives against a wartime presidency, it soon became clear that a key goal was to undercut the FEPC.[36]

Once again, a dispute between the president and Congress over the extent of executive authority evolved in ways that demonstrate the president's ability to maneuver within legislative constraints. Both the first and the second FEPCs were funded outside the normal congressional appropriations process, using "emergency" funds appropriated to the presidency for discretionary use. But in 1944 Senator Richard Russell (D-Ga.) sponsored an amendment to an appropriations bill that restricted the president's ability to spend money on agencies created by executive order. The Russell amendment "prohibited federal funding of any agency that had been in existence for more than one year (including those established by executive order) without a specific congressional appropriation," and included language that apparently would prohibit a president from creating a new FEPC without explicit congressional approval.[37] Although the amendment was written in general terms, Russell was clearly targeting the FEPC.[38] With this legislative language in place, Congress abolished the FEPC in 1946, appropriating funds only so that the FEPC could liquidate.[39] In five years, the FEPC had failed, on the whole, to dislodge persistent discrimination either in the federal government or among private contractors. It was a potent symbol, however, and had an impact that extended far beyond its narrow administrative borders. In establishing the precedent of federal government action, it ensured that "all subsequent debate was cast in its image and defined by its terms."[40]

But the Russell amendment proved to be only a minor impediment to the creation of new presidential committees. Some committees, such as Truman's Committee on Civil Rights, served for less than one year. Others were created on the basis of a distinction made between *presidential* commissions, which relied on legislative appropriations or allocations from the president's discretionary funds, and *interdepartmental* commissions, which were funded through contributions by executive branch departments. The Russell amendment made it more difficult for presidents to fund the former, so Truman (and later Eisenhower) reconfigured the committees as interdepartmental, something which required only that the committee address an issue relevant to more than one executive department. In December 1951 Truman established by executive order a Committee on Government Contract Compliance (CGCC) and charged it with investigating and reporting on the enforcement of nondiscrimination clauses in federal government contracts.[41]

The CGCC was only a small part of Truman's broad civil rights agenda. In December 1946 Truman issued Executive Order 9808, establishing the President's committee on Civil Rights.[42] Truman established the committee after a surge of racially motivated attacks—some against black veterans recently returned from World War II service—seemed to portend an era of violent racial tension. At a September 1946 meeting with civil rights groups, "David K. Niles, a Truman administrative assistant . . . suggested that a committee be created to investigate the problem and to recommend a program of corrective action. When Walter White [executive secretary of the NAACP] remarked that Congress might not be amenable to such a proposal, the President replied that he would act by creating the committee by executive order and finance it out of the president's contingent fund."[43] Truman's decision to issue the order was based at least partly on the belief that the Democratic Party had to do something to maintain the allegiance of blacks; the 1946 midterm elections had produced Republican congressional majorities for the first time since 1930, and demonstrated that "blacks might be drifting back to the Republican party after years of supporting the New Deal."[44]

The committee's report, *To Secure These Rights*, released in 1947, recommended a stunning sweep of civil rights initiatives: new and more powerful executive branch units to enforce existing civil rights laws; a permanent Commission on Civil Rights in the EOP; new laws to provide more protection against state action, including antilynching legislation; legislation protecting voting rights; an end to discrimination in the military; a ban on discrimination in all federal government activities, contracting, grants, and services; state laws guaranteeing equal access to public accommodations. The report put Truman in the midst of a crucial dilemma: whether to push the report's recommendations and destroy his base in the South or to move slowly and alienate key northern supporters.

Congress was in no hurry to adopt the legislative recommendations in the report, and Truman continued to rely on executive authority to advance his civil rights agenda and contrast himself with the Republican-controlled 80th Congress. In a special message to Congress on civil rights, delivered in February 1948, Truman advanced most of the proposals suggested by the 1947 committee, asking for congressional action on a number of fronts. At the same time, he pledged an aggressive presidential agenda, promising an executive order "containing a comprehensive restatement of the Federal non-discrimination policy," and administrative action within the new Department of Defense to end discrimination in the military.[45]

From this point on, Truman's action on civil rights was to be tied closely to strategic considerations surrounding the 1948 presidential election. Truman needed the support of blacks and he also had to fend off a challenge from the left by Henry Wallace. Heated opposition to Truman's civil rights message from southern legislators convinced Truman that any attempt to push legislation would fail, so he fell back on the executive order strategy in an attempt to prevent a complete revolt within the party. When Truman appeared to retreat too far, producing a "weasely and unsatisfactory" draft nondiscrimination order, civil rights groups once again mobilized to apply political pressure. The NAACP and A. Philip Randolph declared flatly that without strong executive action Truman could not count on their support in 1948.[46]

Truman could not prevent the schism with southern Democrats from widening, but he ultimately surmised that he could offset his increasing weakness in the South by bolstering his support among minorities there and in the North. In August 1948 Clark Clifford urged Truman to "speak out fully on his Civil Rights record," including his executive orders and support for FEPC legislation. Black votes in key states, Clifford argued, "will more than cancel out any votes the President may lose in the South."[47] As part of this strategy, Truman issued two major executive orders in June 1948 that were timed to maximize their electoral impact and boost his campaign just after the Democratic Convention.

The first of these two orders, E.O. 9980, established a Fair Employment Board as a unit of the Civil Service Commission, and charged it with enforcing nondiscrimination in employment within the federal government.[48] Although it had a much narrower reach than the earlier FEPCs— it applied only to government employment, and did not extend to government contractors, thus covering only 2 million government employees, against 20 million workers for contractors[49]—it received a warm reception from civil rights groups.[50]

Truman's second order was more significant, and once again highlights the close connection between the president's legal authority and the political imperatives of presidential leadership. Through World War II and demobilization, all branches of the military were strictly segregated, although on a few occasions acute military needs led to short-term integration of some units. Blacks were typically restricted to menial jobs (cooks, stewards, and so on), and had limited opportunities for training and advancement (in 1947, there were only two black officers in the navy, and none in the marine corps; the army had a better record, but blacks were still concentrated in the lower grades of the enlisted ranks[51]). A postwar study on the military's racial policy—the Gillem Board Report—had recommended expanded opportunities for blacks, but it also recommended the continuation of segregated units and limiting black personnel to 10 percent of overall military strength. A public backlash against military segregation grew, fueled by the view that it was indefensible in light of the contribution of black soldiers during the war and inconsistent with U.S. foreign policy values. Civil rights groups took advantage of opportunities to make their case in Washington. When confronted with the possibility of another mass demonstration, this time in the form of a campaign to urge blacks to refuse induction into the military, Truman moved quickly to issue an executive order (E.O. 9881, July 26, 1948) that, in effect, established a nondiscrimination policy for the military and established a commission (the Committee on Equality of Treatment and Opportunity in the Armed Forces) to oversee implementation of the policy.[52] Truman opted for an executive order to do this largely because of the president's discretion in military administration and the relative flexibility and speed that executive action offered over legislation: "By seizing this opportunity, the Truman Administration hoped to demonstrate its dedication to legal equality for racial minorities without waiting for congressional approval—approval that a conservative Congress, faced with controversial issues in an election year, was highly unlikely to grant."[53]

There is little doubt that the timing of the orders was motivated by a desire to maximize their political impact and improve Truman's electoral prospects. The orders, along with the dramatic Democratic Convention civil rights plank, recaptured the initiative from the Republicans, who had made their own forays into the question in an attempt to woo blacks back to their historical allegiances. "The Truman orders were timed perfectly . . . to focus attention on Congress, and, concurrently, to undercut [Henry] Wallace's standing with many Negroes. In all probability, Executive Order 9981 was also designed to reduce the possibility of an immediate confrontation between the administration and A. Philip Randolph," who had promised an active campaign of civil disobedience—including refusals to respond to induction—if Truman did not issue the order.[54] But since the order did not specify a deadline for ending all discrimination—instead, it called for the policy to be implemented "as rapidly as possible . . . without impairing efficiency or morale," it was seen as a reasonable compromise that would avoid antagonizing southern Democrats.[55]

In issuing E.O. 9981, Truman stepped into a process that had been emerging since the end of World War II. It was less a revolutionary policy change than it was a critical step in harnessing the developing momentum and establishing concrete steps to carry out the task of nondiscrimination: "By placing presidential authority squarely behind an official commitment to end such discrimination [in the military], and by publicly stating that he sought to eliminate racial segregation from the military, Truman broke with prior national policy and altered the course of the debate. His intervention emboldened advocates of racial equality, put supporters of segregation on the defensive, and opened a path leading toward the completion of formal racial integration."[56]

Compared with Truman, Eisenhower was less inclined to rely on executive power to promote a civil rights agenda. Nevertheless, the executive orders in the 1940s had firmly established that the presidency was the focal point of racial progress, and the Eisenhower White House recognized that a retreat was politically impossible. In his 1953 State of the Union Address, Eisenhower pledged his dedication to "equality of opportunity for all," and promised to use "whatever authority exists in the office of the president" to end segregation in Washington, D.C., in federal government employment, and in the military. It is clear, though, that Eisenhower took a restrictive view of how far that authority would extend. During the 1952 campaign, he told Herbert Brownell that if elected he would work to end discrimination in those areas under federal jurisdiction. Although Eisenhower took a progressive stance on the issue, Brownell found that "the qualifier *federal* jurisdiction was quite limiting in his 1952 position."[57]

After the inauguration, Eisenhower's staff attempted to walk this fine line in considering the future of the various presidential committees responsible for civil rights issues. The work of the Committee on Equality of Treatment in the Armed Services continued; "by the end of 1953," writes Stephen Ambrose, "Eisenhower could boast that segregation in the Navy and the Air Force was 'a thing of the past.' "[58] In a memorandum to White House Chief of Staff Sherman Adams, Max Rabb noted that a failure to continue the general policy of nondiscrimination in government contracts "would be regarded in many quarters as evidence of an unsympathetic attitude on the part of the Administration towards those civil rights."[59] Rabb recommended that the existing committee be replaced by a new and restructured organization. The existing Committee on Government Contract Compliance, he thought, was too reminiscent of the Truman administration: "the general idea has merit but there is no need to rubber stamp [Truman's] brainchild."[60] Yet the administration moved on this issue only after being questioned by reporters about the fate of Truman's CGCC,[61] and Eisenhower remained reluctant to move beyond those areas in which presidential and federal authority were unambiguous.

The most significant executive action in the Eisenhower years was the president's decision to federalize the Arkansas National Guard in September 1957 in order to enforce the federal court order to desegregate Little Rock schools.[62] Eisenhower issued Executive Order 10730 on September 25, 1957, relying on his authority as commander in chief and on statutory provisions that permit the president to use militia and military forces when normal law enforcement authorities are unable to enforce federal law. The attorney general concluded that it was well within the president's authority to take this step, citing precedents dating back eighty years.[63]

Despite this dramatic step, which he took reluctantly, Eisenhower was never able to overcome the impression that he was unsympathetic to a civil rights agenda. Part of the problem was his hesitation in speaking out forcefully, as well as his general inattentiveness to civil rights issues. When pressed in 1957 to comment on the Civil Rights Act then pending in the Senate, Eisenhower admitted that he hadn't read the legislation. "It was," writes Ambrose, "a stunning confession of ignorance."[64] Eisenhower's failure to assert his prerogative reflected his limited view of how far the executive power extended, rather than any political calculations about maintaining or expanding the Republican coalition.[65]

This limited interpretation of presidential power was apparent in the limp performance of the Committee on Government Contracts. The committee, despite being headed by Vice President Nixon, lacked the authority and resources to take significant action. Most of its activities consisted of broad educational efforts, and when it did investigate specific complaints of discriminatory activity it relied more on voluntary compliance than on sanctions. Responsibility for enforcing nondiscrimination, in any case, remained with the individual contracting agencies, which were reluctant to cancel contracts or debar contractors in response to complaints.[66]

Moreover, the nondiscrimination clauses required in most contracts exempted eighteen different types of federal activity, leaving "gaping holes in the compliance program."[67]

This lack of progress was reflected in the lukewarm support Eisenhower received from minorities. By the summer of 1957 (before the Little Rock crisis of the fall), E. Frederick Morrow, the first African American to serve as assistant to the president, was warning Sherman Adams that Eisenhower's repeated refusals to meet with black leaders was undercutting political support for the administration.[68] The following year, Morrow attributed the drubbing that Republicans took in the 1958 congressional elections—losing forty-nine seats in the House and fifteen in the Senate, a showing worse than the post-Watergate debacle in 1974—to a lack of responsiveness to minority concerns. After the elections, Morrow warned "emphatically and categorically that there cannot be a Republican victory in 1960 until this situation is faced squarely and honestly."[69]

Indeed, as Morrow predicted, the executive's role in civil rights played a significant role in the 1960 presidential election. Kennedy and his staff made it clear from the earliest days of the campaign that they intended to use the president's executive powers to make progress on civil rights. In contrast to Eisenhower's narrower view of presidential authority, Kennedy pictured that power as far more expansive. In January 1960, Kennedy argued that the president "must above all be the Chief Executive in every sense of the word. He must be prepared to exercise the fullest powers of his office—all that are specified and some that are not." Again and again during the 1960 presidential campaign, Kennedy criticized Eisenhower and Nixon for not taking more decisive action on civil rights. Kennedy charged that Eisenhower could have—indeed, should have—ended discrimination in federal housing programs and by government contractors with a stroke of the presidential pen. Nixon's Committee on Government Contracts, Kennedy claimed had been "completely ineffective" in enforcing the nondiscrimination orders, but could be transformed into an effective tool of presidential leadership.[70]

Executive Orders versus Legislation: Kennedy, Civil Rights, and Energy in the Executive

Eisenhower's failure to issue an executive order banning housing discrimination became a lightning rod for Kennedy's supporters, and a potent symbol of energy (or lack thereof) in the executive. And, as in presidential initiatives in employment discrimination, executive action was to forge a path for legislation, first through the Civil Rights Act of 1964 and later through the Fair Housing Act of 1969.

"Federal housing" was a catch-all phrase referring to low-income housing units owned by the federal government as well as to federal loans and grants to private organizations and firms constructing privately owned housing. Unlike federal employment and contracting, where presidents had been trying for two decades to implement nondiscrimination policy, there had been no movement at all to end such practices in federal housing programs. Federally owned housing—usually run by local public agencies—practiced blatant discrimination against minorities, shunting blacks into segregated areas. Federally chartered and insured banks often refused to issue mortgages to nonwhites. Until 1947, the Federal Housing Administration (FHA) actually encouraged housing segregation and recommended the use of restrictive covenants, arguing that neighborhood property values declined when minorities moved in. Even after the Supreme Court declared restrictive covenants unconstitutional in 1948, the FHA still provided subsidies to builders who refused to sell or rent to minorities.[71]

Pressure for executive action came late; in its section on housing, the 1947 Committe on Civil Rights focused on restrictive covenants, and although it criticized in passing the use of federal grants and funding for private entities that discriminated, it did not call for strong executive action.[72] Indeed, Truman specifically avoided any mention of housing in his civil rights message to Congress in 1947, out of fear that asking for legislation would do nothing but provoke a sharp negative reaction.[73] The 1949 National Housing Act set as a policy goal "a decent home and suitable living environment for every American family," but there was no specific mention of nondiscrimination; and after even stronger policy declarations in other areas had gone unenforced, there was little hope that this language could be used as a foundation for equal housing.[74] Throughout the 1950s, members of both houses of Congress tried to insert nondiscrimination language in housing bills, but their efforts always failed.

Nevertheless, within the civil rights community pressure for executive leadership was building. In 1955 a coalition of groups offered a detailed proposal for a housing executive order, but Eisenhower evinced no enthusiasm for this or any other version of a housing order.[75] In 1959, the Commission on Civil Rights—a body established by the 1957 Civil Rights Act—called for an executive order banning discrimination in all federal housing programs, but the issue was overshadowed by broader efforts to make progress on voting rights, which was seen as a higher priority.[76]

Kennedy's campaign staff recognized that highlighting civil rights would produce a political payoff; from the beginning, there were plans for maximizing the visibility of civil rights throughout the campaign. These efforts ranged from Kennedy's repeated and unambiguous promises to take decisive action on housing and employment to the organization and sponsorship of a Conference on Constitutional Rights, explicitly designed to focus attention on the issue, in October 1960.

Executive action formed the core of Kennedy's civil rights platform. In 1959 Harris Wofford, who would play a critical role in the Kennedy White House, urged a strategy of both "talk and action," combining "White House conferences and executive orders" to raise the profile of racial nondiscrimination and provide the issues with a public platform.[77] Wofford recommended that Kennedy endorse the 1959 report of the Commission on Civil Rights, which strongly backed an executive order on housing discrimination.

The executive order strategy was based on a combination of political necessity and moral imperatives. Executive action was preferable to legislation, at least for the first few years, because Congress would likely "go up in flames" if the president pushed a strong civil rights agenda (including measures such as school desegregation). In a twist, though, Wofford also noted that Kennedy could hang executive orders over the heads of southern legislators by hinting that if they opposed the orders, he would follow up with legislation that they would like even less. In a transition memo to the president-elect, Wofford set out the thinking behind this strategy:

> Even if you now decide on a course of executive action with practically no legislation this year *it would be impolitic to announce or acknowledge any such decision*. Negro and civil rights groups are not yet adjusted to the idea of the primacy of executive action in this field. They have so long operated in the absence of Presidential action, with all attention given to legislation, that they would greet such a decision as a sell-out. After they have tasted the fruits of executive action, they will know the barrenness of their legislative lobbying, and see that the logic of such executive action will lead to complementary legislation—and lead there sooner than a party-splitting legislation battle at the beginning of your Administration. Moreover, you probably need the possibility of Administration support for far-reaching legislation this session as a threat to use in the recurring negotiation with southern political leaders. You can explain your executive actions to them as the only alternative to bringing forward such legislation.[78]

Kennedy's repeated pledges to issue executive orders early in his term created unusual pressure for executive action, and the promises would come to haunt him as his initial enthusiasm was tempered by the realities of presidential governance. Having raised expectations so high, he faced growing criticism as he found one reason after another for delaying, in particular, his housing order. Kennedy had to walk the fine lines between arousing the wrath of southern legislators (which would put the rest of his legislative agenda at risk), satisfying a constituency that was crucial to his narrow electoral victory, and crafting an order that would stand up to legal scrutiny. None of these paths was easy to traverse, and the process took almost two years to complete.

Kennedy did move quickly in those areas where the president's authority was well established. During the transition, Wofford advised the president that there was plenty of room for executive action on government contracting, and in April 1961 Kennedy created, via Executive Order 10925, the President's Committee on Equal Employment Opportunity (PCEEO), placing Vice President Lyndon Johnson at the head and giving the committee broad powers to oversee the contracting and employment activity of federal agencies.[79] In doing so, he expanded the authority of previous contract oversight bodies, and gave the committee heightened visibility by putting the vice president in charge.

On housing, Kennedy had more trouble making progress. Wofford urged the president to issue the housing nondiscrimination order quickly, but recognized that it would have to take its place alongside housing legislation and a proposal to create a new executive Department of Housing and Urban Development.[80] The legal issues surrounding the order proved unexpectedly complicated and controversial, and Kennedy was soon devoting his attention to other higher-priority issues: the Bay of Pigs in April 1961, the Berlin crisis in the summer. In October 1961 Kennedy reportedly promised not to issue the order until after the 1962 midterm elections, a delay that Robert Weaver, head of the Housing and Home Finance Agency, attributed to political considerations. White House aides Kenneth O'Donnell and Larry O'Brien, Weaver believed, "recognized that the open occupancy Executive order had to be issued but urged that the timing was terribly important and said let's not muddy the water right now until we get some of these other things that we've got to get out."[81]

The delay galvanized supporters. Wofford notes ruefully that the "stroke of the pen" metaphor came back to haunt him, as the National Committee against Discrimination in Housing (NCDH) organized a campaign to send pens to the White House by the thousands to dramatize the lack of action. Since Kennedy remembered that Wofford had originally coined the phrase, all of the pens that came in were forwarded to his office, where they piled up.[82]

The most difficult legal decisions involved the scope of the order and which federal organizations would be covered: would the order apply only to agencies directly involved in constructing or administering federally funded housing, or would it extend to home mortgage lending by federally insured financial institutions? Proponents of the order pushed for broad coverage, as did the Civil Rights Commission in its 1961 report, but there were legal questions regarding how much authority the president had over the independent regulatory agencies that exercised oversight over commercial banks and lenders (especially the Federal Reserve and the Federal Deposit Insurance Corporation). The idea behind the executive order was that the FDIC would make deposit insurance conditional on a bank's lending practices; insurance would be denied to banks that discriminated. It was not clear, for one thing, that the president could rely solely on executive authority: a 1962 Justice Department analysis concluded that it was possible to construct a reasonable argument in favor of FDIC regulation through an executive order, although the question was "close" and there was "a substantial chance that the courts would reach an opposite conclusion."[83] The legislative history of congressional efforts to ban housing discrimination was so uniformly negative that many legislators and legal scholars doubted that the president could accomplish the feat through executive action of any sort.[84] Politically, housing discrimination was an especially sensitive policy area, since opponents saw it as a particularly intrusive federal invasion of property rights and private decisions about one's living arrangements.[85]

These political and legal concerns hindered quick action, even as pressure to issue the order mounted steadily through 1961 and 1962. An early version of a housing executive order, prepared in the fall of 1961 by Assistant Attorney General Nicholas Katzenbach, sought the middle ground by exempting the Federal Reserve and the FDIC from coverage, but applying the order to other lending activities (by savings and loans and lenders covered by the Veterans Administration and Federal Housing Administration).[86] By this point, however, Kennedy had little stomach for controversial civil rights action, a result of his bruising early battles with Congress and "legitimate constitutional reservations over the extent of his executive authority."[87] After word leaked in November that the executive order was sitting on Kennedy's desk waiting for his signature, the White House backed down in the face of congressional pressure for more time.[88] Harris Wofford explained that the order "had been cleared through all the agencies, and the press release had been written, and the date had been set." But Kennedy was furious about the leak, and decided the day before the order was to be issued to wait for another six months.[89]

In January 1962 Kennedy's proposal to establish a cabinet-level Housing and Urban Development Agency was rebuffed by the House Rules Committee, leaving him even more reluctant to further antagonize Congress by issuing the housing order while it was in session.[90] But civil rights groups kept up their pressure on the administration, and by mid-1962 even opponents of a housing order conceded that the question was not whether an order would be issued, but when. Even the National Association of Home Builders had concluded that the order—which the association opposed—would reduce the amount of uncertainty surrounding the home construction industry, and that eventually everybody would learn to live with it.[91] Even so, Kennedy chose to announce the order in as low profile a setting as possible: he signed the order (E.O. 11063) on November 20, 1962, the same day that he announced the end of the Cuban missile crisis.[92]

Although the order was hailed as a major victory, many supporters considered it a disappointment after such a long wait. Kennedy overruled the strong recommendations of the Civil Rights Commission and the Housing and Home Finance Agency that the order cover commercial banks as well as federally guaranteed lending activity, and applied the order only to new housing instead of making it retroactive to existing loans and projects.[93]

The prospective application of Kennedy's order severely limited its effectiveness; it did not reach into the existing housing base, and much of the new housing that came under its aegis was beyond the means of most black families. In practice, the order extended only to new homes constructed with FHA- or VA- guaranteed loans. Within a few years, the Johnson administration was facing pressure from both inside and outside of the government to expand the order's range and tighten its enforcement provisions.[94] The President's Committee on Equal Opportunity in Housing (PCEOH) concluded in March 1965 that Executive Order 11063 was "not as helpful as many had hoped or expected" because it failed to cover federally insured mortgage lenders, and several members of the committee threatened to resign unless Johnson corrected the deficiencies.[95] The committee itself was pushing hard for executive action, and Johnson was warned that a failure to act quickly could provoke a public rebuke from committee members.[96] The success of the Civil Rights Act and Voting Rights Act left housing discrimination—which all conceded was rampant—as the last major policy area "as yet untouched by the Great Society."[97] By the end of 1965 White House domestic policy head Joseph Califano was warning the president that there would be "an explosion" without swift action.[98]

In thinking about broadening E.O. 11063, Johnson faced the same legal questions that Kennedy had in determining how far presidential power could extend over independent regulatory agencies and private financial institutions. The constitutional issues were little changed from 1963 and were no more favorable to the president. Justice and Treasury both advised Johnson that he lacked the authority to extend Kennedy's order, although Califano had passed along the attorney general's view that the courts "would find some way to sustain" the president.[99] Even the PCEOH, which six months earlier had given strong support to the legality of a broadened order, was persuaded that the legal questions could not be dismissed.[100] Califano summarized the pros and cons of both the executive order and legislative strategies: "The advantages of the Executive Order route are that the civil rights leaders and your housing committee would applaud you, and you avoid the difficulties of a tough legislative battle. The disadvantages are the opposition you would get from bankers (from using them as an instrument), the chance that you would lose in court and be accused of overextending your authority and the fact that you would be moving in the most sensitive of civil rights areas all alone, without Congressional back-up."[101] In Congress, Senator Jacob Javits (R-N.Y.) was pushing hard for an executive order, arguing that extending 11063 to cover federally insured banks and savings and loans was constitutionally sound and could cover 80 percent of all housing in the country. Javitz also worried that if Johnson proposed legislation and failed to secure passage, future executive initiatives in housing would face even higher constitutional hurdles.[102]

The legal objections and political risks surrounding aggressive executive action once again proved compelling, and Johnson elected to go the legislative route despite what were seen as dim chances of congressional approval. In his 1966 State of the Union Address, he called for "legislation, resting on the fullest constitutional authority of the federal government, to prohibit racial discrimination in the sale or rental of housing." The House did manage to pass compromise housing language as part of a 1966 civil rights bill, but the legislation died when its supporters quickly gave up the fight in the Senate. The defeat created additional pressure on Johnson to issue an executive order, and the White House established a civil rights task force to make policy recommendations on housing and other civil rights issues. After yet another review of the legal questions, and another Department of Justice opinion that the president did not have the necessary authority to broaden the housing order, the task force recommended abandoning the executive approach altogether in favor of a new statute.[103]

In 1967 the White House tried again and failed to secure congressional enactment of an open housing law, but Congress unexpectedly passed the legislation after a flurry of activity in early 1968 (days after the assassination of Martin Luther King, Jr.). The fair housing law, which was added as a Senate amendment to a broader civil rights bill, went well beyond what any executive order could have done. On the basis of the interstate commerce clause in Article I and the equal protection clause in the Fourteenth Amendment, Congress barred discrimination in home sales, rentals, and mortgages. There were narrowly carved out exceptions (such as private individuals who owned fewer than four homes and who did not work with a broker or real estate agent), but the law covered 80 percent of the housing units in the United States.[104] Kennedy's housing executive order had covered perhaps 2 percent.[105]

In employment and housing, executive action led to significant episodes of lawmaking that settled the question of federal enforcement of nondiscrimination policies. The scope of Roosevelt's FEPC and Eisenhower's Committee on Government Contracts appears timid when compared with the sweeping language in the 1964 Civil Rights Act, but there is no question that the initial presidential forays advanced the agenda. Each step was incremental, to be sure, but each successive order secured the gains that had been made, solidified the precedent of federal involvement, and gave sharper definition to the moral imperatives of racial equality. Most of the controversial aspects of the various civil rights orders that presidents issued between 1941 and 1965 were given broad legislative imprimatur in the Civil Rights Act of 1964 and follow-up legislation in the late 1960s. The general path from executive initiative to legislative entrenchment is clear, although sometimes decades elapsed before Congress put its full weight behind the initial executive efforts. Pointing to Truman's executive orders (9808, 9980, and 9981), Gerald Rosenberg notes that "the civil rights movement that burst forth in the 1960s had been growing for three decades. While the pot did not boil over until the 1960s, it had been simmering for a long time."[106]

Not all episodes of presidential involvement in civil rights policy, however, followed this progression. As I show in the following section on affirmative action policy, there are times when presidents create institutions and expectations that even they cannot control.

The Unresolved Question: Presidential Power and "Affirmative Action"

In a recent analysis of affirmative action, sociologist John David Skrenty concludes that the emphasis on proportional hiring originated in the 1940s and 1950s, when the FEPC and its progeny focused on employment statistics as the only way to identify and root out discriminatory employment practices. "Throughout the 1950s and 1960s," he argues, "agencies in search of a useful tool for fighting discrimination were continually led to the affirmative action approach, monitoring numbers and percentages of African-Americans hired as a measure of discrimination."[107] In his view, affirmative action was an administrative solution to the complex problem of discrimination.

Affirmative action—or the practice of granting preferences in employment, contracting, or education on the basis of race or gender—is largely a creature of executive action, even though the presidents who crafted the language showed no inkling that the concept would eventually become the lightning rod of civil rights policy. Kennedy's Executive Order 10925 contained the first use of the term at the presidential level, with its mandate that government contractors "take affirmative action to ensure that applicants are employed, and that employees are treated during employment, without regard to their race, creed, color, or national origin."[108] There was, though, no indication that Kennedy had given much thought to this wording, and the term did not have the meaning that it would take on in the following decade.

Indeed, notes Graham, the term "affirmative action" had long been used by civil rights groups to mean aggressive efforts to recruit minority applicants, instead of the "passive nondiscrimination" of the Eisenhower administration. The phrase was put into E.O. 10925 almost as an afterthought, and it was not considered especially controversial at the time.[109] The vice president's aides spent far more time worrying about the administrative structure of the committee and resisting pressure to add sex and age to the list of prohibited grounds for discrimination.[110] In 1982, James E. Jones, Jr., a staff lawyer in the Department of Labor who assisted in the initial organization of the PCEEO, referred to a "collective failure in 1961 to appreciate the overriding significance of the affirmative action element of Executive Order 10925."[111]

Similarly, Johnson's Executive Order 11246, which is generally considered to have established the legal basis for a wider application and broader construction of affirmative action, was not intended to be a blueprint for such a policy but was instead motivated by a need to rationalize a complicated administrative structure that had evolved since the Civil Rights Act of 1964; the specific language about the goals was almost identical to what Kennedy had used in Executive Order 10925: "The internal debate leading to Johnson's new executive orders in September 1965 focused almost exclusively on structural arrangements, administrative jurisdictions, bureaucratic politics, and to some degree on questions of leadership and staff personalities. Affirmative action had simply not been fundamentally at issue in the tortured evolution of E.O. 11246 . . . the potential sword was mighty, as it had always been. But the language was vintage 1961."[112] The key differences between E.O. 11246 and its predecessors were the provisions that transferred enforcement authority from a presidential commission to the secretary of labor, gave the secretary of labor authority to require compliance reports on hiring practices before companies could bid on government contracts, and required that contractors comply with the order in all of their activities, not just those directly related to federal contract activities. Even civil rights groups failed to appreciate the potential that this new authority created, and many criticized the order for not doing more. Yet it "potentially possessed the awesome power of the federal contract purse."[113] Almost immediately administrators in the newly created Office of Federal Contract Compliance (OFCC),

established by 11246 to oversee administration of the order, began flesh-
ing out what affirmative action consisted of, although the initial statements suggested that no one was quite sure what the term meant. In 1967
OFCC director Edward C. Sylvester admitted that "I don't pretend to
have a definition of affirmative action that is going to satisfy everybody
here. . . . There is no fixed and firm definition of affirmative action. I
would say that in a general way, affirmative action is anything that you
have to do to get results."[114]

Congress had given legislative notice to affirmative action in Title VII
of the Civil Rights Act of 1964, allowing courts to "order such affirmative
action as may be appropriate" to remedy a history of intentional discriminatory practices by private employers. Even so, it was Nixon, a Republican president, who infused the full measure of the federal government's
power into E.O. 11246. In 1969 the secretary of labor issued a directive,
under the authority of 11246, requiring certain construction unions in
Philadelphia to adopt "specific goals and timetables" for the hiring of
minorities. On all construction contracts, bidders had to submit an affirmative action plan outlining "specific goals of minority manpower utiliza-
tion" based on standards issued by local Department of Labor officials.
The order was a response to the long-standing practice by construction
contractors of allowing unions to determine the makeup of their labor
force on a government contract. Local unions commonly denied membership or apprenticeship slots to minorities, so contractors would end up
relying on a segregated workforce. The "Philadelphia Plan" put the burden on the contractors themselves to ensure a representative workforce.
It was an indirect way of attacking the problem that had bedeviled earlier
attempts to end discrimination in contracts by ending the "union-refer-
ral" loophole (in which contractors claimed they had no control over the
personnel sent to them by unions). The step was controversial from the
beginning. Comptroller General Elmer Staats issued an opinion declaring
the Philadelphia Plan illegal, arguing that the goals and timetables requirement flatly contradicted language in Title VII of the Civil Rights Act prohibiting discrimination on the basis of race, color, gender, religion, or national origin.[115]

In a second implementing order issued in 1970, the Department of
Labor extended the previous order to all government contractors, and
stipulated that contractors recruit a workforce that approximated the racial composition of the applicant pool in the local geographic area. Thus
did Executive Order 11246 create the modern structure of affirmative
action, through administrative action that has repeatedly been upheld as
a valid exercise of the president's executive authority.[116] Even now 11246
is the focal point. The Congressional Research Service concluded in a
1995 review that 11246 and its predecessors "served as the historical

model for federal laws and regulations establishing minority participation 'goals.' "[117]

In an indication of the immense controversy that affirmative action would provoke, almost nobody was satisfied with the Philadelphia Plan. Criticism came from all sides: labor unions and traditional conservatives resented what they saw as excessive federal intrusion, while the NAACP argued that the order failed to go far enough.[118]

As with so many other examples in which the courts have upheld executive action, judges have found a basis for presidential authority in implicit congressional approval. In *U.S. v. New Orleans Public Service, Inc.*, 553 F.2d 458 (5th Cir, 1977), the court noted the long history of presidential nondiscrimination orders in upholding the regulations that implemented 11246. Moreover, the court also found that Congress had granted at least implicit authority through the Civil Rights Act of 1964, the Federal Administrative Property and Services Act of 1949, and the Equal Employment Opportunity Act of 1972:

> To be sure, the legislative history does not show, in so many words, congressional ratification of the particular aspect of the Executive Order program here at issue, *viz.*, the imposition by operation of the order of the nondiscrimination clause on all government contractors, regardless of whether the employers have expressly consented to the clause. However, Congress not only has refused to circumscribe the role of the Office of Federal Contract Compliance in combating employment discrimination, but has indicated a concern for the efficacy of such efforts and an intent that they would continue. The regulation in controversy is an integral part of a long-standing program which Congress has recognized and approved.[119]

The decisions upholding the order and the associated regulations have been the subject of a great deal of criticism, particularly over their view that the president possesses the constitutional authority to issue such an order.

The disputes typically center on an apparent conflict between E.O. 11246 and its implementing regulations, which must themselves be based on presidential authority, and Title VII of the 1964 Civil Rights Act. The argument is that affirmative action programs—with their attendant goals and timetables, and proportionality requirements—run counter to the clear language of Title VII, which prohibits employment discrimination on the basis of race, color, sex, religion, or national origin. Since affirmative action, at least as implemented by the OFCC and E.O. 11246, requires contractors to take race et al. into account in hiring and promotions, it follows that those who are not members of the favored categories suffer illegal discrimination based on their race, color, or sex.[120] Executive Order 11246, the interpretation of Title VII, the Philadelphia Plan, and the concept of affirmative action remain the most significant unresolved issues in civil rights.

The Philadelphia Plan spurred multiple legal and congressional challenges to the president's right to mandate such a program. Questions arose over the president's authority to implement such a program through executive action; whether Congress had given implicit approval of Executive Order 11246; and whether Congress, in enacting Title VII of the Civil Rights Act, had intended that the legislation serve as the exclusive remedy for discrimination claims.

But in a pattern almost identical to that of intelligence organization or budget politics, Congress has failed—repeatedly—in its efforts to wrest the policy initiative back from the president. Not all legislative efforts have been devoted to taking power away from the president, and some have clearly been devoted to granting explicit congressional recognition to the affirmative action orders. As with classified information, emergency powers, or intelligence organization, however, the courts interpret legislative action in a way that puts Congress at a disadvantage: judges often find congressional authorization of presidential power in implicit legislative action, but require explicit and unambiguous expressions of congressional sentiment in order to limit the president's power.

The question of affirmative action in employment is inextricably linked with congressionally authorized racial and gender-specific preferences in government contract awards, and controversies around both have grown. Supporters see such provisions as crucial remedies that address entrenched discriminatory practices, while opponents argue that they have led to rigid quotas and indefensible reverse discrimination.

In the face of sustained controversy, however, even presidents firmly opposed to affirmative action have resisted the idea of backing away from E.O. 11246. As with the earlier orders, successive presidents have had the authority to rescind or modify the specifics of 11246, but they have had to take into consideration the symbolic problems in retreating from a well-established precedent. By the 1980s affirmative action had become synonymous with "quotas," anathema to the Reagan administration; there were moves both within the White House and the Department of Justice to modify 11246 or change the administrative enforcement mechanisms.

Despite this strong opposition and repeated efforts, and despite considerable support in Congress, the Reagan administration was unable to make any major changes to affirmative action programs or 11246. William Bradford Reynolds, whom Reagan appointed as assistant attorney general for civil rights, made no secret of his opposition to affirmative action, telling the Senate Judiciary Committee in 1981 that he favored a strict and race-neutral definition of what constituted discriminatory employment practices.[121] Several months later Reynolds announced his opposition to numerical goals and his intention to find a test case with which to seek Supreme Court reversal of its *Weber* decision (a 1979 case in which the Court upheld the use of racial employment quotas in as consistent with the Civil Rights Act when the purpose was to remedy past discrimination).[122] In August 1981, the Office of Federal Contract Compliance Programs (OFCCP) proposed a change in the thresholds used to determine whether a contractor was covered under 11246's requirements or had to submit a written affirmative action plan. The proposed regulations exempted all contractors with fewer than one hundred employees from coverage regardless of the amount of contracts they received, and contractors would be freed from the need to submit a formal affirmative action plan unless they received $1 million in contracts, up from $50,000 in the existing regulations.[123] These changes provoked blistering criticism, and the White House quietly dropped the proposal, switching to an effort to secure change through the courts.[124] It would be fifteen years until the next attempt to revise the regulatory regime surrounding 11246.[125]

But opponents of 11246 did not abandon their efforts to rescind the order altogether. After Reagan's landslide victory in 1984, Reynolds once again proposed altering Executive Order 11246, suggesting " 'with the stroke of a pen' the President should replace this executive order with one that makes clear that the federal government does not require, authorize, or permit the use of goals, or any other form of race- or gender-conscious preferential treatment by federal contractors."[126] When Edwin Meese became attorney general in 1985, he agreed to take up the issue,. but ultimately decided that any changes in E.O. 11246 would be politically costly. Terry Eastland recalled: "Meese came to believe that changing the executive order would be a largely symbolic act too costly in political terms to undertake. . . . Meese thought that any change might (1) provoke Congress to pass law requiring the Executive Order regime; (2) weaken political support in Congress for the President as a general matter; (3) hurt the President as a matter of perception generally, and (4) also hurt the Republican Party. . . . With Don Regan, then the White House Chief of Staff, not inclined to pursue reform either, the issue died in the Domestic Policy Council."[127] With his own advisors split, and a well-organized coalition arguing loudly against repeal, the president "recognized that he had no politically viable alternative but to abandon his plan to reform affirmative action."[128]

By this point even congressional Republicans had grown weary of the persistent charge that the GOP was unsympathetic to minority interests, and Reagan, distracted by the upcoming 1986 Geneva Summit with Russian premier Mikhail Gorbachev and increasingly committed to tax reform as his highest domestic priority, was unwilling to resolve the open feud. In any case, proponents of a major revision lost much of their momentum when the Supreme Court upheld affirmative action as constitutionally permissible in two key cases during the 1987 term, thus undermining Reynolds's central argument that racial preferences were legally questionable.[129]

The resilience of affirmative action programs during the Reagan years confirms a central premise of the new institutional economics paradigm: institutions, once they are created, can resist attempts to impose significant change. Institutional creation is a double-edged sword: presidents can create new administrative capabilities, and they will exert control over these new capabilities more often than not, but there is no guarantee that they will be able to do so. The case of affirmative action also demonstrates how executive orders can bind successive presidents. In this instance, change was blocked by the emergence of an institutional capacity to protect existing programs. Within the executive branch, those who favored altering 11246 ran into opposition from the Department of Labor and its congressional allies, the Equal Employment Opportunities Commission (EEOC, created in the Civil Rights Act to enforce language in the act banning workplace discrimination), and the broader civil rights community. Surprisingly, even the business community expressed ambivalence about changing the 11246 program, with many CEOs indicating that their companies would retain affirmative action programs no matter what the government did (although some groups, such as the Chamber of Commerce, favored repeal). The 1985–1986 dispute between Labor and Justice engendered a contentious, public, and cabinetwide split, and Reagan ultimately refused to step in.[130] This episode tells us that "intuition notwithstanding, preexisting executive orders are not always so easy to change. Ronald Reagan was a popular president whose view of civil rights was most definitely in conflict with an executive order program inherited from previous administrations. Yet despite having the legal and constitutional wherewithal to bring the order into line with his own administration's views on civil rights issues, [he] apparently felt obligated to maintain the status quo."[131]

With one brief but notable exception, the specifics of 11246 faded into the background during the Bush administration, pushed off the stage by the controversy over the 1990 and 1991 civil rights bills. These bills originated as part of an effort to reverse six Supreme Court cases, the most prominent of which was *Ward's Cove Packing Co., Inc. v. Antonio,* 490 U.S. 642 (1989), that made it more difficult to sue over discriminatory employment practices. In *Ward's Cove,* the Court ruled that plaintiffs in job bias lawsuits had to prove that an employer *intended* to discriminate, shifting the burden of proof that had up to this point been on the employer. The decision reversed two decades of jurisprudence on the so-called disparate impact test, under which courts had held that even race-neutral job requirements (such as a having a high school diploma) could be biased if they had an especially adverse impact on minorities, even if there was no intent to discriminate.[132]

In 1990 Congress passed a bill to reverse these decisions and restore what had been, until *Ward's Cove*, the controlling legal interpretations on employment discrimination law. It also expanded the reach of the Civil Rights Act of 1964 and the remedies available to plaintiffs, allowing for punitive damages in both civil rights and sexual harassment lawsuits. Critics argued that employers would have to adopt rigid racial hiring quotas in order to avoid lawsuits under the restored disparate impact standard, and Bush vetoed the bill after months of negotiations failed to secure any acceptable compromises.[133]

A renewed effort to pass a civil rights bill in 1991 appeared to be heading in the same direction as the 1990 failure, but the debacle of the Clarence Thomas Supreme Court confirmation hearings in October 1991 intensified the pressure on both Democrats and Republicans to show progress. Within days of the hearings, the White House and Congress agreed on a compromise civil rights bill, which was presented to the president in November. But in an excruciatingly embarrassing misstep, Bush's signing of the 1991 civil rights act was marred by the release, the day before, of a directive to all federal agencies ordering them to end any programs that involved quotas, preferences, or set-asides.[134] The draft order, which was to be attached to the civil rights bill as a signing statement (a statement that the president issues when signing a bill, which is supposed to serve as an interpretive guide to agencies and the courts),[135] was quickly withdrawn when opponents characterized it "as a deliberate presidential effort to repudiate by executive order the very legislation that Bush was signing."[136] Bush excluded the most controversial language from his final signing statement, but he found it difficult to distance himself from the fact that it was his own White House counsel who had drafted the order, and the miscommunication played into what had become a standard refrain: that Republican presidents were unsympathetic, at best, to the civil rights cause. Representative William Clay (D-Mo.) drew parallels between Bush and David Duke, the Klansman and self-avowed white supremacist who had recently lost in his attempt to become governor of Louisiana. House Speaker Thomas Foley (D-Wash.) warned that "if [the draft statement] were to be issued as an executive order, I think it would be a tragedy."[137]

Bush's relationships with minority groups were hardly helped when a Department of Education official announced, in December 1990, that the department would end federal assistance to colleges and universities that offered scholarships designated for racial minorities. The decision, if implemented, would have eliminated these programs. Within a week, President Bush reversed the decision, but the flap occurred just after the veto of the 1990 civil rights bill and was "particularly damaging to the White House."[138]

Twelve years of Republican control of the White House, and almost uniform opposition to 11246, had produced no significant change in the affirmative action practices under the order. But by 1995, affirmative action faced a frontal assault from the courts and in the states. In January, the Supreme Court heard oral arguments in the case that would a few months later significantly restrict the breadth of affirmative action programs in federal contracting.[139] The 104th Congress convened, with the first Republican majorities in four decades and a committed core group dedicated to ending affirmative action in federal programs; even those legislators not unalterably opposed to affirmative action promised a careful review of such programs.[140] One of the first actions taken by the House was an overwhelming vote, on February 21, to eliminate a lucrative tax break for broadcasters who sell their FCC licenses to minority-owned companies; the provision would become law less than two months later. Leading contenders for the Republican presidential nomination announced their intention to rescind Executive Order 11246 if they were elected.[141] In February, the Congressional Research Service produced a report, at the behest of Senator Robert Dole (R-Kans.), which detailed the existence of 160 federal laws and programs that involved some sort of racial preference or classification.[142] After receiving the report, Dole introduced legislation to explicitly overturn E.O. 11246. This was hardly the first time a legislator had tried to take this step, but in the context of the upcoming presidential election it was a signal that the effort to scale back affirmative action was a high priority for the Republican leadership.

In California, a referendum proposal banning affirmative action in all state government activities was gaining momentum and by the end of the year would secure enough signatures to qualify for the November 1996 ballot as Proposition 209 (it would pass, 54%–46%). Governor Pete Wilson ended affirmative action in state government hiring and contracting in June, one month before the University of California Board of Regents voted to end all racial preferences in UC admissions and hiring.[143]

This rapidly growing pressure on affirmative action rebounded back to the presidency, and both sides looked to Clinton for some sort of resolution. Clinton, like Lyndon Johnson and Kennedy before him, faced the well-established expectation that this was the president's responsibility, and he struggled to find a good way to proceed. Opponents of affirmative action once again noted that the president could eliminate most federal requirements just by rescinding Executive Order 11246, but Clinton knew that any backtracking would infuriate critical components of the Democratic constituency (including African Americans, Hispanics, and women). Proponents expected Clinton to reiterate his strong support for the concept, and the Reverend Jesse Jackson threatened an independent presidential campaign if Clinton or the Democrats backpedaled.[144] This time around, Clinton struggled to maintain control of an issue so controversial and seemingly devoid of middle ground that doing anything—including doing nothing—could trigger explosive political reactions.[145]

Clinton did his best to steer a middle course, expressing his support for the concept of affirmative action but also ordering a review of federal affirmative action programs and suggesting that he was open to modifying existing practices.[146] Yet even the slogan—"mend it, don't end it"—suggested a defensiveness born from the realization that the choice was not whether or not to back away from current practices, but by how much.

Ironically, the group charged with the review issued its report just as the Supreme Court announced its decision in *Adarand*.[147] In *Adarand*, the Court held that all racial classifications were subject to the highest level of judicial examination, or "strict scrutiny." Under this doctrine, such programs must be narrowly tailored and further a compelling state interest. Unlike previous decisions which had also applied the strict scrutiny test, *Adarand* declared all racial preferences inherently suspect; more important, the Court rejected the program at issue, whereas previous court decisions had upheld them. The program in question in *Adarand* gave contractors a financial incentive to use minority-owned subcontractors, by paying them a bonus of up to 10 percent of the value of each subcontract awarded to "socially or economically disadvantaged" firms. In the wake of *Adarand*, Clinton directed every executive branch agency to review its affirmative action policies to ensure compliance with the Court decision.[148] By early 1998 the Clinton administration had modified or eliminated seventeen different affirmative action programs, although the changes were confined to contracting set-asides, not to the affirmative action employment practices required of government contractors.[149]

Ultimately the White House opted for a finesse, by narrowing the circumstances in which affirmative action could be used while keeping the core principle of racial preferences intact. In one key decision, the White House modified the set-aside contracting rules, applying them only when minority-owned firms made up a disproportionately small percentage of contract awards relative to minority firms' overall market share. In keeping with the contentious history of affirmative action, both supporters and opponents were dissatisfied with Clinton's attempt to split the difference.[150] In August 1997, the OFCCP made minor revisions to the compliance and record-keeping requirements under E.O. 11246, but the underlying framework of contractor affirmative action programs remained in place.[151]

Congress could have eliminated the 11246 regime by enacting legislation that explicitly overturned it, by refusing to appropriate funds for the OFCCP, by attaching appropriations riders that prohibit expenditures of public funds to enforce the order, or by clarifying the meaning of the Title VII language in the 1964 Civil Rights Act and thus countermanding the court decisions upholding 11246's legality. Here, though, the chronicle of efforts to overturn this executive order merge with the stories of attempts to overturn other orders (whether in intelligence organization, regulatory reform, or classified information, as detailed in the earlier chapters): Congress has failed to make any significant alterations to the affirmative action framework created via 11246.

This is not for lack of trying: there have been dozens of attempts since the early 1970s to eliminate affirmative action requirements generally and to nullify E.O. 11246 specifically. Few of them have made any headway, though, with only a handful even progressing to the floor; not once has Congress actually passed any legislation that bears directly on 11246, failing even when Republicans had majority control of both chambers. Beginning with the 104th Congress, both the House and the Senate have held hearings on legislation to nullify 11246, but without any effect. Much more common have been congressional efforts to create or expand race-conscious preferences, usually in contracting set-asides for minority or socially disadvantaged businesses.

Congress has actually managed to sidestep entirely the question of modifying or eliminating 11246, even when it considered major changes to civil rights laws. Both the 1990 and the 1991 versions of the civil rights bill specified that they were to have no effect on court-ordered affirmative action agreements or consent decrees, and Dole inserted the following language into the *Congressional Record* as part of the legislative history of the 1991 act:

> This legislation does not purport to resolve the question of the legality under Title VII of affirmative action programs that grant preferential treatment to some on the basis of race, color, religion, sex or national origin, and thus "tend to deprive" other "individual[s] of employment opportunities . . . on the basis of race, color, religion, sex, or national origin." In particular, this legislation should in no way be seen as expressing approval or disapproval of *United Steelworkers* v. *Weber*, 443 U.S. 193 (1979), or *Johnson* v. *Transportation Agency* 480 U.S. 616 (1987), or any other judicial decision affecting court-ordered remedies, affirmative action, or conciliation agreements.[152]

At a time when legislators grappled with the controversial issues of sex discrimination, the balance of power between Congress and the courts in interpreting civil rights laws, and the damages that could be assessed against employers who discriminated, Congress explicitly left Executive Order 11246 alone.

Despite two contentious decades and accumulating evidence of successful state and local efforts to move away from state-sanctioned racial preferences,[153] the federally mandated affirmative action programs created by Executive Order 11246 have proved amazingly durable. The affirmative action requirements on government contractors have not been modified—not by Congress, the president, or the courts—even as the public sentiment against affirmative action had grown to the point that Princeton University political scientist Carol Swain wrote in January 1998 that "race-conscious affirmative action is on life support, and the only remaining questions are who will pull the plug and when."[154] The federal courts, even though they have been more willing to reject race-based preferences in the past few years, have still not restricted the scope of affirmative action plans by private employers who wish to contract with the federal government; the initial decisions which upheld 11246's legality are still valid.

Extending 11246's Coverage

The language of Executive Orders 10925 and 11246 prohibited discrimination on the basis of race, color, religion, or national origin. Conspicuously absent in these provisions was any reference to sex. Far from reflecting an oversight, the exclusion of gender from these early nondiscrimination orders was intentional. Gender issues were viewed as distinct from, and less important than, race discrimination, and civil rights activists fought efforts to merge the two (in part because few people truly saw sex discrimination as a serious issue, but also because there was no broad pressure to "support the inclusion of a prohibition on sex-based discrimination in an executive order to ban racial bias in private employment").[155]

Nevertheless Kennedy recognized the importance of political support from women, and in December 1961 established (via Executive Order 10980) the President's Commission on the Status of Women (PCSW).[156] The commission quickly zeroed in on the president's power to extend the nondiscrimination language in 10925 to sex, although members split on the wisdom of the addition and the commission ultimately refused to recommend it. The PCSW, along with two other groups—the Citizens' Advisory Council on the Status of Women, and the Interdepartmental Commit-

tee on the Status of Women, both created by Executive Order 11126[157]—
played a key role in placing sex discrimination on the public agenda, and
was instrumental in persuading Johnson to amend 11246 to include sex
as a protected category, in October 1967. Cynthia Harrison describes the
PCSW and its successors: "The president's commission and its state-level
offspring helped to legitimize the issue of sex discrimination, made data
available to support allegations that discrimination against women constituted a serious problem, drew up agendas to ameliorate inequities, raised
expectations that responsible parties would take action, and, most important, sensitized a nationwide network of women to the problems
women faced."[158]

Clinton provides another example of how presidents have used executive orders to extend the protection of earlier civil rights orders, particularly when doing so offers a way around a recalcitrant Congress. In May
1998 Clinton issued Executive Order 13087,[159] which prohibited federal
agencies from discriminating in employment on the basis of sexual orientation. In doing so, Clinton continued the pattern of adding to the list of
prohibited bases for discrimination first established by Kennedy's 1962
executive order establishing the PCEEO.

Clinton's order provoked an immediate reaction. Congressional Republicans and conservative religious organizations denounced Clinton for
creating a new protected class eligible for affirmative action benefits.[160]
Donald Devine, who headed the Office of Personnel Management from
1981 to 1995, was especially critical of the way Clinton implemented the
policy, arguing that Clinton had circumvented public deliberation and
congressional involvement by resorting to an executive order and calling
on Congress to overturn it:

> President Clinton's Executive Order 13087 was issued out of the glare of public
> attention but can have far-reaching implications in both the short- and long-
> term. In my opinion, this order mandates a completely unwise, unworkable,
> and unenforceable policy that will make the government even more difficult to
> manage. Far-reaching policies such as these should be developed with the bene-
> fit of reasoned debate and public consensus, two things obviously lacking here.
> The courts are not properly situated to act decisively and quickly enough to
> prevent the damage this order will do. Congress alone is properly positioned to
> take action correcting this order before it can do much damage both to the
> orderly management of the government and to its equal employment policies
> generally.[161]

Within a few months, legislators had introduced several bills and amendments designed to explicitly overturn 13087 or to prohibit agencies from
using any public funds to enforce it.[162] For all of the huffing and puffing
about presidential imperialism, though, Congress did nothing about the

order itself. On the one floor vote on the matter, a spending prohibition amendment to the Commerce, Justice, State, Judiciary, and Related Agencies appropriations bill, the proposal lost by a wide margin in early 1998, 176–252.[163] The fate of 13087 offers yet another example of Congress's relative inability to counter executive orders through legislation.

Executive Orders and Social Change

Why has affirmative action taken a path different from that of the other issues originally raised by civil rights executive orders? Unlike the fair employment and nondiscrimination orders, which are now considered routine, the controversy over affirmative action has only grown with time. To historian Graham, the difference is that Executive Order 11246, the Philadelphia Plan, and affirmative action marked a change in the substance of civil rights policy, from one enjoying a broad consensus in favor to one fraught with conflicting loyalties and contradictory impulses. After 1965 the civil rights agenda shifted from equality of opportunity and passive nondiscrimination to equality of results. This changed the focus of political debate from individual-level discrimination to a zero-sum game of preferences, compensation for past discrimination, and group identity, with the goal of ensuring equality as a fact: "It is this policy watershed, between classic liberalism's core command against discrimination on the one hand, and the new theory of compensatory justice on the other, that was crossed in 1967–68. After 1965 the civil rights era moved from Phase I, when anti-discrimination policy was enacted into federal law, to Phase II, when the problems and politics of implementation produced a shift of administrative and judicial enforcement from a goal of equal treatment to one of equal results."[164] Compensatory justice is inevitably a more complex and controversial concept than equality of opportunity, and it pits conflicting interests directly against each other.

Whether Graham is correct or not in his assessment of why affirmative action remains contentious, there is no question that the institutions and doctrines surrounding affirmative action have proved remarkably resistant to presidential change. Federal affirmative action was an executive creation, and as such is susceptible to revision or outright retraction. Yet even Reagan, whose administration was openly opposed to the policy, found the costs of repeal too high. The result has been, at least insofar as Congress and the presidency are concerned, a stalemate, with neither branch able to move one way or the other (the judiciary is another matter, as are the states, which is why opponents of affirmative action have directed their efforts at them).

The story of presidential action in civil rights, from Roosevelt's establishment of the Fair Employment Practices Committee in 1941, to Truman's integration of the military in 1941, through Kennedy's efforts to ban discrimination in federal housing programs in 1962, displays many of the same dynamics seen in the previous chapters on presidential control of institutions and defense policy. In this area, presidents had to rely on executive authority to outmaneuver a Congress that was less enamored of civil rights, and to secure political advantages by responding to an increasingly important and well-organized set of interests. Presidents since Roosevelt have tried to do this without arousing the wrath of southern political interests that have been both opposed to federal intervention and a critical bloc in Congress. And when their executive authority lacked the necessary reach, presidents relied on their ability to focus public attention on civil rights.

The civil rights executive orders issued by presidents from Roosevelt to Nixon did not originate spontaneously in a political vacuum: they were spurred by a complicated mix of moral arguments, raw political calculations, cultural and demographic shifts in the populace, and particular pressure strategies adopted by those who wanted the orders issued. All of these forces played a role, and none of them alone would have been sufficient to spur the executive to action (indeed, William Monroe Trotter's entreaty to Woodrow Wilson in 1914 was similar in many respects to A. Philip Randolph's to FDR in1941, but the contexts in which the appeals took place and the strategies available to each were sufficiently different that Randolph succeeded in getting a nondiscrimination executive order whereas Trotter did not). Beginning with Executive Order 8802, successive presidential actions took their place within a broader political context of racial politics at the same time that they helped shape that context.

Presidents used executive orders to prod and drag Congress when the legislature refused to enact significant new protections, and to steer a middle course that would not prove excessively antagonizing to the South. By relying on executive orders to embark on such a difficult course, "presidents began to pick their way warily through the minefield" of racial politics.[165] Presidential involvement was crucial, in that it established the federal government's role in civil rights enforcement: scarcely a decade after Roosevelt's 1941 establishment of the Fair Employment Practices Committee in 1941 (an important but ultimately ineffective organization), the validity of presidential nondiscrimination efforts was "assumed,"[166] and White House officials recognized that efforts to back away from the precedent of nondiscrimination in federal activities would provoke sharp opposition.[167]

The use of executive orders in civil rights demonstrates in one sense the limits of executive power to foster broad and enduring social change. In this regard civil rights falls into the theoretical predictions of the "politics of structure" model I employed in chapters four and five to analyze the use of executive orders to expand the president's control over government institutions and processes. The expectation is that the farther an executive action reaches beyond the government in requiring changes in private behavior, the greater the controversy about the legitimacy and authority of the action. Executive action can serve as a spark to ignite a broader dialogue by placing an issue on the national agenda and extending the envelope of acceptable social policies. It can establish an anchor point for political debate, and can help draw Congress and the courts along. By itself, though, it cannot create consensus where the middle ground does not otherwise exist; the persistence of the affirmative action controversy nearly four decades after Executive Orders 10925 and 11246, and more than thirty years after the Philadelphia Plan established the baseline for "goals and timetables," attests to the limits of the president's ability to force a policy on a skeptical public. The discretion and flexibility of executive action as opposed to legislation can, to use Graham's language, help presidents "pick their way" carefully through complicated policies, but on some issues the trail is so narrow and convoluted that no path is clear of mines.

Seven

Conclusion

JOSEPH STORY, in his venerable *Commentaries on the Constitution,* found that the proper scope and organization of the executive power are "problems among the most important, and probably the most difficult to be satisfactorily resolved, of all which are involved in the theory of free governments."[1] Missing the mark on achieving the proper balance leads directly to the pathologies of republican governments that the Framers feared. An executive that is too strong would re-create monarchy; a weak executive would prove unable to stop the government from tumbling into chaos and paralysis.

In constructing the presidency, and the other institutions of the federal government, the Framers strove to get that balance right. But as is the case with trying to balance majority rule with protection of minority rights, it is hard to accommodate such contradictory—if not mutually exclusive—imperatives. We want a president who is empowered to deal effectively with emergencies, but not one who can usurp popular sovereignty or exercise power without accountability. We impose constitutional constraints—checks and balances, explicit limits on presidential power, congressional removal—but fret when the president appears paralyzed by forces he cannot control.

The Framers, in creating a presidency with limited powers and an enhanced ability to act, along with a Congress with broader powers, but subject to majoritarian and collective constraints, got the balance right. This is reflected in the remarkable self-correcting attributes of our constitutional system. Presidents who push too far find themselves the object of broad political condemnation (Reagan, with Iran-Contra) or formal sanction (Nixon, Clinton). But the predictions of either the imperial presidency or the paralyzed presidency have proved wrong; the office is both resilient *and* subject to moderating influences. The president occupies an office beset by contradictory impulses, or ambivalence (to use Harvey Mansfield's term): the occupant "innovates and initiates" at the same time that he seeks to portray himself as merely an agent of the popular will, "now subordinate, now independent."[2]

President Clinton's travails in 1998 and 1999 highlighted this duality. His affair with Monica Lewinsky, subsequent independent counsel investigation, impeachment, and trial provoked sharply different reactions. To many, Clinton represented the worst of presidential imperialism: shocking lapses in moral and ethical behavior, legalistic and evasive hairsplitting, subversion of the judicial process for personal gain, and an avoidance of individual and legal accountability outrageous enough to justify his removal from office. Many others saw the impeachment process as little more than an effort to topple a president by any means possible—a case of score settling for the highest of constitutional stakes, fueled by an independent counsel who appeared to have no sense of proportion.

Yet even as the House was poised to begin its deliberations over the articles of impeachment approved by the Judiciary Committee, Clinton again demonstrated the power of the president's unilateral authority. On December 16, 1998, Clinton ordered a military attack on Iraq in response to Saddam Hussein's defiance of United Nations arms inspectors. Unlike the August 1998 military attack, this time members of Congress were openly skeptical about Clinton's motives. Senate Majority Leader Trent Lott (R-Miss.) questioned both "the timing and the policy." House Majority Leader Richard Armey (R-Tex.) argued that "the suspicion some people have about the president's motives in this attack is itself a powerful argument for impeachment. After months of lies, the president has given millions of people around the world reason to doubt that he has sent Americans into battle for the right reasons."[3] But Clinton was still able to commit the United States to military action on his word. More pointedly, with his legal protections steadily eroding and his political support weakening (the Supreme Court had declined to give the president immunity from civil suits while in office, and Independent Counsel Starr successfully challenged assertions of confidentiality with close advisors, government lawyers, and the Secret Service), Clinton appeared to thrive: after the House voted to impeach him, his approval rating rose.

Congressional Republicans strenuously objected to what they saw as Clinton's excessive use of executive orders to circumvent the legislative process. It is, however, hard to take many of the claims seriously, and most were motivated more by the substance of what Clinton was doing than by any sincere concerns over the legitimate scope of presidential authority (Representative Chenoweth's fuming over the American Heritage Rivers Initiative as a violation of limited government did not impede her efforts to declare a national day of day of "prayer, fasting and humiliation before God," a bill that left civil libertarians and First Amendment proponents aghast).[4] The dire warnings of impending dictatorship through executive orders are overstated, and they serve not only to exaggerate the nature of the president's authority but also to divert attention from more serious issues involving government accountability and the development of unwarranted federal government power. Concerns about presidential power are functionally tied to concerns about government power since, as I have tried to show, the expansion in the president's executive authority corresponds to the rise of the modern administrative state.

"Energy in the executive," insisted Hamilton in *Federalist* 70, "is a leading character in the definition of good government." The president's ability to reorganize institutions, alter administrative procedures, and generally act like a chief executive is an important power, one with consequences beyond what appears to be, at first glance, the sort of issue that could only be of interest to bureaucratic junkies or devotees of organizational theory. Presidents, by using their formal powers to capture new capabilities as they develop and by reshaping processes to link their preferences more directly with outcomes, have taken advantage of their unique position and powers to exert significant control over federal government activities. This does not deny the realities of separated powers, or what presidency scholar Charles O. Jones calls the "separated system," and we need not view the executive-legislative relationship as a zero-sum game. It does suggest, however, that studies of presidential power should pay more attention to the legal and institutional sources of presidential authority, and that political scientists should mend the split in the literature between the legal and the political aspects of the institution and individual presidents.

But the "institutional" model I set out in chapters one and two clearly predicts a gradual expansion of presidential power. Over time, presidents have taken control of significant areas of government policy, typically by taking the initiative and relying on Congress's relative inability to respond effectively. Presidents have engaged in these struggles throughout the twentieth century, not because of their personal predilections but because the institutional resources for leadership with which they are endowed fall well short of the leadership expectations with which they are burdened. In the long run, presidents have prevailed in these struggles. With the advantage of superior information and the capacity to act unilaterally or "go first," modern presidents have succeeded in creating institutional capabilities for influence—over budgets, over agency rulemaking, over foreign affairs and intelligence—that have far surpassed those of their predecessors. If, as the case study chapters have shown, it is the president who is better positioned to expand institutional boundaries and legal authority (as opposed to Congress), the inevitable result appears to be a steady concentration of power within the executive branch.

Such a concentration of power, especially in combination with an inefficient Congress and a deferential judiciary, poses the clear risk for misuse.[5] Can presidents use executive orders to resurrect the imperial presidency? My answer is no. The key is that the use of executive orders is conditioned on presidents' overall political situation: presidents balance the benefits of issuing an order against the costs of doing so. Despite fears that executive orders can undermine popular sovereignty, it is also possible that they can *enhance* accountability by creating a clear decision trail that leads directly to the president.[6] Despite the often arcane language and obscure provisions in many executive orders, the orders themselves leave no doubt about who is speaking. There are limits to what presidents can accomplish with executive orders (as Truman discovered in *Youngstown*), but this does not negate the fact that presidents can use them strategically. It is, ultimately, possible to unite the legal approach to presidential power with the behavioral approach epitomized by Neustadt's *Presidential Power*. In that connection lies the ultimate protection against abuse of executive authority, for it is not simply words on a legal document that give rise to power, but the context that surrounds them as well.

Norton Long, in a classic work on public administration, asked what precisely gives the written law its force and effect. He distinguished force and effect from the law's formal authority, a classification that parallels the behavioral paradigm's distinction between influence and formal power. In doing so, he drew direct comparisons between executive orders and legislation as instruments of government authority.

At the time Long wrote, just after World War II, the governing assumption of public administration was that bureaucrats got all of the authority and power they needed through statutes, and that implementation was automatic. Congress says "Do this, do that" with a statute, and the bureaucracy and public respond. Yet in a work that challenged the existing notions of administrative science, Long argued that this was a one-dimensional view of legal authority. The legal authority of statutes, he concluded, depended not only on the formal declaration of policy but also on the constellation of political and social forces that surround any complex policy:

> Neither statute nor executive order, however, confers more than the legal authority to act. Whether Congress or President can impart the substance of power as well as the form depends upon the line-up of forces in the particular case. A price control law wrung from a reluctant Congress by an amorphous and unstable combination of consumer and labor groups is formally the same as a law enacting a support price program for agriculture backed by the disciplined organizations of farmers and their congressmen. The differences for the scope and effectiveness of administration are obvious. The Presidency, like Congress, responds to and translates the pressures that play upon it. The real mandate contained in an Executive order varies with the political strength of the group demand embodied in it, and the context of other group demands.[7]

In other words, the concept that formal authority cannot serve as the sole source of presidential power and influence applies no differently to

Congress and the laws *it* enacts. The corollary is that the existence of formal authority does not, by itself, automatically mean that every action taken thereby is immediately implemented.

Identifying a central tendency, in any case, does not eliminate the importance of outlying cases that prove to be exceptions. Congress can, if sufficiently provoked, respond with enough force to convince the president to back down, even when there is no question about where the legal authority lies. One example, identified in chapter one, was Clinton's imminent order to overturn the military's ban on gay and lesbian personnel. There was no doubt whatsoever about Clinton's authority to make the policy change, but in the face of enormous congressional opposition and a legislative battle that he knew he would lose, Clinton demurred. A second case occurred in 1998. In May, Clinton issued Executive Order 13083, which suspended a Reagan-era order implementing procedural and substantive requirements on federal actions affecting state and local governments.[8] The Reagan order imposed limits on the ability of federal agencies to preempt state and local law via the rulemaking process, and Clinton's replacement order instituted a far more elastic standard for justifying federal involvement. The reaction to the order was quick, extremely negative, and unusually broad. Congressional critics mobilized along with the National Governors' Association, the U.S. Conference of Mayors, the National League of Cities, the National Association of County Officials, and the National Conference of State Legislators to protest what they argued was an ill-conceived encroachment on state and local government autonomy.[9] Many pointed out the irony that the order explicitly required extensive consultation with local governments on federalism issues, but was drafted with no consultation at all. Faced with such strong opposition, the administration backtracked immediately; Clinton suspended Executive Order 13083 in August 1998 with Executive Order 13095.[10]

The ultimate check on executive energy is—and should be—political. Congress can step in to reclaim the ground it has lost to the executive, and its failure to do so is much more a function of political will than of any flaws in constitutional arrangements. If, say, the 105th Congress had successfully overturned the affirmative action requirements in Executive Order 11246, the ban on assassinations included in the intelligence orders, or the secrecy regulations in Executive Order 12356, its success would not be viewed as a destruction of constitutional foundations (although, to be sure, there would be vigorous debate about the merits). More important, a president would be hard pressed to defy such a legislative statement, although we might expect chief executives to exploit any residual discretion that Congress left them. When presidents have ignored statutory limits on their power, as exemplified by the ineffective 1973 War Powers Resolution, they are often able to do so because Congress has either left them with more than enough residual decision space (or, to use a less technical term, "wriggle room") to permit broad discretion or has passed legislation with poorly worded or ineffective restrictions. The history of executive-legislative relations strongly suggests that overreaching by one branch often leads to a clear response from the other. Fisher notes: "At some point, after passing beyond a threshold of common sense and prudence, aggressive actions become counterproductive. They trigger revolts, leading to the recapture of ground taken not only in the most recent assault but in earlier offenses as well."[11] The boundaries of executive power might be ambiguous, but they are not invisible.

The importance of the legal construction of the executive has not been matched by a commensurate level of attention, at least among political scientists, to the empirical, historical, or normative aspects of the question of just how much executive power is enough. This in part reflects both the ambiguities that surrounded the original debates about the presidency and the initial decisions concerning its structure, which lacked a coherent theory of executive power and which were the product more of compromise than of consistency. What the Framers ultimately created was an office that was designed to be strong in order that the country could respond to emergencies; at the same time, it was an office that concealed much of that power in conceptions that viewed it as merely an agent for carrying out the will of Congress.[12]

The tangled history of the executive power points to the conclusion that executive orders matter. Presidents, particularly in the twentieth century (although there are crucial examples from earlier history), have pushed the boundaries of presidential power by taking advantage of gaps in constitutional and statutory language that allow them to fill power vacuums and gain control of emerging capabilities. Because of the inherent ambiguities of the constitutional vestments of executive authority, presidents have expanded their powers outward as a function of precedent, public expectations, and deference from the legislative and judicial branches. Executive orders have played a central role in this expansion.

In order to see the importance of constitutional form to the presidency, studies of presidential power must include a broader understanding of the president's formal powers. The notion that studying the president's constitutional authority will not produce useful or interesting findings is shortsighted, and it obscures important elements of the institution. A president's willingness to exercise formal legal authority is conditioned on broader strategic considerations, to be sure, but that does not diminish the powers available. Even within the constitutional constraints of the separation of powers, presidents can use executive orders to alter and adapt government structure, processes, and policies. A president's ability to effect major policy change on his own is in many instances less dependent on personality or powers of persuasion than on the office's formal authority and the inherent characteristics of governing institutions. To understand the nature of the president's legal power, executive orders are a good place to start.

List of Abbreviations

CF	Confidential Files
DDEL	Dwight D. Eisenhower Library, Abilene, Kans.
FDRL	Franklin D. Roosevelt Library, Hyde Park, N.Y.
GRFL	Gerald R. Ford Library, Ann Arbor, Mich.
HSTL	Harry S Truman Library, Independence, Mo.
JCL	Jimmy Carter Library, Atlanta, Ga.
JFKL	John F. Kennedy Library, Boston, Mass.
LBJL	Lyndon Baines Johnson Library, Austin, Tex.
NPMP	Nixon Presidential Materials Project, National Archives, College Park, Md.
O/A	Oversize/Attachment files
OF	Official Files
RCGS	Records of the Commission on Government Security, 1955–1957. National Archives, College Park, Md.
RRL	Ronald Reagan Library, Simi Valley, Calif.
SMOF	Staff Member Office Files
WHCF	White House Central Files
WHSF	White House Staff Files
WHO/OSANSA	White House Office/Office of the Special Assistant for National Security Affairs
WHO/OSS	White House Office/Office of the Staff Secretary
WHORM	White House Office of Records Management

Notes

1. The immediate cause of the crisis was the Mexican government's December 1994 decision to devalue the peso in an unsuccessful attempt to stem the flow of capital out of the country and allow the government to repay loans that were coming due. If the crisis was left unchecked, some thought, Mexico faced severe economic hardship that could interfere with political reforms instituted in recent years. In addition, the effects threatened to spill over internationally by destroying investor confidence in emerging markets worldwide, which would in turn hurt the U.S. and European economies. See James D. Humphrey III, "Foreign Affairs Power and 'The First Crisis of the 21st Century': Congressional vs. Executive Authority and the Stabilization Plan for Mexico," *Michigan Journal of International Law* 17 (1995): 181–220.

2. Carroll J. Doherty, "Rank and File Draw Line against Aid for Mexico," *Congressional Quarterly Weekly Report* (January 21, 1995): 214.

3. The authorizing statute, 31 U.S.C. § 5302 (b), allows the secretary of the treasury to deal in international financial transactions "consistent with the obligations of the [United States] Government in the International Monetary Fund on orderly exchange arrangements and a stable system of exchange rates," subject to the president's approval.

4. Congress held several hearings on Clinton's decision, and the House asked the president to submit all relevant documents pertaining to the loan guarantees (H. Res. 80). Yet Congress failed in attempts to limit the president's ability to authorize the loan guarantees or alter the basic Exchange Stabilization Fund statute. House Committee on Banking and Financial Services, *U.S. and International Response to the Mexican Financial Crisis*, 104th Cong., 1st sess., 1995, Serial no. 104–1; Senate Committee on Banking, Housing, and Urban Affairs, *The Mexican Peso Crisis*. 104th Cong., 1st sess., 1995, S. Hrg. 104–164; House Committee on Banking and Financial Services, Subcommittee on General Oversight and Investigations, *Administration's Response to the Mexican Financial Crisis*, 104th Cong., 1st sess., 1995, Serial no. 104–13.

5. Executive Order 13099, 63 *Federal Register* 45167 (August 20, 1998).

6. Richard E. Neustadt, *Presidential Power and the Modern Presidents* (New York: Free Press, 1990), 11.

7. E. Donald Elliot, "Why Our Separation of Powers Jurisprudence Is So Abysmal," *George Washington Law Review* 57, no. 3 (January, 1989): 525.

8. Louis Fisher, "Laws Congress Never Made," *Constitution* (fall 1993): 59.

9. Executive Order 8248, 4 *Federal Register* 3864 (September 8, 1939).

10. Clinton L. Rossiter, *The American Presidency*, rev. ed. (New York: New American Library, 1960), 129.

11. Executive Order 9066, 7 *Federal Register* 1407 (February 19, 1942).

12. Executive Order 9981, 13 *Federal Register* 4313 (July 26, 1948).

13. Executive Order 10730, 22 *Federal Register* 7628 (September 25, 1957).

14. American Council on Race Relations, *Report: Executive Orders on Race Discrimination* 3, no. 3 (August 1948): 3.

15. Martin Luther King, Jr., "Equality Now: The President Has the Power," *The Nation* (February 4, 1961): 93.

16. Kennedy's order was Executive Order 10925, 26 *Federal Register* 1977 (March 6, 1961); Johnson's was Executive Order 11246, 30 *Federal Register* 12319 (September 24, 1965). Although these orders made "affirmative action" part of the national lexicon, historian Hugh Davis Graham traces the origins of the phrase to the 1935 Wagner Act and a 1945 New York State antidiscrimination law. Within the civil rights community, the term was routinely used by 1960. See Hugh Davis Graham, *The Civil Rights Era: Origins and Development of National Policy, 1960–1972* (New York: Oxford University Press, 1990), 33–34.

17. Nixon originally formed a group called the Plumbers to investigate and combat leaks in his administration; it sprang from his outrage over the publication of the *Pentagon Papers* in the *New York Times*. In 1971 the Plumbers broke into the office of Daniel Ellsberg's psychiatrist to search for incriminating information about Ellsberg. The Plumbers were also responsible for the Watergate break-in. See Stanley I. Kutler, ed., *Abuse of Power: The New Nixon Tapes* (New York: Free Press, 1997), 1–9.

18. Robert J. Spitzer, "The President, Congress, and the Fulcrum of Foreign Policy," in *The Constitution and the Conduct of American Foreign Policy*, ed. David Gray Adler and Larry N. George (Lawrence: University Press of Kansas, 1996), 102.

19. 16 *Federal Register* 3503 (April 8, 1952).

20. The decision is central to my argument that an emphasis on the president's executive power in studies of the office does not require an assumption that the president is not constrained by the law. As the definitive study of the steel seizure concluded, "When the *Youngstown* decision was made, it seemed dramatic, but more an aberration than the culmination or beginning of a legal trend. It has proved, however, to be an important foundation for the reaffirmation of the proposition that the President is not above the law." Maeva Marcus, *Truman and the Steel Seizure Case* (New York: Columbia University Press, 1977), 248.

21. 46 *Federal Register* 13193 (February 19, 1981).

22. Terry Moe and Scott A. Wilson, "Presidents and the Politics of Structure," *Law and Contemporary Problems* 57, no. 2 (spring 1994): 38.

23. Lawrence Lessig and Cass R. Sunstein, "The President and the Administration," *Columbia Law Review* 94, no. 1 (January 1994): 5.

24. C. Boyden Gray, "Special Interest Regulation and the Separation of Powers," in *The Fettered Presidency: Legal Constraints on the Executive Branch*, ed. L. Gordon Crovitz and Jeremy A. Rabkin (Washington, D.C.: American Enterprise Institute, 1989), 221.

25. Senate Special Committee on National Emergencies and Delegated Emergency Powers, *National Emergencies and Delegated Emergency Powers*, 94th Cong., 2d sess., 1976, 5.

26. House Committee on Expenditures in the Executive Departments, *Investigation of Charges That Proposed Security Regulations under Executive Order 9835 Will Limit Free Speech and a Free Press*, 80th Cong., 1st sess., 1947; House Committee on Government Operations, *Executive Orders and Proclamations: A Study of a Use of Presidential Power*, 85th Cong., 1st sess., Committee Print, December 1957; Senate Special Committee on National Emergencies and Delegated Emergency Powers, *Executive Orders in Times of War and National Emergency*, 93d Cong., 2d sess., 1974, Committee Print; House Committee on Government Operations, Subcommittee on Government Information and Individual Rights, *Executive Order on Security Classification*, 97th Cong., 2d sess., 1982; House Committee on Economic and Educational Opportunities, *Nullifying an Executive Order That Prohibits Federal Contracts with Companies That Hire Permanent Replacements for Striking Employees*, 104th Cong., 1st sess., 1995, Committee Report no. 104–163; House Committee on the Judiciary, Subcommittee on Civil and Constitutional Rights, *Executive Order on Intelligence Activities*, 97th Cong., 2d sess., 1982, Serial no. 112.

27. Fisher, "Laws Congress Never Made," 60.

28. Douglas Jehl, "One Hand Tied, Clinton Offers the Other," *New York Times*, November 10, 1994.

29. James Bennett, "True to Form, Clinton Shifts Energies Back to U.S. Focus," *New York Times*, July 5, 1995.

30. Richard L. Berke, "A Conservative Sure His Time Has Come," *New York Times*, May 30, 1995.

31. "The 2000 Campaign: Excerpts from Democratic Candidates' Debate at the Apollo Theater," *New York Times*, February 23, 2000.

32. William Safire, *Safire's Political Dictionary* (New York: Ballantine Books, 1978), 701. Madison's journal of the Constitutional Convention records John Dickinson arguing the merits of a limited monarchy as a form of Republican government, although he felt such a system was impossible in the United States as it required the existence of nobility. "A house of nobles was essential to such a government,—could these be created by a breach, or by a stroke of the pen? No. They were the growth of ages, and could only arise under a complication of circumstances none of which existed in this country." James Madison, *Notes of Debates in the Federal Convention of 1787* (New York: W. W. Norton & Co., 1987), 57. Kennedy's remarks are recorded in "Transcript of the Second Nixon-Kennedy Debate on National TV," *New York Times*, October 8, 1960.

33. King, "Equality Now," 93.

34. Executive Order 12954, 60 *Federal Register* 13023 (March 10, 1995).

35. *Congressional Record*, March 9, 1995, H2899.

36. Carl Sagan, *The Demon-Haunted World: Science as a Candle in the Dark* (New York: Ballantine Books, 1996), 90–91.

37. Executive Orders 10997 through 11005, 27 *Federal Register* 1522–1544, February 20, 1962.

38. Letter, William A. Geoghegan (assistant deputy attorney general) to Senator Mike Mansfield, October 28, 1963, White House Central Files, Box 2, Folder: FE-6 (Executive Orders), GRFL. These orders, and follow-on orders, are a staple of right-wing literature. See, for example, George Nicholas, "Secret Plan (PRM

32) Gives Total Control to President," *The Spotlight* (May 5, 1980); Eugene Schroder, *Constitution: Fact or Fiction?* (Cleburne, Tex.: Buffalo Creek Press, 1997).

39. Keith Russell, "Stroke of His Pen Subverts the Law," *Insight* (July 27, 1998): 15.

40. Executive Order 13061, 62 *Federal Register* 178, 48445 (September 15, 1997).

41. *Congressional Budget Office Analysis of H.R. 1842*, reprinted in House Committee on Resources, *Terminate Further Development and Implementation of the American Heritage Rivers Initiative*, 105th Cong., 2d sess., 1998, Report no. 105–781.

42. Michael Satchell, "A U.N. 'Plot' on U.S. Rivers: How a Tiny Conservation Idea Became a Global Conspiracy," *U.S. News & World Report* (October 27, 1997): 42.

43. Remarks in *Congressional Record*, June 10, 1997, H3653. Chenoweth introduced H.R. 1842, a bill to terminate the rivers initiative, and filed a lawsuit in federal court claiming that the program was an unconstitutional usurpation of Congress's legislative power. The D.C. District Court dismissed the suit, finding that Chenoweth and other legislators lacked standing; the decision was upheld on appeal (*Chenoweth et al. v. Clinton*, 997 F. Supp. 36 1998; affirmed by the D.C. Court of Appeals in a decision released on July 2, 1999 [no. 98–5905]). In March 2000 the Supreme Court refused to hear an appeal of this decision.

44. Senate Committee on the Judiciary, Subcommittee on Terrorism, Technology, and Government Information, *The Militia Movement in the United States*, 104th Cong., 1st sess., 1997, 84.

45. Phillip J. Cooper, "By Order of the President: Administration by Executive Order and Proclamation," *Administration and Society* 18 (1986): 233–262; George A. Krause and David B. Cohen, "Presidential Use of Executive Orders, 1953–1994," *American Politics Quarterly* 25, no. 4 (October 1997): 458–481; Dennis W. Gleiber and Steven A. Shull, "Presidential Influence in the Policymaking Process," *Western Political Quarterly* 45 (1992):441–468; Fisher, "Laws Congress Never Made."

46. Sara Schramm, "The Politics of Executive Orders" (Ph.D. diss., George Washington University, 1981); Robert A. Shanley, "Presidential Executive Orders and Environmental Policy," *Presidential Studies Quarterly* 13 (1983): 405–416; Joseph Cooper and William West, "Presidential Power and Republican Government: The Theory and Practice of OMB Review," *Journal of Politics* 50 (1988): 864–895.

47. Cooper, "By Order of the President," 234.

48. Schramm, "The Politics of Executive Orders," 155.

49. Shanley, "Presidential Executive Orders and Environmental Policy," 405.

50. Paul C. Light, *The President's Agenda,* rev. ed. (Baltimore: Johns Hopkins UniversityPress, 1991), 117.

51. Mark A. Peterson, *Legislating Together: The White House and Capitol Hill from Eisenhower to Reagan* (Cambridge: Harvard University Press, 1990), 88.

52. The term comes from Charles O. Jones, *The Presidency in a Separated System* (Washington, D.C.: Brookings Institution, 1994).

53. Abner S. Greene, "Checks and Balances in an Era of Presidential Lawmaking," *University of Chicago Law Review* 61 (1994): 123–196; David Schoenbrod, *Power without Responsibility: How Congress Abuses the People through Delegation* (New Haven: Yale University Press, 1993).

54. See, for example, Louis Fisher, *Presidential War Power* (Lawrence: University Press of Kansas, 1995), and Harold Hongju Koh, *The National Security Constitution: Sharing Power after the Iran-Contra Affair* (New Haven: Yale University Press, 1990).

55. The Supreme Court has, on more than one occasion, sidestepped constitutional confrontations with the president out of fear that it would be unable to enforce its decisions and would lose legitimacy as a result. In the most famous of these cases, *Ex Parte Merryman,* 17 Fed. Case no. 9, 487 (1861), Chief Justice of the United States Roger Brooke Taney issued a writ of habeas corpus requiring the commander of Fort McHenry to produce in court Merryman, who had been arrested for leading a secessionist drill company. The commander refused, citing Lincoln's order suspending habeas corpus. At this point Taney backed down, writing that even though he considered Lincoln's suspension of habeas to be illegal, he had done all he could do as an officer of the court and would leave the matter to Lincoln for resolution. Merryman was soon released to civil authorities in any case, and the charges against him were eventually dropped. See J. G. Randall, *Constitutional Problems under Lincoln,* rev. ed. (Urbana: University of Illinois Press, 1951), 162n.

56. Richard Pious, *The American Presidency* (New York: Basic Books, 1979), 16.

57. Norman C. Thomas and Joseph A. Pika, "Institutions and Personalities in Presidency Research," paper delivered at the 1996 annual meeting of the American Political Science Association, August 29–September 1, San Francisco, 6. This view has a distinguished pedigree. Woodrow Wilson, in his 1885 classic *Congressional Government*, urged readers to keep in mind that "the business of the President, occasionally great, is usually not above routine. Most of the time it is *mere* administration" (253–254).

58. In my references to Neustadt, I cite the most recent edition of the book, which was published in 1990. Although Neustadt has added material in successive editions to account for new administrations, he has not revised the chapters in which he sets out his basic argument.

59. Other works in this tradition are Louis W. Koenig, *The Chief Executive* (New York: Harcourt, Brace & World, 1964), and Rossiter, *The American Presidency*, rev. ed.

60. Edward S. Corwin, *The President: Office and Powers* (New York: New York University Press, 1948), 353.

61. Ibid., vii.

62. Joseph M. Bessette and Jeffrey Tulis, "The Constitution, Politics, and the Presidency," in *The Presidency in the Constitutional Order,* ed. Joseph M. Bessette and Jeffrey Tulis (Baton Rouge: Louisiana State University Press, 1981), 4–5.

63. Presidency scholarship was not the only subfield in political science that moved away from formal legal studies. The shift in presidential studies paralleled developments in the way political scientists and legal scholars viewed the courts,

as scholars moved from strictly legal analyses to studies of the dynamics of judicial decision making and judicial values, most notably in the "attitudinal model," which posits that law matters less than judges' attitudes and preferences. See Jeffrey A. Segal and Harold J. Spaeth, *The Supreme Court and the Attitudinal Model* (New York: Cambridge University Press, 1993).

64. Lyn Ragsdale, *Vital Statistics on the Presidency: Washington to Clinton* (Washington, D.C.: Congressional Quarterly, 1996), 2.

65. Pious, *The American Presidency*, 17.

66. Henry P. Monaghan, "The Protective Power of the Presidency," *Columbia Law Review* 93, no. 1 (January 1993): 2.

67. Robert J. Spitzer, "The Constitutionality of the Presidential Line-Item Veto," *Political Science Quarterly* 112, no. 2 (1997): 280.

68. Bessette and Tulis, "The Constitution, Politics, and the Presidency," 6.

69. James Sterling Young, "Thinking about the Purposes of Presidential Power," *Miller Center Journal* 2 (1995): 179–188.

70. Steven Skowronek, *The Politics Presidents Make: Leadership from John Adams to George Bush* (Cambridge: Harvard University Press, 1993), 6.

71. A sampling of the legal literature: Andrée Blumstein, "Doing Good the Wrong Way: The Case for Delimiting Presidential Powers under Executive Order No. 11246," *Vanderbilt Law Review* 33, no. 4 (May 1980): 921–953; Robert B. Cash, "Presidential Power: Use and Enforcement of Executive Orders," *Notre Dame Lawyer* 39 (1963): 44–55; Frank B. Cross, "Executive Orders 12,291 and 12,498: A Test Case in Presidential Control of Executive Agencies," *Journal of Law and Politics* 4 (1988): 483–541; Kimberly A. Egerton, "Presidential Power over Federal Contracts under the Federal Property and Administrative Services Act: The Close Nexus Test of *AFL-CIO v. Kahn*," *Duke Law Journal* 1980, no. 1 (February 1980): 205–233; Joel L. Fleishman and Arthur H. Aufses, "Law and Orders: The Problem of Presidential Legislation," *Law and Contemporary Problems* 40 (1976): 1–45. Michael D. Fricklas, "Executive Order 12356: The First Amendment Rights of Government Grantees," *Boston University Law Review* 64, no. 2 (March 1984): 447–519; John E. Noyes, "Executive Orders, Presidential Intent, and Private Rights of Action," *Texas Law Review* 59 (1981): 836–878; William Neighbors, "Presidential Legislation by Executive Order," *University of Colorado Law Review* 37 (1964): 105–118; Morton Rosenberg, "Beyond the Limits of Executive Power: Presidential Control of Agency Rulemaking under Executive Order 12291," *Michigan Law Review* 80 (1981): 193–247; Morton Rosenberg, "Presidential Control of Agency Rulemaking: An Analysis of Constitutional Issues That May Be Raised by Executive Order 12,291," *Arizona Law Review* 23 (1981): 1199–1234; Cass R. Sunstein, "Cost-Benefit Analysis and the Separation of Powers," *Arizona Law Review* 23 (1981): 1267–1282; Joseph Tauber, "*Dames & Moore v. Regan*: The Constitutionality of the Executive Orders Implementing the Agreement with Iran," *Ohio Northern University Law Review* 9 (1982): 519–527.

72. Peter M. Shane and Harold H. Bruff, *Separation of Powers Law* (Durham, N.C.: Carolina Academic Press, 1996), 131.

73. William F. Fox, Jr., *Understanding Administrative Law*, 3d ed. (New York: Matthew Bender & Co., 1997), 84.

74. Spitzer, "The Constitutionality of the Presidential Line-Item Veto," 280.

75. George C. Edwards III and Stephen J. Wayne, *Presidential Leadership: Politics and Policy Making* (New York: St. Martin's Press, 1994), 448.

76. Bessette and Tulis, "The Constitution, Politics, and the Presidency," 7.

77. Louis Fisher, *Constitutional Conflicts between Congress and the President*, 4th ed. (Lawrence: University Press of Kansas, 1997), x.

78. Cass R. Sunstein, "An Eighteenth Century Presidency in a Twenty-First Century World," *Arkansas Law Review* 48 (1993): 1.

79. Ibid., 15.

80. Peterson, *Legislating Together*; Richard Rose, *The Postmodern President: The White House Meets the World* (Chatham, N.J.: Chatham House, 1988); Gary L. Rose, *The American Presidency under Siege* (Albany: State University of New York Press, 1997). "The mainstream view [of the presidency] has long been that presidents must operate within a basic structural framework, anchored in separation of powers, granting them far less power than the need for strong leadership, and that their key to success is the resourceful pursuit of bargaining and cooperation within this framework" (Moe and Wilson, "Presidents and the Politics of Structure," 13).

81. Rose, *The American Presidency under Siege*, 12.

82. Rose, *The American Presidency under Siege*; Michael A. Genovese, *The Presidency in an Age of Limits* (Westport, Conn.: Greenwood Press, 1993).

83. Neustadt, *Presidential Power and the Modern Presidents*, 24.

84. Peter W. Sperlich, "Bargaining and Overload: An Essay on *Presidential Power*," in *The Presidency*, ed. Aaron Wildavsky (Boston: Little, Brown, 1969), 186.

85. Neustadt, *Presidential Power and the Modern Presidents*, 184.

86. Sperlich, "Bargaining and Overload," 186.

87. Neustadt, *Presidential Power and the Modern Presidents*, 18.

88. Ibid., 23–24.

89. Shane and Bruff, *Separation of Powers Law*, 41. In contrast, one struggles in vain to find a similar expression from the Nixon administration.

90. Douglas W. Kmiec, "The OLC's Opinion Writing Function: The Legal Adhesive for a Unitary Executive," *Cardozo Law Review* 15 (October 1993): 359.

91. Ibid., 361.

92. "Wartime Interpretation of Legislative and Executive Orders. Speech delivered to the Society for Advancement of Management," August 13, 1942, Oscar Cox Papers, Folder: Wartime Interpretation of Legis. and Exec. Orders, FDRL.

93. Louis Fisher, *American Constitutional Law*, 3d ed. (Durham, N.C.: Carolina Academic Press, 1999), 11. The exchange, which took place at an April 17, 1952, press conference, was as follows: "*Q*: Mr. President, if you can seize the steel mills under your inherent powers, can you, in your opinion, also seize the newspapers and/or the radio stations? *The President*: Under similar circumstances the President of the United States has to act for whatever is for the best of the country. That's the answer to your question." *Public Papers of the Presidents— Harry S Truman, 1952–53* (Washington, D.C.: Federal Register Division, National Archives, 1953), 273.

94. *Public Papers of the President, 1952–53*, 301.

95. Bessette and Tulis, "The Constitution, Politics, and the Presidency," 10.

96. Ibid., 10.

97. Edwards and Wayne, *Presidential Leadership*, 148.

98. Bessette and Tulis, "The Constitution, Politics, and the Presidency," 27.

99. Michael J. Horowitz, "Commentary and Exchanges on Politics and Public Debate," in Crovitz and Rabkin, *The Fettered Presidency*, 318.

100. L. Gordon Crovitz and Jeremy A. Rabkin, "Introduction," in Crovitz and Rabkin, *The Fettered Presidency*, 11.

101. *Chamber of Commerce of the United States et al. v. Reich*, 74 F.3d 1322, 1338. The court reasoned that the executive order "applies to all contracts over $100,000, and federal government purchases totaled $437 billion in 1994, constituting approximately 6.5% of the gross domestic product. Federal contractors employ 26 million workers, 22% of the labor force" (1338).

102. Fleishman and Aufses, "Law and Orders," 6.

103. Krause and Cohen, "Presidential Use of Executive Orders, 1953–1994."

104. Gary King, "The Methodology of Presidency Research," in *Researching the Presidency: Vital Questions, New Approaches*, ed. George C. Edwards III, John H. Kessel, and Bert A. Rockman (Pittsburgh: University of Pittsburgh Press, 1993), 387–388.

105. Ibid., 393.

106. Terry M. Moe, "The New Economics of Organization," *American Journal of Political Science* 28, no. 4 (November 1984): 739–777; Terry M. Moe, "Presidents, Institutions, and Theory," in Edwards, Kessel, and Rockman, *Researching the Presidency*.

107. Terry M. Moe, "The Politicized Presidency," in *The New Direction in American Politics*, ed. John E. Chubb and Paul E. Peterson (Washington, D.C.: Brookings Institution, 1985), 238.

108. Thomas J. Weko, *The Politicizing Presidency: The White House Personnel Office, 1948–1994* (Lawrence: University Press of Kansas, 1995), 11.

109. Moe and Wilson, "Presidents and the Politics of Structure," 4.

110. Moe, "Presidents, Institutions, and Theory," 366.

111. Moe and Wilson, "Presidents and the Politics of Structure," 14.

112. Gordon Silverstein, *Imbalance of Powers: Constitutional Interpretation and the Making of American Foreign Policy* (New York: Oxford University Press, 1997), 145.

113. Senate Special Committee on National Emergencies and Delegated Emergency Powers, *Executive Orders in Times of War and National Emergency*, 93d Cong., 2d sess., 1974, Committee Print. The attorney general's opinion to the secretary of commerce about the legality of Johnson's executive order on currency controls traces the history of the Trading with the Enemy Act and presidential reliance on the law. Letter, Attorney General to Alexander B. Trowbridge, February 3, 1968, White House Central Files, EX-FO, Folder: EX-FO 4–1, 1/3/68–1/10/68. LBJL.

114. Koh, *The National Security Constitution*, 46–47.

115. The act, as it existed in 1977, authorizes the president, during "time of war or during any other period of national emergency dictated by the President,"

to regulate "under such rules and regulations as he may prescribe," foreign exchange transactions, the import and or export of gold and silver, and to broadly control how foreign countries or citizens conduct transactions within the United States (50 U.S.C. § 5(b)).

116. *Dames & Moore v. Regan,* 453 U.S. 654, 677 (1981).

117. Koh, *The National Security Constitution,* 48. In contrast, Silverstein attributes the failure of the IEEPA to constrain the president on, in part, bad drafting: "It contained no hard definitions of emergencies, no penalty for failure to consult with Congress, and the burden remained on Congress to revoke an emergency, rather than on the president to demonstrate its necessity." Silverstein, *Imbalance of Powers;* 154.

118. Moe and Wilson, "Presidents and the Politics of Structure," 14.

119. Larry Evans, Jarrell Wright, and Neal Devins, "Congressional Procedure and Statutory Interpretation," *Administrative Law Review* 45 (1993): 239.

120. Jessica Korn, *The Power of Separation: American Constitutionalism and the Myth of the Legislative Veto* (Princeton: Princeton University Press, 1996). In fact, Korn argues that the legislative veto was never useful as a policy tool. Its defenders mistook its "symbolic importance for actual policy making power" (p. 122).

121. Ibid., 116–117.

122. Steven G. Calabresi, "Some Normative Arguments for the Unitary Executive," *Arkansas Law Review* 48 (1995): 30.

123. Terry M. Moe and William G. Howell, "The Presidential Power of Unilateral Action," *Journal of Law, Economics and Organization* 15, no. 1 (April 1999). Moe and Howell identify a handful of cases in which Congress overturned other forms of executive action. An example occurred in 1995, when the 1996 Department of Defense Authorization Act prohibited spending funds on any abortion services at U.S. military installations. This overturned one of Clinton's first actions as president, but that action was an administrative directive to the secretary of defense, not an executive order.

124. Noyes, "Executive Orders, Presidential Intent, and Private Rights of Action," 846.

125. Public Law 105–261, § 3161.

126. "Congress Suspends Declassification Order," *News Media & the Law* (winter 1999): 15.

127. In the case of Clinton's federalism order, his original order rescinded an earlier Reagan administration order, so when he rescinded *that* order it left the Reagan order intact and in force. I discuss this order in more detail in chapter seven.

128. In this framework presidents are assumed to be less affected by electoral and interest group pressures, and are better equipped to think about how government as a whole works (Moe and Wilson, "Presidents and the Politics of Structure," 11–13). Legislators, in contrast, are consumed with reelection goals and are more concerned with creating institutions that deliver services to constituents than they are with ensuring overall government responsiveness and efficiency. Not everyone agrees with the veracity of these assumptions; see, for example,

Jonathan R. Macey, "Comment: Confrontation or Cooperation for Mutual Gain?" *Law and Contemporary Problems* 57, nos. 1–2 (1994): 45–57.

129. Neustadt, *Presidential Power and the Modern Presidents*, 17.

Chapter Two
Executive Orders and the Law

1. Peter M. Shane and Harold H. Bruff, *Separation of Powers Law* (Durham, N.C.: Carolina Academic Press, 1996), 130.

2. Senate Special Committee on National Emergencies and Delegated Emergency Powers, *Executive Orders in Times of War and National Emergency*, 93d Cong., 2d sess., 1974, 2.

3. House Committee on Government Operations, *Executive Orders and Proclamations: A Study of a Use of Presidential Power*, 85th Cong., 1st sess., 1957.

4. Robert B. Cash, "Presidential Power: Use and Enforcement of Executive Orders," *Notre Dame Lawyer* 39, no. 1 (1963): 44.

5. William D. Neighbors, "Presidential Legislation by Executive Order," *University of Colorado Law Review* 37 (1964): 106.

6. Edward S. Corwin, *The President: Office and Powers* (New York: New York University Press, 1948), 440n.

7. Henry P. Monaghan, "The Protective Power of the Presidency," *Columbia Law Review* 93, no. 1 (January 1993): 1–74.

8. Terry Eastland, *Energy in the Executive: The Case for the Strong Presidency* (New York: Free Press, 1992), 351.

9. Joel L. Fleishman and Arthur H. Aufses, "Law and Orders: The Problem of Presidential Legislation," *Law and Contemporary Problems* 40 (1976): 5.

10. Corwin, *The President*, 440n. Some proclamations, to be sure, have important substantive impact (particularly Lincoln's Emancipation Proclamation).

11. Louis Fisher, *Constitutional Conflicts between Congress and the President*, 4th ed. (Lawrence: University Press of Kansas, 1997), 110.

12. Memo, William Nichols to Staff Secretary, February 13, 1975, Folder "ND-13-3: Security—Classified Information, 8/9/74–2/29/75, Box 26, White House Central Files, GRFL.

13. Fleishman and Aufses, "Law and Orders," 5.

14. Corwin, *The President*, 149.

15. Louis Fisher, *American Constitutional Law*, 3d ed. (Durham, N.C.: Carolina Academic Press, 1999), 225.

16. *Jenkins v. Collard*, 145 U.S. 557, 560–561 (1891).

17. *Little v. Barreme*, 2 Cranch 170 (1804).

18. Lawrence Lessig and Cass R. Sunstein, "The President and the Administration," *Columbia Law Review* 94 (1994): 1–123; Steven Calabresi and Saikrishna Prakash, "The President's Power to Execute the Laws," *Yale Law Journal* 104 (1994): 541–663.

19. Monaghan, "The Protective Power of the Presidency," 6.

20. *Youngstown Sheet and Tube v. Sawyer*, 343 U.S. 579 (1952), 635–663.

21. This term comes from A. Michael Froomkin, "The Imperial Presidency's New Vestments," *Northwestern University Law Review* 88, no. 4 (1994): 1349.

22. Calabresi and Prakash, "The President's Power to Execute the Laws," 599.

23. Lessig and Sunstein, "The President and the Administration," 2.

24. Shane and Bruff, *Separation of Powers Law*, 420.

25. John P. Roche, "Executive Power and Domestic Emergency: The Quest for Prerogative," in *The Presidency*, ed. Aaron Wildavsky (Boston: Little, Brown, 1969), 713.

26. *Myers v. United States*, 272 U.S. 52, 135.

27. *Humphrey's Executor v.s. United States*, 295 U.S. 602 (1935).

28. Froomkin, "The Imperial Presidency's New Vestments," 1349.

29. 478 U.S. 714, 734.

30. E. Donald Elliot, "Why Our Separation of Powers Jurisprudence Is So Abysmal," *George Washington Law Review* 57, no. 3 (January 1989): 506–532.

31. Lessig and Sunstein, "The President and the Administration," 6–7.

32. *Youngstown Sheet and Tube v. Sawyer*, 634–635.

33. Ibid., 635.

34. Shane and Bruff, *Separation of Powers Law*, 14.

35. J. G. Randall, *Constitutional Problems under Lincoln*, rev. ed. (Urbana: University of Illinois Press, 1951), 35.

36. Steven G. Calabresi and Kevin H. Rhodes, "The Structural Constitution: Unitary Executive, Plural Judiciary," *Harvard Law Review* 105, no. 6 (April 1992): 1176.

37. Lessig and Sunstein, "The President and the Administration," 68.

38. Calabresi and Prakash, "The President's Power to Execute the Laws," 570.

39. Monaghan, "The Protective Power of the Presidency," 22.

40. James Thomas Flexner, *Washington: The Indispensable Man* (Boston: Little, Brown, 1974), 277.

41. Louis Fisher, *Presidential War Power* (Lawrence: University Press of Kansas, 1995), 20.

42. *Federalist* 70–77.

43. Fisher, *Presidential War Power*, 21.

44. Ruth Wiessbourd Grant and Stephen Grant, "The Madisonian Presidency," in *The Presidency in the Constitutional Order*, ed. Joseph M. Bessette and Jeffrey Tulis (Baton Rouge: Louisiana State University Press, 1981), 50.

45. In 1890 the Supreme Court resolved the question of implied powers in favor of the president, ruling in *In re Neagle*, 135 U.S. 1, 27 (1890), that the constitutional directive that the president "shall take care that the laws be faithfully executed" indicated the existence of implied administrative powers not directly mentioned.

46. James Rogers Sharp, *American Politics in the Early Republic* (New Haven: Yale University Press, 1993), 91.

47. *In re Neagle*, 27.

48. Shane and Bruff, *Separation of Powers Law*, 51.

49. There is no doubt that they recognized the legitimacy of government secrecy on the whole, as the Constitutional Convention itself was conducted in secret. See Mark J. Rozell, *Executive Privilege: The Dilemma of Secrecy and Democratic Accountability* (Baltimore: Johns Hopkins University Press, 1994), 27–28.

50. *Chicago and Southern Airlines v. Waterman Steamship Corp.*, 333 U.S. 103, 111 (1948).

51. *New York Times Co. v. United States*, 403 U.S. 713, 728 (1971), J. Stewart, concurring.

52. *United States v. Nixon*, 418 U.S. 684, 706 (1974).

53. *United States v. Nixon* remains the most important case in this area.

54. Fisher, *Constitutional Conflicts between Congress and the President*, 88–89.

55. Ibid., 87.

56. See, for example, R. Kent Weaver, *Automatic Government: The Politics of Indexation* (Washington, D.C.: Brookings Institution, 1988); Theodore J. Lowi, *The End of Liberalism: The Second Republic of the United States* (New York: W. W. Norton, 1979); David Schoenbrod, *Power without Responsibility: How Congress Abuses the People through Delegation* (New Haven: Yale University Press, 1993).

57. *J. W. Hampton, Jr. & Co. v. United States*, 276 U.S. 394, 409 (1928). The Court reaffirmed this principle in *Loving v. United States*, 116 S. Ct. 1737 (1996).

58. Shane and Bruff, *Separation of Powers Law*, 112.

59. The first—and only other—case was *Panama Refining Co. v. Ryan*, 293 U.S. 388 (1935), in which the Court rejected a legislative delegation that authorized the president to bar shipments of oil in excess of quotas established by individual states.

60. *A.L.A. Schecter Poultry Corp. v. United States*, 295 U.S. 495 (1935).

61. U.S. Department of Commerce, Division of Press Intelligence, "Subject Index of Executive Orders, March 8, 1933–October 1, 1935," Papers of Samuel L. Rosenman, File: Subject Index of Executive Orders, FDRL.

62. *A.L.A. Schechter Poultry Corp. v. United States*, 542.

63. Fisher, *Constitutional Conflicts between Congress and the President*, 100.

64. *American Trucking Associations v. Environmental Protection Agency*, 175 F.3d 1027, 1033 (1999).

65. The Walsh-Healy Act (41 U.S.C. 35–45) sets wage, hour, and working-condition requirements for government contractors. The Davis-Bacon Act (40 U.S.C. 276a et seq.) requires contractors to pay the "prevailing wage" for local workers. The Competition in Contracting Act of 1984 requires civilian and military procurement agencies to award contracts on the basis of "full and open competition." The statute specified the conditions under which agencies could award noncompetitive contracts (for example, when only one source could provide the government with what it needed, or when government needs are of "unusual and compelling urgency"), but leaves it up to the agencies to determine when these conditions are met.

66. John Cibinc, Jr., and Ralph C. Nash, Jr., *Formation of Government Contracts*, 2d ed. (Washington, D.C.: Government Contracts Program, George Washington University, 1986), 14.

67. Letter, Robert F. Kennedy to Lyndon Johnson, September 26, 1961, George Reedy Papers, Folder: Committee on Equal Employment, LBJL.

68. *AFL–CIO v. Kahn*, 618 F. 2d 784, 794, D.C. Cir. (1979).

69. Executive Order 6246, August 10, 1933; "Memorandum—Executive Orders," Papers of Samuel L. Rosenman, National Recovery Administration, FDRL.

70. Ibid.

71. Andrée Blumstein, "Doing Good the Wrong Way: The Case for Delimiting Presidential Powers under Executive Order No. 11246," *Vanderbilt Law Review* 33, no. 4 (May 1980): 924.

72. 43 *Federal Register* 51375 (November 3, 1978).

73. Kimberly A. Egerton, "Presidential Power over Federal Contracts under the Federal Property and Administrative Services Act: The Close Nexus Test of *AFL-CIO v. Kahn*," *Duke Law Journal* 1980, no. 1 (February 1980): 210.

74. *AFL-CIO v. Kahn*, 789–790. Egerton interprets the decision as recognizing a "presidential power to use government contract leverage to implement broader national policies" ("Presidential Power over Federal Contracts," 218). Ironically, although the appeals court cited past antidiscrimination executive orders to support its argument about the president's procurement authority under the Federal Property and Administrative Services Act, Egerton concludes that the president may not have needed to rely on FPASA to issue them: none of the orders cited the act, and a 1969 Opinion of the Attorney General on the legality of the Philadelphia Plan (a system of specific goals for minority hiring and promotion in the construction trades around Philadelphia) argues only that Executive Order 11246 "is a lawful exercise of the Federal Government's authority to determine the terms and conditions under which it is willing to enter into contracts." Letter, Attorney General John Mitchell to Secretary of Labor, September 22, 1969, Papers of John Dean III, F: Equal Employment Opportunity Commission, NPMP.

75. Egerton, "Presidential Power over Federal Contracts," 212.

76. 60 *Federal Register* 13023 (March 10, 1995).

77. *Chamber of Commerce of the United States et al. v. Reich*, 74 F.3d 1322 (D.C. Cir. 1996).

78. Ibid., 1322.

79. Ibid., 1325.

80. Ibid., 1338.

81. Bruce Ledewitz, "The Uncertain Power of the President to Execute the Laws," *Tennessee Law Review* 46, no. 4 (summer 1979): 770.

82. Donald L. Robinson, "Presidential Prerogative and the Spirit of American Constitutionalism," in *The Constitution and the Conduct of American Foreign Policy*, ed. David Gray Adler and Larry N. George (Lawrence: University Press of Kansas, 1996), 114.

83. Memorandum, Jackson to Roosevelt, August 27, 1940, 4, Presidential Subject Files, Departmental File, Box 62: Defense Program Reports, September and October 1941—Navy: Reports and Bulletins: 1939–March 1940, Folder: Departmental File, Navy: Destroyers and Naval Bases, 1940, Part I, FDRL.

84. Cited in Corwin, *The President*, 189.

85. William Howard Taft, *The Chief Magistrate and His Powers* (New York: Columbia University Press, 1916), 144.

86. Ibid., 139–140.

87. Forrest McDonald, *The American Presidency: An Intellectual History* (Lawrence: University Press of Kansas, 1994), 295–297.

88. In his second term, 1905–1908, Roosevelt issued 830 executive orders, more than five times as many as any previous president had issued in a four-year term. Lyn Ragsdale, *Vital Statistics on the Presidency: Washington to Clinton* (Washington, D.C.: Congressional Quarterly, 1996), 337–340.

89. Clifford L. Lord, *Presidential Executive Orders*, comp. WPA Historical Records Survey (New York: Archives Publishing Co., 1944), 1.

90. Phillip Shaw Paludan, *The Presidency of Abraham Lincoln* (Lawrence: University Press of Kansas, 1994), 71.

91. McDonald, *The American Presidency*, 398. Although the federal judiciary in several cases did view these acts as unconstitutional, they were powerless to intercede when Lincoln refused to accept the rulings. Ultimately "the courts had no option but to let the president do as he pleased" (ibid., 399).

92. James D. Richardson, *A Compilation of the Messages and Papers of the Presidents, 1789–1897*, vol. 6 (Washington, D.C.: Government Printing Office, 1896–1899), 20–31.

93. Corwin, *The President*, 280. Emphasis omitted.

94. Memorandum, "Regulation of Prices and Wages by Executive Order, after Suspension of the Price Control Act," August 27, 1942, Oscar Cox Papers, Folder: Stabilization of the National Economy I, FDRL. For a detailed analysis of the offending provisions, see Bureau of the Budget, *The United States at War: Development and Administration of the War Program by the Federal Government* (Committee of Records of War Administration, War Records Section, Bureau of the Budget), Historical Reports on War Administration, 1946, chap. 9.

95. Assistant Solicitor General, "Wage and Agricultural Price Control under Existing Law," July 23, 1942, Oscar Cox Papers, Folder: Stabilization of the National Economy I, FDRL. In June 1941 Roosevelt seized the North American Aviation plant in California, which was embroiled in a strike. In doing so, he relied upon his "duty constitutionally and inherently resting upon the President to exert his civil and military as well as his moral authority to keep the defense efforts of the United States as a going concern" (Corwin, *The President*, 297, citing Attorney General Robert Jackson's opinion).

96. Corwin, *The President*, 304.

97. "The War Powers of the President: Historical Illustrations," August 25, 1942, Oscar Cox Papers, F: Stabilization of the National Economy I, FDRL.

98. Corwin, *The President*, 304–305.

99. Quoted in Albert L. Sturm, "Emergencies and the Presidency," *Journal of Politics* 11, no. 1 (February 1949): 134.

100. Doris Kearns Goodwin, *No Ordinary Time: Franklin and Eleanor Roosevelt and the Home Front in World War II* (New York: Simon and Schuster, 1994), 359.

101. Memorandum, Oscar Cox to Harry L. Hopkins, February 11, 1943, Oscar Cox Papers, Folder: War Powers of the President, FDRL.

102. *Youngstown Sheet and Tube v. Sawyer*, 646, J. Jackson, concurring.

103. E. Donald Elliot, "Why Our Separation of Powers Jurisprudence Is So Abysmal," *George Washington Law Review* 67, no. 3 (January 1989): 527.

104. Ledewitz, "The Uncertain Power of the President to Execute the Laws," 762.

105. "The legislature not only commands the purse but prescribes the rules by which the duties and rights of every citizen are to be regulated." Hamilton, *Federalist* 78.

106. 43 Op. A.G. no. 29 (1981), reprinted in Shane and Bruff, *Separation of Powers Law*, 185–189.

107. Executive Order 10924, 26 *Federal Register* 1789 (March 2, 1961).

108. Louis Fisher, *Presidential Spending Power* (Princeton: Princeton University Press, 1975), 67–68.

109. Comp. Stat. 1913, 4614, 4628. Cited in *U.S. v. Midwest Oil*, 465.

110. *U.S. v. Midwest Oil*, 474.

111. Fisher, *American Constitutional Law*, 220.

112. The Supreme Court cited the *Midwest Oil* reasoning in, for example, *Youngstown* and *Dames & Moore v. Regan*.

113. Fisher, *Presidential War Power*, 21. Glennon argued that the use of "custom" in interbranch disputes should be conditioned on the finer points of the practice in question. In addition to the frequency and duration of the practice, he also suggests examining its consistency and continuity as well as the institutional capacity to express objections. This last condition places Congress at a serious disadvantage with respect to the president, since the collective nature of Congress means by definition that it will find it harder to articulate a meaningful position through, say, legislation or committee documents, than the president will in his public statements. Michael J. Glennon, "The Use of Custom in Resolving Separation of Powers Disputes," *Boston University Law Review* 64 (1984): 109–151.

114. *Youngstown Sheet and Tube v. Sawyer*, 610–611.

115. Ibid., 598.

116. Lawrence H. Tribe, "Toward a Syntax of the Unsaid: Construing the Sounds of Congressional and Constitutional Silence," *Indiana Law Journal* 57 (1982): 520. Emphasis in original.

117. Ibid., 527.

118. *Dames & Moore v. Regan*, 453 U.S. 654 (1981), 677.

119. Ibid., 678; Joseph Tauber, "*Dames & Moore v. Regan*: The Constitutionality of the Executive Orders Implementing the Agreement with Iran," *Ohio Northern University Law Review* 9 (1982): 526–527.

120. *Immigration and Naturalization Service vs. Chadha*, 462 U.S. 919 (1983).

121. Harold Horgju Koh, *The National Security Constitution: Sharing Power after the Iran-Contra Affair* (New Haven: Yale University Press, 1990), 142.

122. *Jenkins v. Collard* 145 U.S. 546 (1891); *Independent Meat Packers Association, et al. v. Butz* 526 F.2d 228 (8th Cir., 1975), rehearing and rehearing en banc denied December 15, 1975, *cert. denied* March 22, 1976, 424 U.S. 966; *Marks v. Central Intelligence Agency* 590 F.2d 997 (D.C. Cir., 1978).

123. House Committee on Government Operations, *Executive Orders and Proclamations: A Study of a Use of Presidential Power*, 85th Cong., 1st sess., 1957, Committee Print, 4–5.

124. Fisher, *Presidential War Powers*, 19; Fisher notes that in 1807, Congress enacted a law that held navy captain Little blameless for obeying a presidential order, and also reimbursed him for the damages he paid (ibid.).

125. Examples of the Court's overturning executive orders on constitutional grounds include *Youngstown*. Examples of orders overturned on the grounds that the president exceeded or failed to comply with statutory authorities include *Chamber of Commerce v. Reich* (Clinton's replacement worker order) and *Cole v. Young*, 351 U.S. 536 (1956), in which the Court ruled that Eisenhower's imposition of a "loyalty" standard for security clearances exceeded the scope of powers that Congress had delegated in a 1950 statute. More often the courts uphold executive orders.

126. This is true even if the underlying order itself is valid: though the president's ability to mandate affirmative action programs in government contractors has been upheld as a valid exercise of statutory authority, the courts "uniformly have refused to infer private rights of action under Executive Order 11,246 and other nondiscrimination executive orders." John E. Noyes, "Executive Orders, Presidential Intent, and Private Rights of Action," *Texas Law Review 59* (1981): 848.

127. *Zhang v. Slattery*, 55 F.3d 732 (2d Cir. 1995); *Facchiano Construction Co., Inc. v. U.S. Department of Labor*, 987 F.2d 206 (3d Cir. 1993), *cert. denied*, 114 S. Ct. 80, 126; *Chen Zhou Chai v. Carroll*, 48 F.3d 1331 (4th Cir. 1995). Citations taken from *Federal Practice Digest 4th*, vol. 93, 1995 Cumulative Annual Pocket Part (St. Paul, Minn.: West Publishing Co., 1995), 28–29.

128. Noyes, "Executive Orders, Presidential Intent, and Private Rights of Action," 854.

129. *Watershed Associates Rescue v. Alexander*, 586 F. Supp. 978 (D.C. Neb. 1982); *National Indian Youth Council v. Andrus*, 501 F. Supp. 649 (D.C. N.M. 1980), *affirmed* 644 F.2d 220.

130. *Dalton v. Specter*, 114 S. Ct. 1719 (1994). The Clinton administration claimed that the president's decision to bar replacement workers under the FPASA was this sort of nonreviewable discretionary act, drawing direct parallels with *Dalton*. An appeals court found this argument unpersuasive, holding that it "would permit the President to bypass scores of statutory limitations on governmental authority." *Chamber of Commerce v. Reich*, 1332.

131. *Independent Meat Packers Association et al. v. Butz*, 526 D.2d 228 (8th Cir. 1975), *cert. denied*, 96 S. Ct. 1461.

132. *Watershed Associates Rescue v. Alexander*, 586 F. Supp. 978 (D.C. Neb. 1982).

133. *Legal Aid Society v. Brennan*, 608 F.2d 1319 (9th Cir. 1979), *cert. denied* 447 U.S. 921 (1980); *Sierra Club v. Peterson*, 705 F.2d 1475 (9th Cir. 1982). See Steven Ostrow, "Enforcing Executive Orders: Judicial Review of Agency Action under the Administrative Procedures Act," *George Washington Law Review 55*, no. 3 (March 1987): 668–670.

134. *Michigan v. Thomas*, 805 F.2d 176 (6th Cir. 1986); *Center for Science in the Public Interest v. Department of the Treasury*, 797 F.2d 995 (D.C. Cir. 1986).

135. *Public Citizen Health Research Group v. Tyson*, 796 F.2d 1479 (D.C. Cir. 1986).

136. Noyes, "Executive Orders, Presidential Intent, and Private Rights of Action."

137. Executive Order 11030, 27 *Federal Register* 5847 (June 21, 1962); Executive Order 11354, 32 *Federal Register* 7695 (May 26, 1967).

138. Memorandum, William M. Nichols to Richard Darman, February 12, 1981, "Proposed Executive Order Entitled 'Federal Regulation,' " WHORM Subject File, FG—Federal Government—Organizations (000167) [1 of 2], RRL. The Office of Legal Counsel did, however, prepare a memorandum in support of the proposed order. See Office of Legal Counsel, "Proposed Executive Order Entitled 'Federal Regulation,' " *Opinions of the Office of Legal Counsel*, vol. 5 (1981), 59–68.

139. Attorney General Herbert Brownell did not issue a formal written opinion on Eisenhower's actions until November. Memorandum for the President, November 7, 1957, Papers of Gerald D. Morgan, Box 6, Folder: Civil Rights, DDEL.

140. Executive Order 12114, 44 *Federal Register* 1957 (January 9, 1979).

141. 42 U.S.C. § 4332 (2) (C). The environmental impact statement requirement has spurred an avalanche of litigation, because groups or individuals opposed to a particular agency action can delay or even prevent it by challenging the sufficiency and accuracy of the EIS itself.

142. 42 U.S.C. § 4332 (2) (F). One source argued that the ambiguities appeared "attributable either to poor drafting, or, more likely, to the fact that none of the principal authors of the Act gave hard thought to the applicability of the impact statement requirement to extraterritorial federal actions." "President Orders Environmental Review of International Actions," *Environmental Law Reporter* 9 (January 1979): 10011.

143. The Atomic Energy Commission eventually agreed to produce a general EIS on the overall nuclear export program. This had the effect of putting off, for a time, the question of whether the National Environmental Policy Act applied to the Export-Import Bank. "Renewed Controversy over the International Reach of NEPA," *Environmental Law Reporter* 7 (November 1977): 10205–10206.

144. *National Organization for the Reform of Marijuana Laws v. United States Department of State*, 452 F. Supp. 1226 (D.D.C. 1978); *Sierra Club v. Coleman*, 421 F. Supp. 63 (D.D.C. 1976); *Sierra Club v. Adams*, 578 F.2d 389 (D.C. Cir. 1978).

145. The Council Environmental Quality outlined its position in a series of memoranda to agency heads issued between 1976 and 1978. "Renewed Controversy over the International Reach of NEPA," 10207. See also Note, "Agency Responses to Executive Order 12,114: A Comparison and Implications," *Cornell International Law Journal* 14 (summer 1981): 484.

146. A few other subcabinet agencies, including the Agency for International Development, the Federal Highway Administration, and the National Oceanic and Atmospheric Administration, prepared at least one environmental impact statement between 1975 and 1977 even though the law was unclear. "President Orders Environmental Review of International Actions," 10011 nn8, 10.

147. Executive Order 11991, 42 *Federal Register* 26967 (May 25, 1977).

148. Office of Legal Counsel, Memorandum for Associate Attorney General Michael Egan, "Nature of the Department's Representation of the Export-Import Bank," January 18, 1978, Margaret McKenna Files, Box 129, Folder: Executive

Order 12114—National Environmental Policy Act, 7/77–2/88 [CF, O/A 421], JCL.

149. Dick Kirschten, "Should Environmental Statements Have an Impact Abroad?" *National Journal* (September 16, 1978), 1471.

150. *Natural Resources Defense Council v. Export-Import Bank*, Civ. no. 77–0080 (D.D.C.).

151. Margaret McKenna, "Memorandum for the File: NEPA," February 3, 1978, Margaret McKenna Files, Box 129, Folder: Executive Order 12114—National Environmental Policy Act, 7/77–2/78 [CF, O/A 421], JCL; McKenna, Memorandum to Files: NEPA, May 30, 1978, Margaret McKenna Files, Box 129, Folder: Executive Order 12114—National Environmental Policy Act, 5/78 [CF, O/A 421],

152. Office of Legal Counsel, "Nature of the Department's Representation of the Export-Import Bank," 22. Justice's preference was to settle the lawsuit by having Eximbank issue its own regulations for extraterritorial projects. See McKenna, "Memorandum for the File: NEPA," February 3, 1978, 2.

153. "Administration Favors 'Flexibility' in Foreign Environmental Assessments," *Environment Reporter* 9, no. 11 (July 14, 1978): 438.

154. Kirschten, "Should Environmental Statements Have an Impact Abroad?" 1471.

155. Robert Lipshutz, Memorandum for the President: The Need for a Policy Decision with Regard to the Extraterritorial Application of the National Environmental Policy Act, July 5, 1978, Margaret McKenna Files, Box 126, Folder: Executive Order 12114—National Environmental Policy Act, 6/78–7/8/78 [CF, O/A 420], JCL.

156. Memorandum, Herbert J. Hansell to Lipshutz and Eizenstat, n.d., "Proposed Executive Order on the Environmental Effects Abroad of Major Federal Actions," Margaret McKenna Files, Box 128, Folder: Executive Order 12114 For Signature, 7/78–8/9/78 [CF, O/A 420], JCL.

157. Robert Lipshutz and Margaret McKenna, Memorandum for the President, "Proposed Executive Order on the Environmental Effects Abroad of Major Federal Actions," August 18, 1978, Margaret McKenna Files, Box 127, Folder: Executive Order 12114, 9/78–1/79 [CF, O/A 420], JCL.

158. Memo, Warren to Mondale and Eizenstat, September 8, 1978, Margaret McKenna Files, Box 128, Folder: Executive Order 12114 9/78–1/79, JCL.

159. Glenn Pincus, "The 'NEPA-Abroad' Controversy: Unresolved by an Executive Order," *Buffalo Law Review* 30, no. 3 (summer 1981): 639.

160. The exemptions are (1) actions that do not have significant environmental effects; (2) actions taken by the president; (3) actions involving national security or armed conflicts; (4) intelligence or arms transfer activities; (5) nuclear power programs; (6) activities at international conferences and organizations; and (7) disaster and emergency relief.

161. "President Orders Environmental Review of International Actions," 10013.

162. Therese M. Welsh, "Agency Responses to Executive Order 12,114: A Comparison and Implications," *Cornell International Law Journal* 14, no. 2 (summer 1981): 481–506.

163. *National Resources Defense Council v. Nuclear Regulatory Commission*, 647 F.2d 1345 (D.C. Cir. 1981); *Greenpeace U.S.A. v. Stone*, 748 F. Supp. 749 (D. Hawaii 1990).

164. *Environmental Defense Fund v. Massey*, 986 F.2d 528 (D.C. Cir. 1993).

165. Karen A. Klick, "The Extraterritorial Reach of NEPA's EIS Requirement after *Environmental Defense Fund v. Massey*," *American University Law Review* 44 (October 1994): 291–322.

166. *Greenpeace U.S.A. v. Stone*, 749.

167. Ibid., 762.

168. Klick, "The Extraterritorial Reach of NEPA's EIS Requirement," 318–320.

Chapter Three
Patterns of Use

1. House Committee on Government Operations, *Executive Orders and Proclamations: A Study of a Use of Presidential Power*, 85th Cong., 1st sess., December 1957, Committee Print, 35.

2. The State Department has maintained proclamations in a numbered series since the late eighteenth century, although even this formal collection is incomplete: a later accounting concluded that Washington issued the first formal proclamation in October 1789, but the State Department series does not begin until January 1791. See Congressional Information Service (CIS), *CIS Index to Presidential Executive Orders and Proclamations* (Washington, D.C.: Congressional Information Service, 1988), viii.

3. *Executive Orders and Proclamations*, 38.

4. Clifford L. Lord, *Presidential Executive Orders*, vol. 1, comp. WPA Historical Records Survey (New York: Archives Publishing Co., 1944), 1.

5. James Hart, *The Ordinance Making Powers of the President of the United States* (Baltimore: Johns Hopkins University Press, 1925), 318.

6. *CIS Index to Presidential Executive Orders and Proclamations*, x; Clifford L. Lord, ed., *List and Index of Presidential Executive Orders,Unnumbered Series*, New Jersey Historical Records Survey Project (Newark, N.J.: Historical Records Survey, Works Progress Administration, 1943), v.

7. *CIS Index to Presidential Executive Orders and Proclamations*, ix.

8. American Bar Association, *Report of the Special Committee on Administrative Law* (Chicago: American Bar Association, 1934), 214. Cited in Erwin N. Griswold, "Government in Ignorance of the Law," *Harvard Law Review* 43 (1934): 199.

9. Griswold, "Government in Ignorance of the Law," 199; Department of Commerce, Division of Press Intelligence, *Subject Index of Executive Orders*, March 8, 1933–October 1, 1935, and October 1, 1935–September 1, 1936, Papers of Samuel Rosenman, Folder: Subject Index of Executive Orders, FDRL.

10. Minutes of the National Emergency Council meeting of December 11, 1934, reprinted in Lester G. Seligman and Elmer E. Cornwell, Jr., *New Deal Mosaic: Roosevelt Confers with His National Emergency Council, 1933–1936* (Eugene: University of Oregon Press, 1965), 362–364.

11. Robert H. Jackson, *The Struggle for Judicial Supremacy* (New York: Alfred A. Knopf, 1949), 90–91.

12. Letter, Ickes to FDR, September 25, 1934, Official Files, OF 56g—Administrator for the Petroleum Industry, FDRL. Some of this history is recounted in a brief submitted by the solicitor general to the Court in response to the questions raised in oral argument. The brief ("Supplemental Memorandum for Respondent") is reprinted in volume 28 of Phillip B. Burland and Gerhard Casper, *Landmark Briefs and Arguments of the Supreme Court of the United States: Constitutional Law* (Washington, D.C.: University Press of America, 1975). The Court took note of the petroleum code's tangled history in the *Panama* decision, 293 U.S. 388, 412–413.

13. Franklyn Waltman, Jr., "NRA Set-Up Made Target in High Court," *Washington Post*, December 11, 1934.

14. Edward S. Corwin, *The President: Office and Powers* (New York: New York University Press, 1948), 441.

15. Griswold, "Government in Ignorance of the Law."

16. Memorandum for the Attorney General, from Stephen Early, March 13, 1934, Official Files, OF-285 (Government Departments, 1934), FDRL.

17. *Executive Orders and Proclamations*, 5.

18. *Federal Crop Insurance Corporation v. Merril*, 387. This "voluminous and dull publication" has grown sixfold since Jackson and Douglas wrote, from an average of approximately 60 pages per day in 1945 to over 270 per day in 1997.

19. Senate Special Committee on National Emergencies and Delegated Emergency Powers, *Executive Orders in Times of War and National Emergency*, 93d Cong., 2d sess., 1974, Committee Print, 17–19; U.S. Office of War Information, *Presidential Orders Pertaining to the National Emergency and the War, July 1 1939 – July 1 1942* (Washington, D.C.: Bureau of Public Inquiries,1942).

20. In the example cited in chapter two, in which Roosevelt demanded that Congress repeal provisions of the Emergency Price Control Act of 1942, Corwin argued that Roosevelt was "suggesting, if not threatening, a virtually complete suspension of the Constitution" (Corwin, *The President*, 306).

21. Office of Price Administration, *The Beginnings of OPA* (Historical Reports on War Administration, Office of Temporary Controls, Office of Price Administration General Publication no. 1, 1946), 44–45.

22. Arthur M. Schlesinger, Jr., *The Imperial Presidency* (New York: Houghton Mifflin, 1973), 115.

23. Corwin, *The President*, 296.

24. Ibid., 298–299.

25. Executive Order 9047, 7 *Federal Register* 629 (January 30, 1942).

26. Executive Order 9154, 7 *Federal Register* 3275 (May 1, 1942).

27. Executive Order 12077, 43 *Federal Register* 37163 (August 22, 1978).

28. Robert W. Swenson, "Legal Aspcts of Mineral Resources Exploitation," in Paul W. Gates, *History of Public Land Law Development* (Washington, D.C.: Government Printing Office, 1968), 725.

29. Ibid., 733.

30. Charles F. Wheatley, Jr., *Study of Withdrawals and Reservations of Public Domain Lands*, vol. 1 (Washington, D.C.: Public Land Review Commission, 1969), 4.

31. Executive Order 9337, 8 *Federal Register* 5516 (April 24, 1943).

32. Executive Order 10355, 17 *Federal Register* 4831 (May 26, 1952).

33. Peter M. Shane and Harold H. Bruff, *Separation of Powers Law* (Durham, N.C.: Carolina Academic Press, 1996), 62.

34. Proclamation 6290, 61 *Federal Register* 50223 (September 24, 1996).

35. Bureau of the Budget, *The United States at War: Development and Administration of the War Program of the Federal Government* (War Records Section, Bureau of the Budget; Historical Reports on War Administration, no. 1, 1946), 491–501.

36. Glendon A. Schubert, "The Presidential Subdelegation Act of 1950," *Journal of Politics* 13, no. 4 (November 1951): 647–674; letter, Roger W. Jones to Attorney General, April 29, 1952, WHCF, Official Files, Folder: OF-6B, HSTL.

37. These functions were delegated by, respectively, Executive Order 10289, 16 *Federal Register* 9199 (September 17, 1951), and Executive Order 10637, 20 *Federal Register* 7025 (September 16, 1955).

38. The various editions of the *Annual Report of the National Mediation Board* describe the emergency boards set up pursuant to Section 10 of the Railway Labor Act. Between 1934 and 1944, all of the boards were established via proclamations or through the National Railway Labor Panel.

39. Executive Order 9172, 7 *Federal Register* 3913 (May 22, 1942).

40. Thomas R. Wolanin, *Presidential Advisory Commissions* (Madison: University of Wisconsin Press, 1975). Probably the first case was President Washington's use of a special commission in 1794 to mediate the Whiskey Rebellion; see David Flitner, Jr., *The Politics of Presidential Commissions: A Public Policy Perspective* (Dobbs Ferry, N.Y.: Transnational Publishers, 1986), 8.

41. Jay S. Bybee, "Advising the President: Separation of Powers and the Federal Advisory Committee Act," *Yale Law Journal* 104, no. 1 (October 1994): 51–128.

42. Wolanin, *Presidential Advisory Commissions*, 63. The choice of instrument also depends on how the president intends to pay for a commission. Presidents are more likely to use an executive order if they intend to use presidential discretionary funds. Commissions that rely on agency contributions or private funding can be set up through the less formal process of public announcements (*ibid.*, 64).

43. Bybee, "Advising the President," 63.

44. Ibid., 64.

45. Wolanin, *Presidential Advisory Commissions*, 66.

46. Bybee, "Advising the President," 68–69.

47. Ibid., 71.

48. Executive Order 11007, 27 *Federal Register* 1875 (February 28, 1962).

49. Executive Order 11671, 37 *Federal Register* 11307 (June 7, 1972).

50. Wolanin, *Presidential Advisory Commissions*, 71.

51. Lyn Ragsdale and John J. Thies III, "The Institutionalization of the American Presidency, 1924–92," *American Journal of Political Science* 41, no. 4 (October 1997): 1288–1289.

52. Lyn Ragsdale, *Vital Statistics on the Presidency: Washington to Clinton* (Washington, D.C.: Congressional Quarterly, 1996), 297–298.

53. I drew the sample in two lots; the first was a sample of 1,000 orders drawn from the population of orders issued between March 1936 and December 1995. To update the sample to include orders through the end of 1999, I drew exactly the same percentage of orders (17.6 percent) from the population of orders issued between January 1996 and December 1999 (resulting in 28 more orders in the sample). The result is a pooled sample of 1,028 orders.

54. Before then, public land and civil service orders were even more common. Between 1901 and 1916, 86 percent of executive orders dealt with these two areas, and in 1901 and 1904, every executive order fell into these categories. Data from Sara Schramm, "The Politics of Executive Orders" (Ph.D. diss., George Washington University, 1981).

55. David Mayhew, *Divided We Govern* (New Haven: Yale University Press, 1991), 49. During this span Congress enacted a total of 24,671 bills, of which 15,875 were public and the remainder private (data from Norman Ornstein, Thomas E. Mann, and Michael Malbin, *Vital Statistics on Congress, 1995–1996* [Washington, D.C.: Congressional Quarterly Press, 1996],165). By Mayhew's criteria, just over 1 percent of these bills constituted major legislation (267 out of 24,671).

56. Mark A. Peterson, *Legislating Together: The White House and Capitol Hill from Eisenhower to Reagan* (Cambridge: Harvard University Press, 1990), 183.

57. Conversely, the press often refers to presidential executive actions in general as "executive orders," even when the actions do not take that form. When Clinton reversed the existing ban on fetal tissue research and overturned a ban on abortions at overseas military hospitals, he did so through presidential directives to agency heads, not through formal executive orders. Nevertheless, these actions were widely reported to be executive orders.

58. George C. Edwards III and B. Dan Wood, "Who Influences Whom? The President, Congress, and the Media," *American Political Science Review* 93, no. 2 (June 1999): 331.

59. Clinton L. Rossiter, *The American Presidency*, rev. ed. (New York: New American Library, 1960), 59. Rossiter discounts the fact that in 1943 Congress granted the president formal legislative authority to make such seizures and argues that since Roosevelt had relied on the commander-in-chief power to take over plants well before this act, the delegation was "at best declaratory, even supererogatory" (ibid., 60).

60. Corwin, *The President*, 301.

61. Studies supporting the argument that legislative failures spur executive order issuance: Dennis W. Gleiber and Steven A. Shull, "Presidential Influence in the Policymaking Process," *Western Political Quarterly* 45 (1992): 441–468; Joel L. Fleishman and Arthur H. Aufses, "Law and Orders: The Problem of Presidential Legislation," *Law and Contemporary Problems* 40 (1976): 1–45. A study reaching the opposite conclusion: George A. Krause and David B. Cohen, "Presidential Use of Executive Orders, 1953–1994," *American Politics Quarterly* 25, no. 4 (October 1997): 458–481.

62. Theodore B. Olson, "The Impetuous Vortex: Congressional Erosion of Presidential Authority," in *The Fettered Presidency: Legal Constraints on the Executive Branch*, ed. Gordon Crovitz and Jeremy A. Rabkin (Washington, D.C.: American Enterprise Institute, 1989).

63. Gleiber and Shull, "Presidential Influence in the Policymaking Process," 453.

64. Krause and Cohen, "Presidential Use of Executive Orders, 1953–1994."

65. Viveca Novak, "The Stroke of a Pen." *National Journal*, December 5, 1992, 2764.

66. The records of Ford's Domestic Council contain numerous examples of orders that were pushed through under substantial time pressure at the end of his term, without the standard reviews (Folder, Domestic Council Files, 1/18–19/77, Box 72, Robert T. Hartmann Files 1974–1977, GRFL).

67. Richard Whittle, "Glee, Questions Greet Release of Hostages," *Congressional Quarterly Weekly Report*, January 24, 1981, 166.

68. Joseph Tauber, "*Dames & Moore v. Regan*: The Constitutionality of the Executive Orders Implementing the Agreement with Iran," *Ohio Northern University Law Review* 9 (1982): 519–527.

69. Harold Hongju Koh, *The National Security Constitution: Sharing Power after the Iran-Contra Affair* (New Haven: Yale University Press, 1990), 122.

70. Fleishman and Aufses, "Law and Orders," 6.

71. Ruth P. Morgan, *The President and Civil Rights: Policy-Making by Executive Order* (New York: St. Martin's Press, 1970).

72. Jon R. Bond and Richard Fleisher, *The President in the Legislative Arena* (Chicago: University of Chicago Press, 1990), 67.

73. Krause and Cohen, "Presidential Use of Executive Orders, 1953–1994."

74. Phillip J. Cooper, "By Order of the President: Administration by Executive Order and Proclamation," *Administration and Society* 18 (1986): 235.

75. Eizenstat memorandum to Carter, "Your Trip to California Next Week," September 19, 1976, WHCF, Subject File, NR-14, Folder: Executive NR-7 2/16/80–1/20/81, JCL.

76. Executive Order 13017, 61 *Federal Register* 47659 (September 9, 1996); Executive Order 13019, 61 *Federal Register* 51763 (October 3, 1996); Executive Order 13021, 61 *Federal Register* 54929 (October 23, 1996). See Martin Kasindorf, "2 Candidates Hit the Road—Clinton: Weigh Health Care," *Newsday*, September 6, 1996; Todd S. Purdum, "Clinton Sets New Rules on Deadbeat Dads," *New York Times*, September 28, 1996; "More Federal Aid for 29 Tribal Colleges in West," *New York Times*, October 27, 1996.

77. <http://www.nara.gov/fedreg/eo.html>.

78. Gary King, "Variance Specification in Event Count Models: From Restrictive Assumptions to a Generalized Estimator," *American Journal of Political Science* 33, no. 3 (August 1989): 762–784.

79. William H. Greene, *Econometric Analysis*, 3d ed. (Saddle River, N.J.: Prentice-Hall, 1997), 939–940.

80. The test statistic is $\lambda_{LR} = 2(L - L^*)$, with a $\chi^2(1)$ distribution. L is the log-likelihood of the negative binomial estimation, and L^* the log-likelihood of the same model estimated as a Poisson process (the equivalent of estimating the

negative binomial model with the constraint $\alpha = 0$). See George G. Judge, W. E. Griffith, R. Carter Hill, Helmut Lütkepohl, and Tsoung-Chao Lee, *The Theory and Practice of Econometrics* (New York: John Wiley & Sons, 1985), 216–217.

81. Data available on the Gallup web site: <http://www.gallup.com>. Ragsdale, *Vital Statistics on the Presidency*.

82. Judge et al., *The Theory and Practice of Econometrics*, 356–363.

83. I chose the order of the polynomial based on the minimum degree that produced statistically significant results. Because each variable took nonzero values only for the hypothesized 24 periods of the intervention and lagged effects, multicollinearity was a severe problem. The correlation between a_0 and a_1, b_0 and b_1, etc., was .87; between the first- and second-order variables it was .97.

84. Gary King, "Statistical Models for Political Science Event Counts," 857.

85. Douglas Jehl, "One Hand Tied, Clinton Offers the Other," *New York Times*, November 10, 1994.

86. Mayhew, *Divided We Govern*. For a contrasting argument—that divided government *does* make a significant difference—see George C. Edwards III, Andrew Barrett, and Jeffrey Peake, "The Legislative Impact of Divided Government," *American Journal of Political Science* 41, no. 2 (April 1997): 545–564.

87. Charles O. Jones, *The Presidency in a Separated System* (Washington, D.C.: Brookings Institution, 1994), 273.

88. Jeffrey T. Spoeri, "The Pennsylvania Avenue Tug of War: The President vs. Congress over the Ban on Homosexuals in the Military," *Washington University Journal of Urban and Contemporary Law* 45 (1994): 175–218.

89. Pat Towell, "Campaign Promise, Social Debate Collide on Military Battlefield," *Congressional Quarterly*, January 30, 1993.

Chapter Four
Executive Orders and the Institutional Presidency

1. Sidney M. Milkis, *The President and the Parties: The Transformation of the American Party System since the New Deal* (New York: Oxford University Press, 1993), 119–120.

2. Alan Brinkley, *The End of Reform: New Deal Liberalism in Recession and War* (New York: Vintage Books, 1995), 22; Milkis, *The Presidency and the Parties*, 122.

3. Milkis, *The Presidency and the Parties*, 125.

4. Louis Brownlow, *A Passion for Anonymity* (Chicago: University of Chicago Press, 1958), 429.

5. Milkis, *The President and the Parties*, 114.

6. Executive Order 8248, 5 *Federal Register* 3864.

7. Brownlow, *A Passion for Anonymity*, 427–429.

8. L. F. Schmeckebier, "Organization of the Executive Branch of the National Government of the United States: Changes between June 1 and September 30, 1939," *American Political Science Review* 33, no. 6 (December 1939): 1047.

9. Brownlow, *A Passion for Anonymity*, 429.

10. Arthur W. MacMahon, "VI. The Future Organizational Pattern of the Executive Branch," *American Political Science Review* 38, no. 6 (December 1944): 1182.

11. Bureau of the Budget, *The United States at War: Development and Administration of the War Program of the Federal Government* (War Records Section, Bureau of the Budget, Historical Reports on War Administration, no. 1, 1946), 44.

12. Edward S. Corwin, *The President: Office and Powers* (New York: New York University Press, 1948), 295.

13. Herbert Emmerich, *Federal Organization and Administrative Management* (Tuscaloosa: University of Alabama Press, 1971), 72.

14. Corwin, *The Presidency*, 295.

15. Terry M. Moe, "The Politicized Presidency," in *The New Direction in American Politics*, ed. John E. Chubb and Paul E. Peterson (Washington, D.C.: Brookings Institution, 1985), 247.

16. Peri E. Arnold, *Making the Managerial Presidency: Comprehensive Reorganization Planning, 1905–1980* (Princeton: Princeton University Press, 1986), 10–11.

17. James L. Sundquist, *The Decline and Resurgence of Congress* (Washington, D.C.: Brookings Institution, 1981), 39.

18. Steven Skowronek, *Building a New American State: The Expansion of National Administrative Capacities, 1877–1920* (New York: Cambridge University Press, 1982).

19. Ibid., 165.

20. Arnold, *Making the Managerial Presidency*, 11.

21. Skowronek, *Building a New American State*, 169–170.

22. Moe, "The Politicized Presidency"; Larry Berman, *The Office of Management and Budget and the Presidency, 1921–1979* (Princeton: Princeton University Press, 1979).

23. Louis Fisher, *Presidential Spending Power* (Princeton: Princeton University Press, 1975), 27.

24. David Brady and Mark A. Morgan, "Reforming the Structure of the House Appropriations Process: The Effects of the 1885 and 1919–20 Reforms on Money Decisions," in *Congress: Structure and Policy*, ed. Mathew D. McCubbins and Terry Sullivan (New York: Cambridge University Press, 1987).

25. *The Need for a National Budget: Message from the President of the United States Transmitting the Report of the Commission on Economy and Efficiency on the Subject of the Need for a National Budget*, 62d Cong., 2d sess., 1912, H. Doc. no. 854, 10.

26. Lucius Wilmerding, Jr., *The Spending Power: A History of the Efforts of Congress to Control Expenditures* (New Haven: Yale University Press,1943), 149.

27. Executive Order 163, January 31, 1902; Executive Order 402, January 25, 1906. Both orders are indexed in Clifford L. Lord, *Presidential Executive Orders*, vol. 1, comp. WPA Historical Records Survey (New York: Archives Publishing Co., 1944). For the text of the orders, see *Congressional Record*, April 23, 1912, 5223.

28. Fisher, *Presidential Spending Power*, 29.

29. Skowronek, *Building a New American State*, 187.

30. "Copy of Letter Sent by the President to the Secretary of the Treasury Relative to the Submission of a Budget to Congress," September 19, 1912, Series 6, File no. 3868, Reel no. 447, Papers of William Howard Taft, microfilm, Wisconsin State Historical Society, Madison.

31. Fisher, *Presidential Spending Power*, 33.

32. *The Need for a National Budget*, 4.

33. See "Copy of Letter Sent by the President to the Secretary of the Treasury."

34. E. E. Naylor, *The Federal Budget System in Operation* (Washington, D.C.: Hayworth Printing Co., 1941), 25.

35. Moe, "The Politicized Presidency," 247.

36. Charles Wallace Collins, "The Coming of the Budget System," *South Atlantic Quarterly* 15 (1916): 314–315.

37. Arnold, *Making the Managerial Presidency*, 14–15.

38. Executive Office of the President, *Budget of the United States, Fiscal Year 2000: Historical Tables* (Washington, D.C.: Government Printing Office, 1999), 19.

39. Senate Special Committee on the National Budget, *National Budget System*, 66th Cong., 2d sess., 1920, Report no. 524, 6.

40. Milkis, *The President and the Parties*, 104.

41. Fisher, *Presidential Spending Power*, 16.

42. Arnold, *Making the Managerial Presidency*, 54.

43. Charles G. Dawes, *The First Year of the Budget of the United States* (New York: Harper & Brothers Publishers, 1923).

44. Ibid., ix.

45. Ibid., 104–105. Dawes used the term "executive order" loosely, and considered the regulations issued by the bureau as executive orders approved by the president. He took a broad and extremely formal view of presidential power, but his conception of executive discretion fits well into Moe's definition of residual decision rights: "Where the statutes of the United States prescribe methods to be followed in governmental business administration," Dawes wrote in his 1922 report, "they, of course, limit Executive discretion by their terms, but in all routine business of government, where a method is not prescribed by law, it follows of necessity that methods may be imposed by the Executive, as in all other forms of business organization" (131).

46. Budget Circular no. 49, section 3. Reprinted in Dawes, *The First Year of the Budget of the United States*, 162.

47. Richard E. Neustadt, "Presidency and Legislation: The Growth of Central Clearance," *American Political Science Review* 48 (1954): 644.

48. Dawes, *The First Year of the Budget of the United States*, 161.

49. Neustadt, "Presidency and Legislation," 645–646.

50. For bills not dealing the appropriations, legislative clearance originally operated through the National Emergency Council, an ad hoc advisory group Roosevelt established in 1933 to help him coordinate executive branch policy. When Roosevelt disbanded the NEC in 1936, he transferred its clearance functions to the Bureau of the Budget. Berman, *The Office of Management and Budget and the Presidency*, 10.

51. Cited in Neustadt, "Presidency and Legislation," 650.

52. *The President's Committee on Administrative Management, Report of the Committee* (Washington, D.C.: Government Printing Office, 1937), 17. Hereafter cited as *PCAM*.

53. Berman, *The Office of Management and Budget and the Presidency*, 7.

54. Fisher, *Presidential Spending Power*, 44.

55. Berman, *The Office of Management and Budget and the Presidency*, 27–28.

56. Percival Brundage, *The Bureau of the Budget* (New York: Praeger, 1970), 29–30.

57. Neustadt, "Presidency and Legislation," 668.

58. The Supreme Court upheld these protections in *Humphrey's Executor v. United States*, 295 U.S. 602 (1935), ruling that agencies with "quasi-legislative" or "quasi-judicial" powers could be independent of direct presidential control.

59. James Hart, "The Exercise of Rule-Making Power," in *PCAM*.

60. "Memorandum: The President's Powers over Independent Regulatory Commissions," White House Office, Office of the Staff Secretary, Subject Series, White House Subseries, Folder: Rockefeller Committee on Reorganization of the Government [1956–1958] [1], DDEL.

61. Ronald J. Penoyer, *Directory of Federal Regulatory Agencies*, 3d ed. (St. Louis: Center for the Study of American Business, 1981), 1–4.

62. Cornelius M. Kerwin, *Rulemaking: How Government Agencies Write Law and Make Policy*, 2d ed. (Washington, D.C.: Congressional Quarterly Press, 1999), 122.

63. Berman, *The Office of Management and Budget and the Presidency*, chap. 4.

64. Arnold, *Making the Managerial Presidency*, 288.

65. Louis Fisher and Ronald Moe, "Presidential Reorganization Authority: Is It Worth the Cost?" *Political Science Quarterly* 96, no. 2 (summer 1981): 302–304.

66. Berman, *The Office of Management and Budget and the Presidency*, 112.

67. George C. Eads and Michael Fix, *Relief or Reform? Reagan's Regulatory Dilemma* (Washington, DC: Urban Institute Press, 1984), 48. Emphasis in original.

68. Ibid.

69. Senate Committee on Governmental Affairs, *Regulatory Review Sunshine Act*, 102d Cong., 2d sess., 1992, Report no. 102–256, 12; National Academy of Public Administration, *Presidential Management of Rulemaking in Regulatory Agencies* (Washington, D.C.: National Academy of Public Administration, 1987), 9.

70. Penoyer, *Directory of Federal Regulatory Agencies*, 2.

71. Caroline DeWitt, "The President's Council on Competitiveness: Undermining the Administrative Procedure Act with Regulatory Review," *Administrative Law Journal of the American University* 6 no. 4 (winter 1993): 769.

72. 39 *Federal Register* 41501 (November 29, 1974).

73. *Regulatory Review Sunshine Act*, 12.

74. *Independent Meat Packers Association v. Butz*, 395 F. Supp. 923 (1975).

75. *Independent Meat Packers Association v. Butz*, 526 F.2d 228 (8th Cir., 1975), 235–236, rehearing and rehearing en banc denied December 15, 1975, *cert. denied* March 22, 1976.

76. Richard E. Cohen, "A Fight over Independence," *National Journal*, December 31, 1977, 2016.

77. National Academy of Public Administration, *Presidential Management of Rulemaking in Regulatory Agencies*, 9.

78. Bert Lance, Memorandum for the President, "Regulatory Reform Initiatives," August 3, 1977, WHCF Subject File, FG-1, F: Executive FG 7/1/77–8/31/77, JCL.

79. Council of Economic Advisers, Memorandum for the Economic Policy Group, Subject: Economic Impact Analysis, February 21, 1977, 5, Rick Neustadt Files, Box 70, F: Regulatory Reform. JCL.

80. Executive Order 12044, 43 *Federal Register* 12661 (March 24, 1978).

81. Letter to the President, Committee on Government Affairs, December 16, 1977, WHCF Subject File, FG-2, F: Executive FG, 12/1/77–2/28/78, JCL.

82. Memorandum for the President, James T. McIntyre, "Executive Order on Improving Government Regulations," Rick Neustadt Files, Box 70, F: Regulatory Reform—Executive Order 12044 [11/15/77–4/6/78], JCL.

83. Morton Rosenberg, "Presidential Control of Agency Rulemaking: An Analysis of Constitutional Issues That May Be Raised by Executive Order 12, 291." *Arizona Law Review* 23 (1981): 1200n.

84. Executive Order 12291, 46 *Federal Register* 13193 (February 17, 1981).

85. Joseph Cooper and William West, "Presidential Power and Republican Government: The Theory and Practice of OMB Review," *Journal of Politics* 50 (1988): 871.

86. Robert F. Durant, *The Administrative Presidency Revisited: Public Lands, the BLM and the Reagan Revolution* (Albany: State University of New York Press, 1992), 49.

87. Cooper and West. "Presidential Power and Republican Government," 881.

88. Antonin Scalia, "Deregulation HQ: An Interview on the New Executive Order with Murray L. Weidenbaum and James C. Miller III," *Regulation* (March/April 1981): 23.

89. Alan B. Morrison, "OMB Interference with Agency Rulemaking: The Wrong Way to Write a Regulation," *Harvard Law Review* 99 (1986): 1063.

90. Office of Legal Counsel, "Proposed Executive Order Entitled 'Federal Regulation,' " 5 Op. O.L.C. 59 (1981), 60–61. Compare this with Charles Collins's 1916 argument in favor of a presidential budget: "The first essential of a budget system is executive responsibility. The head of the executive branch of the government takes complete responsibility to the people for the financial policy of the nation" (Collins, "The Coming of the Budget System," 314).

91. Office of Legal Counsel, "Proposed Executive Order Entitled 'Federal Regulation,' " 62. This argument is strained, however, since it equates the regulatory activity of any agency with the activities of the "principal officer" of executive departments.

92. Horace W. Wilkie, "Legal Basis for Increased Activities of the Federal Budget Bureau," *George Washington University Law Review* 11, no. 3 (April 1943): 271.

93. Rosenberg, "Presidential Control of Agency Rulemaking," 1205.

94. The key provisions were public notice of proposed rules, solicitation of public comment, and maintenance of public records.

95. W. Andrew Jack, "Note: Executive Orders 12,291 and 12,498: Usurpation of Legislative Power or Blueprint for Legislative Reform?" *George Washington University Law Review* 54, no. 4 (May 1986): 524–525.

96. Frank B. Cross, "Executive Orders 12,291 and 12,498: A Test Case in Presidential Control of Executive Agencies," *Journal of Law and Politics* 4 (1988): 484.

97. Christopher C. DeMuth and Douglas H. Ginsburg, "White House Review of Agency Rulemaking," *Harvard Law Review* 99 (1986): 1082.

98. Cass R. Sunstein, "Cost-Benefit Analysis and the Separation of Powers," *Arizona Law Review* 23 (1981): 1281.

99. In a few cases, regulatory agencies were prohibited from using cost-benefit calculations in forming regulatory policy. The best-known example is the infamous Delaney clause, which was added to the Food Drug and Cosmetics Act in 1958 to regulate food additives. The language prohibits the Food and Drug Administration from declaring a food additive safe if it "is found to induce cancer when ingested by man or animal." The lack of any qualification or balancing language in the clause is generally interpreted to mean that the FDA must ban additives when there is any risk of cancer, no matter how infinitesimal, and no matter what the costs may be. See Lars Noah and Richard A. Merrill, "Starting from Scratch: Reinventing the Food Additive Approval Process," *Boston University Law Review* 78 (April 1998): 329–443.

100. In *Natural Resources Defense Council v. EPA*, 683 F.2d 752 (3d Cir. 1982), an appeals court ruled that the Environmental Protection Agency could not rely on Executive Order 12291 to indefinitely postpone regulations. In *Environmental Defense Fund v. Thomas*, 627 F. Supp. 566, the D.C. District Court similarly ruled that the OMB could not prevent agencies from issuing regulations required by a statutory deadline. See Jack, "Note: Executive Orders 12,291 and 12,498," 524–525.

101. Executive Order 12498, 50 *Federal Register* 1036 (January 8, 1985).

102. Jack, "Note: Executive Orders 12,291 and 12,498," 521.

103. *Youngstown Sheet and Tube v. Sawyer*, 343 U.S. 579, 635 (1952).

104. Cooper and West, "Presidential Power and Republican Government," 873–874.

105. Terry M. Moe, "Presidents, Institutions, and Theory," in *Researching the Presidency: Vital Questions, New Approaches*, ed. George C. Edwards III, John H. Kessel, and Bert A. Rockman (Pittsburgh: University of Pittsburgh Press, 1993), 431.

106. Cooper and West, "Presidential Power and Republican Government," 882.

107. DeWitt, "The President's Council on Competitiveness," 795.

108. There were, however, a few hearings in which opponents publicized the council's activities. Senate Committee on Governmental Affairs, *The Role of the Council on Competitiveness in Regulatory Review*, 102d Cong., 1st sess., 1991, S. Hrg. 102–1135; House Committee on Government Operations, Subcommittee on Legislation and National Security, *The Secret Interference by the Vice President's Staff with HUD's Guidelines for Access by Handicapped Persons to Multifamily Dwellings*, 102d Cong., 2d sess., 1992.

109. For a general review, see Cass R. Sunstein, "Health-Health Trade-offs," *University of Chicago Law Review* 63 (Fall 1996): 1533–1571.

110. Letter, James MacRae to Nancy Risque-Rorbach, March 10, 1992. Reprinted in Senate Committee on Governmental Affairs, *Is the Office of Management and Budget Interfering with Workers Health and Safety Protection?* 102d Cong., 2d sess., 1992, S. Hrg. 102–144.

111. *Is the Office of Management and Budget Interfering with Workers Health and Safety Protection?* 59. Taken at face value, this estimate could lead to the conclusion that federal regulation actually causes nearly 70,000 deaths each year: OMB estimated that the total cost of federal regulation in 1991 was in the neighborhood of $400 billion to $500 billion. $500 billion divided by $7.5 million is 66,667.

112. Risque-Rorbach to MacRae, March 13, 1992. Reprinted in *Is the Office of Management and Budget Interfering with Workers Health and Safety Protection?* 61–63.

113. Frank Swoboda, "OMB's Logic: Less Protection Saves Lives; Letter Blocking Health Standards for 6 Million Workers Shocks Officials at Labor Dept." *Washington Post*, March 17, 1992.

114. *Is the Office of Management and Budget Interfering with Workers Health and Safety Protection?* 5.

115. General Accounting Office, *Risk-Risk Analysis: OMB's Review of a Proposed OSHA Rule*, GAO/PEMD-92-33 (1992). OSHA's proposed rule was blocked, in any event, by a successful lawsuit against a 1989 workplace pollution rule. In *AFL-CIO v. OSHA*, 965 F.2d 962 (11th Cir., 1992), a federal appeals court held that OSHA's workplace chemical exposure limits were based on flawed analysis. This ruling forced OSHA to revamp its process for setting exposure limits and invalidated the proposed regulations then in the pipeline. The final rules have still not been issued as of June 2000.

116. E. Donald Elliott, "TQM-ing OMB: Or Why Regulatory Review under Executive Order 12,291 Works Poorly and What President Clinton Should Do About It," *Law and Contemporary Problems* 57, no. 2 (spring 1994).

117. Moe and Wilson, "Presidents and the Politics of Structure," 41.

118. Richard H. Pildes and Cass R. Sunstein, "Reinventing the Regulatory State," *University of Chicago Law Review* 62 (1995): 6.

119. Testimony of Sally Katzen, OIRA Administrator, in Senate Committee on Governmental Affairs, Subcommittee on Financial Management and Accountability, *Oversight of Regulatory Review Activities of the Office of Information and Regulatory Affairs*, 104th Cong., 2d sess., 1996, S. Hrg. 104–825, 9.

120. House Committee on Government Reform and Oversight, Subcommittee on National Economic Growth, Natural Resources, and Regulatory Affairs, *H.R.*

1704, Congressional Office of Regulatory Analysis Creation Act, 105th Cong., 2d sess., 1998, Serial no. 105–146, 80.

121. Executive Order 12898, "Environmental Justice," 58 *Federal Register* 7629 (February 11, 1994); Executive Order 13045, "Protection of Children from Environmental Health Risks and Safety Risks," 62 *Federal Register* 19885 (April 21, 1997); Executive Order 13084, "Consultation and Coordination with Indian Tribal Governments," 63 *Federal Register* 27655 (May 14, 1998).

122. Statement of David C. Vladeck, in Senate Committee on Governmental Affairs, *OMB's Office of Information and Regulatory Affairs Information Management, Paperwork, and Regulatory Review*, 103d Cong., 2d sess., 1994, S. Hrg. 103–1030, 197.

123. The Congressional Review Act, Section E of Public Law 104–121 (May 29, 1996), included in 5 U.S.C. §§ 801–808. An example of a required report is General Accounting Office, *Securities and Exchange Commission: Regulation of Exchanges and Alternative Trading Systems*, B-281761, (January 6, 1999).

124. Testimony of Representative Sue Kelly (R-N.Y.), in U.S. Congress, *The Role of Congress in Monitoring Agency Rulemaking*, 105th Cong., 1st sess., 1997, Serial no. 54, 32.

125. As of March 1999, only eight disapproval resolutions had been introduced (House Committee on the Judiciary, *Congressional Office of Regulatory Analyses Creation Act*, Report no. 105–441, 105th Cong., 2d sess., 1998, 20). Between March 1998 and March 1999, only two more had been introduced, both addressing the same rule.

126. *H.R. 1704, Congressional Office of Regulatory Analysis Creation Act*, 6.

127. "Dissenting Views to H.R. 1704," in ibid., 18–22.

128. Testimony of Sally Katzen, OIRA Administrator, in Senate Committee on Governmental Affairs, Subcommittee on Financial Management and Accountability, *Oversight of Regulatory Review Activities of the Office of Information and Regulatory Affairs*, 104th Cong., 2d sess., 1996, S. Hrg. 104–825, 8.

129. Executive Order 12866, 58 *Federal Register* 51735 (October 4, 1993), section 6. General Accounting Office, *Regulatory Reform: Changes Made to Agencies' Rules Are Not Always Clearly Documented*, GAO/GGD-98–31 (January 1998).

130. Lyn Ragsdale and John J. Thies III, "The Institutionalization of the American Presidency, 1924–92," *American Journal of Political Science* 41, no. 4 (October 1997): 1280–1318.

131. For example, the Brownlow Report made very clear the characteristics of ideal presidential aides: these who have "no power to make decisions or issue instructions in their own right; they would not be interposed between the President and the heads of his departments. They would not be assistant presidents in any sense . . . they should be possessed of high competence, great physical vigor, and a passion for anonymity." *PCAM*, 5.

132. George Reedy, *The Twilight of the Presidency* (New York: World Publishing, 1970); Arthur M. Schlesinger, Jr., *The Imperial Presidency* (New York: Houghton Mifflin, 1973).

133. Matthew J. Dickinson, *Bitter Harvest: FDR, Presidential Power, and the Growth of the Presidential Branch* (New York: Cambridge University Press, 1996), 35.

134. Ibid., 40.

135. Ibid.

136. *Referral from Independent Counsel Kenneth W. Starr in Conformity with the Requirements of Title 28, United States Code, Section 595(c)*, 105th Cong., 2d sess., 1998, H. Doc. 105–310, 42–43.

137. Ibid., 55–6.

138. Terry M. Moe, "The New Economics of Organization," *American Journal of Political Science* 28, no. 4 (November 1984): 739–777.

Chapter Five
Executive Orders and Foreign Affairs

1. Arthur Schlesinger, *The Imperial Presidency* (Boston: Houghton, Mifflin, 1973), 345.

2. Commission on Protecting and Reducing Government Secrecy, *Secrecy: Report of the Commission on Protecting and Reducing Government Secrecy*, 105th Cong., 1st sess., 1997, S. Doc 105–2, 8.

3. Harold Hongju Koh, *The National Security Constitution: Sharing Power after the Iran-Contra Affair* (New Haven: Yale University Press, 1990), 172.

4. Robert J. Spitzer, "The President, Congress, and the Fulcrum of Foreign Policy," in *The Constitution and the Conduct of American Foreign Policy*, ed. David Gray Adler and Larry N. George (Lawrence: University Press of Kansas, 1996), 102.

5. Mark J. Rozell, *Executive Privilege: The Dilemma of Secrecy and Accountability in a Democratic Society* (Baltimore: Johns Hopkins University Press, 1995), 3.

6. New York City Bar Association, *The Federal Loyalty-Security Program* (New York: Dodd, Mead & Co., 1956), 80.

7. *Albertson and Procter v. Subversive Activities Control Board*, 382 U.S. 70 (1965); *Communist Party of the United States v. Subversive Activities Control Board*, 367 U.S. 1 (1961). See also Alan I. Bigel, "The First Amendment and National Security: The Court Responds to Governmental Harassment of Alleged Communist Sympathizers," *Ohio Northern University Law Review* 19 (1993): 885–925.

8. Senate Committee on the Judiciary, Subcommittee on the Separation of Powers, *President Nixon's Executive Order 11605 Relating to the Subversive Activities Control Board*, 92d Cong., 1st sess., 1971, 7.

9. Ibid., 7.

10. Memorandum, Bud Krogh to John Erlichman, June 1, 1970, WHSF/SMOF, Egil Kroch chronological files, Box 3, Folder: memos, June 1970, NPMP.

11. Memorandum, Robert C. Mardian to Attorney General John Mitchell, "Proposals to Transfer Additional Functions to the Subversive Activities Control Board," December 4, 1970, Papers of John Dean III, Box 69, Folder: SACB (2 of 4), NPMP.

12. Memorandum, "Re: Proposed Executive order entitled Amendment of Executive Order No. 10450 of April 27, 1953, Relating to Security Requirements for Government Employment," May 6, 1971. Papers of John Dean III, Box 69, Folder: SACB (2 of 4), NPMP.

13. Executive Order 1605, 36 *Federal Register* 12831 (July 8, 1971).

14. *President Nixon's Executive Order 11605*, 13–14.

15. Louis Fisher, *Constitutional Conflicts between Congress and the President*, 4th ed. (Lawrence: University Press of Kansas, 1997),113.

16. Cited in ibid., 112.

17. Memorandum, Bud Krogh to John Erlichman, "Subversive Activities Control Board," June 1, 1970, WHSF/SMOF, Krogh Chronological File 1969–1973, Box 3, Folder: Memos, June 1970, NPMP.

18. See, for example, the testimony of Arthur Miller in *President Nixon's Executive Order 11605*, 56.

19. *Secrecy: Report of the Commission on Protecting and Reducing Government Secrecy*, 5.

20. These include the 1911 Defense Secrets Act, the Espionage Act of 1917, and the 1917 Trading with the Enemy Act.

21. Senate Select Committee on Intelligence, *The Disclosure to Congress Act of 1998*, 105th Cong., 2d sess., 1998, Report no. 105–165, 4–5.

22. Bruce E. Fein, "Access to Classified Information: Constitutional and Statutory Dimensions," *William and Mary Law Review* 26 (1985): 817–818.

23. *National Federation of Federal Employees v. U.S.*, 688 F. Supp. 671, 685 (D.D.C. 1983).

24. House Select Committee on Intelligence, *A Statutory Basis for Classifying Information*, 103d Cong., 2d sess., 1994, 49; Schlesinger, *The Imperial Presidency*, 334.

25. J. G. Randall, "The Newspaper Problem in Its Bearing upon Military Secrecy during the Civil War," *American Historical Review* 23 (January 1918): 311–312.

26. *A Statutory Basis for Classifying Information*, 50.

27. U.S. Commission on Government Security, *Report of the Commission on Government Security* (June 1957), 153.

28. Executive Order 8381, 5 *Federal Register* 1147 (March 22, 1940).

29. Richard C. Ehlke and Harold C. Relyea, "The Reagan Administration Order on Security Classification: A Critical Assessment," *Federal Bar & News Journal* 30, no. 2 (February 1983): 92.

30. Note, "Developments in the Law: The National Security Interest and Civil Liberties," *Harvard Law Review* 85 (1972): 1194.

31. Executive Order 8985, 6 *Federal Register* 6625 (December 18, 1941).

32. Executive Order 9182, 7 *Federal Register* 4468 (June 13, 1942).

33. Report to the National Security Council by the Executive Secretary, June 28, 1948, President's Secretary's File: National Security Council, HSTL.

34. Executive Order 10104, 15 *Federal Register* 597 (February 1, 1950).

35. *A Statutory Basis for Classifying Information*, 51.

36. Memorandum for the Files, Raymond P. Whearty, Chairman of the Interdepartmental Committee on Internal Security, June 17, 1952, Official Files, Box 928, Folder: 285M (June 25–October 1952), HSTL.

37. Executive Order 10290, 16 *Federal Register* 9795 (September 24, 1951), § 25(c).

38. Col. J. M. Worthington, letter to the White House, July 2, 1953, WHCF, OF-72, Executive Office of the President (1), DDEL.

39. House Committee on Government Operations, *Availability of Information from Federal Departments and Agencies, Part 13—Department of Defense, Sixth Section*, 85th Cong., 1st sess. (1957), 155.

40. Brownell to Eisenhower, June 15, 1953, WHCF, OF Box 468, OF-103-K, Executive Order on Classified Information, DDEL.

41. Executive Order 10501, 18 *Federal Register* 7049 (November 10, 1953).

42. *Availability of Information from Federal Departments and Agencies, Part 13—Department of Defense, Sixth Section*, 3291; House Committee on Government Operations, *Freedom of Information Legislation during the 85th Congress*, 85th Cong., 2d sess. (1958), 174–175.

43. Cabinet Paper, CI-59–64, December 7, 1959, Papers of Dwight D. Eisenhower as President 1953–1961 (Whitman Files), Cabinet Series, Box 15, F: Cabinet Meeting of December 11, 1959, DDEL.

44. Executive Order 11652, 37 *Federal Register* 5209 (March 10, 1972).

45. Schlesinger, *The Imperial Presidency*, 349.

46. John W. Dean III, "Memorandum for the Attorney General," November 13, 1970; William H. Rehnquist, "Memorandum for the Honorable John W. Dean III," July 9, 1971. Both documents: Papers of John Dean III, Box 20, Folder: Classification [2 of 2], NPMP.

47. Memorandum for the President, from Stu Eizenstat, "Proposals on Openness in Government," February 17, 1977, White House Central Files, Subject File FG-1, Folder: Executive FG 1/20/77–3/15/77, JCL.

48. Executive Order 12065, 43 *Federal Register* 28949 (July 3, 1978).

49. Memorandum for the President, from David Aaron and Stu Eizenstat, "PRM/NSC-29: Comprehensive Review of the Classification System," August 17, 1977, Rick Neustadt Files, Box 26, Folder: Declassification Correspondence and Memoranda, 4/5/77–8/29/77, JCL.

50. Office of the White House Press Secretary, "Fact Sheet: The New Executive Order on the Security Classification System," Rick Neustadt Files, Box 26, Folder: Declassification 6/16/78–11/26/79, JCL.

51. Executive Order 12356, 47 *Federal Register* 14874 (April 6, 1982).

52. House Committee on Government Operations, *Security Classification Policy and Executive Order 12356*, 97th Cong., 2d sess., 1982; Michael D. Fricklas, "Executive Order 12356: The First Amendment Rights of Government Grantees," *Boston University Law Review* 64, no. 2 (March 1984).

53. Testimony of Steven Garfinkel, Director, Information Security Oversight Office, in House Government Information and Individual Rights Subcommittee, Committee on Government Operations, *Executive Order on Security Classification*, 97th Cong., 2d sess., 1982, 133.

54. Ehlke and Relyea, "The Reagan Administration Order on Security Classification," 91.

55. Executive Order 12958, 60 *Federal Register* 19825 (April 20, 1995).

56. Information Security Oversight Office (ISOO), *1996 Annual Report to the President* (Washington, D.C.: National Archives and Records Administration, June 30, 1997); ISOO, *1998 Annual Report to the President.*

57. Letter, Erwin Seago to Howard Pyle, November 6, 1956, with attachments, WHCF, Official Files, Box 467, Folder 103-K: Executive Order on Classified Information, DDEL. Ironically, this study itself was labeled "For Official Use Only."

58. In the Lloyd-LaFollette Act, for example, Congress gave the president the authority to remove employees "only for such cause as will promote the efficiency of the service," and imposed notification and adjudication requirements; Peter M. Shane and Harold H. Bruff, *Separation of Powers Law* (Durham, N.C.: Carolina Academic Press 1996), 390–391. A contemporary, sympathetic review of Truman's loyalty program argued that "under the American system of balance of powers, the President must retain broad authority to hire and fire. If the courts could review his reasons and reverse his decisions, the Chief Executive would cease to control the administration of government and the entire machinery might bog down in sloth and incompetence." Nathaniel Weyl, *The Battle against Disloyalty* (New York: Thomas Y. Crowell Co., 1951), 192.

59. Executive Order 9835, 12 *Federal Register* 1935 (March 21, 1947). Truman established the Temporary Commission on Employee Loyalty with Executive Order 9806, 11 *Federal Register* 13863 (November 25, 1946).

60. Executive Order 9835, 5(1).

61. Executive Order 9835, 5(2)a–f. The first attorney general's list appeared on March 20, 1948.

62. Executive Order 10450, 18 *Federal Register* 2489 (April 27, 1953).

63. Memorandum, E. C. Kennelly to Stanley J. Tracy, "Civilian Employee Security Program: Executive Order 10450; Preliminary Interview with Mr. Robert W. Minor," November 9, 1956, RCGS, Box 17, Folder: Executive Order 10450, National Archives.

64. Guenther Lewy, *The Federal Loyalty-Security Program: The Need for Reform* (Washington, D.C.: American Enterprise Institute, 1983), 34–35.

65. *Weiman v. Updegraff*, 344 U.S. 183 (1952). In the 1960s the Court extended this holding, concluding that even membership in a communist organization was not a sufficient reason, by itself, to deny government employment; the government had to show that an individual had a "specific intent" to further a group's illegal goals (Lewy, *The Federal-Security Program*, 25; *Elfbrandt v. Russell*, 348 U.S. 11 (1966); *Keyishian v. Board of Regents*, 385 U.S. 589 (1967)).

66. 351 U.S. 536 (1956).

67. "In the absence of an immediate threat of harm to the 'national security,' the normal dismissal procedures seem fully adequate and the justification for summary dismissal powers disappears." 351 U.S. 536, 546.

68. Lewy, *The Federal Loyalty-Security Program*, 19.

69. *Greene v. McElroy*, 360 U.S. 474 (1959).

70. Phillip Areeda, Memorandum to David Kendall, July 23, 1959, WHCF/OF, Box 103, Folder: 103-K: Executive Order re: Classified Information (4), DDEL.

71. 25 *Federal Register* 1583 (February 20, 1960). E.O. 10865 permits cross-examination of adverse witnesses unless the informant is dead or ill (in which case the identity will be disclosed), cannot attend due to "good and sufficient" cause, or when the agency head certifies that revealing the informant's identity would "be substantially harmful to the national interest."

72. 60 *Federal Register* 40243, August 7, 1995.

73. *Secrecy: Report of the Commission on Protecting and Reducing Government Secrecy*, 75.

74. Eleanor Bontecou, *The Federal Loyalty-Security Program* (Ithaca, New York: Cornell University Press, 1953), 103.

75. Adam Yarmolinksy, *Case Studies in Personnel Security* (Washington, D.C.: Bureau of National Affairs, August 1955).

76. John Earl Haynes and Harvey Klehr, *Venona: Decoding Soviet Espionage in America* (New Haven: Yale University Press, 1999), 13–14.

77. *Secrecy: Report of the Commission on Protecting and Reducing Government Secrecy*, 85.

78. House Committee on Government Operations, Special Subcommittee on Government Information, *Availability of Information from Federal Departments and Agencies*, part 3, 84th Cong., 2d sess., 1956, 449.

79. *Secrecy: Report of the Commission on Protecting and Reducing Government Secrecy*, 30.

80. Carole M. Barker and Matthew H. Fox, *Classified Files: The Yellowing Pages, a Report on Scholars' Access to Government Documents* (New York: Twentieth Century Fund, 1972); House Subcommittee of the Committee on Government Operations, *U.S. Government Information Policies and Practices—Security Classification Problems Involving Subsection (b) (1) of the Freedom of Information Act (Part 7)*, 92d Cong., 2d sess., 1972; House Committee on Armed Services, Special Subcommittee on Intelligence, *Hearings on Proper Classification and Handling of Government Information Involving the National Security*, 92d Cong., 2d sess., 1972.

81. Senate Permanent Select Committee on Intelligence, *Special Report: Committee Activities*, S. Report no. 104–4, 104th Cong., 1st sess., 1995.

82. Lewy, *The Federal Loyalty-Security Program*, 4.

83. Harold M. Hyman, *Try Men's Souls: Loyalty Tests in American History* (Berkeley: University of California Press, 1959), 317.

84. Laws barring payment to employees deemed subversive were rejected by the Supreme Court as unconstitutional bills of attainder in *United States v. Lovett*, 328 U.S. 303 (1946).

85. Robert J. Donovan, *Conflict and Crisis: The Presidency of Harry S Truman, 1945–1948* (New York: W. W. Norton, 1977), 293. John E. Haynes makes the same point in *Red Scare or Red Menace: American Communism and Anticommunism in the Cold War Era* (Chicago: Ivan R. Dee, 1996): "The Truman administration implemented a broader-than-needed security system to protect its flank from Republican criticism" (174).

86. Donovan, *Conflict and Crisis*, 294.

87. Hyman, *To Try Mens' Souls*, 334.

88. David McCullough, *Truman* (New York: Simon and Schuster, 1992), 553.

89. *Congressional Record*, July 15, 1947, 8943.

90. Robert J. Donovan, *Tumultuous Years: The Presidency of Harry S Truman, 1949–1953* (New York: W. W. Norton, 1982), 366.

91. 16 *Federal Register* 3690 (April 28, 1951). On the criticism of the loyalty program that preceded Executive Order 10241, see Hyman, *To Try Mens' Souls*, 334.

92. John Lord O'Brian, "New Encroachments on Individual Freedom," *Harvard Law Review* 66, no. 1 (November 1952): 19.

93. Donovan, *Tumultuous Years*, 366.

94. Anthony Leviero, "New Security Plan Issued: Thousands Face Re-Inquiry," *New York Times*, April 28, 1953.

95. Robert N, Johnson, "The Eisenhower Security Program," *Journal of Politics* 18, no. 4 (November 1956): 625. In contrast, Anthony Lewis argued that Congress had in fact put the president on the defensive until McCarthy's Senate censure in 1954. Anthony Lewis, "Eisenhower's Four Years: An Analysis of Policy on Loyalty and Problems in Red Investigations," *New York Times*, June 12, 1956.

96. House Committee on Government Operations, *Freedom of Information Legislation during the 85th Congress*, 85th Cong., 2d sess., 1958.

97. Note, "National Security Information Disclosure under the FOIA: The Need for Effective Judicial Enforcement," *Boston College Law Review* 25 (May 1984): 614.

98. *EPA v. Mink*, 410 U.S. 73 (1973).

99. Note, "Keeping Secrets: Congress, the Courts, and National Security Information," *Harvard Law Review* 103, no. 4 (February 1990).

100. House of Representatives, *Freedom of Information Act Amendments: Conference Report to Accompany H.R. 12471*, 93d Cong., 2d sess., 1974, Report no. 93–1380, 11.

101. *Taylor v. Department of the Army*, 684 F.2d 99 (D.C. Cir. 1982); *Goldberg v. United States Department of State*, 818 F.2d 71 (D.C. Cir. 1987).

102. *Rosenfeld v. United States Department of Justice*, 57 F.3d 803 (9th Cir. 1995); Justin D. Franklin and Robert F. Bouchard, *Guidebook to the Freedom of Information and Privacy Acts*. 2d ed., 2 vols., Update 21 (Deerfield, Ill.: Clark, Boardman, Callaghan, April 1997), I-65.

103. James T. O'Reilly, *Federal Information Disclosure*, 2d ed. (Rochester, N.Y.: Lawyers Cooperative Publishing, 1996), 11–27.

104. Documents in White House Central Files, FE-6, Folder: FE 10–1 7/1/77–12/31/77, JCL.

105. Louis Fisher, "Congressional-Executive Struggles over Information: Secrecy Pledges," *Administrative Law Review* 42, no. 1 (winter 1990): 92. See also Lewis Chimes, "National Security and the First Amendment: The Proposed Use of Government Secrecy Agreements under National Security Directive 84," *Columbia Journal of Law and Social Problems* 19, no. 3 (1985).

106. Fisher, "Congressional-Executive Struggles over Information," 93.

107. Michael J. Glennon, "Congressional Access to Classified Information," *Berkeley Journal of International Law* 16 (1998): 129–137.

108. Tim Weiner, "Guatemalan Agent of CIA Tied to Killing of American," *New York Times*, March 23, 1995.

109. Tim Weiner, "In Furor over Killings, President Warns of Shake-up in the CIA," *New York Times*, March 25, 1995.

110. Tim Weiner, "A Secret Disclosed Imperils the Career of State Dept. Aide," *New York Times*, November 16, 1996.

111. Thomas W. Lippman, "Under Fire by CIA, State Department Official Takes Case to Public," *Washington Post*, November 25, 1996; Tim Weiner, "CIA Chief Disciplines Official for Disclosure," *New York Times*, December 6, 1996.

112. David C. Morrison, "When Should Top Secrets Be Disclosed?" *National Journal*, April 22, 1995, 984.

113. Office of Legal Counsel Memorandum, 1996. The passage from which this quotation is taken is reprinted in House Select Committee on Intelligence, *Intelligence Community Whistleblower Protection Act of 1998*, 105th Cong., 2d sess., 1998, Report no. 105–747, part 1, 11.

114. Senate Permanent Select Committee on Intelligence, *Authorizing Appropriations for Fiscal Year 1998 for the Intelligence Activities of the United States Government*, Report no. 105–24, June 9, 1997, 105th Cong., 1st sess., 27. A subsequent House report stated that the Senate action was "in response to the OLC memo." *Intelligence Community Whistleblower Protection Act of 1998*, 11.

115. House Select Committee on Intelligence, *Intelligence Authorization Act for Fiscal Year 1998—Conference Report*, 105th Cong., 1st sess., 1997, Report no. 105–350, 22–23.

116. Testimony of Randolph Moss, Deputy Assistant Attorney General, Office of Legal Counsel, in Senate Permanent Select Committee on Intelligence, *The Disclosure to Congress Act of 1998*, 105th Cong., 2d sess., 1998, Report no. 105–165, 4.

117. 5 U.S. Code App., § 8H (d)(2)(A).

118. Neil King Jr., "Case of Lost-and-Found Disk Drives Demonstrates Weakness of U.S. Systems for Protecting Secrets," *Wall Street Journal*, July 5, 2000.

119. Executive Order 10656, 21 *Federal Register* 859 (February 8, 1956); Executive Order 10938, 26 *Federal Register* 3951 (May 6, 1961).

120. *Chicago and Southern Airlines v. Waterman Steamship Corp*, 333 U.S. 103, 111 (1948).

121. American Bar Association, Working Group on Intelligence Oversight and Accountability, *Oversight and Accountability of the U.S. Intelligence Agencies: An Evaluation* (Chicago: American Bar Association, 1985), 13.

122. Harold C. Relyea, *The Evolution and Organization of the Federal Intelligence Organization: A Brief Overview (1776–1975)*, reprinted in Senate Select Committee to Study Governmental Operations with Respect to Intelligence Activities, *Supplementary Reports on Intelligence Activities: Book VI*, 94th Cong., 2d sess., 1976, Report no. 94–755, 25.

123. Relyea, *The Evolution and Organization of the Federal Intelligence Organization*, 51.

124. Ibid., 59.

125. From its establishment in 1882 until 1899, the Office of Naval Intelligence (ONI) operated without any funding or statutory authorization, relying on clerks detailed from other offices. The outbreak of the Spanish-American War prompted Congress to formally authorize a staff for ONI (ibid., 62).

126. Ibid., 64.

127. John M. Oseth, *Regulating U.S. Intelligence Operations: A Study in the Definition of the National Interest* (Lexington: University Press of Kentucky, 1985), 33.

128. Ibid., 33.

129. John Ranlelagh, *CIA: A History* (London: BBC Books, 1992), 24. A declassified history of the CIA argued that in establishing the post of Coordinator of Information, Roosevelt and Donovan had "taken a giant step in the establishment of the country's pioneer organization for central intelligence and special operations." Thomas F. Troy, *Donovan and the CIA: A History of the Establishment of the Central Intelligence Agency* (Frederick, Md.: University Press of America, 1981), 63.

130. Relyea, *The Evolution and Organization of the Federal Intelligence Organization*, 141.

131. Executive Order 9182, 7 *Federal Register* 4468 (June 13, 1942); Center for the Study of Intelligence, *The Origin and Development of the CIA in the Administration of Harry Truman* (Washington, D.C.: CSI, March 1995), 11.

132. Troy, *Donovan and the CIA*, 133.

133. Military Order of June 13, 1942.

134. Troy, *Donovan and the CIA*, 428.

135. Arthur B. Darling, *The Central Intelligence Agency: An Instrument of Government, to 1950* (University Park: Pennsylvania State University Press, 1990), 29–38.

136. Troy, *Donovan and the CIA*, 220.

137. Memorandum for the President, November 18, 1944, reprinted in Troy, *Donovan and the CIA*, 445–447.

138. Darling, *The Central Intelligence Agency*, 46; letter, Truman to Secretary of State James Byrnes, September 20, 1945, reprinted in Troy, *Donovan and the CIA*, 463.

139. Sidney W. Souers, Memorandum for Commander Clifford, December 27, 1945, Reprinted in Michael Warner, *CIA Cold War Records: The CIA under Harry Truman* (Washington, D.C.: CIA History Staff, Center for the Study of Intelligence, 1994), 17–19.

140. Darling, *The Central Intelligence Agency*, 71.

141. Troy, *Donovan and the CIA*, 346.

142. Senate Select Committee to Study Governmental Operations with Respect to Intelligence Activities [the Church Committee], *Supplemental Detailed Staff Reports on Foreign and Military Intelligence: Book IV*, 94th Cong., 2d sess. Report no. 94–755 (1976), 14.

143. Darling, *The Central Intelligence Agency*, 75.

144. Ibid., 77.

145. Sidney W. Souers, Memorandum to the National Intelligence Authority, *Progress Report on the Central Intelligence Group*, June 7, 1946, p. 10; reprinted in Warner, *CIA Cold War Records*, 41–51.

146. Troy, *Donovan and the CIA*, 365.

147. Ludwell Lee Montague, *General Walter Bedell Smith as Director of Central Intelligence: October 1950–February 1953* (University Park: Penn State University Press, 1992), 34.

148. Clark Clifford, *Counsel to the President* (New York: Random House, 1991), 168. Others have argued that the clause was intended to authorize only espionage, or clandestine information collection, not covert operations; see Jeffrey Richelson, *The U.S. Intelligence Community*, 2d ed. (Cambridge, Mass.: Ballinger, 1989), 12.

149. Troy, *Donovan and the CIA*, 389.

150. Ibid., 394. In its new function the CIA would advise the National Security Council on intelligence activities.

151. Ibid., 410.

152. Senate Select Committee to Study Governmental Operations with Respect to Intelligence Activities [the Church Committee], *Foreign and Military Intelligence, Final Report: Book I*, 94th Cong., 2d sess., 1976, Report no. 94–755, 39.

153. Ibid., 141.

154. John Steelman, Memorandum for the President, April 24, 1948, Official Files, 1290-B [Central Intelligence Agency], HSTL.

155. Senate Committee on Rules and Administration, *Joint Committee on the Central Intelligence Agency*, 84th Cong., 2d sess., 1956, Report no. 1570, 11.

156. Memorandum, Allan W. Dulles, "Proposed Legislation to Establish a Joint Committee on Foreign Intelligence," January 6, 1956, 4–5, WHO/OSANSA Records, 1952–1961, Special Assistant Series, Subject Subseries, Box 2, F: Central Intelligence Agency (1) [August 1955–February 1958], DDEL. This document, originally classified as secret, was declassified in September 1998.

157. Executive Order 10656, 21 *Federal Register* 859, February 8, 1956.

158. *Supplemental Detailed Staff Reports on Foreign and Military Intelligence*, 63.

159. *Joint Committee on the Central Intelligence Agency*, 15.

160. Memorandum, "Discussion at the Special Meeting in the President's Office on Thursday, January 17, 1957," WHO/OSANA Records 1952–61, NSC Series, Subject Subseries, Box 7, F: PBCFIA First Report to the President [December 1956–August 1958], DDEL.

161. Executive Order 10938, 26 *Federal Register* 3951 (May 6, 1961).

162. Executive Order 11460, 34 *Federal Register* 5535 (March 22, 1969).

163. Executive Order 11905, 41 *Federal Register* 7703 (February 19, 1976).

164. Frank J. Smist, Jr., *Congress Oversees the United States Intelligence Community, 1947–1994*, 2d. (Knoxville: University of Tennessee Press, 1994), 79.

165. Memorandum for the President, Walter Mondale and Stansfield Turner, April 14, 1977, Robert Lipshutz files, Folder: Intelligence Overview Notebook I 6/77 [CF, O/A 716], JCL.

166. Ibid., 2.

167. Zbigniew Brzezinski, "Meeting with Senate Select Committee on Intelligence," August 3, 1977, Robert Lipshutz Files, Folder: Intelligence Community (EO, January 1978) 8/77 [CF O/A 711], JCL.

168. Executive Order 12036, 43 *Federal Register* 3674 (January 26, 1978).

169. Executive Order 11905, § 5(b)(6).

170. Griffin B. Bell, Memorandum for the President, "Intelligence Executive Order," Robert Lipshutz Files, Folder: Intelligence Overview Notebook, 6/77, CF, O/A 716, JCL.

171. Executive Order 12036, Section 2–207.

172. Richelson, *The United States Intelligence Community* 2d ed., 366.

173. Executive Order 12333, 46 *Federal Register* 59941 (December 8, 1981).

174. Bretton G. Sciaroni, "The Theory and Practice of Executive Branch Intelligence Oversight," *Harvard Journal of Law and Public Policy* 12, no. 2, (spring 1989): 409.

175. Ibid., 417. Under § 2–306 of Carter's order, the NSC would have been prohibited from engaging in any "special operations" if it were, as Sciaroni argued, not a member of the intelligence community.

176. Rhodri Jeffreys-Jones, *The CIA and American Democracy* (New Haven: Yale University Press, 1989), 198.

177. Koh, *The National Security Constitution*, 58.

178. Those interested in a fuller exposition should turn to Koh, *The National Security Constitution*, or the *Report of the Congressional Committees Investigating the Iran-Contra Affair, with Supplemental, Minority, and Additional Views*, 100th Cong., 1st sess., 1987, H. Rept. no. 100–433.

179. *Report of the Congressional Committees Investigating the Iran-Contra Affair*, 491–496.

180. Ibid., 545

181. Ibid.

182. Office of Legal Counsel, *Memorandum for the Attorney General: The President's Compliance with the "Timely Notification" Requirement of Section 501(b) of the National Security Act*, December 17, 1986, 5, 24.

183. Commission on Roles and Capabilities of the United States Intelligence Community, *Preparing for the 21st Century: An Appraisal of U.S. Intelligence*, March 1, 1996, A-22.

184. Smist, *Congress Oversees the United States Intelligence Community*, 312.

185. Joint Hearing of the Senate Select Committee on Intelligence and House Permanent Select Committee on Intelligence, *S. 2198 and S. 421 to Reorganize the United States Intelligence Community*, 102d Cong., 2d sess., 1992, 19.

186. Commission on the Roles and Capabilities of the United States Intelligence Community, *Preparing for the 21st Century: An Appraisal of U.S. Intelligence* (Washington, D.C.: Government Printing Office,) 1.

187. Richard Pipes, "What to Do about the CIA," *Commentary* 99 (March 1995): 36.

188. Commission on the Roles and Capabilities of the United States Intelligence Community, *Preparing for the 21st Century*, 140.

189. Ibid., 143.

190. Ibid., 144.

191. Ibid., 143–44. For a critical review of the Commission's report, see Bruce D. Berkowitz, "Reform of the Intelligence Community," *Orbis* 40, no. 4 (fall 1996): 653–663, and John Prados, "No Reform Here," *Bulletin of the Atomic Scientists*, September/October 1996.

192. House Permanent Select Committee on Intelligence, *IC21: Intelligence Community in the 21st Century*, 104th Cong., 1996, Staff Study, 2.

193. Carroll J. Doherty, "Hill Clears Modest Overhaul of Spy Organizations," *Congressional Quarterly Weekly Report*, September 28, 1996, 2769.

194. Ibid.

195. Executive Order 11905, § 5(g)).

196. Boyd M. Johnson III, "Executive Order 12333: The Permissibility of an American Assassination of a Foreign Leader," *Cornell International Law Journal* 25, no. 2 (spring 1992): 417–426.

197. "Memorandum from the Judge Advocate General," *Army Lawyer* (December 1989): 4–9, 8.

198. Michael N. Schmitt, "State-Sponsored Assassination in International and Domestic Law," *Yale Journal of International Law* 17, no. 2 (summer 1992): 679.

199. Ibid., 667.

200. Abraham Sofaer, quoted in ibid., 668.

201. Scmitt, "State-Sponsored Assassination in International and Domestic Law," 668–669.

202. Ibid., 674.

203. Robert F. Teplitz, "Taking Assassination Attempts Seriously: Did the United States Violate International Law in Forcefully Responding to the Iraqi Plot to Kill George Bush?" *Cornell International Law Journal* 28, no. 2 (spring 1995): 570.

204. Scmitt, "State-Sponsored Assassination in International and Domestic Law," 661–662.

205. H. Con. Res. 39, 102d Cong.

206. Paul Richter, "Congress Ponders Whether the U.S. Should Ease Ban on Assassinations," *Los Angeles Times*, September 18, 1998.

Chapter Six
Executive Orders and Civil Rights

1. Russell L. Riley, *The Presidency and the Politics of Racial Inequality: Nation-Keeping from 1831 to 1965* (New York: Columbia University Press, 1999), 236–237.

2. Ibid., 238.

3. Hugh Davis Graham, *The Civil Rights Era: Origins and Development of National Policy, 1960–1972* (New York: Oxford University Press, 1990), 9.

4. Ibid., 152.

5. Cited in Stephan Thernstrom and Abigail Thernstrom, *America in Black and White* (New York: Simon and Schuster, 1997), 157.

6. *Plessy v. Ferguson*, 163 U.S. 537 (1896); *Civil Rights Cases*, 109 U.S. 3 (1883).

7. Will Maslow and Joseph B. Robinson, "Civil Rights Legislation and the Fight for Equality," *The University of Chicago Law Review* 20, no. 3 (spring 1953): 389.

8. Linda Weiss, *Farewell to the Party of Lincoln: Black Politics in the Age of FDR* (Princeton: Princeton University Press, 1983), 4.

9. Seth M. Scheiner, "President Theodore Roosevelt and the Negro, 1901–1908," *Journal of Negro History* 47, no. 3 (July 1962); Ann J. Lane, *The Brownsville Affair: National Crisis and Black Reaction* (Port Washington, N.Y.: National University Publications, 1971).

10. Weiss, *Farewell to the Party of Lincoln*, 6.

11. Henry Blumenthal, "Woodrow Wilson and the Race Question," *Journal of Negro History* 48, no. 1 (January 1963): 5.

12. Leon A. Ransom, "Combatting Discrimination in the Employment of Negroes in War Industries and Government Agencies," *Journal of Negro Education* 12, no. 3 (summer 1943): 409.

13. Stephen R. Fox, *The Guardian of Boston: William Monroe Trotter* (New York: Atheneum Press, 1970), 179–181.

14. Charles Johnson, "The Army, the Negro, and the Civilian Conservation Corps, 1933–1942," *Military Affairs* 36, no. 3 (October 1972): 82.

15. Ruth P. Morgan, *The President and Civil Rights: Policy Making by Executive Order* (New York: St. Martin's Press, 1970), 30.

16. Graham, *The Civil Rights era*, 9.

17. "It was absolutely vital for the President to respond to the concerns of the southern senators and congressmen who could determine the fate of his legislative program. . . . Roosevelt needed their votes to put through what he regarded as 'must' recovery legislation, and he was unwilling to risk alienating them by championing racial causes. Refusing to risk his legislative program by pushing unpopular civil rights measures was practical politics: it was clearly more important to the administration to keep southern political support than it was to court blacks." Weiss, *Farewell to the Party of Lincoln*, 39–40.

18. Ibid., 35.

19. Ibid., 50.

20. Harvard Sitkoff, *A New Deal for Blacks: The Emergence of Civil Rights as a National Issue*, vol. 1 (New York: Oxford University Press, 1978), 67.

21. Executive Order 7046, May 20, 1936. See Sitkoff, *A New Deal for Blacks*, 69.

22. Alan Brinkley, *The End of Reform: New Deal Liberalism in Recession and War* (New York: Vintage Books, 1995), 165.

23. Ibid., 165–166.

24. Executive Order 8802, 6 *Federal Register* 3109 (June 25, 1941).

25. See, for example, Gunnar Myrdal's characterization of the Fair Employment Practices Committee in *An American Dilemma* (New York: Harper & Row, 1944), 415.

26. Louis Ruchames, *Race, Jobs, and Politics: The Story of the FEPC* (New York: Columbia University Press, 1953), 22.

27. Paula F. Pfeiffer, *A. Philip Randolph, Pioneer of the Civil Rights Movement* (Baton Rouge: Louisiana State University Press, 1990), 47.

28. "Proposals of the Negro March-On-Washington Committee to President Roosevelt for Urgent Consideration," June 21, 1941, OF-391-Marches on Washington, 1937–1945, FDRL.

29. Ruchemes, *Race, Jobs, and Politics*, 17.

30. Gerald N. Rosenberg, *The Hollow Hope* (Chicago: University of Chicago Press, 1991), 168.

31. Graham, *The Civil Rights Era*, 11.

32. Ruchames, *Race, Jobs, and Politics*, 46. The transferred FEPC was thereafter headed by Paul McNutt, who was viewed as indifferent to the committee's goals.

33. Graham, *The Civil Rights Era*, 11.

34. Ruchemes, *Race, Jobs, and Politics*, 57; Graham, *The Civil Rights Era*, 12.

35. A report to Truman's Presidential Committee on Civil Rights identified repeated unsuccessful efforts in 1942, 1944, 1945, and 1947 to enact permanent FEPC legislation.

36. Graham, *The Civil Rights Era*, 12–13.

37. Ibid., 13.

38. See, for example, Russell's remarks in *Independent Offices Appropriation Bill for 1945*, Hearing of the Senate Committee on Appropriations, 78th Cong., 2d sess., 1944, 332–336.

39. Paul H. Norgren and Samuel E. Hill, *Toward Fair Employment* (New York: Columbia University Press, 1964), 156.

40. Graham, *The Civil Rights Era*, 14.

41. Executive Order 10308, 16 *Federal Register* 12303 (December 3, 1951).

42. Executive Order 9808, 11 *Federal Register* 14153 (December 5, 1946).

43. William C. Berman, *The Politics of Civil Rights in the Truman Administration* (Columbus: Ohio State University Press, 1970), 51.

44. Robert J. Donovan, *Conflict and Crisis: The Presidency of Harry S Truman, 1945–1948* (New York: W. W. Norton, 1977), 333.

45. *Public Papers of the Presidents—Harry S Truman, 1948* (Washington, D.C.: Federal Register Division, National Archives, 1953), 125–126.

46. Berman, *The Politics of Civil Rights in the Truman Administration*, 95–98.

47. Morris J. MacGregor and Bernard C. Nalty, *Blacks in the United States Armed Forces: Basic Documents*, vol. 8: *Segregation under Siege* (Wilmington, Del.: Scholarly Resources, 1977), 685–686.

48. Executive Order 9980, 13 *Federal Register* 4311 (July 26, 1948).

49. Graham, *The Civil Rights Era*, 15.

50. American Council on Race Relations, "Executive Orders on Discrimination," *Report on Race Relations*, August 1948.

51. Presidential Committee on Civil Rights, *To Secure These Rights* (Washington, D.C.: Government Printing Office, 1947), 44–45.

52. Executive Order 9981, 13 *Federal Register* 4313 (July 26, 1948).

53. Sherie Mershon and Steven Schlossman, *Foxholes and Color Lines: Desegregating the U.S. Armed Forces* (Baltimore: Johns Hopkins University Press, 1998), 167–168.

54. Berman, *The Politics of Civil Rights in the Truman Administration*, 117. See also Riley, *The Presidency and the Politics of Racial Inequality*, 163–164.

55. Morgan, *The President and Civil Rights*, 20.

56. Merson and Schlossman, *Foxholes and Color Lines*, 158.

57. Herbert Brownell, *Advising Ike: The Memoirs of Herbert Brownell* (Lawrence: University Press of Kansas, 1993), 98.

58. Stephen Ambrose, *Eisenhower*, Vol. 2: *The President* (New York: Simon and Schuster, 1984), 126.

59. Max Rabb, Memorandum to Adams, "The President's Committee on Government Contract Compliance," undated, WHCF, OF Box 440, Folder: 102-1-2, Government Contracts Committee (1), DDEL.

60. Ibid.

61. Morgan, *The President and Civil Rights*, 43.

62. Executive Order 10730, 22 *Federal Register* 7628 (September 25, 1957).

63. Memorandum for the President, from Herbert Brownell, November 7, 1957, Papers of Gerald Morgan, Box 6, Folder: Civil Rights, DDEL.

64. Ambrose, *Eisenhower*, Vol. 2: *The President*, 407.

65. Anthony Lewis, *Portrait of a Decade: The Second American Revolution* (New York: Random House, 1964), 105.

66. Robert Frederick Burk, *The Eisenhower Administration and Black Civil Rights* (Knoxville: University of Tennessee Press, 1984), 98.

67. Ibid., 99.

68. E. Frederick Morrow, Memorandum to Sherman Adams, June 4, 1957, WHCF-OF, Box 731, F: 142A (2), DDEL. Burk notes that most of the White House staff viewed Morrow as a symbolic appointee, and he was usually shut out of substantive policy decisions. *The Eisenhower Administration and Black Civil Rights*, 77–88.

69. Memo, Morrow to Gerald Morgan, November 10, 1958, Morgan Papers, Box 6, F: Civil Rights, DDEL.

70. Senate Committee on Commerce, *Freedom of Communications*, 87th Cong., 1st sess., 1961, 432, 576. This report compiled Kennedy's campaign speeches and press releases into a single document. See also Daniel H. Pollitt, "The President's Power in Areas of Race Relations: An Exploration," *North Carolina Law Review* 39 (1961): 238–281.

71. Morgan, *The President and Civil Rights*, 62.

72. Presidential Committee on Civil Rights, *To Secure These Rights*, 166–168.

73. Morgan, *The President and Civil Rights*, 63.

74. The courts had played a role as well, striking down racially restrictive covenants in 1948 and prohibiting lawsuits seeking to enforce existing restrictive covenants in 1953 (*Shelley v. Kraemer*, 334 U.S. 1 [1948]; *Barrows v. Jackson*, 346 U.S. 249 [1953]).

75. Irving Berg, "Racial Discrimination in Housing: A Study in the Quest for Governmental Access by Minority Interest Groups, 1945–1962" (Ph.D. diss., University of Florida, 1967), 265.

76. *Report of the U.S. Commission on Civil Rights, 1959*, 538; Burk, *The Eisenhower Administration and Black Civil Rights*, 232.

77. Wofford letter to Theodore Sorenson, June 9, 1959, Files of the Democratic National Committee, Box 223, Folder: Civil Rights—Other Drafts, Memoranda, Correspondence 6/6/59–8/9/60 and undated, JFKL.

78. Wofford, "Memorandum to President-elect Kennedy on Civil Rights, 1961," December 30, 1960, Pre-Presidential Papers, Box 1071, Folder: Civil Rights—Harris Wofford Memorandum, JFKL, 15–16. Emphasis in original.

79. Executive Order 10925, 26 *Federal Register* 1977 (March 6, 1961).

80. Wofford, "Memorandum to President-elect Kennedy on Civil Rights, 1961," 23.

81. Robert C. Weaver, recorded interview by Daniel Patrick Moynihan, July 9, 1964, 159. JFKL Oral History Project.

82. Harris Wofford, recorded interview by Larry Hackman, May 22, 1968,. 46. JFKL Oral History Project.

83. Norbert Schlei to Lee White, September 10, 1962, 2, White Papers, Box 21, F: Housing Executive Order Background 9/30/62–11/20/62, JFKL.

84. Morgan, *The President and Civil Rights*, 69.

85. See, for example, Senator John Sparkman's (D-Ala.) argument in his article "Civil Rights and Property Rights," *Federal Bar Journal* 24, no. 1 (winter 1964): 31–46.

86. Memorandum, Katzenbach to Lee White, "Housing Discrimination Executive Order," October 20 1961, Sorenson Papers, Folder: Civil Rights 2/6/61–12/26/61, JFKL.

87. Graham, *The Civil Rights Era*, 65.

88. Anthony Lewis, "Kennedy Decides on Housing Edict," *New York Times*, October 21, 1961.

89. Wofford Oral History, JFKL, February 3, 1969, 154–155.

90. *Trends in Housing* 6, no. 5 (September-October 1962): 3.

91. See Berg, "Racial Discrimination in Housing," 301.

92. Executive Order 11603, 27 *Federal Register* 11527 (November 24, 1962).

93. William L. Taylor, Assistant Staff Director, U.S. Commission on Civil Rights to Lee C. White, August 9, 1962; memo, Milton Semer, General Counsel, Housing and Home Finance Agency, to Lee C. White, August 17, 1962. Both documents in White Papers, Box 21, Folder: Housing E.O. Background 8/1/62–8/16/62, JFKL.

94. Graham, *The Civil Rights Era*, 259.

95. President's Committee on Equal Opportunity in Housing, "Recommendation to the President," March 16, 1965, WHCF, CF Box 40, FG-743, LBJL; Lee White memo to LBJ, May 19, 1965, WHCF, SF Box 47, Ex HU 2-2, Housing 11/12/65–12/9/66, LBJL.

96. Memorandum from the Attorney General, September 20, 1965, WHCH Subject Files, FG Box 403, Ex FG 731 1/1/65–, LBJL.

97. Graham, *The Civil Rights Era*, 259.

98. Califano to LBJ, October 28, 1965, WHCF, Subject Files, Box 47, Ex HU-2-2 Housing 11/23/63–11/11/65, LBJL.

99. Ibid., 2.

100. Memorandum, David Lawrence to LBJ, November 10, 1965, WHCF SF, HU Box 47, Ex HU 2-2 Housing 11/23/63–11/11/65, LBJL.

101. Califano to LBJ, October 28, 1965, WHCF, Subject Files, Box 47, Ex HU-2-2 Housing 11/23/63–11/11/65, LBJL.

102. See, for example, the exchange between Javitz and Roy Wilkins, chair of the Leadership Council on Civil Rights, in Senate Committee on the Judiciary, Subcommittee on Constitutional Rights, *Civil Rights*. 89th Cong., 2d sess., part 1, 1966, 565–569.

103. Graham, *The Civil Rights Era*, 258, 262–264.

104. *Congressional Quarterly Almanac* 24 (1968), 152–154.

105. The President's Committee on Equal Employment Opportunity estimated that out of 60 million housing units in the country, E.O. 11063 covered about one million units. *Recommendation to the President*, March 16, 1965, 7–8.

106. Rosenberg, *The Hollow Hope*, 168.

107. John David Skrenty, *The Ironies of Affirmative Action* (Chicago: University of Chicago Press, 1996), 115.

108. Executive Order 10925, Section 301 (1).

109. Graham, *The Civil Rights Era*, 33.

110. Letter, George Reedy to Johnson, March 3, 1961, Vice Presidential Papers 1961–63, Box 86, Folder: Labor—President's Committee on EEO Executive Order, LBJL.

111. James E. Jones, Jr., "Twenty-One Years of Affirmative Action: The Maturation of the Administrative Enforcement Provisions under Executive Order 11246 As Amended," *Chicago-Kent Law Review*, 59, no. 1 (1985): 68.

112. Graham, *The Civil Rights Era*, 188; Executive Order 11246, 30 *Federal Register* 12319 (September 28, 1965).

113. For an analysis of these provisions, see Andrée Blumstein, "Doing Good the Wrong Way: The Case for Delimiting Presidential Power under Executive Order 11246," *Vanderbilt Law Review* 33, no. 4 (May 1980): 925.

114. Quoted in Richard P. Nathan, *Jobs and Civil Rights: The Role of the Federal Government in Promoting Equal Opportunity in Employment and Training* (Washington, D.C.: Commission on Civil Rights, April 1969), 93.

115. Graham, *The Civil Rights Era*, 296.

116. Executive Order 10925 was upheld in general terms in *Farkas v. Texas Instruments*, 335 F.2d 629, *cert. denied* (5th Cir. 1967). Executive Order 11246 and the Philadelphia Plan in particular were upheld in *Contractors Association of Eastern Pennsylvania v. Secretary of Labor*, 442 F.2d 159 (3rd Cir. 1971).

117. Congressional Research Service, *Compilation and Overview of Federal Laws and Regulations Establishing Affirmative Action Goals or Other Preference Based on Race, Gender, or Ethnicity*, February 17, 1995.

118. Graham, *The Civil Rights Era*, 346.

119. *U.S. v. New Orleans Public Service, Inc.*, 553 F. 2d 458, 467 (5th Cir. 1977).

120. For example, see Nelson Lund, *Reforming Affirmative Action in Employment: How to Restore the Law of Equal Treatment* (Washington, D.C.: Heritage Foundation Reports, 1995).

121. Senate Committee on the Judiciary, *Department of Justice Confirmations*, part 2, 97th Cong., 1st sess., 1981, Serial no. J-97-7.

122. Washington Council of Lawyers, Civil Rights Task Force, "Reagan Civil Rights: The First Twenty Months," in Senate Committee on the Judiciary, *Nomi-*

nation of William Bradford Reynolds to Be Associate Attorney General of the United States, 99th Cong, 1st sess., 1985, Serial no. J-99-29, S. Hrg. no. 99-374, 717–718; *Steelworkers v Weber*, 443 U.S. 193 (1979).

123. 46 *Federal Register* 42698 (1981). (The Office of Federal Contract Compliance had been renamed the Office of Federal Contract Compliance Programs in 1971.)

124. Kathy Sawyer, "Civil Rights Leaders Rally around the Affirmative-Action Flag," *Washington Post*, December 9, 1981.

125. 62 *Federal Register* 44174 (1997).

126. Terry Eastland, *Energy in the Executive: The Case for a Strong Presidency* (New York: Free Press, 1992), 355–356.

127. Ibid., 356. See also Gary L. McDowell, "Affirmative Inaction: The Brock-Meese Standoff on Federal Racial Quotas," *Policy Review* (spring 1989): 32–37.

128. Nicholas Laham, *The Reagan Presidency and the Politics of Race: In Pursuit of Colorblind Justice and Limited Government* (Westport, Conn.: Praeger Press, 1998), 34.

129. *United States v. Paradise*, 480 U.S. 149 (1987); *Johnson v. Transportation Agency of Santa Clara County*, 480 U.S. 616 (1987). Each case involved the use of race-conscious hiring programs by a government agency in order to compensate for a history of discriminatory employment practices. The Court upheld the use of race and sex as a factor in hiring and promotions.

130. George de Lama, "Affirmative Action Divides White House," *Chicago Tribune*, January 19, 1986.

131. Robert R. Detlefsen, "Affirmative Action and Business Deregulation: On the Reagan Administration's Failure to Revise Executive Order No. 11246," in *Presidential Leadership and Civil Rights Policy*, ed. James W. Riddlesperger, Jr., and Donald W. Jackson (Westport, Conn.: Greenwood Press, 1995).

132. The disparate impact doctrine originated in *Griggs v. Duke Power Co.*, 401 U.S. 414 (1971).

133. Joan Biskupic, "Failure to Enact Civil Rights Bill Laid to Political Miscalculation," *Congressional Quarterly Weekly Report*, October 27, 1990, 3610–3611. See also Roger Clegg, "Introduction: A Brief Legislative History of the Civil Rights Act of 1991," *Louisiana Law Review* 54 (1994).

134. Steven A. Holmes, "Bush to Order End of Rules Allowing Race-Based Hiring," *New York Times*, November 21, 1991.

135. On signing statements generally, see Kristy L. Carroll, "Whose Statute Is It Anyway? Why and How Courts Should Use Presidential Signing Statements When Interpreting Federal Statutes," *Catholic University Law Review* 46 (winter 1997): 475–531.

136. Ann Devroy, "President Signs Civil Rights Bill; White House Disavows Proposed Directive to End Affirmative Action," *Washington Post*, November 22, 1991.

137. Joan Biskupic, "Bush Signs Anti-Job Bias Bill amid Furor over Preferences," *Congressional Quarterly Weekly Report*, November 23, 1991, 3463.

138. Maureen Dowd, "President Orders Aide to Review New Minority Scholarship Policy," *New York Times*, December 14, 1990.

139. *Adarand Construction v. Pena*, 515 U.S. 200 (1995).

140. House Committee on the Judiciary, *Group Preferences and the Law*, 104th Cong., 1st sess., 1995, Serial no. 74; Senate Committee on Labor and Human Resources, *Affirmative Action and the Office of Federal Contract Compliance*,. 104th Cong., 1st sess., 1995, S. Hrg. 104–14.

141. Bennett Roth, "Gramm Vows to Kill Affirmative Action if Elected President," *Houston Chronicle*, February 9, 1995.

142. The report is reprinted in the *Congressional Record*, S3930–S3938, March 15, 1995.

143. B. Drummond Ayres, Jr., "California Board Ends Preferences in College System," *New York Times*, July 20, 1995.

144. Ibid.

145. Ann Devroy, "Clinton Orders Affirmative Action Review; at Stake: Principles and Political Base," *Washington Post*, February 24, 1995.

146. Steven A. Holmes, "White House Signals an Easing on Affirmative Action," *New York Times*, February 25, 1995.

147. *Adarand Construction v. Pena*, 515 U.S. 200 (1995).

148. *Weekly Compilation of Presidential Documents*, July 19, 1995, 1264–1265.

149. Steven A. Holmes, "Administration Cuts Affirmative Action While Defending It," *New York Times*, March 16, 1998.

150. Michael A. Fletcher, "Weighing Profits and Preference: Clinton Affirmative Action Plan for Contractors Vexes Critics," *Washington Post*, July 10, 1998.

151. 61 *Federal Register* 44174 (August 19, 1997).

152. *Congressional Record*, October 30, 1991, S15477.

153. In November 1998 Washington State voters approved a ballot initiative prohibiting racial preferences in public contracting, hiring, and higher education. The one referendum example that runs counter to this trend was in Houston, where in November 1997 voters rejected a citywide initiative that would have ended affirmative action by city agencies. A state judge, however, threw out the election results, citing a wording change by the city council—deleting references to "preferential treatment" in the proposal and inserting "affirmative action" in its place—that critics charged was made to make voters more likely to reject it. See Richard T. Seymour and Barbara Berish Brown, *Equal Employment Law Update* spring (Washington, D.C.: American Bar Association, spring 1998); "Judge Rejects Last Fall's Vote; Ballot Language at Issue on Affirmation Action Program," *Houston Chronicle*, June 27, 1998.

154. Carol M. Swain, "Black and White and Read All Over" [review of Stephan and Abigail Thernstrom, *America in Black and White*], *The New Democrat* (January/February 1998): 23.

155. Cynthia Harrison, *On Account of Sex: The Politics of Women's Issues, 1945–1968* (Berkeley: University of California Press, 1988), 148.

156. Executive Order 10980, 26 *Federal Register* 12059 (December 16, 1961).

157. Executive Order 11126, 28 *Federal Register* 11717 (November 1, 1963).

158. Harrison, *On Account of Sex*, 216.

159. Executive Order 13087, 63 *Federal Register* 30097 (June 2, 1998).

160. Sean Scully, "Conservatives Vow Effort to Undo Directive on Gays," *Washington Times*, July 7, 1998.

161. Testimony before the House Judiciary Committee, Subcommittee on the Constitution, July 17, 1998, *Federal Document Clearing House Congressional Testimony*, July 17, 1998.

162. H.R. 4318, introduced by Bob Barr (R-Ga.) on July 23, 1988, which would repeal Executive Order 11478; H. Amdt. 855, an amendment to an appropriations bill, introduced by Joel Heflen (R-Co.).

163. Roll call vote no. 398, *Congressional Record*, August 5, 1998, H7263.

164. Graham, *The Civil Rights Era*, 456.

165. Ibid., 9.

166. J. Lee Rankin, "Memorandum to the Attorney General," June 3, 1953, 3, WHCF, OF Box 440, F:102-1-1, President's Committee on Contract Compliance, DDEL.

167. Sherman Adams, "Memorandum to the Attorney General, April 14, 1953, WHCF, OF Box 440, F:102-1-1, President's Committee on Contract Compliance, DDEL.

Chapter Seven
Conclusion

1. Joseph Story, *Commentaries on the Constitution of the United States*, 5th ed., ed. Melvin Bigelow (Boston: Little, Brown and Co., 1891), 280.

2. Harvey C. Mansfield, Jr., "The Ambivalence of Executive Power," in *The Presidency in the Constitutional Order*, ed. Joseph M. Bessette and Jeffrey Tulis (Baton Rouge: Louisiana State University Press, 1981), 331.

3. Helen Dewar and Eric Pianin, "This Time, Partisanship Doesn't Stop with Strikes," *Washington Post*, December 17, 1998.

4. H. Con. Res. 94, 106th Cong.

5. Both Harold Hongju Koh and Louis Fisher argue that presidents have assumed far more unilateral authority in foreign affairs than is constitutionally warranted. Harold Hongju Koh, *The National Security Constitution: Sharing Power after The Iran-Contra Affair* (New Haven: Yale University Press, 1990); Louis Fisher, *Presidential War Power* (Lawrence: University Press of Kansas, 1995). Charles Tiefer, in *The Semi-Sovereign Presidency: The Bush Administration's Strategy for Governing without Congress* (Boulder: Westview Press, 1994), claims that Bush in particular simply arrogated legislative authority in domestic (especially regulatory) policy as well.

6. Phillip J. Cooper, "Power Tools for an Effective and Responsible Presidency," *Administration and Society* 29, no. 5 (November 1997): 537.

7. Norton E. Long, "Power and Administration," *Public Administration Review* 9, no. 4 (autumn 1949): 257.

8. Executive Order 13083, 63 *Federal Register* 27651 (May 19, 1998). The Reagan order, issued in 1987, was Executive Order 12612, 52 *Federal Register* 41685 (October 30, 1987).

9. House Committee on Government Reform and Oversight, Subcommittee on National Economic Growth, Natural Resources, and Regulatory Affairs, *Clinton-*

Gore v. State and Local Governments, 105th Cong., 2d sess., 1998, Serial no. 105–164; David S. Broder, "White House to Rewrite Federalism Order, Now with State-Local Input," *Washington Post*, July 29, 1998.

10. Executive Order 13095, 63 *Federal Register* 42565 (August 7, 1998).

11. Louis Fisher, *Constitutional Conflicts between Congress and the President*, 4th ed. (Lawrence: University Press of Kansas, 1997), 299.

12. Harvey C. Mansfield Jr., *Taming the Prince: The Ambivalence of Modern Executive Power* (Baltimore: Johns Hopkins University Press, 1993).

Index